PRIVACY AND THE MEDIA

Aspen Custom Publishing Series

PRIVACY AND THE MEDIA

SECOND EDITION

Daniel J. Solove
John Marshall Harlan Research Professor of Law
George Washington University Law School

Paul M. Schwartz
Jefferson E. Peyser Professor of Law
U.C. Berkeley School of Law
Faculty Director, Berkeley Center for Law & Technology

Wolters Kluwer

Published by Wolters Kluwer in New York.

Wolters Kluwer serves customers worldwide with CCH, Aspen Publishers, and Kluwer Law International products. (www.wolterskluwerlb.com)

To contact Customer Care, e-mail customer.service@wolterskluwer.com, call 1-800-234-1660, fax 1-800-901-9075, or mail correspondence to:

Wolters Kluwer
Attn: Order Department
PO Box 990
Frederick, MD 21705

Printed in the United States of America.

1 2 3 4 5 6 7 8 9 0

ISBN 978-0-7355-1043-2

About Wolters Kluwer Law & Business

Wolters Kluwer Law & Business is a leading global provider of intelligent information and digital solutions for legal and business professionals in key specialty areas, and respected educational resources for professors and law students. Wolters Kluwer Law & Business connects legal and business professionals as well as those in the education market with timely, specialized authoritative content and information-enabled solutions to support success through productivity, accuracy and mobility.

Serving customers worldwide, Wolters Kluwer Law & Business products include those under the Aspen Publishers, CCH, Kluwer Law International, Loislaw, ftwilliam.com and MediRegs family of products.

CCH products have been a trusted resource since 1913, and are highly regarded resources for legal, securities, antitrust and trade regulation, government contracting, banking, pension, payroll, employment and labor, and healthcare reimbursement and compliance professionals.

Aspen Publishers products provide essential information to attorneys, business professionals and law students. Written by preeminent authorities, the product line offers analytical and practical information in a range of specialty practice areas from securities law and intellectual property to mergers and acquisitions and pension/benefits. Aspen's trusted legal education resources provide professors and students with high-quality, up-to-date and effective resources for successful instruction and study in all areas of the law.

Kluwer Law International products provide the global business community with reliable international legal information in English. Legal practitioners, corporate counsel and business executives around the world rely on Kluwer Law journals, looseleafs, books, and electronic products for comprehensive information in many areas of international legal practice.

Loislaw is a comprehensive online legal research product providing legal content to law firm practitioners of various specializations. Loislaw provides attorneys with the ability to quickly and efficiently find the necessary legal information they need, when and where they need it, by facilitating access to primary law as well as state-specific law, records, forms and treatises.

ftwilliam.com offers employee benefits professionals the highest quality plan documents (retirement, welfare and non-qualified) and government forms (5500/PBGC, 1099 and IRS) software at highly competitive prices.

MediRegs products provide integrated health care compliance content and software solutions for professionals in healthcare, higher education and life sciences, including professionals in accounting, law and consulting.

Wolters Kluwer Law & Business, a division of Wolters Kluwer, is headquartered in New York. Wolters Kluwer is a market-leading global information services company focused on professionals.

To my parents and grandparents—DJS

To Steffie, Clara, and Leo—PMS

SUMMARY OF CONTENTS

CONTENTS

PREFACE

This text aims to provide a comprehensive and accessible introduction to the legal, social, and political issues involving information privacy and the media. The book contains three chapters. Chapter 1 provides a basic introduction to the issues and range of laws that address information privacy. Chapter 2 explores the definition, meaning, and value of privacy. Chapter 3 examines the complex relationship between privacy and the media.

In this text, we focus extensively on tort law and the First Amendment. The defamation and privacy torts have an important impact on media dissemination of personal information. In addition, the First Amendment has a complex relationship to privacy. In many instances, the First Amendment and privacy prove to be mutually reinforcing. For example, privacy is often essential to freedom of assembly. But privacy can also come into conflict with the First Amendment. Protecting privacy can restrict freedom of the press and freedom of speech. It can restrict the media's ability to gather and disclose information. We explore topics such as anti-paparazzi laws, gossip and rumor on blogs and social network websites, and the use of people's names or photographs for commercial purposes, among many other issues.

As the reference above to blogs indicates, we have incorporated material about the new media landscape in this casebook. For example, the Internet presents interesting problems for the application of defamation law and the privacy torts. Previously, it was primarily the mainstream news media that communicated libelous or private information to the public. Today, anybody can disseminate information around the world over the Internet. Rumor and gossip are increasingly spreading through blogs and social network sites. These new forms of media are giving rise to many difficult new problems, which we cover in depth.

We have also included extensive notes and commentary, and have integrated cases and statutes with theoretical and policy perspectives. To facilitate discussion and debate, we have included excerpts from commentators with a wide range of viewpoints. Technical terms are clearly explained. When selecting cases, we have included the leading cases as well as endeavored to provide a solid historical background and a timely and fresh perspective. We have strived to make this text a lively, thorough, and insightful introduction to the issues of privacy and the media that is accessible to those studying law, journalism, philosophy, and other fields.

A Note on the Casebook Website. We strive to keep the book up to date between editions, and we maintain a web page for the book with downloadable updates and other useful information. We invite you to visit the website:

http://informationprivacylaw.com

A Note on the Editing. We have deleted many citations and footnotes from the cases to facilitate readability. The footnotes that have been retained in the cases have been renumbered. When discussing books, articles, and other materials in the notes and commentary, we have included full citations in footnotes in order to make the text easier to read. We have also included many citations to additional works in the footnotes that may be of interest to the reader.

Daniel J. Solove
Paul M. Schwartz

November 2014

ACKNOWLEDGMENTS

Daniel J. Solove: I would like to thank Carl Coleman, Scott Forbes, Susan Freiwald, Tomás Gómez-Arostegui, Stephen Gottlieb, Marcia Hofmann, Chris Hoofnagle, John Jacobi, Orin Kerr, Raymond Ku, Peter Raven-Hansen, Joel Reidenberg, Neil Richards, Michael Risinger, Lior Strahilevitz, Peter Swire, William Thompson, and Peter Winn for helpful comments and suggestions. Charlie Sullivan and Jake Barnes provided indispensable advice about how to bring this project to fruition. Special thanks to Richard Mixter at Aspen Publishers for his encouragement and faith in this project. Thanks as well to the other folks at Aspen who have contributed greatly to the editing and development of this book: John Devins, Christine Hannan, Carmen Reid, Jessica Barmack, John Burdeaux, and Sandra Doherty. I would like to thank my research assistants Peter Choy, Monica Contreras, Carly Grey, Maeve Miller, James Murphy, Poornima Ravishankar, Sheerin Shahinpoor, Vladimir Semendyai, John Spaccarotella, Tiffany Stedman, Lourdes Turrecha, Eli Weiss, and Kate Yannitte. I would also like to thank Dean Blake Morant for providing the resources I needed. And thanks to my wife Pamela Solove and son Griffin Solove, who kept me in good cheer throughout this project.

Paul M. Schwartz: For their suggestions, encouragement, and insights into information privacy law, I would like to thank Ken Bamberger, Fred Cate, Malcolm Crompton, Chris Gulotta, Andrew Guzman, Chris Hoofnagle, Ted Janger, Ronald D. Lee, Lance Liebman, Steven McDonald, Deirdre Mulligan, Joel Reidenberg, Ira Rubinstein, Pam Samuelson, Lior Strahilevitz, Viktor Mayer-Schönberger, Peter Swire, Peter Winn, and William M. Treanor. I benefited as well from the help of my talented research assistants: Cesar Alvarez, Kai-Dieter Classen, Alpa Patel, Karl Saddlemire, and Laura Sullivan. Many thanks to my co-author, Daniel Solove. Many thanks as well to my mother, Nancy Schwartz, and to Laura Schwartz and Ed Holden; David Schwartz and Kathy Smith; and Daniel Schwartz.

A profound debt is owed Spiros Simitis. My interest in the subject of information privacy began in 1985 with his suggestion that I visit his office of the Hessian Data Protection Commissioner in Wiesbaden and sit in on meetings there. Through his scholarship, example, and friendship, Professor Simitis has provided essential guidance during the decades since that initial trip to Wiesbaden. My portion of the book is dedicated to Steffie, Clara, and Leo, with my gratitude and love.

Finally, both of us would like to thank Marc Rotenberg, who helped us shape the book in its first two editions and provided invaluable input.

We are grateful to the following sources for their permission to reprint excerpts of their scholarship:

Anita L. Allen, *Coercing Privacy*, 40 William & Mary L. Rev. 723 (1999). Used by permission. © 1999 by William & Mary Law Review and Anita L. Allen.

Julie E. Cohen, *Examined Lives: Informational Privacy*, 52 Stan. L. Rev. 1371 (2000). © 2000. Reprinted by permission of the Stanford Law Review in the format textbook via Copyright Clearance Center and Julie Cohen.

Amitai Etzioni, The Limits of Privacy 2-3, 213-214 (1999). © 1999 by Amitai Etzioni. Reprinted by permission of Basic Books, a member of Perseus Books, LLC and Amitai Etzioni.

Catharine A. MacKinnon, Toward a Feminist Theory of the State 190-193 (1989). © 1989 by Harvard University Press. Reprinted with permission.

Richard A. Posner, *The Right of Privacy,* 12 Ga. L. Rev. 393 (1978). Reprinted with permission.

Paul M. Schwartz, *Privacy and Democracy in Cyberspace*, 52 Vand. L. Rev. 1609 (1999). Reprinted with the permission of Paul Schwartz.

Reva B. Seigel, *The Rule of Love: Wife Beating as Prerogative of Privacy*, 105 Yale L.J. 2117 (1996). Reprinted by permission of the *Yale Law Journal* Company and the William S. Hein Company, from the *Yale Law Journal,* vol. 105, pages 2117-2207.

Spiros Simitis, *Reviewing Privacy in an Informational Society*, 135 U. Pa. L. Rev. 707, 709-710, 724-726, 732-738, 746 (1987). © 1987 by the University of Pennsylvania Law Review. Reprinted by permission of the University of Pennsylvania Law Review and Spiros Simitis.

Daniel J. Solove, *Conceptualizing Privacy,* 90 California Law Review 1087 (2002). © 2002 by the California Law Review.

Daniel J. Solove, The Virtues of Knowing Less: Justifying Privacy Protections Against Disclosure, 53 Duke Law Journal 967 (2003). © 2003 by Daniel J. Solove.

Alan Westin, Privacy and Freedom 7, 31-38 (1967). A study sponsored by the Association of the Bar of the City of New York. Reprinted with permission.

PRIVACY AND THE MEDIA

CHAPTER 1

INTRODUCTION

CHAPTER OUTLINE

A. INFORMATION PRIVACY, TECHNOLOGY, AND THE LAW

We live in a world shaped by technology and fueled by information. Technological devices — such as mobile phones, video and audio recording devices, computers, and the Internet — have revolutionized our ability to capture information about the world and to communicate with each other. Information is the lifeblood of today's society. Increasingly, our everyday activities involve the transfer and recording of information. The government collects vast quantities of personal information in records pertaining to an individual's birth, marriage, divorce, property, court proceedings, motor vehicles, voting activities, criminal transgressions, professional licensing, and other activities. Private sector entities also amass gigantic databases of personal information for marketing purposes or to prepare credit histories. Wherever we go, whatever we do, we could easily leave behind a trail of data that is recorded and gathered together.

These new technologies, coupled with the increasing use of personal information by business and government, pose new challenges for the protection of privacy. This book is about the law's response to new challenges to privacy. A significant amount of law regulates information privacy in the United States and around the world. Is this law responsive to the present and future dangers to privacy? Can information privacy itself endanger other important values? What duties and responsibilities must corporations, government agencies, and other private and public sector entities have with regard to personal data? What rights do individuals have to prevent and redress invasions to their privacy? When and how should privacy rights be limited? Does the war on terrorism require less privacy and more sharing of information? How should the law respond to an age of rapid technological change? Has the meaning of privacy changed in the age of social media and powerful search engines? These are some of the questions that this text will address.

This book's topic is information privacy law. Information privacy concerns the collection, use, and disclosure of personal information. Information privacy is often contrasted with "decisional privacy," which concerns the freedom to make decisions about one's body and family. Decisional privacy involves matters such as contraception, procreation, abortion, and child rearing, and is at the center of a series of Supreme Court cases often referred to as "substantive due process" or "the constitutional right to privacy." But information privacy increasingly incorporates elements of decisional privacy as the use of data both expands and limits individual autonomy.

Information privacy law is an interrelated web of tort law, federal and state constitutional law, federal and state statutory law, evidentiary privileges, property law, contract law, and criminal law. Information privacy law is relatively new, although its roots reach far back. It is developing coherence as privacy doctrines in one area are being used to inform and structure legal responses in other areas. Information privacy law raises a related set of political, policy, and philosophical questions: What is privacy? Why is privacy important? What is the impact of technology on privacy? How does privacy affect the efforts of law enforcement and national security agencies to protect the public? What is the role of the courts, the legislatures, and the law in safeguarding, or in placing limits on, privacy?

Furthermore, one might wonder: Why study information privacy law? There are a number of answers to this question. First, in today's Information Age, privacy is an issue of paramount significance for freedom, democracy, and security. One of the central issues of information privacy concerns the power of commercial and government entities over individual autonomy and decision making. Privacy also concerns the drawing of rules that may limit this autonomy and decision making by necessarily permitting commercial and government entities access to personal information. Understood broadly, information privacy plays an important role in the society we are constructing in today's Information Age.

Second, information privacy is an issue of growing public concern. Information privacy has become a priority on the legislative agenda of Congress and many state legislatures. Information privacy problems are also timely, frequently in the news, and often the subject of litigation.

Third, there are many new laws and legal developments regarding information privacy. It is a growth area in the law. Increased litigation, legislation, regulation, as well as public concern over privacy are spurring corporations in a variety of businesses to address privacy. Lawyers are drafting privacy policies, litigating privacy issues, and developing ways for dot-com companies, corporations, hospitals, insurers, and banks to conform to privacy regulations. A new position, the Chief Privacy Officer, is a mainstay at most corporations. The leading organization of these officers, the International Association of Privacy Professionals (IAPP), boasts thousands of members. Attorneys increasingly are grappling with privacy issues — either through litigation of privacy violations or through measures to comply with privacy regulations and to prevent litigation. All of these developments demand lawyers who are well-versed in the grand scheme and subtle nuances of information privacy law.

Fourth, information privacy law is an engaging and fascinating topic. The issues are controversial, complex, relevant, and current. Few areas of law are more closely intertwined with our world of rapid technological innovation. Moreover, concerns regarding information privacy play an important role in debates regarding security in post-9/11 America. The study of privacy law also helps us understand how our legal institutions respond to change and may help prepare us for other challenges ahead.

SIDIS V. F-R PUBLISHING CORP.

113 F.2d 806 (2d Cir. 1940)

[William James Sidis (1898–1944) was perhaps the most famous child prodigy of his day. According to Amy Wallace's biography of Sidis, *The Prodigy*, he was able to read the *New York Times* at the age of 18 months.[1] By the time he was three, William had learned to operate a typewriter and used it to compose a letter to Macy's to order toys. At that age, he also learned Latin "as a birthday present for his father." That year, after his father taught him the Greek alphabet, he taught himself to read Homer with the aid of a Greek primer. By the time he started elementary school, at the age of six, he could speak and read at least eight languages. At the age of five, he had already devised a method for calculating the day of the week on which any given date occurred, and when he was seven years old, he wrote a book about calendars. At that time, he had already prepared manuscripts about anatomy, astronomy, grammar, linguistics, and mathematics. At the age of eight, he created a new table of logarithms, which used a base of 12 instead of the conventional ten. From early childhood on, Sidis was also passionately interested in politics and world events. According to Wallace, Sidis was one of the few child prodigies in world history whose talents were not limited to a single field.

---

[1] Amy Wallace, *The Prodigy* (1986).

In 1909, Harvard University permitted Sidis to enroll in it; he was 11 years old and the youngest student in the history of Harvard. Sidis also made the front pages of newspapers around the nation when on January 5, 1910, he delivered a two-hour lecture to the Harvard Mathematics Club. The *New York Times* featured Sidis on its front page of October 11, 1909, as "Harvard's Child Prodigy."[2]

Boris Sidis, William's father, was a distinguished physician, early pioneer of American psychology (and opponent of Sigmund Freud), and prolific author. In 1911, Boris published a book about his educational theories and his virulent opposition to the educational institutions of the day. At the time of the publication of this book, *Philistine and Genius*, William was 13, and in Wallace's description, "teetering on the edge of his endurance to public exposure." Although the book did not mention his son by name, it did discuss him and his accomplishments, which brought William additional publicity. Sarah Sidis, William's mother and herself a physician, had a domineering and deeply troubled relationship with her son. Neither she nor Boris did anything to shelter William from the great publicity that followed him from an early age and the tremendous stress that it created in his life.

When he graduated from Harvard at age 16, William told reporters: "I want to live the perfect life. The only way to live the perfect life is to live it in seclusion. I have always hated crowds." After graduating from college, Sidis accepted a teaching position at the Rice University in Houston. After a difficult eight months as a professor of mathematics there, William returned to Boston and enrolled in Harvard Law School in 1916. He left the law school in his last semester there without taking a degree.

From 1918 until a *New Yorker* article about him in 1937, Sidis engaged in socialist and other radical politics, published numerous newsletters, lived an active social life, addressed a monthly study group, wrote a treatise about the classification of streetcar transfers, and financed his life through a series of modest clerical jobs and sales of his patented "perpetual calendar." During this period, in 1925, Sidis also published *The Animate and the Inanimate*. In Wallace's view, this book is the first work on the subject of "black holes" in space as well as an extraordinary work in the field of cosmogony, or the study of the origins of the universe. The book did not receive a single review at the time and was ignored by academia.

Before 1937, Sidis had done an excellent job of avoiding publicity for a decade. In that year, however, a local paper, the *Boston Sunday Advertiser*, published an article about him. This was followed by the August 14, 1937, issue of the *New Yorker*, which contained a brief biographical sketch about Sidis, his life following his graduation from Harvard, and the subsequent decades during which he lived in obscurity.[3] The article was part of a regular feature of the magazine called "Where Are They Now?," which provided brief updates on the lives of famous figures of the past. The article was printed under the subtitle *April Fool*, a reference to the fact that Sidis was born on April Fool's Day. The article recounted the history of Sidis's life and his current whereabouts: "William

[2] *Harvard's Child Prodigy: All Amazed at Mathematical Grasp of Youngest Matriculate, Aged 13 Years*, N.Y. Times, Oct. 10, 1909, at A1.

[3] J.L. Manley, *Where Are They Now?: April Fool!*, New Yorker 22 (Aug. 14, 1937).

James Sidis lives today, at the age of thirty-nine, in a hall bedroom of Boston's shabby south end." The article also contained numerous errors about Sidis's life.

A mystery still exists regarding the interview at the basis of this article. According to Wallace, Sidis's contemporary biographer, a member of the monthly study group, whom she refers to only as "John," had brought along a friend to one meeting. Several members of this group suspected that this woman, who was the daughter of a publisher at a large company, served as the basis for the *New Yorker*'s report. Yet, the mystery remains as this individual did not interview Sidis at the time of the monthly meeting. Wallace writes: "William always maintained that the entire article was a combination of imagination and old stories about him, and no strangers had gained access to his room." Another possibility is that Sidis spoke to someone without knowing that she was a reporter, which seems unlikely due to his aversion to publicity.

The *New Yorker* article described Sidis's famous childhood and then recounted his subsequent career as an insignificant clerk: "He seems to get a great and ironic enjoyment out of leading a life of wandering irresponsibility after a childhood of scrupulous regimentation." Sidis never remained at one job for too long because "his employers or fellow-workers [would] soon find out that he is the famous boy wonder, and he can't tolerate a position after that." According to Sidis: "The very sight of a mathematical formula makes me physically ill. . . . All I want to do is run an adding machine, but they won't let me alone." The article also described Sidis's dwelling, a small bedroom in a poor part of Boston and his personal activities, interests, and habits.

In his legal action against the *Boston Sunday Advertiser*, Sidis won a settlement of $375. Sidis also sued F-R Publishing Corporation, the publisher of the *New Yorker*. Among his claims were a violation of his privacy rights under §§ 50-51 of the N.Y. Civil Rights Law.]

CLARK, C.J. . . . It is not contended that any of the matter printed is untrue. Nor is the manner of the author unfriendly; Sidis today is described as having "a certain childlike charm." But the article is merciless in its dissection of intimate details of its subject's personal life, and this in company with elaborate accounts of Sidis' passion for privacy and the pitiable lengths to which he has gone in order to avoid public scrutiny. The work possesses great reader interest, for it is both amusing and instructive; but it may be fairly described as a ruthless exposure of a once public character, who has since sought and has now been deprived of the seclusion of private life.

The article of December 25, 1937, was a biographical sketch of another former child prodigy, in the course of which William James Sidis and the recent account of him were mentioned. The advertisement published in the New York World-Telegram of August 13, 1937, read: "Out Today. Harvard Prodigy. Biography of the man who astonished Harvard at age 11. Where are they now? by J.L. Manley. Page 22. The New Yorker."

The complaint contains a general allegation, repeated for all the claims, of publication by the defendant of *The New Yorker*, "a weekly magazine of wide circulation throughout the United States." Then each separate "cause" contains an allegation that the defendant publicly circulated the articles or caused them to be circulated in the particular states upon whose law that cause is assumed to be founded. Circulation of the New York World-Telegram advertisement is, however, alleged only with respect to the second "cause," for asserted violation of New York law.

Under the first "cause of action" we are asked to declare that this exposure transgresses upon plaintiff's right of privacy, as recognized in California, Georgia, Kansas, Kentucky, and Missouri. Each of these states except California grants to the individual a common law right, and California a constitutional right, to be let alone to a certain extent. The decisions have been carefully analyzed by the court below, and we need not examine them further. None of the cited rulings goes so far as to prevent a newspaper or magazine from publishing the truth about a person, however intimate, revealing, or harmful the truth may be. Nor are there any decided cases that confer such a privilege upon the press. . . .

It must be conceded that under the strict standards suggested by [Warren and Brandeis in their article, *The Right to Privacy*] plaintiff's right of privacy has been invaded. Sidis today is neither politician, public administrator, nor statesman. Even if he were, some of the personal details revealed were of the sort that Warren and Brandeis believed "all men alike are entitled to keep from popular curiosity."

But despite eminent opinion to the contrary, we are not yet disposed to afford to all of the intimate details of private life an absolute immunity from the prying of the press. Everyone will agree that at some point the public interest in obtaining information becomes dominant over the individual's desire for privacy. Warren and Brandeis were willing to lift the veil somewhat in the case of public officers. We would go further, though we are not yet prepared to say how far. At least we would permit limited scrutiny of the "private" life of any person who has achieved, or has had thrust upon him, the questionable and indefinable status of a "public figure."

William James Sidis was once a public figure. As a child prodigy, he excited both admiration and curiosity. Of him great deeds were expected. In 1910, he was a person about whom the newspapers might display a legitimate intellectual interest, in the sense meant by Warren and Brandeis, as distinguished from a trivial and unseemly curiosity. But the precise motives of the press we regard as unimportant. And even if Sidis had loathed public attention at that time, we think his uncommon achievements and personality would have made the attention permissible. Since then Sidis has cloaked himself in obscurity, but his subsequent history, containing as it did the answer to the question of whether or not he had fulfilled his early promise, was still a matter of public concern. The article in *The New Yorker* sketched the life of an unusual personality, and it possessed considerable popular news interest.

We express no comment on whether or not the newsworthiness of the matter printed will always constitute a complete defense. Revelations may be so intimate and so unwarranted in view of the victim's position as to outrage the community's notions of decency. But when focused upon public characters, truthful comments upon dress, speech, habits, and the ordinary aspects of personality will usually not transgress this line. Regrettably or not, the misfortunes and frailties of neighbors and "public figures" are subjects of considerable interest and discussion to the rest of the population. And when such are the mores of the community, it would be unwise for a court to bar their expression in the newspapers, books, and magazines of the day.

Plaintiff in his first "cause of action" charged actual malice in the publication, and now claims that an order of dismissal was improper in the face of such an allegation. We cannot agree. If plaintiff's right of privacy was not invaded by the article, the existence of actual malice in its publication would not change that result. Unless made so by statute, a truthful and therefore non-libelous statement will not become libelous when uttered maliciously. A similar rule should prevail on invasions of the right of privacy. "Personal ill-will is not an ingredient of the offence, any more than in an ordinary case of trespass to person or to property." Warren and Brandeis, supra at page 218. Nor does the malice give rise to an independent wrong based on an intentional invasion of the plaintiff's interest in mental and emotional tranquility.

If the article appearing in the issue of August 14, 1937, does not furnish grounds for action, then it is clear that the brief and incidental reference to it contained in the article of December 25, 1937, is not actionable. . . .

[The court concluded that the second cause of action under N.Y. Civil Rights Law was properly dismissed as well. The second cause of action charged invasion of the rights conferred on plaintiff by §§ 50 and 51 of the N.Y. Civil Rights Law. Section 50 states: "A person, firm or corporation that uses for advertising purposes, or for the purposes of trade, the name, portrait or picture of any living person without having first obtained the written consent of such person, or if a minor of his or her parent or guardian, is guilty of a misdemeanor." Section 51 gives the injured person an injunction remedy and damages. The court found: "Though a publisher sells a commodity, and expects to profit from the sale of his product, he is immune from the interdict of Secs. 50 and 51 so long as he confines himself to the unembroidered dissemination of facts. . . . *The New Yorker* articles limit themselves to the unvarnished, unfictionalized truth."]

NOTES & QUESTIONS

1. ***Involuntary Public Figures.*** After losing his privacy suit against the *New Yorker*, Sidis sued it for libel for the false information in the story. Among his charges, he claimed that a reader of the article would think that he was a reprehensible character, disloyal to his country, a loathsome and filthy person in personal habits, suffered a mental breakdown, and was a fool, who lived in misery and poverty. The *New Yorker* settled this case out of court for a small amount of money, which Wallace estimates in her biography of Sidis at between $500 and $600.

   Sidis suffered from high blood pressure, and, approximately three months after receiving the settlement from the *New Yorker*, on July 17, 1944, he died from a cerebral hemorrhage and pneumonia. He was 46 years old and had $652.81 in his bank account.

   The life of William Sidis illustrates a man profoundly disturbed by being thrust by his parents into the limelight as a child and by the media hounding him. He tried to spend his adult life fleeing from being the focus of any public attention. If he had been an involuntary public figure in the past, should this affect whether he should be able to retreat from the public eye in the future? Does it matter that he became a public figure as a child, that is, that he did not voluntarily choose this status as an adult?

The *Sidis* case suggests the principle that once one is a public figure, one is always a public figure. Can people who were once famous ever retreat into obscurity?

2. ***Who Was J.L. Manley? What Did He Try to Convey in His Article?*** The Sidis article was written by a "J.L. Manley." In a biography of James Thurber, the famous American humorist, Burton Bernstein reveals that Thurber used Jared L. Manley as a pseudonym.[4] Under this signature, Thurber wrote 24 profiles of onetime celebrities, including the Sidis piece. All pieces were based on the research of other reporters at the *New Yorker*, including the unnamed reporter who actually interviewed Sidis.

   In Thurber's own account of his time at the *New Yorker*, he faulted the *Sidis* court on one matter: "[N]owhere was there any indication of what I thought had stood out all through my story, implicit though it was — my feeling that the piece would help to curb the great American thrusting of talented children into the glare of fame or notoriety, a procedure in so many cases disastrous to the later career and happiness of the exploited youngsters."[5]

3. ***J.D. Salinger's Letters.*** In 1998, Joyce Maynard wrote an autobiography, *At Home in the World*, that describes her romance with J.D. Salinger in the 1970s. J.D. Salinger, an acclaimed author who wrote *The Catcher in the Rye*, had long ago completely retreated from public life and adopted a highly secluded existence in New Hampshire. In 1999, Maynard auctioned the letters J.D. Salinger wrote to her. She received $156,500 for the letters from the auction at Sotheby's. CNN reported at that time, "California philanthropist Peter Norton, who bought the letters, said he plans to return them to Salinger." Should Salinger have a right to privacy in the disclosure of the letters? Copyright law does create a copyright interest in unpublished letters — which prevents not only the publication of the entire contents of the letters, but a paraphrase of the letters that is too close to the actual text of the letters. *See Salinger v. Random House, Inc.*, 811 F.2d 90 (2d Cir. 1987). Should privacy law provide Salinger with the right to sue over the writing of Maynard's book?

---

[4] *See* Burton Bernstein, *Thurber* 261 (1975). Bernstein writes:

> For all the distractions of city life and his sleepless schedule, Thurber was getting a lot of good work done. In early 1936, he began to write (really rewrite, since some of the New Yorker's best reporters, like Eugene Kinkead, were doing the research) a number of short, retrospective Profiles. His nonfiction craft rose to a new high in these excellent pieces, which lent themselves to his human approach.

Id. Bernstein also reveals that Jared L. Manley was a name that Thurber cobbled together when writing his first piece about an old boxer based on the initials of the boxer John L. Sullivan and "Manley" based on "the manly art of self-defense."

[5] James Thurber, *My Years with Ross* (1959).

4. ***Girls Gone Wild.*** A company markets videotapes of young college women at spring break or Mardi Gras flashing and undressing. The women, often intoxicated, reveal their nudity in public and give their permission to use the video footage on the company's videotapes, which are called "Girls Gone Wild." Later on, when sober, some of the women regret their decision to be in the video. Have they waived all privacy rights to their nude images on the video if they sign a consent form? Or should they be entitled to have some time to reconsider? Should they not be able to sign away these rights even when sober? Others have sued claiming that they were just filmed in public without signing a consent form. Do they have a valid privacy claim even when they exposed themselves in public?
5. ***Privacy Inalienability.*** Do we care whether or not Sidis knew he was talking to a reporter as opposed to a new neighbor? Can we assume that anyone who talks to a reporter has abandoned a privacy interest in the information that she shares with the journalist? More broadly, to what extent should privacy interests be tradable, waiveable, or otherwise alienable?[6]
6. ***Googleization.*** The Internet makes the preservation and dissemination of information much easier. Information about a person can be easily discovered by "Googling" them. Google will pull up dozens, sometimes hundreds of thousands, of information fragments about a person. It is becoming increasingly difficult for people to hide their personal information, which once would fade into obscurity but is now preserved forever on the Internet. Youthful indiscretions become permanent baggage. Consider the plight of one Michael, who was briefly imprisoned as a minor. The information comes up on a Google search, and Michael finds that it is inhibiting his ability to date, since many of the women he dates inquire about his time in prison. They have obviously Googled him:

   > "When you meet someone," Michael says, "you don't say, 'I had an affair one time,' or 'I was arrested for DUI once,' or 'I cheated on my taxes in 1984.' "... [W]hat Michael finds most disturbing are the sudden silences. "Instead of thinking, 'Was I curt last week?' or 'Did I insult this political party or that belief?' I have to think about what happened when I was 17."[7]

   Is Sidis's claim to privacy quaint by today's standards? How do we protect privacy in a post-Google world?
7. ***The* Star Wars *Kid and the Numa Numa Dance.*** An overweight, awkward 15-year-old kid videotaped himself pretending to be a character from a *Star Wars* movie.[8] He swung around a golf ball retriever pretending that it was a light saber and made his own sound effects. Somebody found the video,

---

[6] Paul M. Schwartz, *Property, Privacy, and Personal Data*, 117 Harv. L. Rev. 2055, 2074 (2004).

[7] Neil Swidey, *A Nation of Voyeurs: How the Internet Search Engine Google Is Changing What We Can Find Out About Each Other and Raising Questions About Whether We Should,* Boston Globe Mag., Feb. 2, 2003, at 10.

[8] Amy Harmon, *Fame Is No Laughing Matter for the "Star Wars" Kid,* N.Y. Times, May 19, 2003, at C3.

digitized it, and posted it on the Internet. The video created a buzz, and it was downloaded millions of times around the world. Versions of the video with music and special effects were soon posted. People made fun of the kid in various discussions throughout the Internet.

In December 2005, Gary Brolsma placed on the Internet a clip of himself lip-synching and dancing in a chair to a Romanian pop song.[9] He called his performance the "Numa Numa Dance." The video was featured on newsgrounds.com, a website devoted to animation and videos, as well as elsewhere on the Internet. Newsgrounds.com alone soon received almost two million hits for the "Numa Numa Dance." Brolsma appeared on Good Morning America, and CNN and VHI showed his clip.

Suddenly, however, he decided that he disliked the attention. The *New York Times* reported that Brolsma "has now sought refuge from his fame in his family's small house on a gritty street in Saddle Brook." The article added: "According to his relatives, he mopes around the house. . . . He is distraught, embarrassed." His grandmother quoted him as saying: "I just want this to end."

Is this simply life in the Internet Age? Does it matter that the parents of the "*Star Wars* kid" alleged that the clip of their son was placed online without his permission? In contrast, Brolsma posted the video of his dance himself. Is there something that the law can do to protect people like the *Star Wars* kid or the Numa Numa dancer? If so, what?

As an update to the story of the Numa Numa Dance, Brolsma has moved beyond any anguish at his fame or notoriety. In September 2006, he released a second video, "New Numa," with corporate sponsorship at newnuma.com. The new video features Brolsma and members of a rock band, the Nowadays, and a new song. The video was released along with a promotion that allowed the public to submit their own videos and win a share of $45,000 in prizes. Brolsma also offered a selection of t-shirts and a coffee mug for sale to the public. In 2008, he started a website, the Numa Network, which has grown to include a YouTube channel and a Facebook presence.

B. INFORMATION PRIVACY LAW: ORIGINS AND TYPES

Information privacy law is a wide-ranging body of law, encompassing common law, constitutional law, statutory law, and international law. This section will provide a brief introduction to the various strands of information privacy law that will be covered throughout this book. It begins by looking in detail at the most important article ever written about privacy.

---

[9] Alan Feuer & Jason George, *Internet Fame Is Cruel Mistress for Dancer of the Numa Numa,* N.Y. Times, Feb. 26, 2005, at A1.

1. COMMON LAW

(a) The Warren and Brandeis Article

The common law's development of tort remedies to protect privacy is one of the most significant chapters in the history of privacy law. In the late nineteenth century, considerable concerns about privacy captured the public's attention, ultimately resulting in the 1890 publication of Samuel Warren and Louis Brandeis's pathbreaking article, *The Right to Privacy*.[10] According to Roscoe Pound, the article did "nothing less than add a chapter to our law."[11] Harry Kalven even hailed it as the "most influential law review article of all."[12] The clearest indication of the article's ongoing vitality can be found in the Supreme Court's decision *Kyllo v. United States*, 533 U.S. 27 (2001). The Brandeis and Warren article is cited by the majority, those in concurrence, and even those in dissent.

Several developments in the late nineteenth century created a growing interest in privacy. First, the press became increasingly sensationalistic. Prior to the Civil War, wide-circulation newspapers were rare. However, the development of a new form of sensationalistic journalism, known as "yellow journalism," made newspapers wildly successful. In 1833, Benjamin Day began publishing a newspaper called *The Sun* patterned after the "penny presses" in London (so named because they sold for a penny). The *Sun* contained news of scandals, such as family squabbles, public drunkenness, and petty crimes. In about four months, the *Sun* had a circulation of 4,000, almost the same as the existing New York daily papers. Just two months later, the *Sun* was reaching 8,000 in circulation. Other penny press papers soon followed. In reporting on his travels in America, Charles Dickens observed that New York newspapers were "pulling off the roofs of private houses."[13] In his great novel of 1844, *The Life and Adventures of Martin Chuzzlewit*, he listed (imaginary) New York newspapers called *The Sewer, The Stabber, The Family Spy, The Private Listener, The Peeper, The Plunderer,* and *The Keyhole Reporter*.[14]

Between 1850 and 1890, newspaper circulation increased about 1,000 percent — from 100 papers with 800,000 readers to 900 papers with more than 8 million readers. Joseph Pulitzer and William Randolph Hearst became the leading rivals in the newspaper business, each amassing newspaper empires. Their highly sensationalistic journalism became the paradigm for yellow journalism.[15]

Second, technological developments caused great alarm for privacy. In their article, Warren and Brandeis pointed to the invention of "instantaneous

---

[10] Samuel Warren & Louis Brandeis, *The Right to Privacy*, 4 Harv. L. Rev. 193 (1890).

[11] Quoted in Alpheus Mason, *Brandeis: A Free Man's Life* 70 (1946).

[12] Harry Kalven, Jr., *Privacy in Tort Law — Were Warren and Brandeis Wrong?*, 31 Law & Contemp. Probs. 326, 327 (1966).

[13] Charles Dickens, *American Notes* (1842).

[14] Charles Dickens, *The Life and Adventures of Martin Chuzzlewit* (1844).

[15] For more information about yellow journalism, *see generally* Gini Graham Scott, *Mind Your Own Business: The Battle for Personal Privacy* 37-38 (1995); Robert Ellis Smith, *Ben Franklin's Web Site: Privacy and Curiosity from Plymouth Rock to the Internet* 102-20 (2000).

photography" as a new challenge to privacy. Photography had been around for many years before Warren and Brandeis penned their article. However, the equipment was expensive, cumbersome, and complicated to use. In 1884, the Eastman Kodak Company introduced the "snap camera," a handheld camera that was small and cheap enough for use by the general public. The snap camera allowed people to take candid photographs in public places for the first time. In the late nineteenth century, few daily newspapers even printed drawings, let alone photographs. Warren and Brandeis, however, astutely recognized the potential for the new technology of cameras to be used by the sensationalistic press.

The question of the origin of Warren and Brandeis's article has led to considerable debate. Some scholars suggest that Warren and Brandeis were strongly influenced by an article written in 1890 by E.L. Godkin, a famous social commentator in his day.[16] In the article, Godkin observed:

> . . . Privacy is a distinctly modern product, one of the luxuries of civilization, which is not only unsought for but unknown in primitive or barbarous societies. . . .
>
> The chief enemy of privacy in modern life is that interest in other people and their affairs known as curiosity, which in the days before newspapers created personal gossip. . . . [A]s long as gossip was oral, it spread, as regarded any one individual, over a very small area, and was confined to the immediate circle of his acquaintances. It did not reach, or but rarely reached, those who knew nothing of him. It did not make his name, or his walk, or his conversation familiar to strangers. . . . [G]ossip about private individuals is now printed, and makes its victim, with all his imperfections on his head, known to hundreds or thousands miles away from his place of abode; and, what is worst of all, brings to his knowledge exactly what is said about him, with all its details. It thus inflicts what is, to many men, the great pain of believing that everybody he meets in the street is perfectly familiar with some folly, or misfortune, or indiscretion, or weakness, which he had previously supposed had never got beyond his domestic circle. . . .
>
> In truth, there is only one remedy for the violations of the right to privacy within the reach of the American public, and that is but an imperfect one. It is to be found in attaching social discredit to invasions of it on the part of conductors of the press. At present this check can hardly be said to exist. It is to a large extent nullified by the fact that the offence is often pecuniarily profitable.[17]

Warren and Brandeis referred to Godkin's essay, and their article does bear some similarities to his work. One difference is that Godkin, although recognizing the growing threats to privacy, remained cynical about the possibility of a solution, expressing only the hope that attitudes would change to be more respectful of privacy. Warren and Brandeis had a different view. In their judgment, the law could and should provide protection for privacy.

---

[16] *See* Elbridge L. Adams, *The Right to Privacy and Its Relation to the Law of Libel*, 39 Am. L. Rev. 37 (1905); Dorothy J. Glancy, *The Invention of the Right to Privacy*, 21 Ariz. L. Rev. 1 (1979).

[17] E.L. Godkin, *The Rights of the Citizen: To His Own Reputation*, Scribner's Mag. (1890); *see also* E.L. Godkin, *The Right to Privacy*, The Nation (Dec. 25, 1890).

Another theory suggests that incursions by journalists into the privacy of Samuel Warren inspired the article. Warren, a wealthy and powerful attorney in Boston, practiced law with Louis Brandeis, who later went on to become a U.S. Supreme Court Justice. In 1883, Samuel Warren married Mabel Bayard, the daughter of a prominent senator from Delaware, and set up house in Boston's Back Bay. The Warrens were among the Boston elite and were frequently reported on in the *Saturday Evening Gazette*, "which specialized in 'blue blood items,' " and "reported their activities in lurid detail."[18]

According to William Prosser, Warren was motivated to write the article because reporters intruded upon his daughter's wedding. However, this certainly could not have been the reason because in 1890, Warren's oldest daughter was not even ten years old![19] Most likely, the impetus for writing the article was Warren's displeasure about a number of stories in the *Gazette* about his dinner parties.[20]

Whatever inspired them to write, Warren and Brandeis published an article that profoundly shaped the development of the law of privacy.

SAMUEL D. WARREN AND LOUIS D. BRANDEIS, *THE RIGHT TO PRIVACY*

4 Harv. L. Rev. 193 (1890)

> It could be done only on principles of private justice, moral fitness, and public convenience, which, when applied to a new subject, make common law without a precedent; much more when received and approved by usage.
>
> — Willes, J., in *Millar v. Taylor,* 4 Burr. 2303, 2312

That the individual shall have full protection in person and in property is a principle as old as the common law; but it has been found necessary from time to time to define anew the exact nature and extent of such protection. Political, social, and economic changes entail the recognition of new rights, and the common law, in its eternal youth, grows to meet the demands of society. Thus, in very early times, the law gave a remedy only for physical interference with life and property, for trespasses *vi et armis*.[21] Then the "right to life" served only to protect the subject from battery in its various forms; liberty meant freedom from actual restraint; and the right to property secured to the individual his lands and his cattle. Later, there came a recognition of man's spiritual nature, of his feelings and his intellect. Gradually the scope of these legal rights broadened;

---

[18] Mason, *Brandeis, supra*, at 46.

[19] *See* James H. Barron, *Warren and Brandeis*, The Right to Privacy, 4 Harv. L. Rev. 193 (1890): *Demystifying a Landmark Citation*, 13 Suffolk L. Rev. 875 (1979).

[20] *See* Smith, *Ben Franklin's Web Site, supra*, at 118-19. For further discussion of the circumstances surrounding the publication of the article, see Martin Burgess Green, *The Mount Vernon Street Warrens: A Boston Story, 1860–1910* (1989); Morris L. Ernst & Alan U. Schwartz, *Privacy: The Right to Be Let Alone* 45-46 (1962); Philippa Strum, *Brandeis: Beyond Progressivism* (1993); Lewis J. Paper, *Brandeis* (1983); Irwin R. Kramer, *The Birth of Privacy Law: A Century Since Warren and Brandeis*, 39 Cath. U. L. Rev. 703 (1990); Dorothy Glancy, *The Invention of the Right to Privacy*, 21 Ariz. L. Rev. 1, 25-27 (1979); Symposium, *The Right to Privacy One Hundred Years Later*, 41 Case W. Res. L. Rev. 643-928 (1991).

[21] Editors' Note: Latin — By or with force and arms.

and now the right to life has come to mean the right to enjoy life, — the right to be let alone; the right to liberty secures the exercise of extensive civil privileges; and the term "property" has grown to comprise every form of possession — intangible, as well as tangible.

Thus, with the recognition of the legal value of sensations, the protection against actual bodily injury was extended to prohibit mere attempts to do such injury; that is, the putting another in fear of such injury. From the action of battery grew that of assault. Much later there came a qualified protection of the individual against offensive noises and odors, against dust and smoke, and excessive vibration. The law of nuisance was developed. So regard for human emotions soon extended the scope of personal immunity beyond the body of the individual. His reputation, the standing among his fellow-men, was considered, and the law of slander and libel arose. Man's family relations became a part of the legal conception of his life, and the alienation of a wife's affections was held remediable. Occasionally the law halted, — as in its refusal to recognize the intrusion by seduction upon the honor of the family. But even here the demands of society were met. A mean fiction, the action *per quod servitium amisit*,[22] was resorted to, and by allowing damages for injury to the parents' feelings, an adequate remedy was ordinarily afforded. Similar to the expansion of the right to life was the growth of the legal conception of property. From corporeal property arose the incorporeal rights issuing out of it; and then there opened the wide realm of intangible property, in the products and processes of the mind, as works of literature and art, goodwill, trade secrets, and trademarks.

This development of the law was inevitable. The intense intellectual and emotional life, and the heightening of sensations which came with the advance of civilization, made it clear to men that only a part of the pain, pleasure, and profit of life lay in physical things. Thoughts, emotions, and sensations demanded legal recognition, and the beautiful capacity for growth which characterizes the common law enabled the judges to afford the requisite protection, without the interposition of the legislature.

Recent inventions and business methods call attention to the next step which must be taken for the protection of the person, and for securing to the individual what Judge Cooley calls the right "to be let alone."[23] Instantaneous photographs and newspaper enterprise have invaded the sacred precincts of private and domestic life; and numerous mechanical devices threaten to make good the prediction that "what is whispered in the closet shall be proclaimed from the house-tops." For years there has been a feeling that the law must afford some remedy for the unauthorized circulation of portraits of private persons; and the evil of invasion of privacy by the newspapers, long keenly felt, has been but recently discussed by an able writer. The alleged facts of a somewhat notorious case brought before an inferior tribunal in New York a few months ago, directly involved the consideration of the right of circulating portraits; and the question whether our law will recognize and protect the right to privacy in this and in other respects must soon come before our courts for consideration.

---

[22] Editors' Note: Latin — Whereby he lost the services (of his servant).

[23] Cooley on Torts, 2d ed., p. 29.

Of the desirability — indeed of the necessity — of some such protection, there can, it is believed, be no doubt. The press is overstepping in every direction the obvious bounds of propriety and of decency. Gossip is no longer the resource of the idle and of the vicious, but has become a trade, which is pursued with industry as well as effrontery. To satisfy a prurient taste the details of sexual relations are spread broadcast in the columns of the daily papers. To occupy the indolent, column upon column is filled with idle gossip, which can only be procured by intrusion upon the domestic circle. The intensity and complexity of life, attendant upon advancing civilization, have rendered necessary some retreat from the world, and man, under the refining influence of culture, has become more sensitive to publicity, so that solitude and privacy have become more essential to the individual; but modern enterprise and invention have, through invasions upon his privacy, subjected him to mental pain and distress, far greater than could be inflicted by mere bodily injury. Nor is the harm wrought by such invasions confined to the suffering of those who may be made the subjects of journalistic or other enterprise. In this, as in other branches of commerce, the supply creates the demand. Each crop of unseemly gossip, thus harvested, becomes the seed of more, and, in direct proportion to its circulation, results in a lowering of social standards and of morality. Even gossip apparently harmless, when widely and persistently circulated, is potent for evil. It both belittles and perverts. It belittles by inverting the relative importance of things, thus dwarfing the thoughts and aspirations of a people. When personal gossip attains the dignity of print, and crowds the space available for matters of real interest to the community, what wonder that the ignorant and thoughtless mistake its relative importance. Easy of comprehension, appealing to that weak side of human nature which is never wholly cast down by the misfortunes and frailties of our neighbors, no one can be surprised that it usurps the place of interest in brains capable of other things. Triviality destroys at once robustness of thought and delicacy of feeling. No enthusiasm can flourish, no generous impulse can survive under its blighting influence.

It is our purpose to consider whether the existing law affords a principle which can properly be invoked to protect the privacy of the individual; and, if it does, what the nature and extent of such protection is.

Owing to the nature of the instruments by which privacy is invaded, the injury inflicted bears a superficial resemblance to the wrongs dealt with by the law of slander and of libel, while a legal remedy for such injury seems to involve the treatment of mere wounded feelings, as a substantive cause of action. The principle on which the law of defamation rests, covers, however, a radically different class of effects from those for which attention is now asked. It deals only with damage to reputation, with the injury done to the individual in his external relations to the community, by lowering him in the estimation of his fellows. The matter published of him, however widely circulated, and however unsuited to publicity, must, in order to be actionable, have a direct tendency to injure him in his intercourse with others, and even if in writing or in print, must subject him to the hatred, ridicule, or contempt of his fellow-men, — the effect of the publication upon his estimate of himself and upon his own feelings not forming an essential element in the cause of action. In short, the wrongs and correlative rights recognized by the law of slander and libel are in their nature material rather than spiritual. That branch of the law simply extends the protection surrounding physical property to certain of the conditions necessary or helpful to worldly prosperity. On the other hand, our law recognizes no principle upon which compensation can be granted for mere injury to the feelings. However painful the mental effects upon another of an act, though purely wanton or even malicious, yet if the act itself is otherwise lawful, the suffering inflicted is *damnum absque injuria.*[24] Injury of feelings may indeed be taken account of in ascertaining the amount of damages when attending what is recognized as a legal injury; but our system, unlike the Roman law, does not afford a remedy even for mental suffering which results from mere contumely and insult, from an intentional and unwarranted violation of the "honor" of another.

It is not however necessary, in order to sustain the view that the common law recognizes and upholds a principle applicable to cases of invasion of privacy, to invoke the analogy, which is but superficial, to injuries sustained, either by an attack upon reputation or by what the civilians called a violation of honor; for the legal doctrines relating to infractions of what is ordinarily termed the common-law right to intellectual and artistic property are, it is believed, but instances and applications of a general right to privacy, which properly understood afford a remedy for the evils under consideration.

The common law secures to each individual the right of determining, ordinarily, to what extent his thoughts, sentiments, and emotions shall be communicated to others. Under our system of government, he can never be compelled to express them (except when upon the witness-stand); and even if he has chosen to give them expression, he generally retains the power to fix the limits of the publicity which shall be given them. The existence of this right does not depend upon the particular method of expression adopted. It is immaterial whether it be by word or by signs, in painting, by sculpture, or in music. Neither does the existence of the right depend upon the nature or value of the thought or emotion, nor upon the excellence of the means of expression. The same protection is accorded to a casual letter or an entry in a diary and to the most valuable poem or essay, to a botch or daub and to a masterpiece. In every such case the individual is entitled to decide whether that which is his shall be given to the public. No other has the right to publish his productions in any form, without his consent. This right is wholly independent of the material on which, or the means by which, the thought, sentiment, or emotion is expressed. It may exist independently of any corporeal being, as in words spoken, a song sung, a drama acted. Or if expressed on any material, as in a poem in writing, the author may have parted with the paper, without forfeiting any proprietary right in the composition itself. The right is lost only when the author himself communicates his production to the public, — in other words, publishes it. It is entirely independent of the copyright laws, and their extension into the domain of art. The aim of those statutes is to secure to the author, composer, or artist the entire profits arising from publication; but the common-law protection enables him to control absolutely the act of publication, and in the exercise of his own discretion, to decide whether there shall be any publication at all. The statutory

[24] Editors' Note: Latin — Loss or harm from something other than a wrongful act and which occasions no legal remedy.

right is of no value, *unless* there is a publication; the common-law right is lost *as soon as* there is a publication.

What is the nature, the basis, of this right to prevent the publication of manuscripts or works of art? It is stated to be the enforcement of a right of property; and no difficulty arises in accepting this view, so long as we have only to deal with the reproduction of literary and artistic compositions. They certainly possess many of the attributes of ordinary property: they are transferable; they have a value; and publication or reproduction is a use by which that value is realized. But where the value of the production is found not in the right to take the profits arising from publication, but in the peace of mind or the relief afforded by the ability to prevent any publication at all, it is difficult to regard the right as one of property, in the common acceptation of that term. A man records in a letter to his son, or in his diary, that he did not dine with his wife on a certain day. No one into whose hands those papers fall could publish them to the world, even if possession of the documents had been obtained rightfully; and the prohibition would not be confined to the publication of a copy of the letter itself, or of the diary entry; the restraint extends also to a publication of the contents. What is the thing which is protected? Surely, not the intellectual act of recording the fact that the husband did not dine with his wife, but that fact itself. It is not the intellectual product, but the domestic occurrence. A man writes a dozen letters to different people. No person would be permitted to publish a list of the letters written. If the letters or the contents of the diary were protected as literary compositions, the scope of the protection afforded should be the same secured to a published writing under the copyright law. But the copyright law would not prevent an enumeration of the letters, or the publication of some of the facts contained therein. The copyright of a series of paintings or etchings would prevent a reproduction of the paintings as pictures; but it would not prevent a publication of list or even a description of them. Yet in the famous case of *Prince Albert v. Strange*, the court held that the common-law rule prohibited not merely the reproduction of the etchings which the plaintiff and Queen Victoria had made for their own pleasure, but also "the publishing (at least by printing or writing), though not by copy or resemblance, a description of them, whether more or less limited or summary, whether in the form of a catalogue or otherwise." Likewise, an unpublished collection of news possessing no element of a literary nature is protected from piracy.

That this protection cannot rest upon the right to literary or artistic property in any exact sense, appears the more clearly when the subject-matter for which protection is invoked is not even in the form of intellectual property, but has the attributes of ordinary tangible property. Suppose a man has a collection of gems or curiosities which he keeps private: it would hardly be contended that any person could publish a catalogue of them, and yet the articles enumerated are certainly not intellectual property in the legal sense, any more than a collection of stoves or of chairs.

The belief that the idea of property in its narrow sense was the basis of the protection of unpublished manuscripts led an able court to refuse, in several cases, injunctions against the publication of private letters, on the ground that "letters not possessing the attributes of literary compositions are not property entitled to protection;" and that it was "evident the plaintiff could not have considered the letters as of any value whatever as literary productions, for a letter cannot be considered of value to the author which he never would consent to have published." But those decisions have not been followed, and it may now be considered settled that the protection afforded by the common law to the author of any writing is entirely independent of its pecuniary value, its intrinsic merits, or of any intention to publish the same and, of course, also, wholly independent of the material, if any, upon which, or the mode in which, the thought or sentiment was expressed.

Although the courts have asserted that they rested their decisions on the narrow grounds of protection to property, yet there are recognitions of a more liberal doctrine. Thus in the case of *Prince Albert v. Strange*, already referred to, the opinions both of the Vice-Chancellor and of the Lord Chancellor, on appeal, show a more or less clearly defined perception of a principle broader than those which were mainly discussed, and on which they both placed their chief reliance. Vice-Chancellor Knight Bruce referred to publishing of a man that he had "written to particular persons or on particular subjects" as an instance of possibly injurious disclosures as to private matters, that the courts would in a proper case prevent; yet it is difficult to perceive how, in such a case, any right of privacy, in the narrow sense, would be drawn in question, or why, if such a publication would be restrained when it threatened to expose the victim not merely to sarcasm, but to ruin, it should not equally be enjoined, if it threatened to embitter his life. To deprive a man of the potential profits to be realized by publishing a catalogue of his gems cannot *per se* be a wrong to him. The possibility of future profits is not a right of property which the law ordinarily recognizes; it must, therefore, be an infraction of other rights which constitutes the wrongful act, and that infraction is equally wrongful, whether its results are to forestall the profits that the individual himself might secure by giving the matter a publicity obnoxious to him, or to gain an advantage at the expense of his mental pain and suffering. . . .

These considerations lead to the conclusion that the protection afforded to thoughts, sentiments, and emotions, expressed through the medium of writing or of the arts, so far as it consists in preventing publication, is merely an instance of the enforcement of the more general right of the individual to be let alone. It is like the right not [to] be assaulted or beaten, the right not [to] be imprisoned, the right not to be maliciously prosecuted, the right not to be defamed. In each of these rights, as indeed in all other rights recognized by the law, there inheres the quality of being owned or possessed — and (as that is the distinguishing attribute of property) there may be some propriety in speaking of those rights as property. But, obviously, they bear little resemblance to what is ordinarily comprehended under that term. The principle which protects personal writings and all other personal productions, not against theft and physical appropriation, but against publication in any form, is in reality not the principle of private property, but that of an inviolate personality.

If we are correct in this conclusion, the existing law affords a principle which may be invoked to protect the privacy of the individual from invasion either by the too enterprising press, the photographer, or the possessor of any other modern device for recording or reproducing scenes or sounds. For the protection afforded is not confined by the authorities to those cases where any particular medium or form of expression has been adopted, not to products of the intellect. The same protection is afforded to emotions and sensations expressed in a musical composition or other work of art as to a literary composition; and words spoken, a pantomime acted, a sonata performed, is no less entitled to protection than if each had been reduced to writing. The circumstance that a thought or emotion has been recorded in a permanent form renders its identification easier, and hence may be important from the point of view of evidence, but it has no significance as a matter of substantive right. If, then, the decisions indicate a general right to privacy for thoughts, emotions, and sensations, these should receive the same protection, whether expressed in writing, or in conduct, in conversation, in attitudes, or in facial expression.

It may be urged that a distinction should be taken between the deliberate expression of thoughts and emotions in literary or artistic compositions and the casual and often involuntary expression given to them in the ordinary conduct of life. In other words, it may be contended that the protection afforded is granted to the conscious products of labor, perhaps as an encouragement to effort. This contention, however plausible, has, in fact, little to recommend it. If the amount of labor involved be adopted as the test, we might well find that the effort to conduct one's self properly in business and in domestic relations had been far greater than that involved in painting a picture or writing a book; one would find that it was far easier to express lofty sentiments in a diary than in the conduct of a noble life. If the test of deliberateness of the act be adopted, much casual correspondence which is now accorded full protection would be excluded from the beneficent operation of existing rules. After the decisions denying the distinction attempted to be made between those literary productions which it was intended to publish and those which it was not, all considerations of the amount of labor involved, the degree of deliberation, the value of the product, and the intention of publishing must be abandoned, and no basis is discerned upon which the right to restrain publication and reproduction of such so-called literary and artistic works can be rested, except the right to privacy, as a part of the more general right to the immunity of the person, — the right to one's personality.

It should be stated that, in some instances where protection has been afforded against wrongful publication, the jurisdiction has been asserted, not on the ground of property, or at least not wholly on that ground, but upon the ground of an alleged breach of an implied contract or of a trust or confidence. . . .

This process of implying a term in a contract, or of implying a trust (particularly where the contract is written, and where there is no established usage or custom), is nothing more nor less than a judicial declaration that public morality, private justice, and general convenience demand the recognition of such a rule, and that the publication under similar circumstances would be considered an intolerable abuse. So long as these circumstances happen to present a contract upon which such a term can be engrafted by the judicial mind, or to supply relations upon which a trust or confidence can be erected, there may be no objection to working out the desired protection through the doctrines of contract or of trust. But the court can hardly stop there. The narrower doctrine may have satisfied the demands of society at a time when the abuse to be guarded against could rarely have arisen without violating a contract or a special confidence; but now that modern devices afford abundant opportunities for the perpetration of such wrongs without any participation by the injured party, the protection granted by the law must be placed upon a broader foundation. While, for instance, the state of the photographic art was such that one's picture could seldom be taken without his consciously "sitting" for the purpose, the law of contract or of trust might afford the prudent man sufficient safeguards against the improper circulation of his portrait; but since the latest advances in photographic art have rendered it possible to take pictures surreptitiously, the doctrines of contract and of trust are inadequate to support the required protection, and the law of tort must be resorted to. The right of property in its widest sense, including all possession, including all rights and privileges, and hence embracing the right to an inviolate personality, affords alone that broad basis upon which the protection which the individual demands can be rested.

Thus, the courts, in searching for some principle upon which the publication of private letters could be enjoined, naturally came upon the ideas of a breach of confidence, and of an implied contract; but it required little consideration to discern that this doctrine could not afford all the protection required, since it would not support the court in granting a remedy against a stranger; and so the theory of property in the contents of letters was adopted. Indeed, it is difficult to conceive on what theory of the law the casual recipient of a letter, who proceeds to publish it, is guilty of a breach of contract, express or implied, or of any breach of trust, in the ordinary acceptation of that term. Suppose a letter has been addressed to him without his solicitation. He opens it, and reads. Surely, he has not made any contract; he has not accepted any trust. He cannot, by opening and reading the letter, have come under any obligation save what the law declares; and, however expressed, that obligation is simply to observe the legal right of the sender, whatever it may be, and whether it be called his right or property in the contents of the letter, or his right to privacy. . . .

We must therefore conclude that the rights, so protected, whatever their exact nature, are not rights arising from contract or from special trust, but are rights as against the world; and, as above stated, the principle which has been applied to protect these rights is in reality not the principle of private property, unless that word be used in an extended and unusual sense. The principle which protects personal writings and any other productions of the intellect of or the emotions, is the right to privacy, and the law has no new principle to formulate when it extends this protection to the personal appearance, sayings, acts, and to personal relation, domestic or otherwise.

If the invasion of privacy constitutes a legal *injuria*, the elements for demanding redress exist, since already the value of mental suffering, caused by an act wrongful in itself, is recognized as a basis for compensation.

The right of one who has remained a private individual, to prevent his public portraiture, presents the simplest case for such extension; the right to protect one's self from pen portraiture, from a discussion by the press of one's private affairs, would be a more important and far-reaching one. If casual and unimportant statements in a letter, if handiwork, however inartistic and valueless, if possessions of all sorts are protected not only against reproduction, but against description and enumeration, how much more should the acts and sayings of a man in his social and domestic relations be guarded from ruthless publicity. If you may not reproduce a woman's face photographically without her consent, how much less should be tolerated the reproduction of her face, her form, and her actions, by graphic descriptions colored to suit a gross and depraved imagination.

The right to privacy, limited as such right must necessarily be, has already found expression in the law of France.

It remains to consider what are the limitations of this right to privacy, and what remedies may be granted for the enforcement of the right. To determine in advance of experience the exact line at which the dignity and convenience of the individual must yield to the demands of the public welfare or of private justice would be a difficult task; but the more general rules are furnished by the legal analogies already developed in the law of slander and libel, and in the law of literary and artistic property.

1. The right to privacy does not prohibit any publication of matter which is of public or general interest.

In determining the scope of this rule, aid would be afforded by the analogy, in the law of libel and slander, of cases which deal with the qualified privilege of comment and criticism on matters of public and general interest. There are of course difficulties in applying such a rule; but they are inherent in the subject-matter, and are certainly no greater than those which exist in many other branches of the law, — for instance, in that large class of cases in which the reasonableness or unreasonableness of an act is made the test of liability. The design of the law must be to protect those persons with whose affairs the community has no legitimate concern, from being dragged into an undesirable and undesired publicity and to protect all persons, whatsoever; their position or station, from having matters which they may properly prefer to keep private, made public against their will. It is the unwarranted invasion of individual privacy which is reprehended, and to be, so far as possible, prevented. The distinction, however, noted in the above statement is obvious and fundamental. There are persons who may reasonably claim as a right, protection from the notoriety entailed by being made the victims of journalistic enterprise. There are others who, in varying degrees, have renounced the right to live their lives screened from public observation. Matters which men of the first class may justly contend, concern themselves alone, may in those of the second be the subject of legitimate interest to their fellow-citizens. Peculiarities of manner and person, which in the ordinary individual should be free from comment, may acquire a public importance, if found in a candidate for public office. Some further discrimination is necessary, therefore, than to class facts or deeds as public or private according to a standard to be applied to the fact or deed *per se*. To publish of a modest and retiring individual that he suffers from an impediment in his speech or that he cannot spell correctly, is an unwarranted, if not an unexampled, infringement of his rights, while to state and comment on the same characteristics found in a would-be congressman could not be regarded as beyond the pale of propriety.

The general object in view is to protect the privacy of private life, and to whatever degree and in whatever connection a man's life has ceased to be private, before the publication under consideration has been made, to that extent the protection is to be withdrawn. Since, then, the propriety of publishing the very same facts may depend wholly upon the person concerning whom they are published, no fixed formula can be used to prohibit obnoxious publications. Any rule of liability adopted must have in it an elasticity which shall take account of the varying circumstances of each case, — a necessity which unfortunately renders such a doctrine not only more difficult of application, but also to a certain extent uncertain in its operation and easily rendered abortive. Besides, it is only the more flagrant breaches of decency and propriety that could in practice be reached, and it is not perhaps desirable even to attempt to repress everything which the nicest taste and keenest sense of the respect due to private life would condemn.

In general, then, the matters of which the publication should be repressed may be described as those which concern the private life, habits, acts, and relations of an individual, and have no legitimate connection with his fitness for a public office which he seeks or for which he is suggested, or for any public or quasi public position which he seeks or for which he is suggested, and have no legitimate relation to or bearing upon any act done by him in a public or quasi public capacity. The foregoing is not designed as a wholly accurate or exhaustive definition, since that which must ultimately in a vast number of cases become a question of individual judgment and opinion is incapable of such definition; but it is an attempt to indicate broadly the class of matters referred to. Some things all men alike are entitled to keep from popular curiosity, whether in public life or not, while others are only private because the persons concerned have not assumed a position which makes their doings legitimate matters of public investigation.

2. The right to privacy does not prohibit the communication of any matter, though in its nature private, when the publication is made under circumstances which would render it a privileged communication according to the law of slander and libel.

Under this rule, the right to privacy is not invaded by any publication made in a court of justice, in legislative bodies, or the committees of those bodies; in municipal assemblies, or the committees of such assemblies, or practically by any communication made in any other public body, municipal or parochial, or in any body quasi public, like the large voluntary associations formed for almost every purpose of benevolence, business, or other general interest; and (at least in many jurisdictions) reports of any such proceedings would in some measure be accorded a like privilege. Nor would the rule prohibit any publication made by one in the discharge of some public or private duty, whether legal or moral, or in conduct of one's own affairs, in matters where his own interest is concerned.

3. The law would probably not grant any redress for the invasion of privacy by oral publication in the absence of special damage.

The same reasons exist for distinguishing between oral and written publications of private matters, as is afforded in the law of defamation by the restricted liability for slander as compared with the liability for libel. The injury resulting from such oral communications would ordinarily be so trifling that the law might well, in the interest of free speech, disregard it altogether.

4. The right to privacy ceases upon the publication of the facts by the individual, or with his consent.

This is but another application of the rule which has become familiar in the law of literary and artistic property. The cases there decided establish also what should be deemed a publication, — the important principle in this connection being that a private communication of circulation for a restricted purpose is not a publication within the meaning of the law.

5. The truth of the matter published does not afford a defence. Obviously this branch of the law should have no concern with the truth or falsehood of the matters published. It is not for injury to the individual's character that redress or prevention is sought, but for injury to the right of privacy. For the former, the law of slander and libel provides perhaps a sufficient safeguard. The latter implies the right not merely to prevent inaccurate portrayal of private life, but to prevent its being depicted at all.

6. The absence of "malice" in the publisher does not afford a defence.

Personal ill-will is not an ingredient of the offence, any more than in an ordinary case of trespass to person or to property. Such malice is never necessary to be shown in an action for libel or slander at common law, except in rebuttal of some defence, *e.g.*, that the occasion rendered the communication privileged, or, under the statutes in this State and elsewhere, that the statement complained of was true. The invasion of the privacy that is to be protected is equally complete and equally injurious, whether the motives by which the speaker or writer was actuated are, taken by themselves, culpable or not; just as the damage to character, and to some extent the tendency to provoke a breach of the peace, is equally the result of defamation without regard to the motives leading to its publication. Viewed as a wrong to the individual, this rule is the same pervading the whole law of torts, by which one is held responsible for his intentional acts, even though they are committed with no sinister intent; and viewed as a wrong to society, it is the same principle adopted in a large category of statutory offences.

The remedies for an invasion of the right of privacy are also suggested by those administered in the law of defamation, and in the law of literary and artistic property, namely: —

1. An action of tort for damages in all cases. Even in the absence of special damages, substantial compensation could be allowed for injury to feelings as in the action of slander and libel.

2. An injunction, in perhaps a very limited class of cases.

It would doubtless be desirable that the privacy of the individual should receive the added protection of the criminal law, but for this, legislation would be required. Perhaps it would be deemed proper to bring the criminal liability for such publication within narrower limits; but that the community has an interest in preventing such invasions of privacy, sufficiently strong to justify the introduction of such a remedy, cannot be doubted. Still, the protection of society must come mainly through a recognition of the rights of the individual. Each man is responsible for his own acts and omissions only. If he condones what he reprobates, with a weapon at hand equal to his defence, he is responsible for the results. If he resists, public opinion will rally to his support. Has he then such a weapon? It is believed that the common law provides him with one, forged in the slow fire of the centuries, and to-day fitly tempered to his hand. The common law has always recognized a man's house as his castle, impregnable, often, even to its own officers engaged in the execution of its command. Shall the courts thus close the front entrance to constituted authority, and open wide the back door to idle or prurient curiosity?

NOTES & QUESTIONS

1. ***The Need for a New Right.*** The article argued for the creation of a new right — the right to privacy. Why did the authors believe that other legal claims were inadequate? For example, why does the law of defamation or the law of contracts not provide a sufficient remedy for the harm described by the authors? Why do Warren and Brandeis reject property rights and copyright as tools to protect privacy?
2. ***Deriving a Right to Privacy in the Common Law.*** How do Warren and Brandeis derive a right to privacy from the common law? Under what principle do they locate this right? In a footnote in the article, Warren and Brandeis observe:

   > The application of an existing principle to a new state of facts is not judicial legislation. To call it such is to assert that the existing body of law consists practically of the statutes and decided cases, and to deny that the principles (of which these cases are ordinarily said to be evidence) exist at all. It is not the application of an existing principle to new cases, but the introduction of a new principle, which is properly termed judicial legislation.
   >
   > But even the fact that a certain decision would involve judicial legislation should not be taken against the property of making it. This power has been commonly exercised by our judges, when applying to a new subject principles of private justice, moral fitness, and public convenience. Indeed, the elasticity of our law, its adaptability to new conditions, the capacity for growth, which has enabled it to meet the wants of an ever changing society and to apply immediate relief for every recognized wrong, have been its greatest boast. . . .

   Why do they include this footnote? Do you agree with their argument?
3. ***Inviolate Personality in the United States and Germany.*** The authors describe privacy as not "the principle of private property but that of inviolate personality." What does that mean? James Whitman traces the idea of the personality right from Warren and Brandeis back to nineteenth-century German legal philosophy:

   > . . . [N]ineteenth-century Germans often thought of "freedom" as opposed primarily to determinism. To be free was, in the first instance, not to be free from government control, nor to be free to engage in market transactions. Instead, to be free was to exercise free will, and the defining characteristic of creatures with free will was that they were unpredictably individual, creatures whom no science of mechanics or biology could ever capture in their full richness. For Germans who thought of things in this way, the purpose of "freedom" was to allow each individual fully to realize his potential as an individual: to give full expression to his peculiar capacities and powers.[25]

   Although the Warren and Brandeis article has been highly influential, their concept of a personality right has failed to gain traction in U.S. privacy law.

---

[25] James Q. Whitman, *The Two Western Cultures of Privacy: Dignity Versus Liberty*, 113 Yale L.J. 1151, 1181 (2004).

Nonetheless, the idea of a personality right has formed the basis of modern German information privacy law. As Paul Schwartz and Karl-Nikolaus Peifer state, it is "a 'source right' that has proven a fertile source for the creation of a related series of legal rights" in Germany.[26] More specifically, they note that "the right has been used to protect honor and reputation, privacy in a spatial sense (a '*Privatsphäre*,' or a private area), individuality, and commercial uses of personality." Why do you think the concept of a "right of personality" has been unsuccessful as a legal concept for privacy in the United States?

4. ***"The Right to Be Let Alone."*** Warren and Brandeis refer to privacy as "the right to be let alone." This phrase was coined by Judge Thomas Cooley earlier in his famous treatise on torts.[27] Do Warren and Brandeis define what privacy is or elaborate upon what being "let alone" consists of? If so, what do they say privacy is? Is this a good account of what constitutes privacy?
5. ***The Scope of the Right to Privacy.*** Brandeis and Warren were careful not to describe privacy as an absolute right. They set out six limitations on the right to privacy. Consider the first limitation and the relationship between the right to privacy and the need for publication on matters of public concern. What conclusions do the authors reach about these competing claims? According to Warren and Brandeis, would the reporting that a public official engaged in illegal business practices be protected by a right to privacy? What about illicit sexual activity? Consider the holding of the *Sidis* court regarding a person who was once of public interest due to his great achievements. Do you think that Warren and Brandeis would agree with the conclusion of *Sidis*?
6. ***The Economics of Gossip.*** Warren and Brandeis begin with a startling observation about the economics of gossip: "In this, as in other branches of commerce, the supply creates the demand." Have Warren and Brandeis inverted the normal concept in which demand drives supply? Note that already in the early nineteenth century, Jean-Baptiste Say, the French economist, famously expressed the idea, henceforth known as Say's Law, that the supply of a product would inherently create demand for it. Is gossip such a product?
7. ***The Nature of the Injury Caused by Privacy Invasions.*** Warren and Brandeis argue that privacy invasions are more harmful than bodily injuries. Do you agree? Warren and Brandeis characterize the injury caused by the violation of privacy as an injury to the feelings. Do you agree? Or do you think that the injury extends beyond an injury to the feelings?
8. ***Remedies.*** Brandeis and Warren suggest two remedies for an invasion of privacy — an action in tort and injunction. These remedies are similar to those in defamation and copyright. What do the authors say about a criminal remedy?

---

[26] Paul M. Schwartz & Karl-Nikolaus Peifer, *Prosser's Privacy and the German Right of Personality*, 98 Cal. L. Rev. 1925, 1952 (2010).

[27] Thomas M. Cooley, *Law of Torts* 29 (2d ed. 1888).

9. ***Criticisms.*** Some have argued that the article is a defense of bourgeois values, i.e., the freedom of an elite group to avoid public scrutiny.[28] Which aspects of the article support this view? Do parts of the article suggest otherwise? Is privacy, as described in the Warren and Brandeis article, a class-based right?
10. ***Did Brandeis Change His Mind?*** Neil Richards argues that Brandeis's views about the importance of publicity and free speech eventually eclipsed the views he set forth in his article with Warren. According to Richards, the First Amendment views that Brandeis developed in the 1920s are "inconsistent with many aspects of the right to privacy that he called for in 1890." As a further matter, Richard contends that "to the extent [Brandeis] retained a belief in tort privacy to the end of his life, it was a narrow category subordinated to the interests of publicity and free speech." At a normative level, Richards builds on Brandeis to develop a "concept of intellectual privacy" — a more focused concept that views privacy as a paramount value when it "is relevant to the activities of thinking, reading, and discussing safeguarded by the First Amendment."[29]

(b) The Recognition of Warren and Brandeis's Privacy Torts

Warren and Brandeis's 1890 article suggested that the existing causes of action under the common law did not adequately protect privacy but that the legal concepts in the common law could be modified to achieve the task. As early as 1903, courts and legislatures responded to the Warren and Brandeis article by creating a number of privacy torts to redress the harms that Warren and Brandeis had noted. In *Roberson v. Rochester Folding Box Co.*, 64 N.E. 442 (N.Y. 1902), the New York Court of Appeals refused to recognize a common law tort action for privacy invasions. Franklin Mills Flour displayed a lithograph of Abigail Roberson (a teenager) on 25,000 advertisement flyers without her consent. The lithograph printed her photograph with the advertising pun: "Flour of the Family." Roberson claimed that the use of her image on the flyer caused her great humiliation and resulted in illness requiring medical help. The court, however, concluded:

> . . . There is no precedent for such an action to be found in the decisions of this court. . . . Mention of such a right is not to be found in Blackstone, Kent, or any other of the great commentators upon the law; nor, so far as the learning of counsel or the courts in this case have been able to discover, does its existence seem to have been asserted prior to about the year 1890. . . .
>
> The legislative body could very well interfere and arbitrarily provide that no one should be permitted for his own selfish purpose to use the picture or the name of another for advertising purposes without his general consent. In such event no embarrassment would result to the general body of law, for the law would be applicable only to cases provided for by statute. The courts, however, being without authority to legislate, are required to decide cases upon principle, and so are necessarily embarrassed by precedents created by

---

[28] *See* Donald R. Pember, *Privacy and the Press* (1972).

[29] Neil Richards, *The Puzzle of Brandeis, Privacy, and Speech*, 63 Vand. L. Rev. 1295, 1312 (2010).

> an extreme, and therefore unjustifiable, application of an old principle. . . . [W]hile justice in a given case may be worked out by a decision of the court according to the notions of right which govern the individual judge or body of judges comprising the court, the mischief which will finally result may be almost incalculable under our system, which makes a decision in one case a precedent for decisions in all future cases which are akin to it in the essential facts. . . .

Shortly after the decision, a note in the *Yale Law Journal* criticized the *Roberson* decision because it enabled the press "to pry into and grossly display before the public matters of the most private and personal concern."[30] One of the judges in the majority defended the opinion in the *Columbia Law Review*.[31]

In 1903, the New York legislature responded to the explicit invitation in *Roberson* to legislate by creating a privacy tort action by statute. *See* N.Y. Civ. Rights Act § 51. This statute is still in use today. As you will see again later in this text, courts are frequently engaged in a dialogue with legislatures about the scope of privacy rights.

In the 1905 case *Pavesich v. New England Life Insurance Co.*, 50 S.E. 68 (Ga. 1905), Georgia became the first state to recognize a common law tort action for privacy invasions. There, a newspaper published a life insurance advertisement with a photograph of the plaintiff without the plaintiff's consent. The court held:

> . . . The right of privacy has its foundation in the instincts of nature. It is recognized intuitively, consciousness being the witness that can be called to establish its existence. Any person whose intellect is in a normal condition recognizes at once that as to each individual member of society there are matters private, and there are matters public so far as the individual is concerned. Each individual as instinctively resents any encroachment by the public upon his rights which are of a private nature as he does the withdrawal of those of his rights which are of a public nature. A right of privacy in matters purely private is therefore derived from natural law. . . .
>
> All will admit that the individual who desires to live a life of seclusion cannot be compelled against his consent, to exhibit his person in any public place, unless such exhibition is demanded by the law of the land. He may be required to come from his place of seclusion to perform public duties — to serve as a juror and to testify as a witness and the like; but, when the public duty is once performed, if he exercises his liberty to go again into seclusion, no one can deny him the right. One who desires to live a life of partial seclusion has a right to choose the times, places, and manner in which and at which he will submit himself to the public gaze. Subject to the limitation above referred to, the body of a person cannot be put on exhibition at any time or at any place without his consent. . . .
>
> It therefore follows from what has been said that a violation of the right of privacy is a direct invasion of a legal right of the individual. . . .

---

[30] *An Actionable Right to Privacy?*, 12 Yale L.J. 34 (1902).

[31] Denis O'Brien, *The Right to Privacy*, 2 Colum. L. Rev. 486 (1902).

In 1960, Dean William Prosser wrote his famous article, *Privacy*, examining the over 300 privacy tort cases decided in the 70 years since the Warren and Brandeis article.

WILLIAM PROSSER, *PRIVACY*

48 Cal. L. Rev. 383 (1960)

. . . The law of privacy comprises four distinct kinds of invasion of four different interests of the plaintiff, which are tied together by the common name, but otherwise have almost nothing in common except that each represents an interference with the right of the plaintiff, in the phrase coined by Judge Cooley, "to be let alone." Without any attempt at exact definition, these four torts may be described as follows:

1. Intrusion upon the plaintiff's seclusion or solitude, or into his private affairs.
2. Public disclosure of embarrassing private facts about the plaintiff.
3. Publicity which places the plaintiff in a false light in the public eye.
4. Appropriation, for the defendant's advantage, of the plaintiff's name or likeness. . . .

Judge Briggs has described the present state of the law of privacy as "still that of a haystack in a hurricane." Disarray there certainly is; but almost all of the confusion is due to a failure to separate and distinguish these four forms of invasion and to realize that they call for different things. . . .

Taking them in order — intrusion, disclosure, false light, and appropriation — the first and second require the invasion of something secret, secluded or private pertaining to the plaintiff; the third and fourth do not. The second and third depend upon publicity, while the first does not, nor does the fourth, although it usually involves it. The third requires falsity or fiction; the other three do not. The fourth involves a use for the defendant's advantage, which is not true of the rest. Obviously this is an area in which one must tread warily and be on the lookout for bogs. Nor is the difficulty decreased by the fact that quite often two or more of these forms of invasion may be found in the same case, and quite conceivably in all four.

NOTES & QUESTIONS

1. ***The Restatement of Torts.*** Prosser's analytical framework imposed order and clarity on the jumbled line of cases that followed the Warren and Brandeis article. The Restatement of Torts recognizes the four torts Prosser described in his article. These torts are known collectively as "invasion of privacy." The torts are: (1) intrusion upon seclusion, (2) public disclosure of private facts, (3) false light, and (4) appropriation.
2. ***The Interests Protected by the Privacy Torts.*** In response to Prosser's assertion that the privacy torts have almost "nothing in common," Edward Bloustein replied that "what provoked Warren and Brandeis to write their

article was a fear that a rampant press feeding on the stuff of private life would destroy individual dignity and integrity and emasculate individual freedom and independence." This underlying principle is a protection of "human dignity" and "personality."[32]

In contrast to Bloustein, Robert Post contends that the privacy torts do "not simply uphold the interests of individuals against the demands of the community, but instead safeguard[ ] rules of civility that in some significant measure constitute both individuals and community." Post argues that the torts establish boundaries between people, which when violated create strife. The privacy torts promote "forms of respect [for other people] by which we maintain a community."[33]

3. ***Prosser's Privacy at 50.*** In 2010, the *California Law Review* held a symposium at Berkeley Law School to celebrate the fiftieth anniversary of the publication of Prosser's *Privacy*. The verdict on the momentous article is mixed. Lior Strahilevitz advocates abandoning the Prosser categories and replacing them with a unitary tort for invasion of privacy. The key under the recast privacy tort would simply be whether "the gravity of the harm to the plaintiff's privacy interest [is] outweighed by a paramount public policy interest."[34]

Along similar negative lines, Neil Richards and Daniel Solove concluded that Prosser's view of the privacy tort has been "rigid and ossifying." Dean Prosser "stunted [privacy law's] development in ways that have limited its ability to adapt to the problems of the Information Age." The authors conclude that tort law should look beyond the narrow categories Prosser proposed in order for it to "regain the creative spirit it once possessed." One way for tort law to do so, in their view, would be to adopt the English approach to the tort of confidentiality.[35]

In contrast, Paul Schwartz and Karl-Nikolaus Peifer praised Prosser: "Prosser pragmatically assessed the kind and amount of privacy that the American legal system was willing to accommodate." In their summary, "Prosser's contribution generated useful doctrinal categories where previously had been unclassified cases and a lingering air of skepticism towards the tort."[36]

Would it be useful to extend the four privacy torts as Richards and Solove propose? Or would a better approach be to replace Prosser's four torts with pure balancing as Strahilevitz advocates? Or do Prosser's categories adequately capture the various privacy interests that should be addressed by tort law?

---

[32] Edward J. Bloustein, *Privacy as an Aspect of Human Dignity: An Answer to Dean Prosser*, 39 N.Y.U. L. Rev. 962, 974, 1000-01 (1964).

[33] Robert C. Post, *The Social Foundations of Privacy: Community and Self in the Common Law Tort*, 77 Cal. L. Rev. 957 (1989).

[34] Lior Strahilevitz, *Reunifying Privacy Law*, 98 Cal. L. Rev. 2007 (2010).

[35] Neil Richards & Daniel Solove, *Prosser's Privacy Law: A Mixed Legacy*, 98 Cal. L. Rev. 1887, 1924 (2010).

[36] Paul M. Schwartz & Karl-Nikolaus Peifer, *Prosser's Privacy and the German Right of Personality*, 98 Cal. L. Rev. 1925, 1982 (2010).

LAKE V. WAL-MART STORES, INC.

582 N.W.2d 231 (Minn. 1998)

BLATZ, C.J. . . . Elli Lake and Melissa Weber appeal from a dismissal of their complaint for failure to state a claim upon which relief may be granted. The district court and court of appeals held that Lake and Weber's complaint alleging intrusion upon seclusion, appropriation, publication of private facts, and false light publicity could not proceed because Minnesota does not recognize a common law tort action for invasion of privacy. We reverse as to the claims of intrusion upon seclusion, appropriation, and publication of private facts, but affirm as to false light publicity.

Nineteen-year-old Elli Lake and 20-year-old Melissa Weber vacationed in Mexico in March 1995 with Weber's sister. During the vacation, Weber's sister took a photograph of Lake and Weber naked in the shower together. After their vacation, Lake and Weber brought five rolls of film to the Dilworth, Minnesota Wal-Mart store and photo lab. When they received their developed photographs along with the negatives, an enclosed written notice stated that one or more of the photographs had not been printed because of their "nature."

In July 1995, an acquaintance of Lake and Weber alluded to the photograph and questioned their sexual orientation. Again, in December 1995, another friend told Lake and Weber that a Wal-Mart employee had shown her a copy of the photograph. By February 1996, Lake was informed that one or more copies of the photograph were circulating in the community.

Lake and Weber filed a complaint against Wal-Mart Stores, Inc. and one or more as-yet unidentified Wal-Mart employees on February 23, 1996, alleging the four traditional invasion of privacy torts — intrusion upon seclusion, appropriation, publication of private facts, and false light publicity. . . . The district court granted Wal-Mart's motion to dismiss, explaining that Minnesota has not recognized any of the four invasion of privacy torts. The court of appeals affirmed.

Whether Minnesota should recognize any or all of the invasion of privacy causes of action is a question of first impression in Minnesota. . . .

This court has the power to recognize and abolish common law doctrines. The common law is not composed of firmly fixed rules. Rather, as we have long recognized, the common law:

> is the embodiment of broad and comprehensive unwritten principles, inspired by natural reason, an innate sense of justice, adopted by common consent for the regulation and government of the affairs of men. It is the growth of ages, and an examination of many of its principles, as enunciated and discussed in the books, discloses a constant improvement and development in keeping with advancing civilization and new conditions of society. Its guiding star has always been the rule of right and wrong, and in this country its principles demonstrate that there is in fact, as well as in theory, a remedy for all wrongs.

As society changes over time, the common law must also evolve:

> It must be remembered that the common law is the result of growth, and that its development has been determined by the social needs of the community which it governs. It is the resultant of conflicting social forces, and those forces which are for the time dominant leave their impress upon the law. It is of judicial origin, and seeks to establish doctrines and rules for the determination, protection, and enforcement of legal rights. Manifestly it must change as society changes and new rights are recognized. To be an efficient instrument, and not a mere abstraction, it must gradually adapt itself to changed conditions.

To determine the common law, we look to other states as well as to England.

The tort of invasion of privacy is rooted in a common law right to privacy first described in an 1890 law review article by Samuel Warren and Louis Brandeis. The article posited that the common law has always protected an individual's person and property, with the extent and nature of that protection changing over time. The fundamental right to privacy is both reflected in those protections and grows out of them:

> Thus, in the very early times, the law gave a remedy only for physical interference with life and property, for trespass vi et armis. Then the "right to life" served only to protect the subject from battery in its various forms; liberty meant freedom from actual restraint; and the right to property secured to the individual his lands and his cattle. Later, there came a recognition of a man's spiritual nature, of his feelings and his intellect. Gradually the scope of these legal rights broadened; and now the right to life has come to mean the right to enjoy life, — the right to be let alone; the right to liberty secures the exercise of extensive civil privileges; and the term "property" has grown to comprise every form of possession — intangible, as well as tangible.

Although no English cases explicitly articulated a "right to privacy," several cases decided under theories of property, contract, or breach of confidence also included invasion of privacy as a basis for protecting personal violations. The article encouraged recognition of the common law right to privacy, as the strength of our legal system lies in its elasticity, adaptability, capacity for growth, and ability "to meet the wants of an ever changing society and to apply immediate relief for every recognized wrong.". . .

Today, the vast majority of jurisdictions now recognize some form of the right to privacy. Only Minnesota, North Dakota, and Wyoming have not yet recognized any of the four privacy torts. Although New York and Nebraska courts have declined to recognize a common law basis for the right to privacy and instead provide statutory protection, we reject the proposition that only the legislature may establish new causes of action. The right to privacy is inherent in the English protections of individual property and contract rights and the "right to be let alone" is recognized as part of the common law across this country. Thus, it is within the province of the judiciary to establish privacy torts in this jurisdiction.

Today we join the majority of jurisdictions and recognize the tort of invasion of privacy. The right to privacy is an integral part of our humanity; one has a public persona, exposed and active, and a private persona, guarded and preserved. The heart of our liberty is choosing which parts of our lives shall become public and which parts we shall hold close. . . .

We decline to recognize the tort of false light publicity at this time. We are concerned that claims under false light are similar to claims of defamation, and to the extent that false light is more expansive than defamation, tension between this tort and the First Amendment is increased.

False light is the most widely criticized of the four privacy torts and has been rejected by several jurisdictions. . . .

Thus we recognize a right to privacy present in the common law of Minnesota, including causes of action in tort for intrusion upon seclusion, appropriation, and publication of private facts, but we decline to recognize the tort of false light publicity. . . .

TOMLJANOVICH, J. dissenting. I would not recognize a cause of action for intrusion upon seclusion, appropriation or publication of private facts. . . .

An action for an invasion of the right to privacy is not rooted in the Constitution. "[T]he Fourth Amendment cannot be translated into a general constitutional 'right to privacy.' " *Katz v. United States*, 389 U.S. 347, 350 (1967). Those privacy rights that have their origin in the Constitution are much more fundamental rights of privacy — marriage and reproduction. *See Griswold v. Connecticut*, 381 U.S. 479, 485 (1965) (penumbral rights of privacy and repose protect notions of privacy surrounding the marriage relationship and reproduction).

We have become a much more litigious society since 1975 when we acknowledged that we have never recognized a cause of action for invasion of privacy. We should be even more reluctant now to recognize a new tort.

In the absence of a constitutional basis, I would leave to the legislature the decision to create a new tort for invasion of privacy.

NOTES & QUESTIONS

1. ***Other Remedies?*** If the Minnesota Supreme Court had rejected the privacy tort, what other legal remedies might be available to Elli Lake?
2. ***Postscript.*** What happened in *Lake* after the Minnesota Supreme Court's decision? In response to a query from the casebook authors, the lead attorney for the *Lake* plaintiff, Keith L. Miller of Miller, Norman & Associates, Ltd., explained that his client lost at the trial that followed the remand. He writes: "The jury found that an invasion of Ms. Lake's privacy had occurred, but that it did not happen 'in the course and scope' of a Wal-Mart worker's employment." In other words, tort notions of agency were found to apply, and a privacy tort violation could be attributed to Wal-Mart only if the employee had carried out the tort in the course and scope of employment. Miller added: "Our proof was problematic because, expectedly, no employee could specifically be identified as the culprit. It was all circumstantial." Finally, he summarized his experience litigating this case: "Gratifying? Certainly. Remunerative? Not so much."
3. ***Legislatures vs. Courts.*** The dissent in *Lake* contends, in a similar way as *Roberson*, that it should be the legislature, not the courts, that recognizes new tort actions to protect privacy. In New York, the statute passed in response to

Roberson remains the state's source for privacy tort remedies. Like New York, some states have recognized the privacy torts legislatively; other states, like Georgia in *Pavesich* and Minnesota in *Lake*, have recognized them judicially. Which means of recognizing the torts do you believe to be most justifiable? Why? Does the legislature have expertise that courts lack? Are courts more or less sensitive to civil rights issues, such as privacy?

(c) Privacy Protection in Tort Law

The Privacy Torts. Prosser's classification of these torts survives to this day. The Restatement (Second) of Torts recognizes four privacy torts:

(1) *Public Disclosure of Private Facts.* This tort creates a cause of action for one who publicly discloses a private matter that is "highly offensive to a reasonable person" and "is not of legitimate concern to the public." Restatement (Second) of Torts § 652D (1977).

(2) *Intrusion upon Seclusion.* This tort provides a remedy when one intrudes "upon the solitude or seclusion of another or his private affairs or concerns" if the intrusion is "highly offensive to a reasonable person." Restatement (Second) of Torts § 652B (1977).

(3) *False Light.* This tort creates a cause of action when one publicly discloses a matter that places a person "in a false light" that is "highly offensive to a reasonable person." Restatement (Second) of Torts § 652E (1977).

(4) *Appropriation.* Under this tort, a plaintiff has a remedy against one "who appropriates to his own use or benefit the name or likeness" of the plaintiff. Restatement (Second) of Torts § 652C (1977).

Today, most states recognize some or all of these torts.

Breach of Confidentiality. The tort of breach of confidentiality provides a remedy when a professional (i.e., doctor, lawyer, banker) divulges a patient's or client's confidential information.

Defamation. The law of defamation existed long before Warren and Brandeis's article. Defamation law, consisting of the torts of libel and slander, creates liability when one makes a false statement about a person that harms the person's reputation. The Supreme Court has held that the First Amendment places certain limits on defamation law.

Infliction of Emotional Distress. The tort of intentional infliction of emotional distress can also serve as a remedy for certain privacy invasions. This tort provides a remedy when one "by extreme and outrageous conduct intentionally or recklessly causes severe emotional distress to another." Restatement (Second) of Torts § 46 (1977). Since privacy invasions can often result in severe emotional distress, this tort may provide a remedy. However, it is limited by the requirement of "extreme and outrageous conduct."

(d) Privacy Protection in Evidence Law

The law of evidence has long recognized privacy as an important goal that can override the truth-seeking function of the trial. Under the common law, certain communications are privileged, and hence cannot be inquired into during a legal proceeding. The law of evidence has recognized the importance of protecting the privacy of communications between attorney and client, priest and penitent, husband and wife, physician and patient, and psychotherapist and patient.

(e) Privacy Protection via Property Rights

Property Rights. Although there are few property laws specifically governing privacy, these laws often implicate privacy. The appropriation tort is akin to a property right, and some commentators suggest that personal information should be viewed as a form of property.[37] If personal information is understood as a form of property, the tort of conversion might apply to those who collect and use a person's private data. Recall, however, that Warren and Brandeis rejected property as an adequate protection for privacy. What kind of market structures might be needed if personal data is to be traded or sold?

Trespass. The law of trespass, which provides tort remedies and criminal penalties for the unauthorized entry onto another's land, can protect privacy. There is some overlap between the torts of intrusion and trespass, as many forms of intrusion involve a trespass as well.

(f) Privacy Protection in Contract Law

Sometimes specific contractual provisions protect against the collection, use, or disclosure of personal information. In certain contexts, courts have entertained actions for breach of implied contract or tort actions based on implicit duties once certain relationships are established, such as physician-patient relationships, which have been analogized to fiduciary relationships. Privacy policies as well as terms of service containing privacy provisions can sometimes be analogized to a contract.

Contract can also function as a way of sidestepping state and federal privacy laws. Many employers make employees consent to drug testing as well as e-mail and workplace surveillance in their employment contracts.

(g) Privacy Protection in Criminal Law

Warren and Brandeis noted that under certain circumstances, criminal law would be appropriate to protect privacy. The criminal law protects bodily invasions, such as assault, battery, and rape. The privacy of one's home is also

[37] *See, e.g.*, Alan Westin, *Privacy and Freedom* 324 (1967); *see also* Richard S. Murphy, *Property Rights in Personal Information: An Economic Defense of Privacy*, 84 Geo. L.J. 2381 (1996); Richard A. Posner, *The Economics of Justice* (1981); Lawrence Lessig, *Code and Other Laws of Cyberspace* 154-62 (1999); Paul M. Schwartz, *Property, Privacy, and Personal Data*, 117 Harv. L. Rev. 2055 (2004).

protected by criminal sanctions for trespass. Stalking and harassing can give rise to criminal culpability. The crime of blackmail prohibits coercing an individual by threatening to expose her personal secrets. Many of the statutes protecting privacy also contain criminal penalties, such as the statutes pertaining to wiretapping and identity theft.

2. CONSTITUTIONAL LAW

Federal Constitutional Law. Although the United States Constitution does not specifically mention privacy, it has a number of provisions that protect privacy, and it has been interpreted as providing a right to privacy. In some instances the First Amendment serves to safeguard privacy. For example, the First Amendment protects the right to speak anonymously. *See McIntyre v. Ohio Election Comm'n*, 514 U.S. 334 (1995). The First Amendment's Freedom of Association Clause protects individuals from being compelled to disclose the groups to which they belong or contribute. Under the First Amendment "Congress shall make no law . . . abridging . . . the right of the people peaceably to assemble. . . ." For example, the Court has struck down the compulsory disclosure of the names and addresses of an organization's members, *see NAACP v. Alabama*, 357 U.S. 449 (1958), as well as a law requiring public teachers to list all organizations to which they belong or contribute. *See Shelton v. Tucker*, 364 U.S. 479 (1960).

The Third Amendment protects the privacy of the home by preventing the government from requiring soldiers to reside in people's homes: "No Soldier shall, in time of peace be quartered in any house, without the consent of the Owner, nor in time of war, but in a manner to be prescribed by law."

The Fourth Amendment provides that people have the right "to be secure in their persons, houses, papers, and effects, against unreasonable searches and seizures. . . ." Almost 40 years after writing *The Right to Privacy*, Brandeis, then a Supreme Court Justice, wrote a dissent that has had a significant influence on Fourth Amendment law. The case was *Olmstead v. United States*, 277 U.S. 438 (1928), where the Court held that wiretapping was not an invasion of privacy under the Fourth Amendment because it was not a physical trespass into the home. Justice Brandeis dissented, contending that the central interest protected by the Fourth Amendment was not property but the "right to be let alone":

> The protection guaranteed by the amendments is much broader in scope. The makers of our Constitution undertook to secure conditions favorable to the pursuit of happiness. They recognized the significance of man's spiritual nature, of his feelings and of his intellect. They knew that only a part of the pain, pleasure and satisfactions of life are to be found in material things. They sought to protect Americans in their beliefs, their thoughts, their emotions and their sensations. They conferred, as against the government, the right to be let alone — the most comprehensive of rights and the right most valued by civilized men. To protect that right, every unjustifiable intrusion by the government upon the privacy of the individual, whatever the means employed, must be deemed a violation of the Fourth Amendment.

Brandeis's dissent demonstrated that the "right to be let alone" did not merely have common law roots (as he had argued in *The Right to Privacy*) but also had constitutional roots as well in the Fourth Amendment.

Modern Fourth Amendment law incorporates much of Brandeis's view. In *Katz v. United States*, 389 U.S. 347 (1967), the Court held that the Fourth Amendment "protects people, not places" and said that the police must obtain a warrant when a search takes place in a public pay phone on a public street. The Court currently determines a person's right to privacy by the "reasonable expectations of privacy" test, a standard articulated in Justice Harlan's concurrence to *Katz*. First, a person must "have exhibited an actual (subjective) expectation of privacy" and, second, "the expectation [must] be one that society is prepared to recognize as 'reasonable.' "

The Fifth Amendment guarantees that: "No person . . . shall be compelled in any criminal case to be a witness against himself. . . ." This right, commonly referred to as the "privilege against self-incrimination," protects privacy by restricting the ability of the government to force individuals to divulge certain information about themselves.

In the landmark 1965 case *Griswold v. Connecticut*, 318 U.S. 479 (1965), the Court declared that an individual has a constitutional right to privacy. The Court located this right within the "penumbras" or "zones" of freedom created by an expansive interpretation of the Bill of Rights. Subsequently, the Court has handed down a line of cases protecting certain fundamental life choices such as abortion and aspects of one's intimate sexual life.

In *Whalen v. Roe*, 429 U.S. 589 (1977), the Court extended its substantive due process privacy protection to information privacy, holding that the "zone of privacy" protected by the Constitution encompasses the "individual interest in avoiding disclosure of personal matters." This offshoot of the right to privacy has become known as the "constitutional right to information privacy."

State Constitutional Law. A number of states have directly provided for the protection of privacy in their constitutions. For example, the Alaska Constitution provides: "The right of the people to privacy is recognized and shall not be infringed." Alaska Const. art. I, § 22. According to the California Constitution: "All people are by their nature free and independent and have inalienable rights. Among these are enjoying and defending life and liberty, acquiring, possessing, and protecting property, and pursuing and obtaining safety, happiness, and privacy." Cal. Const. art. I, § 1. Unlike most state constitutional provisions, the California constitutional right to privacy applies not only to state actors but also to private parties. *See, e.g.*, *Hill v. NCAA*, 865 P.2d 638 (Cal. 1994). The Florida Constitution provides: "Every natural person has the right to be let alone and free from governmental intrusion into his private life except as otherwise provided herein." Fla. Const. art. I, § 23.[38]

---

[38] For more examples, see Ariz. Const. art. II, § 8; Mont. Const. art. II, § 10; Haw. Const. art. I, § 6; Ill. Const. art. I, §§ 6, 12; La. Const. art. I, § 5; S.C. Const. art. I, § 10; Wash. Const. art. I, § 7. For a further discussion of state constitutional protections of privacy, see Timothy O. Lenz, *"Rights Talk" About Privacy in State Courts*, 60 Alb. L. Rev. 1613 (1997); Mark Silverstein, Note, *Privacy Rights in State Constitutions: Models for Illinois?*, 1989 U. Ill. L. Rev. 215.

3. STATUTORY LAW

Federal Statutory Law. From the mid-1960s to the mid-1970s, privacy emerged as a central political and social concern. In tune with the heightened attention to privacy, philosophers, legal scholars, and others turned their focus on privacy, raising public awareness about the growing threats to privacy from technology.[39]

In the mid-1960s, electronic eavesdropping erupted into a substantial public issue, spawning numerous television news documentaries as well as receiving significant attention in major newspapers. A proposal for a National Data Center in 1965 triggered public protest and congressional hearings. At this time, the computer was a new and unexplored technological tool that raised risks of unprecedented data collection about individuals, with potentially devastating effects on privacy. Indeed, toward the end of the 1960s, the issue of the collection of personal information in databases had become one of the defining social issues of American society.

During this time the Supreme Court announced landmark decisions regarding the right to privacy, including *Griswold v. Connecticut* in 1965 and *Roe v. Wade* in 1973, which were landmark decisions regarding the right to decisional/reproductive privacy and autonomy. The famous reasonable expectations of privacy test in Fourth Amendment jurisprudence emerged in 1967 with *Katz v. United States*.

Due to growing fears about the ability of computers to store and search personal information, Congress devoted increasing attention to the issue of privacy. As Priscilla Regan observes:

> In 1965, a new problem was placed on the congressional agenda by subcommittee chairs in both the House and the Senate. The problem was defined as the invasion of privacy by computers and evoked images of *1984*, the "Computerized Man," and a dossier society. Press interest was high, public concern was generated and resulted in numerous letters being sent to members of Congress, and almost thirty days of congressional hearings were held in the late 1960s and early 1970s.[40]

In 1973, in a highly influential report, the United States Department of Health, Education, and Welfare (HEW) undertook an extensive review of data processing in the United States. Among many recommendations, the HEW report proposed that a Code of Fair Information Practices be established. The Fair Information Practices consist of a number of basic information privacy principles that allocate rights and responsibilities in the collection and use of personal information:

---

[39] *See, e.g.*, Vance Packard, *The Naked Society* (1964); Myron Brenton, *The Privacy Invaders* (1964); Alan Westin, *Privacy and Freedom* (1967); Arthur Miller, *The Assault on Privacy* (1971); *Nomos XII: Privacy* (J. Ronald Pennock & J.W. Chapman eds., 1971); Alan Westin & Michael A. Baker, *Databanks in a Free Society: Computers, Record-Keeping and Privacy* (1972); Aryeh Neier, *The Secret Files They Keep on You* (1975); Kenneth L. Karst, *"The Files": Legal Controls over the Accuracy and Accessibility of Stored Personal Data*, 31 Law & Contemp. Probs. 342 (1966); Symposium, *Computers, Data Banks, and Individual Privacy*, 53 Minn. L. Rev. 211-45 (1968); Symposium, *Privacy*, 31 Law & Contemp. Probs. 251-435 (1966).

[40] Priscilla M. Regan, *Legislating Privacy: Technology, Social Values, and Public Policy* 82 (1995).

- There must be no personal-data record-keeping systems whose very existence is secret.
- There must be a way for an individual to find out what information about him is in a record and how it is used.
- There must be a way for an individual to prevent information about him obtained for one purpose from being used or made available for other purposes without his consent.
- There must be a way for an individual to correct or amend a record of identifiable information about him.
- Any organization creating, maintaining, using, or disseminating records of identifiable personal data must ensure the reliability of the data for their intended use and must take reasonable precautions to prevent misuse of the data.[41]

As Marc Rotenberg observes, the Fair Information Practices have "played a significant role in framing privacy laws in the United States."[42]

Beginning in the 1970s, Congress has passed a number of laws protecting privacy in various sectors of the information economy:

- Fair Credit Reporting Act of 1970, Pub. L. No. 90-32, 15 U.S.C. §§ 1681 et seq. — provides citizens with rights regarding the use and disclosure of their personal information by credit reporting agencies.
- Privacy Act of 1974, Pub. L. No. 93-579, 5 U.S.C. § 552a — provides individuals with a number of rights concerning their personal information maintained in government record systems, such as the right to see one's records and to ensure that the information in them is accurate.
- Family Educational Rights and Privacy Act of 1974, Pub. L. No. 93-380, 20 U.S.C. §§ 1221 note, 1232g — protects the privacy of school records.
- Right to Financial Privacy Act of 1978, Pub. L. No. 95-630, 12 U.S.C. §§ 3401–3422 — requires a subpoena or search warrant for law enforcement officials to obtain financial records.
- Foreign Intelligence Surveillance Act of 1978, Pub. L. No. 95-511, 15 U.S.C. §§ 1801-1811 — regulates foreign intelligence gathering within the U.S.
- Privacy Protection Act of 1980, Pub. L. No. 96-440, 42 U.S.C. § 2000aa — restricts the government's ability to search and seize the work product of the press and the media.
- Cable Communications Policy Act of 1984, Pub. L. No. 98-549, 47 U.S.C. § 551 — mandates privacy protection for records maintained by cable companies.

---

[41] *See* U.S. Dep't of Health, Education, and Welfare, *Secretary's Advisory Committee on Automated Personal Data Systems, Records, Computers, and Rights of Citizens* viii (1973).

[42] Marc Rotenberg, *Fair Information Practices and the Architecture of Privacy (What Larry Doesn't Get),* Stan. Tech. L. Rev. 1, 44 (2001).

- Electronic Communications Privacy Act of 1986, Pub. L. No. 99-508 and Pub. L. No. 103-414, 18 U.S.C §§ 2510–2522, 2701–2709 — updates federal electronic surveillance law to respond to the new developments in technology.
- Computer Matching and Privacy Protection Act of 1988, Pub. L. No. 100-503, 5 U.S.C. §§ 552a — regulates automated investigations conducted by government agencies comparing computer files.
- Employee Polygraph Protection Act of 1988, Pub. L. No. 100-347, 29 U.S.C. §§ 2001–2009 — governs the use of polygraphs by employers.
- Video Privacy Protection Act of 1988, Pub. L. No. 100-618, 18 U.S.C. §§ 2710–2711 — protects the privacy of videotape rental information.
- Telephone Consumer Protection Act of 1991, Pub. L. No. 102-243, 47 U.S.C. § 227 — provides certain remedies from repeat telephone calls by telemarketers.
- Driver's Privacy Protection Act of 1994, Pub. L. No. 103-322, 18 U.S.C. §§ 2721–2725 — restricts the states from disclosing or selling personal information in their motor vehicle records.
- Health Insurance Portability and Accountability Act of 1996, Pub. L. No. 104-191 — gives the Department of Health and Human Services (HHS) the authority to promulgate regulations governing the privacy of medical records.
- Identity Theft and Assumption Deterrence Act of 1998, Pub. L. No. 105-318, 18 U.S.C. § 1028 — criminalizes the transfer or use of fraudulent identification with the intent to commit unlawful activity.
- Children's Online Privacy Protection Act of 1998, Pub. L. No. 106-170, 15 U.S.C. §§ 6501–6506 — restricts the use of information gathered from children under age 13 by Internet websites.
- Gramm-Leach-Bliley Act of 1999, Pub. L. No. 106-102, 15 U.S.C. §§ 6801–6809 — requires privacy notices and provides opt-out rights when financial institutions seek to disclose personal data to other companies.
- CAN-SPAM Act of 2003, Pub. L. No. 108-187 — provides penalties for the transmission of unsolicited e-mail.
- Fair and Accurate Credit Transactions Act of 2003, Pub. L. No. 108-159 — amends and updates the Fair Credit Reporting Act, providing (among other things) additional protections against identity theft.
- Video Voyeurism Prevention Act of 2004, Pub. L. No. 108-495, 18 U.S.C. § 1801 — criminalizes the capturing of nude images of people (when on federal property) under circumstances where they have a reasonable expectation of privacy.
- Health Information Technology for Economic and Clinical Health Act (HITECH Act) of 2009, Pub. L. No. 111-5 — expands HIPAA's coverage, strengthens penalties for HIPAA violations, and provides for data breach notification under HIPAA.

Not all of Congress's legislation regarding privacy has been protective of privacy. A number of statutes have mandated the government collection of sensitive personal data or facilitated government investigation techniques:

- Bank Secrecy Act of 1970, Pub. L. No. 91-508 — requires banks to maintain reports of people's financial transactions to assist in government white collar investigations.
- Communications Assistance for Law Enforcement Act of 1994, Pub. L. No. 103-414 — requires telecommunication providers to help facilitate government interceptions of communications and surveillance.
- Personal Responsibility and Work Opportunity Reconciliation Act of 1996, Pub. L. No. 104-193 — requires the collection of personal information (including Social Security numbers, addresses, and wages) of all people who obtain a new job anywhere in the nation, which will be placed into a national database to help track down deadbeat parents.
- USA-PATRIOT Act of 2001, Pub. L. No. 107-56 — amends a number of electronic surveillance statutes and other statutes to facilitate law enforcement investigations and access to information.

State Statutory Law. The states have passed statutes protecting privacy in many contexts, regulating both the public and private sectors. These laws cover a wide range of subjects, from employment records and medical records to library records and student records.

States have led the way in the area of breach notification. Following California's enactment of such a statute, more than 90 percent of the states have now enacted statutes that require organizations to let the affected party know when there is a data leak involving personal data. Many states also have enacted data disposal statutes, and an increasing number of state statutes are setting substantive requirements for data security.

4. INTERNATIONAL LAW

Privacy is a global concern. International law and, more precisely, the privacy laws of other countries and international privacy norms, implicate privacy interests in the United States. For example, commercial firms in the United States must comply with the various standards for global commerce. The Organization of Economic Cooperation and Development (OECD) developed an extensive series of privacy guidelines in 1980 that formed the basis for privacy laws in North America, Europe, and East Asia.

In 1995, the European Union issued the *European Community Directive on Data Protection*, which outlines the basic principles for privacy legislation for European Union member countries.[43] The Directive became effective on October 25, 1998. Currently, the European Union is in the process of debating a sweeping

---

[43] *See* Directive of the European Parliament and the Council of Europe on the Protection of Individuals with Regard to the Processing of Personal Data and on the Free Movement of Such Data (1996).

Data Protection Regulation. Once enacting, this Data Protection Regulation will be immediately binding as law in all EU Member States.[44]

In November 2004, an Asian-Pacific Economic Cooperative (APEC) Privacy Framework was endorsed by the ministers of the APEC countries. The APEC countries are more than 20 nations, mostly in Asia, but also including the United States.

[44] Proposal for a Regulation of the European Parliament and the Council on the Protection of Individuals with Regard to the Processing of Personal Data and on the Free Movement of Such Data (2012).

CHAPTER 2

PERSPECTIVES ON PRIVACY

CHAPTER OUTLINE

A. THE PHILOSOPHICAL DISCOURSE ABOUT PRIVACY

1. THE CONCEPT OF PRIVACY AND THE RIGHT TO PRIVACY

At the outset, it is important to distinguish between the concept of privacy and the right of privacy. As Hyman Gross observed, "[t]he law does not determine what privacy is, but only what situations of privacy will be afforded legal protection."[1] Privacy as a concept involves what privacy entails and how it is to be valued. Privacy as a right involves the extent to which privacy is (and should be) legally protected.

While instructive and illuminative, law cannot be the exclusive material for constructing a concept of privacy. Law is the product of the weighing of competing values, and it sometimes embodies difficult trade-offs. In order to determine what the law *should* protect, we cannot merely look to what the law *does* protect.

[1] Hyman Gross, *The Concept of Privacy*, 42 N.Y.U. L. Rev. 34, 36 (1967).

2. THE PUBLIC AND PRIVATE SPHERES

A long-standing distinction in philosophical discourse is between the public and private spheres. Some form of boundary between public and private has been maintained throughout the history of Western civilization.[2]

Generally, the public sphere is the realm of life experienced in the open, in the community, and in the world of politics. The private sphere is the realm of life where one retreats to isolation or to one's family. At its core is the world of the home. The private sphere, observes Edward Shils, is a realm where the individual "is not bound by the rules that govern public life. . . . The 'private life' is a secluded life, a life separated from the compelling burdens of public authority."[3]

According to Hannah Arendt, both spheres are essential dimensions of human life:

> . . . In ancient feeling, the privative trait of privacy, indicated in the word itself, was all-important; it meant literally a state of being deprived of something, and even of the highest and most human of man's capacities. A man who lived only a private life, who like the slave was not permitted to enter the public realm, or like the barbarian had chosen not to establish such a realm, was not fully human. We no longer think primarily of deprivation when we use the word "privacy," and this is partly due to the enormous enrichment of the private sphere through modern individualism. . . .
>
> To live an entirely private life means above all to be deprived of things essential to a truly human life: to be deprived of the reality that comes from being seen and heard by others, to be deprived of an "objective" relationship with them that comes from being related to and separated from them through the intermediary of a common world of things, to be deprived of the possibility of achieving something more permanent than life itself. . . .
>
> . . . [T]he four walls of one's private property offer the only reliable hiding place from the common public world, not only from everything that goes on in it but also from its very publicity, from being seen and being heard. A life spent entirely in public, in the presence of others, becomes, as we would say, shallow. While it retains visibility, it loses the quality of rising into sight from some darker ground which must remain hidden if it is not to lose its depth in a very real, non-subjective sense. . . .[4]

John Stuart Mill relied upon a notion of the public/private dichotomy to determine when society should regulate individual conduct. Mill contended that there was a realm where people had social responsibilities and where society could properly restrain people from acting or punish them for their deeds. This realm consisted in acts that were hurtful to others or to which people "may rightfully be compelled to perform; such as to give evidence in a court of justice; to bear his fair share in the common defence, or in any other joint work necessary to the interest of the society of which he enjoys the protection." However, "there

---

[2] *See* Georges Duby, *Foreword*, in *A History of the Private Life I: From Pagan Rome to Byzantium* viii (Paul Veyne ed. & Arthur Goldhammer trans., 1987); *see also* Jürgen Habermas, *The Structural Transformation of the Public Sphere* (Thomas Burger trans., 1991).

[3] Edward Shils, *Privacy: Its Constitution and Vicissitudes*, 31 Law & Contemp. Probs. 281, 283 (1966).

[4] Hannah Arendt, *The Human Condition* (1958).

is a sphere of action in which society, as distinguished from the individual, has, if any, only an indirect interest; comprehending all that portion of a person's life and conduct which affects only himself, or if it also affects others, only with their free, voluntary, and undeceived consent and participation." Conduct within this sphere consists of "self-regarding" acts, and society should not interfere with such acts. As Mill further elaborated:

> . . . I fully admit that the mischief which a person does to himself may seriously affect, both through their sympathies and their interests, those nearly connected with him and, in a minor degree, society at large. When, by conduct of this sort, a person is led to violate a distinct and assignable obligation to any other person or persons, the case is taken out of the self-regarding class, and becomes amenable to moral disapprobation in the proper sense of the term. . . . Whenever, in short, there is a definite damage, or a definite risk of damage, either to an individual or to the public, the case is taken out of the province of liberty, and placed in that of morality or law.
>
> But with regard to the merely contingent, or, as it may be called, constructive injury which a person causes to society, by conduct which neither violates any specific duty to the public, nor occasions perceptible hurt to any assignable individual except himself; the inconvenience is one which society can afford to bear, for the sake of the greater good of human freedom. . . . [5]

B. THE DEFINITION AND THE VALUE OF PRIVACY

The following excerpts explore the definition and value of privacy. Those who attempt to define privacy seek to describe what privacy constitutes. Over the past four decades, academics have defined privacy as a right of personhood, intimacy, secrecy, limited access to the self, and control over information. However, defining privacy has proven to be quite complicated, and many commentators have expressed great difficulty in defining precisely what privacy is. In the words of one commentator, "even the most strenuous advocate of a right to privacy must confess that there are serious problems of defining the essence and scope of this right."[6] According to Robert Post, "[p]rivacy is a value so complex, so entangled in competing and contradictory dimensions, so engorged with various and distinct meanings, that I sometimes despair whether it can be usefully addressed at all."[7]

Conceptualizing privacy not only involves defining privacy but articulating the value of privacy. The value of privacy concerns its importance — how privacy is to be weighed relative to other interests and values. The excerpts that follow attempt to grapple with the complicated task of defining privacy and explaining why privacy is worth protecting.

---

[5] John Stuart Mill, *On Liberty* 12, 13, 74-75 (1859).

[6] William M. Beaney, *The Right to Privacy and American Law*, 31 Law & Contemp. Probs. 253, 255 (1966).

[7] Robert C. Post, *Three Concepts of Privacy*, 89 Geo. L.J. 2087, 2087 (2001).

ALAN WESTIN, *PRIVACY AND FREEDOM*

(1967)

. . . Privacy is the claim of individuals, groups, or institutions to determine for themselves when, how, and to what extent information about them is communicated to others. Viewed in terms of the relation of the individual to social participation, privacy is the voluntary and temporary withdrawal of a person from the general society through physical or psychological means, either in a state of solitude or small-group intimacy or, when among larger groups, in a condition of anonymity or reserve. The individual's desire for privacy is never absolute, since participation in society is an equally powerful desire. Thus each individual is continually engaged in a personal adjustment process in which he balances the desire for privacy with the desire for disclosure and communication of himself to others, in light of the environmental conditions and social norms set by the society in which he lives. The individual does so in the face of pressures from the curiosity of others and from the processes of surveillance that every society sets in order to enforce its social norms. . . .

Recognizing the differences that political and sensory cultures make in setting norms of privacy among modern societies, it is still possible to describe the general functions that privacy performs for individuals and groups in Western democratic nations. Before describing these, it is helpful to explain in somewhat greater detail the four basic states of individual privacy[, which are solitude, intimacy, anonymity, and reserve.] . . .

The first state of privacy is solitude; here the individual is separated from the group and freed from the observation of other persons. He may be subjected to jarring physical stimuli, such as noise, odors, and vibrations. His peace of mind may continue to be disturbed by physical sensations of heat, cold, itching, and pain. He may believe that he is being observed by God or some supernatural force, or fear that some authority is secretly watching him. Finally, in solitude he will be especially subject to that familiar dialogue with the mind or conscience. But, despite all these physical or psychological intrusions, solitude is the most complete state of privacy that individuals can achieve.

In the second state of privacy, the individual is acting as part of a small unit that claims and is allowed to exercise corporate seclusion so that it may achieve a close, relaxed, and frank relationship between two or more individuals. Typical units of intimacy are husband and wife, the family, a friendship circle, or a work clique. Whether close contact brings relaxed relations or abrasive hostility depends on the personal interaction of the members, but without intimacy a basic need of human contact would not be met.

The third state of privacy, anonymity, occurs when the individual is in public places or performing public acts but still seeks, and finds, freedom from identification and surveillance. He may be riding a subway, attending a ball game, or walking the streets; he is among people and knows that he is being observed; but unless he is a well-known celebrity, he does not expect to be personally identified and held to the full rules of behavior and role that would operate if he were known to those observing him. In this state the individual is able to merge into the "situational landscape." Knowledge or fear that one is under systematic observation in public places destroys the sense of relaxation and freedom that men seek in open spaces and public arenas. . . .

Still another kind of anonymity is the publication of ideas anonymously. Here the individual wants to present some idea publicly to the community or to a segment of it, but does not want to be universally identified at once as the author — especially not by the authorities, who may be forced to take action if they "know" the perpetrator. The core of each of these types of anonymous action is the desire of individuals for times of "public privacy."

Reserve, the fourth and most subtle state of privacy, is the creation of a psychological barrier against unwanted intrusion; this occurs when the individual's need to limit communication about himself is protected by the willing discretion of those surrounding him. Most of our lives are spent not in solitude or anonymity but in situations of intimacy and in group settings where we are known to others. Even in the most intimate relations, communication of self to others is always incomplete and is based on the need to hold back some parts of one's self as either too personal and sacred or too shameful and profane to express. This circumstance gives rise to what Simmel called "reciprocal reserve and indifference," the relation that creates "mental distance" to protect the personality. This creation of mental distance — a variant of the concept of "social distance" — takes place in every sort of relationship under rules of social etiquette; it expresses the individual's choice to withhold or disclose information — the choice that is the dynamic aspect of privacy in daily interpersonal relations. . . .

This analysis of the various states of privacy is useful in discussing the basic question of the functions privacy performs for individuals in democratic societies. These can also be grouped conveniently under four headings — personal autonomy, emotional release, self-evaluation, and limited and protected communication. . . .

Personal Autonomy. . . . Each person is aware of the gap between what he wants to be and what he actually is, between what the world sees of him and what he knows to be his much more complex reality. In addition, there are aspects of himself that the individual does not fully understand but is slowly exploring and shaping as he develops. Every individual lives behind a mask in this manner; indeed, the first etymological meaning of the word "person" was "mask," indicating both the conscious and expressive presentation of the self to a social audience. If this mask is torn off and the individual's real self bared to a world in which everyone else still wears his mask and believes in masked performances, the individual can be seared by the hot light of selective, forced exposure. . . .

The autonomy that privacy protects is also vital to the development of individuality and consciousness of individual choice in life. . . . This development of individuality is particularly important in democratic societies, since qualities of independent thought, diversity of views, and non-conformity are considered desirable traits for individuals. Such independence requires time for sheltered experimentation and testing of ideas, for preparation and practice in thought and conduct, without fear of ridicule or penalty, and for the opportunity to alter opinions before making them public. The individual's sense that it is he who decides when to "go public" is a crucial aspect of his feeling of autonomy.

Without such time for incubation and growth, through privacy, many ideas and positions would be launched into the world with dangerous prematurity. . . .

Emotional Release. Life in society generates such tensions for the individual that both physical and psychological health demand periods of privacy for various types of emotional release. At one level, such relaxation is required from the pressure of playing social roles. Social scientists agree that each person constantly plays a series of varied and multiple roles, depending on his audience and behavioral situation. On any given day a man may move through the roles of stern father, loving husband, car-pool comedian, skilled lathe operator, union steward, water-cooler flirt, and American Legion committee chairman — all psychologically different roles that he adopts as he moves from scene to scene on the social stage. Like actors on the dramatic stage, Goffman has noted, individuals can sustain roles only for reasonable periods of time, and no individual can play indefinitely, without relief, the variety of roles that life demands. There have to be moments "off stage" when the individual can be "himself": tender, angry, irritable, lustful, or dream-filled. . . .

Another form of emotional release is provided by the protection privacy gives to minor non-compliance with social norms. Some norms are formally adopted — perhaps as law — which society really expects many persons to break. This ambivalence produces a situation in which almost everyone does break some social or institutional norms — for example, violating traffic laws, breaking sexual mores, cheating on expense accounts, overstating income-tax deductions, or smoking in rest rooms when this is prohibited. Although society will usually punish the most flagrant abuses, it tolerates the great bulk of the violations as "permissible" deviations. If there were no privacy to permit society to ignore these deviations — if all transgressions were known — most persons in society would be under organizational discipline or in jail, or could be manipulated by threats of such action. The firm expectation of having privacy for permissible deviations is a distinguishing characteristic of life in a free society. At a lesser but still important level, privacy also allows individuals to deviate temporarily from social etiquette when alone or among intimates, as by putting feet on desks, cursing, letting one's face go slack, or scratching wherever one itches.

Another aspect of release is the "safety-valve" function afforded by privacy. Most persons need to give vent to their anger at "the system," "city hall," "the boss," and various others who exercise authority over them, and to do this in the intimacy of family or friendship circles, or in private papers, without fear of being held responsible for such comments. . . . Without the aid of such release in accommodating the daily abrasions with authorities, most people would experience serious emotional pressure. . . .

Limited and Protected Communication. The greatest threat to civilized social life would be a situation in which each individual was utterly candid in his communications with others, saying exactly what he knew or felt at all times. The havoc done to interpersonal relations by children, saints, mental patients, and adult "innocents" is legendary. . . .

Privacy for limited and protected communication has two general aspects. First, it provides the individual with the opportunities he needs for sharing confidences and intimacies with those he trusts — spouse, "the family," personal friends, and close associates at work. The individual discloses because he knows that his confidences will be held, and because he knows that breach of confidence violates social norms in a civilized society. "A friend," said Emerson, "is someone before . . . [whom] I can think aloud." In addition, the individual often wants to secure counsel from persons with whom he does not have to live daily after disclosing his confidences. He seeks professionally objective advice from persons whose status in society promises that they will not later use his distress to take advantage of him. To protect freedom of limited communication, such relationships — with doctors, lawyers, ministers, psychiatrists, psychologists, and others — are given varying but important degrees of legal privilege against forced disclosure. . . .

NOTES & QUESTIONS

1. ***Privacy as Control over Information.*** A number of theorists, including Westin, conceive of privacy as a form of control over personal information.[8] Consider Charles Fried's definition of privacy:

> At first approximation, privacy seems to be related to secrecy, to limiting the knowledge of others about oneself. This notion must be refined. It is not true, for instance, that the less that is known about us the more privacy we have. Privacy is not simply an absence of information about what is in the minds of others; rather it is the *control* we have over information about ourselves.
>
> To refer for instance to the privacy of a lonely man on a desert island would be to engage in irony. The person who enjoys privacy is able to grant or deny access to others. . . .
>
> Privacy, thus, is control over knowledge about oneself. But it is not simply control over the quantity of information abroad; there are modulations in the quality of the knowledge as well. We may not mind that a person knows a general fact about us, and yet feel our privacy invaded if he knows the details.[9]

Is this a compelling definition of privacy?

In contrast to privacy-as-control, Christena Nippert-Eng, a sociologist, talks about the managerial dimension of privacy. Based on her wide-reaching field interviews, Nippert-Eng concludes that "participants find it incumbent upon themselves to create their own pockets of uninterruptible time and space, or take make decisions without letting anyone else unduly pressure them into a particular choice."[10] She adds that "a need to *manage* one's privacy" runs through all the definitions of privacy offered by her interview participants.

2. ***Privacy as Limited Access to the Self.*** Another group of theorists view privacy as a form of limited access to the self. Consider Ruth Gavison:

---

[8] *See* Adam Carlyle Breckenridge, *The Right to Privacy* 1 (1970); Randall P. Bezanson, *The Right to Privacy Revisited: Privacy, News, and Social Change, 1810–1990*, 80 Cal. L. Rev. 1133 (1992). For a critique of privacy as control, see Anita L. Allen, *Privacy as Data Control: Conceptual, Practical, and Moral Limits of the Paradigm*, 32 Conn. L. Rev. 861 (2000).

[9] Charles Fried, *Privacy*, 77 Yale L.J. 475 (1968).

[10] Christena Nippert-Eng, *Islands of Privacy* 7 (2010).

> . . . Our interest in privacy . . . is related to our concern over our accessibility to others: the extent to which we are known to others, the extent to which others have physical access to us, and the extent to which we are the subject of others' attention. This concept of privacy as concern for limited accessibility enables us to identify when losses of privacy occur. Furthermore, the reasons for which we claim privacy in different situations are similar. They are related to the functions privacy has in our lives: the promotion of liberty, autonomy, selfhood, and human relations, and furthering the existence of a free society. . . .
>
> The concept of privacy suggested here is a complex of these three independent and irreducible elements: secrecy, anonymity, and solitude. Each is independent in the sense that a loss of privacy may occur through a change in any one of the three, without a necessary loss in either of the other two. The concept is nevertheless coherent because the three elements are all part of the same notion of accessibility, and are related in many important ways.[11]

How does this theory of privacy differ from the notion of privacy as "the right to be let alone"? How does it differ from privacy as control over information? How much control should individuals have over access to themselves? Should the decision depend upon each particular person's desires? Or should there be an objective standard — a reasonable degree of control over access?

3. ***Privacy as Intimacy.*** A number of theorists argue that "intimacy" appropriately defines what information or matters are private. For example, Julie Inness argues that "intimacy" is the common denominator in all the matters that people claim to be private. Privacy is "the state of the agent having control over decisions concerning matters that draw their meaning and value from the agent's love, caring, or liking. These decisions cover choices on the agent's part about access to herself, the dissemination of information about herself, and her actions."[12]

Jeffrey Rosen adopts a similar view when he writes:

> . . . Privacy protects us from being misdefined and judged out of context in a world of short attention spans, a world in which information can easily be confused with knowledge. True knowledge of another person is the culmination of a slow process of mutual revelation. It requires the gradual setting aside of social masks, the incremental building of trust, which leads to the exchange of personal disclosures. It cannot be rushed; this is why, after intemperate self-revelation in the heat of passion, one may feel something

---

[11] Ruth Gavison, *Privacy and the Limits of Law*, 89 Yale L.J. 421 (1980); *see also* Edward Shils, *Privacy: Its Constitution and Vicissitudes*, 31 Law & Contemp. Probs. 281, 281 (1996); Sissela Bok, *Secrets: On the Ethics of Concealment and Revelation* 10-11 (1982); Ernest Van Den Haag, *On Privacy*, in *Nomos XII: Privacy* 149 (J. Ronald Pennock & J.W. Chapman eds., 1971); Sidney M. Jourard, *Some Psychological Aspects of Privacy*, 31 L. & Contemp. Probs. 307, 307 (1966); David O'Brien, *Privacy, Law, and Public Policy* 16 (1979); Hyman Gross, *The Concept of Privacy*, 42 N.Y.U. L. Rev. 34 (1967).

[12] Julie C. Inness, *Privacy, Intimacy, and Isolation* 56, 58, 63, 64, 67 (1992). For other proponents of privacy as intimacy, see Robert S. Gerstein, *Intimacy and Privacy*, in *Philosophical Dimensions of Privacy: An Anthology* 265, 265 (Ferdinand David Schoeman ed., 1984); James Rachels, *Why Privacy Is Important*, in *Philosophical Dimensions of Privacy: An Anthology* 290, 292 (Ferdinand David Schoeman ed., 1984); Tom Gerety, *Redefining Privacy*, 12 Harv. C.R.-C.L. L. Rev. 233 (1977).

> close to self-betrayal. True knowledge of another person, in all of his or her complexity, can be achieved only with a handful of friends, lovers, or family members. In order to flourish, the intimate relationships on which true knowledge of another person depends need space as well as time: sanctuaries from the gaze of the crowd in which slow mutual self-disclosure is possible.
>
> When intimate personal information circulates among a small group of people who know us well, its significance can be weighed against other aspects of our personality and character. By contrast, when intimate information is removed from its original context and revealed to strangers, we are vulnerable to being misjudged on the basis of our most embarrassing, and therefore most memorable, tastes and preferences. . . . In a world in which citizens are bombarded with information, people form impressions quickly, based on sound bites, and these impressions are likely to oversimplify and misrepresent our complicated and often contradictory characters.[13]

Does "intimacy" adequately separate private matters from public ones? Can something be private but not intimate? Can something be intimate but not private?

In reaction to Rosen's views on privacy, Lawrence Lessig restates the problem of short attention spans in this fashion: "Privacy, the argument goes, would remedy such a problem by concealing those things that would not be understood with the given attention span. Privacy's function . . . is not to protect the presumptively innocent from true but damaging information, but rather to protect the actually innocent from damaging conclusions drawn from misunderstood information."[14] Lessig notes his skepticism regarding this approach: privacy will not alone solve the problem with the information market. Moreover, there "are possible solutions to this problem of attention span. But what should be clear is that there is no guarantee that a particular problem of attention span will have any solution at all."

JULIE E. COHEN, *EXAMINED LIVES: INFORMATIONAL PRIVACY AND THE SUBJECT AS OBJECT*

52 Stan. L. Rev. 1373 (2000)

Prevailing market-based approaches to data privacy policy — including "solutions" in the form of tradable privacy rights or heightened disclosure requirements before consent — treat preferences for informational privacy as a matter of individual taste, entitled to no more (and often much less) weight than preferences for black shoes over brown or red wine over white. But the values of informational privacy are far more fundamental. A degree of freedom from scrutiny and categorization by others promotes important noninstrumental values, and serves vital individual and collective ends.

First, informational autonomy comports with important values concerning the fair and just treatment of individuals within society. From Kant to Rawls, a central strand of Western philosophical tradition emphasizes respect for the fundamental dignity of persons, and a concomitant commitment to egalitarianism

[13] Jeffrey Rosen, *The Unwanted Gaze: The Destruction of Privacy in America* 8-9 (2000).

[14] Lawrence Lessig, *Privacy and Attention Span*, 89 Geo. L.J. 2063, 2065 (2001).

in both principle and practice. Advocates of strong data privacy protection argue that these principles have clear and very specific implications for the treatment of personally-identified data: They require that we forbid data-processing practices that treat individuals as mere conglomerations of transactional data, or that rank people as prospective customers, tenants, neighbors, employees, or insureds based on their financial or genetic desirability. . . .

Autonomous individuals do not spring full-blown from the womb. We must learn to process information and to draw our own conclusions about the world around us. We must learn to choose, and must learn something before we can choose anything. Here, though, information theory suggests a paradox: "Autonomy" connotes an essential independence of critical faculty and an imperviousness to influence. But to the extent that information shapes behavior, autonomy is radically contingent upon environment and circumstance. . . . Autonomy in a contingent world requires a zone of relative insulation from outside scrutiny and interference — a field of operation within which to engage in the conscious construction of self. The solution to the paradox of contingent autonomy, in other words, lies in a second paradox: To exist in fact as well as in theory, autonomy must be nurtured.

A realm of autonomous, unmonitored choice, in turn, promotes a vital diversity of speech and behavior. The recognition that anonymity shelters constitutionally-protected decisions about speech, belief, and political and intellectual association — decisions that otherwise might be chilled by unpopularity or simple difference — is part of our constitutional tradition. . . .

The benefits of informational privacy are related to, but distinct from, those afforded by seclusion from visual monitoring. It is well-recognized that respite from visual scrutiny affords individuals an important measure of psychological repose. Within our society, at least, we are accustomed to physical spaces within which we can be unobserved, and intrusion into those spaces is experienced as violating the boundaries of self. But the scrutiny, and the repose, can be informational as well as visual, and this does not depend entirely on whether the behavior takes place "in private." The injury, here, does not lie in the exposure of formerly private behaviors to public view, but in the dissolution of the boundaries that insulate different spheres of behavior from one another. The universe of all information about all record-generating behaviors generates a "picture" that, in some respects, is more detailed and intimate than that produced by visual observation, and that picture is accessible, in theory and often in reality, to just about anyone who wants to see it. In such a world, we all may be more cautious.

The point is not that people will not learn under conditions of no-privacy, but that they will learn differently, and that the experience of being watched will constrain, ex ante, the acceptable spectrum of belief and behavior. Pervasive monitoring of every first move or false start will, at the margin, incline choices toward the bland and the mainstream. The result will be a subtle yet fundamental shift in the content of our character, a blunting and blurring of rough edges and sharp lines. . . . The condition of no-privacy threatens not only to chill the expression of eccentric individuality, but also, gradually, to dampen the force of our aspirations to it. . . .

. . . [T]he insulation provided by informational privacy also plays a subtler, more conservative role in reinforcing the existing social fabric. Sociologist Erving Goffman demonstrated that the construction of social facades to mediate between self and community is both instinctive and expected. Alan Westin describes this social dimension of privacy as "reserve." This characterization, though, seems incomplete. On Goffman's account, the construction of social personae isn't just about withholding information that we don't want others to have. It is about defining the parameters of social interaction in ways that maximize social ease, and thus is about collective as well as individual comfort. We do not need, or even want, to know each other that well. Less information makes routine interactions easier; we are then free to choose, consensually and without embarrassment, the interactions that we wish to treat as less routine. Informational privacy, in short, is a constitutive element of a civil society in the broadest sense of that term. . . .

NOTES & QUESTIONS

1. ***Privacy and Respect for Persons.*** Julie Cohen's theory locates the purpose of privacy as promoting the development of autonomous individuals and, more broadly, civil society. Compare her theory to the following theory by Stanley Benn:

   > Finding oneself an object of scrutiny, as the focus of another's attention, brings one to a new consciousness of oneself, as something seen through another's eyes. According to [Jean-Paul] Sartre, indeed, it is a necessary condition for knowing oneself as anything at all that one should conceive oneself as an object of scrutiny. It is only through the regard of the other that the observed becomes aware of himself as an object, knowable, having a determinate character, in principle predictable. His consciousness of pure freedom as subject, as originator and chooser, is at once assailed by it; he is fixed as *something* — with limited probabilities rather than infinite, indeterminate possibilities. . . .
   >
   > The underpinning of a claim not to be watched without leave will be more general if it can be grounded in this way on the principle of respect for persons than on a utilitarian duty to avoid inflicting suffering. . . . But respect for persons will sustain an objection even to secret watching, which may do no actual harm at all. Covert observation — spying — is objectionable because it deliberately deceives a person about his world, thwarting, for reasons that *cannot* be his reasons, his attempts to make a rational choice. One cannot be said to respect a man as engaged on an enterprise worthy of consideration if one knowingly and deliberately alters his conditions of action, concealing the fact from him. . . .[15]

   How is Cohen's theory similar to and/or different from Benn's?

   Benn argues that privacy is a form of respect for persons. By being watched, Benn contends, the observed becomes "fixed as *something* — with limited probabilities rather than infinite indeterminate possibilities." Does Benn adequately capture why surveillance is harmful? Is Benn really

[15] Stanley I. Benn, *Privacy, Freedom, and Respect for Persons*, from *Nomos XIII: Privacy* (J. Ronald Pennock & J.W. Chapman eds., 1971).

concerned about the negative consequences of surveillance on a person's behavior? Or is Benn more concerned about the violation of respect for another?

2. ***Privacy as an Individual Right and as a Social Value.*** Consider the following argument from Priscilla Regan:

> . . . [The] emphasis of privacy as an individual right or an individual interest provides a weak basis for formulating policy to protect privacy. When privacy is defined as an individual right, policy formulation entails a balancing of the individual right to privacy against a competing interest or right. In general, the competing interest is recognized as a social interest. . . . It is also assumed that the individual has a stake in these societal interests. As a result, privacy has been on the defensive, with those alleging a privacy invasion bearing the burden of proving that a certain activity does indeed invade privacy and that the "social" benefit to be gained from the privacy invasion is less important than the individual harm incurred. . . .
>
> Privacy is a *common value* in that all individuals value some degree of privacy and have some common perceptions about privacy. Privacy is also a *public value* in that it has value not just to the individual as an individual or to all individuals in common but also to the democratic political system. . . .
>
> A public value of privacy derives not only from its protection of the individual as an individual but also from its usefulness as a restraint on the government or on the use of power. . . .[16]

DANIEL J. SOLOVE, *CONCEPTUALIZING PRIVACY*

90 Cal. L. Rev. 1087 (2002)

Despite what appears to be a welter of different conceptions of privacy, I argue that they can be dealt with under six general headings, which capture the recurrent ideas in the discourse. These headings include: (1) the right to be let alone — Samuel Warren and Louis Brandeis's famous formulation for the right to privacy; (2) limited access to the self — the ability to shield oneself from unwanted access by others; (3) secrecy — the concealment of certain matters from others; (4) control over personal information — the ability to exercise control over information about oneself; (5) personhood — the protection of one's personality, individuality, and dignity; and (6) intimacy — control over, or limited access to, one's intimate relationships or aspects of life. Some of the conceptions concentrate on means to achieve privacy; others focus on the ends or goals of privacy. Further, there is overlap between conceptions, and the conceptions discussed under different headings are by no means independent from each other. For example, control over personal information can be seen as a subset of limited access to the self, which in turn bears significant similarities to the right to be let alone. . . .

The most prevalent problem with the conceptions is that they are either too narrow or too broad. The conceptions are often too narrow because they fail to include the aspects of life that we typically view as private, and are often too

---

[16] Priscilla M. Regan, *Legislating Privacy: Technology, Social Values, and Public Policy* 213, 225 (1995).

broad because they fail to exclude matters that we do not deem private. Often, the same conceptions can suffer from being both too narrow and too broad. I contend that these problems stem from the way that the discourse goes about the task of conceptualizing privacy. . . .

Most attempts to conceptualize privacy thus far have followed the traditional method of conceptualizing. The majority of theorists conceptualize privacy by defining it *per genus et differentiam*. In other words, theorists look for a common set of necessary and sufficient elements that single out privacy as unique from other conceptions. . . .

[Philosopher Ludwig] Wittgenstein suggests that certain concepts might not share one common characteristic; rather they draw from a common pool of similar characteristics, "a complicated network of similarities overlapping and crisscrossing: sometimes overall similarities, sometimes similarities of detail." . . . Wittgenstein uses the term "family resemblances," analogizing to the overlapping and crisscrossing characteristics that exist between members of a family, such as "build, features, colour of eyes, gait, temperament, etc." For example, in a family, each child has certain features similar to each parent; and the children share similar features with each other; but they may not all resemble each other in the same way. Nevertheless, they all bear a resemblance to each other. . . .

When we state that we are protecting "privacy," we are claiming to guard against disruptions to certain practices. Privacy invasions disrupt and sometimes completely annihilate certain practices. Practices can be disrupted in certain ways, such as interference with peace of mind and tranquility, invasion of solitude, breach of confidentiality, loss of control over facts about oneself, searches of one's person and property, threats to or violations of personal security, destruction of reputation, surveillance, and so on.

There are certain similarities in particular types of disruptions as well as in the practices that they disrupt; but there are differences as well. We should conceptualize privacy by focusing on the specific types of disruption and the specific practices disrupted rather than looking for the common denominator that links all of them. If privacy is conceptualized as a web of interconnected types of disruption of specific practices, then the act of conceptualizing privacy should consist of mapping the typography of the web. . . .

It is reductive to carve the world of social practices into two spheres, public and private, and then attempt to determine what matters belong in each sphere. First, the matters we consider private change over time. While some form of dichotomy between public and private has been maintained throughout the history of Western civilization, the matters that have been considered public and private have metamorphosed throughout history due to changing attitudes, institutions, living conditions, and technology. The matters we consider to be private are shaped by culture and history, and have differed across cultures and historical epochs.

Second, although certain matters have moved from being public to being private and vice versa, the change often has been more subtle than a complete transformation from public to private. Particular matters have long remained private but in different ways; they have been understood as private but because of different attributes; or they have been regarded as private for some people or groups but not for others. In other words, to say simply that something is public or private is to make a rather general claim; what it means for something to be private is the central question. We consider our Social Security number, our sexual behavior, our diary, and our home private, but we do not consider them private in the same way. A number of aspects of life have commonly been viewed as private: the family, body, and home to name a few. To say simply that these things are private is imprecise because what it means for them to be private is different today than it was in the past. . . .

. . . [P]rivacy is not simply an empirical and historical question that measures the collective sense in any given society of what is and has long been considered to be private. Without a normative component, a conception of privacy can only provide a status report on existing privacy norms rather than guide us toward shaping privacy law and policy in the future. If we focus simply on people's current expectations of privacy, our conception of privacy would continually shrink given the increasing surveillance in the modern world. Similarly, the government could gradually condition people to accept wiretapping or other privacy incursions, thus altering society's expectations of privacy. On the other hand, if we merely seek to preserve those activities and matters that have historically been considered private, then we fail to adapt to the changing realities of the modern world. . . .

NOTES & QUESTIONS

1. ***Core Characteristics vs. Family Resemblances.*** Is there a core characteristic common in all the things we understand as being "private"? If so, what do you think it is? Can privacy be more adequately conceptualized by shifting away from the quest to find the common core characteristics of privacy?
2. ***Context.*** Solove contends that the meaning of privacy depends upon context, that there is no common denominator to all things we refer to as "privacy." Does this make privacy too amorphous a concept?

   Consider Helen Nissenbaum:

   > Specifically, whether a particular action is determined a violation of privacy is a function of several variables, including the nature of the situation, or context; the nature of the information in relation to that context; the roles of agents receiving information; their relationships to information subjects; on what terms the information is shared by the subject; and the terms of further dissemination. . . .
   >
   > [N]orms of privacy in fact vary considerably from place to place, culture to culture, period to period; this theory not only incorporates this reality but systematically pinpoints the sources of variation. A second consequence is that, because questions about whether particular restrictions on flow are acceptable call for investigation into the relevant contextual details, protecting privacy will be a messy task, requiring a grasp of concepts and social institutions as well as knowledge of facts of the matter.[17]

[17] Helen Nissenbaum, *Privacy as Contextual Integrity,* 79 Wash. L. Rev. 119, 155-56 (2004). For a more complete account of Nissenbaum's theory, see Helen Nissenbaum, *Privacy in Context: Technology, Policy, and the Integrity of Social Life* (2010).

3. ***Revising the Prosser Taxonomy.*** Daniel Solove contends that the taxonomy of four privacy interests identified by William Prosser, *supra,* must be revised as well as expanded beyond tort law. Solove identifies 16 different kinds of activity that create privacy harms or problems:

> The first group of activities that affect privacy involve information collection. *Surveillance* is the watching, listening to, or recording of an individual's activities. *Interrogation* consists of various forms of questioning or probing for information.
>
> A second group of activities involves the way information is stored, manipulated, and used — what I refer to collectively as "information processing." *Aggregation* involves the combination of various pieces of data about a person. *Identification* is linking information to particular individuals. *Insecurity* involves carelessness in protecting stored information from being leaked or improperly accessed. *Secondary use* is the use of information collected for one purpose for a different purpose without a person's consent. *Exclusion* concerns the failure to allow people to know about the data that others have about them and participate in its handling and use. These activities do not involve the gathering of data, since it has already been collected. Instead, these activities involve the way data is maintained and used.
>
> The third group of activities involves the dissemination of information. *Breach of confidentiality* is breaking the promise to keep a person's information confidential. *Disclosure* involves the revelation of truthful information about a person which impacts the way others judge that person's character. *Exposure* involves revealing another's nudity, grief, or bodily functions. *Increased accessibility* is amplifying the accessibility of information. *Blackmail* is the threat to disclose personal information. *Appropriation* involves the use of another's identity to serve the aims and interests of another. *Distortion* consists of the dissemination of false or misleading information about individuals. Information dissemination activities all involve the spreading or transfer of personal data — or the threat to do so.
>
> The fourth and final group of activities involves invasions into people's private affairs. Invasion, unlike the other groupings, need not involve personal information (although in numerous instances, it does). *Intrusion* concerns invasive acts that disturb one's tranquility or solitude. *Decisional interference* involves the government's incursion into people's decisions regarding their private affairs.[18]

4. ***Reductionists.*** Some theorists, referred to as "reductionists," assert that privacy can be reduced to other concepts and rights. For example, Judith Jarvis Thomson contends that there is nothing particularly distinctive about privacy and to talk about things as violating the "right to privacy" is not all that useful. Privacy is really a cluster of other rights, such as the right to liberty, property rights, and the right not to be injured: "[T]he right to privacy is everywhere overlapped by other rights."[19] Is there something distinctive about privacy? Or can privacy be explained in terms of other, more primary

---

[18] Daniel J. Solove, *A Taxonomy of Privacy,* 154 U. Pa. L. Rev. 477 (2006). For a more complete account of Solove's theory, see Daniel J. Solove, *Understanding Privacy* (2008).

[19] Judith Jarvis Thomson, *The Right to Privacy*, 4 Phil. & Pub. Aff. 295 (1975).

rights and interests? What does privacy capture that these other rights and interests (autonomy, property, liberty, etc.) do not?

ANITA L. ALLEN, *COERCING PRIVACY*

40 Wm. & Mary L. Rev. 723 (1999)

. . . The final decades of the twentieth century could be remembered for the rapid erosion of expectations of personal privacy and of the taste for personal privacy in the United States. . . . I sense that people expect increasingly little physical, informational, and proprietary privacy, and that people seem to prefer less of these types of privacy relative to other goods. . . .

One way to address the erosion would be to stop the avalanche of technology and commercial opportunity responsible for the erosion. We could stop the avalanche of technology, but we will not, if the past is any indication. . . . In the United States, with a few exceptions like government-funded human cloning and fetal tissue research, the rule is that technology marches on.

We could stop the avalanche of commercial opportunity by intervening in the market for privacy; that is, we could (some way or another) increase the costs of consuming other people's privacy and lower the profits of voluntarily giving up one's own privacy. The problem with this suggested strategy is that, even without the details of implementation, it raises the specter of censorship, repression, paternalism, and bureaucracy. Privacy is something we think people are supposed to want; if it turns out that they do not, perhaps third parties should not force it on them, decreasing both their utility and that of those who enjoy disclosure, revelation, and exposure.

Of course, we force privacy on people all the time. Our elected officials criminalize public nudity, even to the point of discouraging breastfeeding. . . . It is one thing, the argument might go, to force privacy on someone by criminalizing nude sun-bathing and topless dancing. These activities have pernicious third-party effects and attract vice. It would be wrong, the argument might continue, to force privacy on someone, in the absence of harm to others, solely on the grounds that one ought not say too much about one's thoughts, feelings, and experiences; one ought not reveal in detail how one spends one's time at home; and one ought not live constantly on display. Paternalistic laws against extremes of factual and physical self-revelation seem utterly inconsistent with liberal self-expression, and yet such laws are suggested by the strong claims liberal theorists make about the value of privacy. Liberal theorists claim that we need privacy to be persons, independent thinkers, free political actors, and citizens of a tolerant democracy. . . .

For people under forty-five who understand that they do not, and cannot, expect to have many secrets, informational privacy may now seem less important. As a culture, we seem to be learning how to be happy and productive — even spiritual — knowing that we are like open books, our houses made of glass. Our parents may appear on the television shows of Oprah Winfrey or Jerry Springer to discuss incest, homosexuality, miscegenation, adultery, transvestitism, and cruelty in the family. Our adopted children may go on television to be reunited with their birth parents. Our law students may compete with their peers for a spot on the MTV program The Real World, and a chance to live with television cameras for months on end and be viewed by mass audiences. Our ten-year-olds may aspire to have their summer camp experiences — snits, fights, fun, and all — chronicled by camera crews and broadcast as entertainment for others on the Disney Channel.

Should we worry about any of this? What values are at stake? Scholars and other commentators associate privacy with several important clusters of value. Privacy has value relative to normative conceptions of spiritual personality, political freedom, health and welfare, human dignity, and autonomy. . . .

To speak of "coercing" privacy is to call attention to privacy as a foundation, a precondition of a liberal egalitarian society. Privacy is not an optional good, like a second home or an investment account. . . .

A hard task seems to lay before us — namely, deciding which forms of privacy are so critical that they should become matters of coercion. . . .

As liberals, we should not want people to sell all their freedom, and, as liberals, we should not want people to sell all their privacy and capacities for private choices. This is, in part, because the liberal conceptions of private choice as freedom from governmental and other outside interference with decision-making closely link privacy and freedom. The liberal conception of privacy as freedom from unwanted disclosures, publicity, and loss of control of personality also closely links privacy to freedom. . . .

Government will have to intervene in private lives for the sake of privacy and values associated with it. . . . The threat to liberalism is not that individuals sometimes expose their naked bodies in public places, display affection with same-sex partners in public, or broadcast personal information on national television. The threat to liberalism is that in an increasing variety of ways our lives are being emptied of privacy on a daily basis, especially physical and informational privacy. . . .

NOTES & QUESTIONS

1. ***Should Privacy Be an Inalienable Right?*** Allen argues that people regularly surrender their privacy and that we should "coerce" privacy. In other words, privacy must be seen as an inalienable right, one that people cannot give away. What if a person wants to live in the spotlight or to give away her personal information? Why shouldn't she be allowed to do so? Recall those who defined privacy as control over information. One aspect of control is that an individual can decide for herself how much privacy she desires. What would Allen say about such a definition of privacy?
2. ***Privacy and Publicity.*** Consider also whether a desire for publicity and a desire for privacy can coexist. Does the person who "tells it all" on the Jerry Springer talk show have any less expectation of privacy when she returns home to be with her family and friends or picks up the telephone to make a private call?
3. ***Eroding Expectations of Privacy and Privacy Paternalism.*** Allen contends that our society is changing by becoming more exhibitionistic and voyeuristic. The result is that expectations of privacy are eroding. In 2011, Allen further

develops these themes in a book, *Unpopular Privacy*. She argues that "privacy is so important and so neglected in contemporary life that democratic states, though liberal and feminist, could be justified in undertaking a rescue mission that includes enacting paternalistic privacy laws for the benefit of uneager beneficiaries."[20]

If people no longer expect privacy in many situations, then why should the law continue to protect it? If people no longer desire privacy, should the law force privacy upon them? Under what circumstances?

PAUL M. SCHWARTZ, *PRIVACY AND DEMOCRACY IN CYBERSPACE*

52 Vand. L. Rev. 1609 (1999)

. . . Self-determination is a capacity that is embodied and developed through social forms and practices. The threat to this quality arises when private or government action interferes with a person's control of her reasoning process. . . . [P]erfected surveillance of naked thought's digital expression short-circuits the individual's own process of decisionmaking. . . .

The maintenance of a democratic order requires both deliberative democracy and an individual capacity for self-determination. . . . [T]he emerging pattern of information use in cyberspace poses a risk to these two essential values. Our task now is to develop privacy standards that are capable of structuring the right kind of information use. . . .

Most scholars, and much of the law in this area, work around a liberal paradigm that we can term "privacy-control." From the age of computer mainframes in the 1960s to the current reign of the Internet's decentralized networks, academics and the law have gravitated towards the idea of privacy as a personal right to control the use of one's data. . . .

. . . [One flaw with the "privacy-control" paradigm is the "autonomy trap."] [T]he organization of information privacy through individual control of personal data rests on a view of autonomy as a given, preexisting quality. . . .

As a policy cornerstone, however, the idea of privacy-control falls straight into the "autonomy trap." The difficulty with privacy-control in the Information Age is that individual self-determination is itself shaped by the processing of personal data. . . .

To give an example of an autonomy trap in cyberspace, the act of clicking through a "consent" screen on a Web site may be considered by some observers to be an exercise of self-reliant choice. Yet, this screen can contain boilerplate language that permits all further processing and transmission of one's personal data. Even without a consent screen, some Web sites place consent boilerplate within a "privacy statement" on their home page or elsewhere on their site. For example, the online version of one New York newspaper states, "By using this site, you agree to the Privacy Policy of the New York Post." This language presents the conditions for data processing on a take-it-or-leave-it basis. It seeks to create the legal fiction that all who visit this Web site have expressed informed

---

[20] Anita L. Allen, *Unpopular Privacy* (2011).

consent to its data processing practices. An even more extreme manifestation of the "consent trap" is a belief that an initial decision to surf the Web itself is a self-reliant choice to accept all further use of one's personal data generated by this activity. . . .

The liberal ideal views autonomous individuals as able to interact freely and equally so long as the government or public does not interfere. The reality is, however, that individuals can be trapped when such glorification of freedom of action neglects the actual conditions of choice. Here, another problem arises with self-governance through information-control: the "data seclusion deception." The idea of privacy as data seclusion is easy to explain: unless the individual wishes to surrender her personal information, she is to be free to use her privacy right as a trump to keep it confidential or to subject its release to conditions that she alone wishes to set. The individual is to be at the center of shaping data anonymity. Yet, this right to keep data isolated quickly proves illusory because of the demands of the Information Age. . . .

NOTES & QUESTIONS

1. ***Privacy and Personhood.*** Like Schwartz, a number of theorists argue that privacy is essential for self-development. According to Jeffrey Reiman, privacy "protects the individual's interest in becoming, being, and remaining a person."[21] The notion that privacy protects personhood or identity is captured in Warren and Brandeis's notion of "inviolate personality." How does privacy promote self-development?

   Consider the following: "Every acceptance of a public role entails the repression, channelizing, and deflection of 'private' or personal attention, motives, and demands upon the self in order to address oneself to the expectations of others."[22] Can we really be ourselves in the public sphere? Is our "public self" any less part of our persona than our "private self"?
2. ***Privacy and Democracy.*** Schwartz views privacy as essential for a democratic society. Why is privacy important for political participation?
3. ***Privacy and Role Playing.*** Recall Westin's view of selfhood:

   > Each person is aware of the gap between what he wants to be and what he actually is, between what the world sees of him and what he knows to be his much more complex reality. In addition, there are aspects of himself that the individual does not fully understand but is slowly exploring and shaping as he develops. Every individual lives behind a mask in this manner; indeed, the first etymological meaning of the word "person" was "mask," indicating both the conscious and expressive presentation of the self to a social audience. If this mask is torn off and the individual's real self bared to a world in which everyone else still wears his mask and believes in masked performances, the individual can be seared by the hot light of selective, forced exposure.

[21] Jeffrey H. Reiman, *Privacy, Intimacy, and Personhood*, in *Philosophical Dimensions of Privacy: An Anthology* 300, 308 (Ferdinand David Schoeman ed., 1984).

[22] Joseph Bensman & Robert Lilienfeld, *Between Public and Private: Lost Boundaries of the Self* 174 (1979).

Is there a "true" or "core" or "authentic" self? Or do we perform many roles and perhaps have multiple selves? Is there a self beneath the roles that we play?

Daniel Solove contends that "[s]ociety accepts that public reputations will be groomed to some degree. . . . Society protects privacy because it wants to provide individuals with some degree of influence over how they are judged in the public arena."[23] To what extent should the law allow people to promote a polished public image and hide the dirt in private?

4. ***Individual Autonomy, Democratic Order, and Data Trade.*** In a later article, Schwartz argues from the premise that "[p]ersonal information is an important currency in the new millennium."[24] He rejects arguments that opposed propertization of personal data, and developed a model to permit data trade consistent with individual autonomy and the maintenance of a democratic order. A key concept in this model is that of the "privacy commons," where privacy is viewed "as a social and not merely an individual good." As a result, Schwartz states, "If sound rules for the use of personal data are not established and enforced, society as a whole will suffer because people will decline to engage in a range of different social interactions due to concerns about use of personal information. A public good — the privacy commons — will be degraded." Do you think that property is a sound concept for building a public goods approach to information privacy?

SPIROS SIMITIS, *REVIEWING PRIVACY IN AN INFORMATION SOCIETY*

135 U. Pa. L. Rev. 707 (1987)

. . . The increased access to personal information resulting from modern, sophisticated techniques of automated processing has sharpened the need to abandon the search for a "neutral" concept in favor of an understanding free of abstractions and fully aware of the political and societal background of all privacy debates. Modern forms of data collection have altered the privacy discussion in three principal ways. First, privacy considerations no longer arise out of particular individual problems; rather, they express conflicts affecting everyone. The course of the privacy debate is neither determined by the caricature of a prominent golfer with a chocolate packet protruding out of his pocket, nor by the hints at the use of a sexual stimulant by a respected university professor, but by the intensive retrieval of personal data of virtually every employee, taxpayer, patient, bank customer, welfare recipient, or car driver. Second, smart cards and videotex make it possible to record and reconstruct individual activities in minute detail.[25] Surveillance has thereby lost its

---

[23] Daniel J. Solove, *The Virtues of Knowing Less: Justifying Privacy Protections Against Disclosure,* 53 Duke L.J. 957 (2003).

[24] Paul M. Schwartz, *Property, Privacy, and Personal Data*, 117 Harv. L. Rev. 2055 (2004).

[25] Editors' Note: Smart cards are also known as "chip cards" or "integrated circuit cards." These devices, generally the size of a credit card, feature an embedded circuit for the processing of data. A precursor of the Internet, Videotex enjoyed its heyday from the late 1970s to mid-1980s.

exceptional character and has become a more and more routine practice. Finally, personal information is increasingly used to enforce standards of behavior. Information processing is developing, therefore, into an essential element of long-term strategies of manipulation intended to mold and adjust individual conduct. . . .

. . . [B]ecause of both the broad availability of personal data and the elaborate matching procedures, individual activities can be accurately reconstructed through automated processing. Surveillance becomes the order of the day. Significantly enough, security agencies were among the first to discover the advantages of automated retrieval. They not only quickly computerized their own data collections but also sought and obtained access to state and private data banks. Entirely new investigation techniques, such as computer profiling, were developed, enabling the agencies to trace wanted persons by matching a presumptive pattern of consumption habits against, for instance, the records of utility companies. The successful attempts at computer-based voice and picture identification will probably influence the work of security agencies even more. . . .

Both the quest for greater transparency and the defense of free speech are legitimated by the goal of allowing the individual to understand social reality better and thus to form a personal opinion on its decisive factors as well as on possible changes. The citizen's right to be "a participator in the government of affairs," to use Jefferson's terms, reflects a profoundly rational process. It presupposes individuals who not only disperse the necessary information but also have the capacity to transform the accessible data into policy expectations. Transparency is, in other words, a basic element of competent communicative action and consequently remains indispensable as long as social discourse is to be promoted, not inhibited.

Inhibition, however, tends to be the rule once automated processing of personal data becomes a normal tool of both government and private enterprises. The price for an undoubted improvement in transparency is a no less evident loss in competence of communication. Habits, activities, and preferences are compiled, registered, and retrieved to facilitate better adjustment, not to improve the individual's capacity to act and to decide. Whatever the original incentive for computerization may have been, processing increasingly appears as the ideal means to adapt an individual to a predetermined, standardized behavior that aims at the highest possible degree of compliance with the model patient, consumer, taxpayer, employee, or citizen. Furthermore, interactive systems do not, despite all contrary assertions, restore a long lost individuality by correcting the effects of mass production in a mass society. On the contrary, the telematic integration forces the individual once more into a preset scheme. The media supplier dictates the conditions under which communication takes place, fixes the possible subjects of the dialogue, and, due to the personal data collected, is in an increasingly better position to influence the subscriber's behavior. Interactive systems, therefore, suggest individual activity where in fact no more than stereotyped reactions occur.

Videotex was typically deployed through a centralized system with one provider of information and involved the display of text on a television screen or dedicated terminal. France Telecom's Minitel was the most successful videotext system in the world.

In short, the transparency achieved through automated processing creates possibly the best conditions for colonization of the individual's lifeworld.[26] Accurate, constantly updated knowledge of her personal history is systematically incorporated into policies that deliberately structure her behavior. The more routinized automated processing augments the transparency, however, the more privacy proves to be a prerequisite to the capacity to participate in social discourse. Where privacy is dismantled, both the chance for personal assessment of the political and societal process and the opportunity to develop and maintain a particular style of life fade. . . .

The processing of personal data is not unique to a particular society. On the contrary, the attractiveness of information technology transcends political boundaries, particularly because of the opportunity to guide the individual's behavior. For a democratic society, however, the risks are high: labeling of individuals, manipulative tendencies, magnification of errors, and strengthening of social control threaten the very fabric of democracy. Yet, despite the incontestable importance of its technical aspects, informatization, like industrialization, is primarily a political and social challenge. When the relationship between information processing and democracy is understood, it becomes clear that the protection of privacy is the price necessary to secure the individual's ability to communicate and participate. Regulations that create precisely specified conditions for personal data processing are the decisive test for discerning whether society is aware of this price and willing to pay it. If the signs of experience are correct, this payment can be delayed no further. There is, in fact, no alternative to the advice of Horace: Seize the day, put not trust in the morrow. . . .

NOTES & QUESTIONS

1. ***Privacy and Democracy.*** As Simitis and other authors in this section observe, privacy is an issue about social structure. What is the relationship between privacy and democracy according to Simitis?
2. ***Privacy Law and Information Flow.*** Generally, one would assume that greater information flow facilitates democracy — it enables more expression, more political discourse, more information about the workings of government. Simitis, however, contends that privacy is "necessary to secure the individual's ability to communicate and participate." How are these two notions about information flow to be reconciled? Consider Joel Reidenberg:

   > Data privacy rules are often cast as a balance between two basic liberties: fundamental human rights on one side and the free flow of information on the other side. Yet, because societies differ on how and when personal information should be available for private and public sector needs, the treatment and

[26] For both the colonization process and the impact of the individual's lifeworld on communicative action, see Jürgen Habermas, 1 *The Theory of Communicative Action* 70-71 (1983) (defining "lifeworld" as shared understandings about what will be treated as a fact, valid norms, and subjective experience). . . .

interaction of these liberties will express a specific delineation between the state, civil society, and the citizen.[27]

Privacy, according to Reidenberg, involves establishing a balance between protecting the rights of individuals and enabling information flow. Do you think these interests always exist in opposition? Consider financial services, communications networks, and medical care. Does privacy impair or enable information flow?[28]

C. CRITICS OF PRIVACY

RICHARD A. POSNER, *THE RIGHT OF PRIVACY*

12 Ga. L. Rev. 393 (1978)

People invariably possess information, including facts about themselves and contents of communications, that they will incur costs to conceal. Sometimes such information is of value to others: that is, others will incur costs to discover it. Thus we have two economic goods, "privacy" and "prying." . . .

[M]uch of the casual prying (a term used here without any pejorative connotation) into the private lives of friends and colleagues that is so common a feature of social life is also motivated, to a greater extent than we may realize, by rational considerations of self-interest. Prying enables one to form a more accurate picture of a friend or colleague, and the knowledge gained is useful in one's social or professional dealings with him. For example, in choosing a friend one legitimately wants to know whether he will be discreet or indiscreet, selfish or generous, and these qualities are not always apparent on initial acquaintance. Even a pure altruist needs to know the (approximate) wealth of any prospective beneficiary of his altruism in order to be able to gauge the value of a transfer to him.

The other side of the coin is that social, like business, dealings present opportunities for exploitation through misrepresentation. Psychologists and sociologists have pointed out that even in every day life people try to manipulate by misrepresentation other people's opinion of them. As one psychologist has written, the "wish for privacy expresses a desire . . . to control others' perceptions and beliefs vis-à-vis the self-concealing person." Even the strongest defenders of privacy describe the individual's right to privacy as the right to "control the flow of information about him." A seldom remarked corollary to a right to misrepresent one's character is that others have a legitimate interest in unmasking the deception.

---

[27] Joel R. Reidenberg, *Resolving Conflicting International Data Privacy Rules in Cyberspace*, 52 Stan. L. Rev. 1315 (2000).

[28] For additional reading about philosophical theories of privacy, see Judith W. DeCew, *In Pursuit of Privacy: Law, Ethics, and the Rise of Technology* (1997) (surveying and critiquing various theories of privacy); Anita L. Allen, *Uneasy Access: Privacy for Women in a Free Society* (1988) (same); Ferdinand David Schoeman, ed., *Philosophical Dimensions of Privacy* (1984) (anthology of articles about the concept of privacy).

Yet some of the demand for private information about other people is not self-protection in the foregoing sense but seems mysteriously disinterested — for example, that of the readers of newspaper gossip columns, whose "idle curiosity" Warren and Brandeis deplored, groundlessly in my opinion. Gossip columns recount the personal lives of wealthy and successful people whose tastes and habits offer models — that is, yield information — to the ordinary person in making consumption, career, and other decisions. . . . Gossip columns open people's eyes to opportunities and dangers; they are genuinely informational. . . .

Warren and Brandeis attributed the rise of curiosity about people's lives to the excesses of the press. The economist does not believe, however, that supply creates demand. A more persuasive explanation for the rise of the gossip column is the secular increase in personal incomes. There is apparently very little privacy in poor societies, where, consequently, people can easily observe at first hand the intimate lives of others. Personal surveillance is costlier in wealthier societies both because people live in conditions that give them greater privacy from such observation and because the value (and hence opportunity cost) of time is greater—too great to make a generous allotment of time to watching neighbors worthwhile. People in wealthier societies sought an alternative method of informing themselves about how others live and the press provided it. A legitimate and important function of the press is to provide specialization in prying in societies where the costs of obtaining information have become too great for the Nosey Parker. . . .

Transaction-cost considerations may also militate against the assignment of a property right to the possessor of a secret. . . . Consider, for example, . . . whether the law should allow a magazine to sell its subscriber list to another magazine without obtaining the subscribers' consent. . . . [T]he costs of obtaining subscriber approval would be high relative to the value of the list. If, therefore, we believe that these lists are generally worth more to the purchasers than being shielded from possible unwanted solicitations is worth to the subscribers, we should assign the property right to the magazine; and the law does this. . . .

Much of the demand for privacy . . . concerns discreditable information, often information concerning past or present criminal activity or moral conduct at variance with a person's professed moral standards. And often the motive for concealment is, as suggested earlier, to mislead those with whom he transacts. Other private information that people wish to conceal, while not strictly discreditable, would if revealed correct misapprehensions that the individual is trying to exploit, as when a worker conceals a serious health problem from his employer or a prospective husband conceals his sterility from his fiancée. It is not clear why society should assign the property right in such information to the individual to whom it pertains; and the common law, as we shall see, generally does not. . . .

We think it wrong (and inefficient) that the law should permit a seller in hawking his wares to make false or incomplete representations as to their quality. But people "sell" themselves as well as their goods. They profess high standards of behavior in order to induce others to engage in social or business dealings with them from which they derive an advantage but at the same time they conceal some of the facts that these acquaintances would find useful in forming an accurate picture of their character. There are practical reasons for not imposing a general legal duty of full and frank disclosure of one's material. . . .

> . . . [E]veryone should be allowed to protect himself from disadvantageous transactions by ferreting out concealed facts about individuals which are material to the representations (implicit or explicit) that those individuals make concerning their moral qualities.
>
> It is no answer that such individuals have "the right to be let alone." Very few people want to be let alone. They want to manipulate the world around them by selective disclosure of facts about themselves. Why should others be asked to take their self-serving claims at face value and be prevented from obtaining the information necessary to verify or disprove these claims?

NOTES & QUESTIONS

1. ***Posner's Conception of Privacy.*** What is Posner's definition of privacy? How does Posner determine the value of privacy (i.e., how it should be weighed relative to other interests and values)? In what circumstances is Posner likely to defend a privacy claim?
2. ***Irrational Judgments.*** One economic argument for privacy is that sometimes people form irrational judgments based upon learning certain information about others. For example, an employer may not hire certain people based on their political views or associations, sexual orientation, mental illness, and prior criminal convictions — even though these facts may have no relevance to a potential employee's abilities to do the job. These judgments decrease efficiency. In *The Economics of Justice*, Posner offers a response:

   > This objection overlooks the opportunity costs of shunning people for stupid reasons, or, stated otherwise, the gains from dealing with someone whom others shun irrationally. If ex-convicts are good workers but most employers do not know this, employers who do know will be able to hire them at a below-average wage because of their depressed job opportunities and will thereby obtain a competitive advantage over the bigots. In a diverse, decentralized, and competitive society, irrational shunning will be weeded out over time. . . [29]

   Will the market be able to eradicate irrational judgments?
3. ***The Dangers of the "Masquerade Ball."*** Consider Dennis Bailey:

   > . . . [I]t is interesting to consider the ways in which the world has become like a giant masquerade ball. Far removed from the tight knit social fabric of the village of the past, we've lost the ability to recognize the people we pass on the street. People might as well be wearing masks because we are likely to know very little about them. In other words, these strangers are anonymous to us, anonymous in the sense that not only their names, but their entire identities, are unknown to us — the intimate details of who they are, where they have come from, and how they have lived their lives.[30]

---

[29] Richard A. Posner, *The Economics of Justice* (1981). Posner further develops his theories about privacy in Richard A. Posner, *Overcoming Law* 531-51 (1995). Posner first set out his views on privacy in Richard A. Posner, *An Economic Theory of Privacy*, Regulations (May/June 1978).

[30] Dennis Bailey, *The Open Society Paradox* 26-27 (2004).

Are we living in a "masquerade ball"? Businesses and the government have unprecedented new technologies to engage in surveillance and gather information. Should the law facilitate or restrict anonymity?

Also consider Steven Nock:

> Any method of social control depends, immediately, on information about individuals. . . . There can be no social control without such information. . . .
>
> Modern Americans enjoy vastly more privacy than did their forebears because ever and ever larger numbers of strangers in our lives are legitimately denied access to our personal affairs. . . . Privacy, however, makes it difficult to form reliable opinions of one another. Legitimately shielded from other's regular scrutiny, we are thereby more immune to the routine monitoring that once formed the basis of our individual reputations.[31]

Does too much privacy erode trust and lessen social control in detrimental ways?

4. ***Information Dissemination and Economic Efficiency.*** Does economic theory necessarily lead to the conclusion that more personal information is generally preferable? Consider the following critique of Posner by Edward Bloustein:

> We must remember that Posner stated in *Economic Analysis of Law* that economics "cannot prescribe social change"; it can only tell us about the economic costs of managing it one way or another. . . . [Posner's] characterization of the privacy of personal information as a species of commercial fraud . . . [is an] extension[ ] of a social value judgment rather than implications or conclusions of economic theory. . . .Our society, in fact, places a very high value on maintaining individual privacy, even to the extent of concealing "discreditable" information. . . .[32]

Also consider Richard Murphy's critique of Posner:

> [D]emarcating a relatively large sphere for the private self creates an opportunity for discovery or actualization of a "true" nature, which may have a value beyond the utility of satisfying preferences. . . . As Roger Rosenblatt put it, "Out of our private gropings and self-inspections grow our imaginative values — private language, imagery, memory. In the caves of the mind one bats about to discover a light entirely of one's own which, though it should turn out to be dim, is still worth a life." Unless a person can investigate without risk of reproach what his own preferences are, he will not be able to maximize his own happiness.[33]

When can the circulation of less personal information be more economically efficient than greater information flow?

5. ***Why Don't Individuals Protect Their Privacy?*** Empirical studies frequently report on growing privacy concerns across the United States. Yet, individuals

---

[31] Steven L. Nock, *The Costs of Privacy: Surveillance and Reputation in America* (1993).

[32] Edward J. Bloustein, *Privacy Is Dear at Any Price: A Response to Professor Posner's Economic Theory*, 12 Ga. L. Rev. 429, 441 (1978). For another critique of Posner's approach, see Kim Lane Scheppele, *Legal Secrets: Equality and Efficiency in the Common Law* (1988).

[33] Richard S. Murphy, *Property Rights in Personal Information: An Economic Defense of Privacy,* 84 Geo. L.J. 2381 (1996).

seem willing to exchange privacy for services or small rewards and generally fail to adopt technologies and techniques that would protect their privacy. If people are willing to sell their privacy for very little in return, isn't this evidence that they do not really value privacy as much as they say they do?

Alessandro Acqusiti and Jens Grossklags have pointed to a number of reasons for this divergence between stated privacy preferences and actual behavior:

> First, incomplete information affects privacy decision making because of externalities (when third parties share personal information about an individual, they might affect that individual without his being part of the transaction between those parties), information asymmetries (information relevant to the privacy decision process — for example, how personal information will be used — might be known only to a subset of the parties making decisions), risk (most privacy related payoffs are not deterministic), and uncertainties (payoffs might not only be stochastic, but dependent on unknown random distributions). Benefits and costs associated with privacy intrusions and protection are complex, multifaceted, and context-specific. They are frequently bundled with other products and services (for example, a search engine query can prompt the desired result but can also give observers information about the searcher's interests), and they are often recognized only after privacy violations have taken place. They can be monetary but also immaterial and, thus, difficult to quantify.
>
> Second, even if individuals had access to complete information, they would be unable to process and act optimally on vast amounts of data. Especially in the presence of complex, ramified consequences associated with the protection or release of personal information, our innate bounded rationality limits our ability to acquire, memorize and process all relevant information, and it makes us rely on simplified mental models, approximate strategies, and heuristics. . . .
>
> Third, even if individuals had access to complete information and could successfully calculate optimization strategies for their privacy sensitive decisions, they might still deviate from the rational strategy. A vast body of economic and psychological literature has revealed several forms of systematic psychological deviations from rationality that affect individual decision making. . . . Research in psychology . . . documents how individuals mispredict their own future preferences or draw inaccurate conclusions from past choices. In addition, individuals often suffer from self-control problems — in particular, the tendency to trade off costs and benefits in ways that damage their future utility in favor of immediate gratification. Individuals' behavior can also be guided by social preferences or norms, such as fairness or altruism. Many of these deviations apply naturally to privacy-sensitive scenarios.[34]

[34] Alessandro Acquisti & Jens Grossklags, *Privacy and Rationality in Decision Making*, IEEE, Security and Privacy 24 (2005).

FRED H. CATE, *PRINCIPLES OF INTERNET PRIVACY*

32 Conn. L. Rev. 877 (2000)

Perhaps the most important consideration when balancing restrictions on information is the historical importance of the free flow of information. The free flow concept is one that is not only enshrined in the First Amendment, but frankly in any form of democratic or market economy. In the United States, we have placed extraordinary importance on the open flow of information. As the Federal Reserve Board noted in its report to Congress on data protection in financial institutions, "it is the freedom to speak, supported by the availability of information and the free-flow of data, that is the cornerstone of a democratic society and market economy."

The significance of open data flows is reflected in the constitutional provisions not only for freedom of expression, but for copyrights — to promote the creation and dissemination of expression, and for a post office — to deliver the mail and the news. Federal regulations demonstrate a sweeping preference for openness, reflected in the Freedom of Information Act, Government in the Sunshine Act, and dozens of other laws applicable to the government. There are even more laws requiring disclosure by private industry, such as the regulatory disclosures required by securities and commodities laws, banking and insurance laws, and many others. This is a very basic tenet of the society in which we live. Laws that restrict that free flow almost always conflict with this basic principle. That does not mean that such laws are never upheld, but merely that they face a considerable constitutional hurdle.

This is done with good reason. Open information flows are not only essential to self-governance; they have also generated significant, practical benefits. The ready availability of personal information helps businesses "deliver the right products and services to the right customers, at the right time, more effectively and at lower cost," Fred Smith, founder and President of the Competitive Enterprise Institute, has written. Federal Reserve Board Governor Edward Gramlich testified before Congress in July 1999 that "[i]nformation about individuals' needs and preferences is the cornerstone of any system that allocates goods and services within an economy." The more such information is available, he continued, "the more accurately and efficiently will the economy meet those needs and preferences."

Federal Reserve Board Chairman Alan Greenspan has been perhaps the most articulate spokesperson for the extraordinary value of accessible personal information. In 1998, he wrote to Congressman Ed Markey (D-Mass.):

> A critical component of our ever more finely hewn competitive market system has been the plethora of information on the characteristics of customers both businesses and individuals. Such information has enabled producers and marketers to fine tune production schedules to the ever greater demands of our consuming public for diversity and individuality of products and services. Newly devised derivative products, for example, have enabled financial institutions to unbundle risk in a manner that enables those desirous of taking on that risk (and potential reward) to do so, and those that chose otherwise, to be

> risk averse. It has enabled financial institutions to offer a wide variety of customized insurance and other products.
>
> Detailed data obtained from consumers as they seek credit or make product choices help engender the whole set of sensitive price signals that are so essential to the functioning of an advanced information based economy such as ours. . . .

In a recent report on public record information, Richard Varn, Chief Information Officer of the State of Iowa, and I examined the critical roles played by public record information in our economy and society. We concluded that such information constitutes part of this nation's "essential infrastructure," the benefits of which are "so numerous and diverse that they impact virtually every facet of American life. . . ." The ready availability of public record data "facilitates a vibrant economy, improves efficiency, reduces costs, creates jobs, and provides valuable products and services that people want."

Perhaps most importantly, widely accessible personal information has helped to create a democratization of opportunity in the United States. Anyone can go almost anywhere, make purchases from vendors they will never see, maintain accounts with banks they will never visit, and obtain credit far from home all because of open information flows. Americans can take advantage of opportunities based on their records, on what they have done rather than who they know, because access to consumer information makes it possible for distant companies and creditors to make rational decisions about doing business with individuals. The open flow of information gives consumers real choice. This is what the open flow of information principle reflects, not just the constitutional importance of information flows, but their significant economic and social benefits as well.

NOTES & QUESTIONS

1. ***The Pros and Cons of the Free Flow of Information.*** In a striking passage, Cate points out that free flows of information create a "democratization of opportunity in the United States." With this phrase, he reminds us that part of the equality at the basis of American life concerns economic opportunity, and that, in his view, a certain kind of flow of personal information will contribute to this goal. While privacy can be problematic, can open access to information also raise difficulties? How should one establish a baseline for open access or restricted access to personal information?
2. ***The Costs of Privacy.*** Can you think of some of the other important values with which privacy might conflict and the costs that privacy can impose? What should be the baseline in measuring costs?
3. ***The Business of Data Trade.*** The trade in personal information is now a valuable part of the U.S. economy. As a single example, Google reached an agreement on April 14, 2007, to purchase DoubleClick, an online advertising company, for $3.1 billion. The deal was driven by Google's interest in behavioral advertising, in which companies use digital data collection techniques to track individuals around the Internet and serve them targeted

ads. Should consumers be allowed to sign up for a National Do Not Track List?

4. ***The Benefits of Information Collection and Use.*** Consider Kent Walker:

> Having some information about yourself out there in the world offers real convenience that goes beyond dollars and cents. Many people benefit from warehousing information — billing and shipping addresses, credit card numbers, individual preferences, and the like — with trustworthy third parties. Such storage of information can dramatically simplify the purchasing experience, ensure that you get a nonsmoking room, or automate the task of ordering a kiddie meal every time your child boards a plane. Likewise, most people prefer to use a credit card rather than a debit card, trading confidentiality of purchases for the convenience of deferred payment. . . .
>
> While there's often little individual incentive to participate in the aggregation of information about people, a great collective good results from the default participation of most people. The aggregation of information often requires a critical mass to be worth doing, or for the results to be worth using. (A phone book with only one out of ten numbers would hardly be worth using, let alone printing.) . . .
>
> Another example is Caller ID, which pits different privacy claims against one another. Many people like the notion of an electronic peephole, letting them know who's at the electronic door before they decide whether to pick up the phone. Yet many people block transmission of their own numbers, valuing protection of their privacy. Neither choice is necessarily right, but it's worth recognizing that the assertion of the privacy claim affects the contending desires of others. The classic Tragedy of the Commons aspects are clear. From my selfish perspective, I want access to information about everyone else — the identity of who's calling me, their listed phone number, etc. I want to be able to intrude on others without their knowing who I am (which I can accomplish by blocking Caller ID), and don't want others to be able to intrude on me unbidden (which I can accomplish by unlisting my phone number). The gain in privacy makes it harder to find the people you want to reach, and harder to know who's calling you.[35]

D. THE FEMINIST PERSPECTIVE ON PRIVACY

Has the legal concept of privacy hurt or helped women throughout history? What is the impact of privacy on women today?

STATE V. RHODES

1868 WL 1278 (N.C. 1868)

[The defendant was indicted for an assault and battery upon his wife, Elizabeth Rhodes. The jury returned the following special verdict: "We find that the defendant struck Elizabeth Rhodes, his wife, three licks, with a switch about the

---

[35] Kent Walker, *Where Everybody Knows Your Name: A Pragmatic Look at the Costs of Privacy and the Benefits of Information Exchange,* 2000 Stan. Tech. L. Rev. 2, 39, 46, 48 (2000).

size of one of his fingers (but not as large as a man's thumb) without any provocation except some words uttered by her and not recollected by the witness." The lower court found that the defendant "had a right to whip his wife with a switch no larger than his thumb, and that upon the facts found in the special verdict he was not guilty in law." Judgment in favor of the defendant was entered from which the State appealed.]

The laws of this State do not recognize *the right of the husband to whip his wife,* but our Courts will not interfere to punish him for moderate correction of her, even if there had been no provocation for it.

Family government being in its nature as complete in itself as the State government is in itself, the Courts will not attempt to control, or interfere with it, in favor of either party, except in cases where permanent or malicious injury is inflicted or threatened, or the condition of the party is intolerable.

In determining whether the husband has been guilty of an indictable assault and battery upon his wife, the criterion is the *effect produced,* and not the manner of producing it or the instrument used. . . .

READE J. The violence complained of would without question have constituted a battery if the subject of it had not been the defendant's wife. The question is how far that fact affects the case.

The courts have been loath to take cognizance of trivial complaints arising out of the domestic relations — such as master and apprentice, teacher and pupil, parent and child, husband and wife. Not because those relations are not subject to the law, but because the evil of publicity would be greater than the evil involved in the trifles complained of; and because they ought to be left to family government. . . .

In this case no provocation worth the name was proved. The fact found was that it was "without any provocation except some words which were not recollected by the witness." The words must have been of the slightest import to have made no impression on the memory. We must therefore, consider the violence as unprovoked. The question is therefore plainly presented, whether the court will allow a conviction of the husband for moderate correction of the wife without provocation.

Our divorce laws do not compel a separation of husband and wife, unless the conduct of the husband be so cruel as to render the wife's condition intolerable, or her life burdensome. What sort of conduct on the part of the husband, would be allowed to have that effect, has been repeatedly considered. And it has not been found easy to lay down any iron rule upon the subject. In some cases it has been held that actual and repeated violence to the person, was not sufficient. In others that insults, indignities and neglect without any actual violence, were quite sufficient. So much does each case depend upon its peculiar surroundings.

We have sought the aid of the experience and wisdom of other times, and of other countries.

Blackstone says "that the husband, by the old law, might give the wife moderate correction, for as he was to answer for her misbehavior, he ought to have the power to control her; but that in the polite reign of Charles the Second, this power of correction began to be doubted." . . . The old law of moderate correction has been questioned even in England, and has been repudiated in

Ireland and Scotland. The old rule is approved in Mississippi, but it has met with but little favor elsewhere in the United States. In looking into the discussions of the other States we find but little uniformity. . . .

Our conclusion is that family government is recognized by law as being as complete in itself as the State government is in itself, and yet subordinate to it; and that we will not interfere with or attempt to control it, in favor of either husband or wife, unless in cases where permanent or malicious injury is inflicted or threatened, or the condition of the party is intolerable. For, however great are the evils of ill temper, quarrels, and even personal conflicts inflicting only temporary pain, they are not comparable with the evils which would result from raising the curtain, and exposing to public curiosity and criticism, the nursery and the bed chamber. Every household has and must have, a government of its own, modeled to suit the temper, disposition and condition of its inmates. Mere ebullitions of passion, impulsive violence, and temporary pain, affection will soon forget and forgive; and each member will find excuse for the other in his own frailties. But when trifles are taken hold of by the public, and the parties are exposed and disgraced, and each endeavors to justify himself or herself by criminating the other, that which ought to be forgotten in a day, will be remembered for life.

It is urged in this case, that as there was no provocation the violence was of course excessive and malicious; that every one in whatever relation of life should be able to purchase immunity from pain, by obedience to authority and faithfulness in duty. . . . Take the case before us. The witness said, there was no provocation except some slight words. But then who can tell what significance the trifling words may have had to the husband? Who can tell what had happened an hour before, and every hour for a week? To him they may have been sharper than a sword. And so in every case, it might be impossible for the court to appreciate what might be offered as an excuse, or no excuse might appear at all, when a complete justification exists. Or, suppose the provocation could in every case be known, and the court should undertake to weigh the provocation in every trifling family broil, what would be the standard? Suppose a case coming up to us from a hovel, where neither delicacy of sentiment nor refinement of manners is appreciated or known. The parties themselves would be amazed, if they were to be held responsible for rudeness or trifling violence. What do they care for insults and indignities? In such cases what end would be gained by investigation or punishment? Take a case from the middle class, where modesty and purity have their abode but nevertheless have not immunity from the frailties of nature, and are sometimes moved by the mysteries of passion. What could be more harassing to them, or injurious to society, than to draw a crowd around their seclusion. Or take a case from the higher ranks, where education and culture have so refined nature, that a look cuts like a knife, and a word strikes like a hammer; where the most delicate attention gives pleasure, and the slightest neglect pain; where an indignity is disgrace and exposure is ruin. Bring all these cases into court side by side, with the same offence charged and the same proof made; and what conceivable charge of the court to the jury would be alike appropriate to all the cases, except, That they all have domestic government, which they have formed for themselves, suited to their own peculiar conditions, and that those governments are supreme, and from them there is no appeal except in cases of great importance requiring the strong arm of the law, and that to those governments they must submit themselves.

It will be observed that the ground upon which we have put this decision, is not, that the husband has the *right* to whip his wife much or little; but that we will not interfere with family government in trifling cases. We will no more interfere where the husband whips the wife, than where the wife whips the husband; and yet we would hardly be supposed to hold, that a wife has a *right* to whip her husband. We will not inflict upon society the greater evil of raising the curtain upon domestic privacy, to punish the lesser evil of trifling violence. Two boys under fourteen years of age fight upon the play-ground, and yet the courts will take no notice of it, not for the reason that boys have the *right* to fight, but because the interests of society require that they should be left to the more appropriate discipline of the school room and of home. . . . The standard is the *effect produced,* and not the manner of producing it, or the instrument used.

Because our opinion is not in unison with the decisions of some of the sister States, or with the philosophy of some very respectable law writers, and could not be in unison with all, because of their contrariety, — a decent respect for the opinions of others has induced us to be very full in stating the reasons for our conclusion.

REVA B. SIEGEL, *"THE RULE OF LOVE": WIFE BEATING AS PREROGATIVE AND PRIVACY*

105 Yale L.J. 2117 (1996)

. . . The Anglo-American common law originally provided that a husband, as master of his household, could subject his wife to corporal punishment or "chastisement" so long as he did not inflict permanent injury upon her. During the nineteenth century, an era of feminist agitation for reform of marriage law, authorities in England and the United States declared that a husband no longer had the right to chastise his wife. Yet, for a century after courts repudiated the right of chastisement, the American legal system continued to treat wife beating differently from other cases of assault and battery. While authorities denied that a husband had the right to beat his wife, they intervened only intermittently in cases of marital violence: Men who assaulted their wives were often granted formal and informal immunities from prosecution, in order to protect the privacy of the family and to promote "domestic harmony." In the late 1970s, the feminist movement began to challenge the concept of family privacy that shielded wife abuse, and since then, it has secured many reforms designed to protect women from marital violence. . . .

Until the late nineteenth century, Anglo-American common law structured marriage to give a husband superiority over his wife in most aspects of the relationship. By law, a husband acquired rights to his wife's person, the value of her paid and unpaid labor, and most property she brought into the marriage. A wife was obliged to obey and serve her husband, and the husband was subject to a reciprocal duty to support his wife and represent her within the legal system. . . .

As master of the household, a husband could command his wife's obedience, and subject her to corporal punishment or "chastisement" if she defied his authority. In his treatise on the English common law, Blackstone explained that a husband could "give his wife moderate correction." . . .

During the 1850s, woman's rights advocates organized numerous conventions throughout the Northeast and Midwest, published newspapers, and conducted petition campaigns seeking for women the right to vote and demanding various reforms of marriage law. And in time the movement did elicit a response. Legislatures and courts began to modify the common law of marital status — first giving wives the right to hold property in marriage, and then the right to their earnings and the rudiments of legal agency: the right to file suit in their own names and to claim contract and tort damages. . . .

. . . By the 1880s, prominent members of the American Bar Association advocated punishing wife beaters at the whipping post, and campaigned vigorously for legislation authorizing the penalty. Between 1876 and 1906, twelve states and the District of Columbia considered enacting legislation that provided for the punishment of wife beaters at the whipping post. The bills were enacted in Maryland (1882), Delaware (1901), and Oregon (1906). . . .

We are left with a striking portrait of legal change. Jurists and lawmakers emphatically repudiated the doctrine of marital chastisement, yet responded to marital violence erratically — often condoning it, and condemning it in circumstances suggesting little interest in the plight of battered wives. Given this record, how are we to make sense of chastisement's demise? . . .

A key concept in the doctrinal regime that emerged from chastisement's demise was the notion of marital privacy. During the antebellum era, courts began to invoke marital privacy as a supplementary rationale for chastisement, in order to justify the common law doctrine within the discourse of companionate marriage, when rationales rooted in authority-based discourses of marriage had begun to lose their persuasive power. . . .

To quote a North Carolina chastisement opinion:

> We know that a slap on the cheek, let it be as light as it may, indeed any touching of the person of another in a rude or angry manner — is in law an assault and battery. In the nature of things it cannot apply to persons in the marriage state, it would break down the great principle of mutual confidence and dependence; throw open the bedroom to the gaze of the public; and spread discord and misery, contention and strife, where peace and concord ought to reign. It must be remembered that rules of law are intended to act in all classes of society. . . .

In *Rhodes*, the defendant whipped his wife "three licks, with a switch about the size of one of his fingers (but not as large as a man's thumb)"; the trial court ruled that a husband had the right to chastise his wife and so was not guilty of assault and battery. On appeal, the North Carolina Supreme Court upheld the verdict but justified it on different grounds. Opening its opinion with the blunt observation that "[t]he violence complained of would without question have constituted a battery if the subject of it had not been the defendant's wife," the court explained why it would not find the defendant guilty:

> The courts have been loath to take cognizance of trivial complaints arising out of the domestic relations — such as master and apprentice, teacher and pupil, parent and child, husband and wife. Not because those relations are not subject

> to law, but because the evil of publicity would be greater than the evil involved in the trifles complained of; and because they ought to be left to family government. . . .

. . . By now it should be clear enough how privacy talk was deployed in the domestic violence context to enforce and preserve authority relations between man and wife. . . .

. . . By the early twentieth century, numerous state supreme courts had barred wives from suing their husbands for intentional torts — typically on the grounds that "the tranquility of family relations" would be "disturb[ed]." . . .

It was not until the late 1970s that the contemporary women's rights movement mounted an effective challenge to this regime. Today, after numerous protest activities and law suits, there are shelters for battered women and their children, new arrest procedures for police departments across the country, and even federal legislation making gender-motivated assaults a civil rights violation. . . .

There is remarkably little scholarship on the social history of privacy discourses; consequently, we know very little about the ways in which conceptions of privacy shaped popular understandings of marriage, or marital violence, in the nineteenth century. But there is no reason to assume that, before demise of the chastisement prerogative, married persons understood a traditional prerogative of marriage, rooted in notions of a husband's authority as master and head of his household, in a framework of "privacy" and "domestic harmony." It seems just as likely that legal elites devised the story linking "privacy" and "domestic harmony" to wife beating in the wake of chastisement's demise (or in anticipation of it). . . .

CATHARINE A. MACKINNON, *TOWARD A FEMINIST THEORY OF THE STATE*

(1989)

The liberal ideal of the private holds that, as long as the public does not interfere, autonomous individuals interact freely and equally. Privacy is the ultimate value of the negative state. Conceptually, this private is hermetic. It means that which is inaccessible to, unaccountable to, unconstructed by, anything beyond itself. By definition, it is not part of or conditioned by anything systematic outside it. It is personal, intimate, autonomous, particular, individual, the original source and final outpost of the self, gender neutral. It is defined by everything that feminism reveals women have never been allowed to be or to have, and by everything that women have been equated with and defined in terms of men's ability to have. To complain in public of inequality within the private contradicts the liberal definition of the private. . . . Its inviolability by the state, framed as an individual right, presupposes that the private is not already an arm of the state. In this scheme, intimacy is implicitly thought to guarantee symmetry of power. Injuries arise through violation of the private sphere, not within and by and because of it.

In private, consent tends to be presumed. Showing coercion is supposed to avoid this presumption. But the problem is getting anything private to be perceived as coercive. This is an epistemic problem of major dimensions and explains why privacy doctrine is most at home at home, the place women experience the most force, in the family, and why it centers on sex. Why a person would "allow" force in private (the "why doesn't she leave" question raised to battered women) is a question given its insult by the social meaning of the private as a sphere of choice. For women the measure of the intimacy has been the measure of oppression. This is why feminism has seen the personal as the political. The private is public for those for whom the personal is political. In this sense, for women there is no private, either normatively or empirically. Feminism confronts the fact that women have no privacy to lose or to guarantee. Women are not inviolable. Women's sexuality is not only violable, it is — hence, women are — seen in and as their violation. To confront the fact that women have no privacy is to confront the intimate degradation of women as the public order. . . .

When the law of privacy restricts intrusions into intimacy, it bars changes in control over that intimacy through law. The existing distribution of power and resources within the private sphere are precisely what the law of privacy exists to protect. . . . [T]he legal concept of privacy can and has shielded the place of battery, marital rape, and women's exploited domestic labor. It has preserved the central institutions whereby women are deprived of identity, autonomy, control, and self-definition. It has protected a primary activity through which male supremacy is expressed and enforced. . . .

This right to privacy is a right of men "to be let alone" to oppress women one at a time. . . .

ANITA L. ALLEN, *UNEASY ACCESS: PRIVACY FOR WOMEN IN A FREE SOCIETY*

(1988)

Critiques of privacy such as MacKinnon's go wrong at the point where the historic unequal treatment of women and the misuse of the private household to further women's domination is taken as grounds for rejecting either the condition of privacy itself or the long-overdue legal rights to effective decision-making that promote and protect that condition. Privacy, here broadly defined as the inaccessibility of persons, their mental states, or information about them to the senses and surveillance devices of others . . . does not pose an inherent threat to women. Nor do sex, love, marriage, and children any longer presume the total abrogation of the forms of privacy a woman might otherwise enjoy. On the contrary, women today are finally in a position to expect, experience, and exploit real privacy within the home and within heterosexual relationships. The women's movement, education, access to affordable birth control, liberalized divorce laws, and the larger role for women in politics, government, and the economy have expanded women's opinions and contributed to the erosion of oppressively nonegalitarian styles of home life. These advances have enhanced the capacity of American men and women, but especially and for the first time women, to secure conditions of adequate and meaningful privacy at home paramount to moral personhood and responsible participation in families and larger segments of society. Instead of rejecting privacy as "male ideology" and subjugation, women can and ought to embrace opportunities for privacy and the exercise of reproductive liberty in their private lives.

NOTES & QUESTIONS

1. ***Privacy and Gender.*** As the *Rhodes* court stated in 1868: "We will not interfere with family government in trifling cases. We will no more interfere where the husband whips the wife, than where the wife whips the husband; and yet we would hardly be supposed to hold, that a wife has a *right* to whip her husband." Is this decision really a neutral one? Does the right to privacy described by Warren and Brandeis apply equally to men and women?[36]
2. ***The Uses of the Public/Private Distinction.*** Reva Siegel points out the troubling use of privacy to protect the oppression of women in the home, which Catharine MacKinnon has discussed at length elsewhere. Is MacKinnon's negative response to the public/private distinction justifiable given the prior uses of this distinction? Or do you agree with Anita Allen that privacy can and should not be abandoned as a value despite its checkered past?[37]
3. ***To What Extent Can Law Change Social Practices?*** According to Frances Olsen, "The notion of noninterference in the family depends upon some shared conception of proper family roles, and 'neutrality' [of the State] can be understood only with reference to such roles."[38] This idea suggests that privacy, within or without the family, might also depend on shared views as to proper social roles. Do you agree?

   Olsen also notes: "The theory of the private family, like free market theory, includes the assertion that particularized adjustments of seemingly unfair or inhumane results will not actually serve anybody's long run interests." Specifically, "it is claimed that state intervention to protect the weaker family members from abuse by the stronger is ineffective because powerful, underlying 'real' relations between family members will inevitably reassert themselves." This argument, which one might term the argument from futility, was rejected in the course of the twentieth century by the powerful social movement to stop spousal abuse and mistreatment of children. Are similar arguments from futility being made today about the "inevitable" erosion of privacy?

---

[36] For a feminist critique of the Warren and Brandeis article, see Anita L. Allen & Erin Mack, *How Privacy Got Its Gender*, 10 N. Ill. U. L. Rev. 441 (1990).

[37] For an overview of the feminist critique of privacy, see generally Judith W. DeCew, *In Pursuit of Privacy: Law, Ethics, and the Rise of Technology* 81-94 (1997); Patricia Boling, *Privacy and the Politics of Intimate Life* (1996); Frances Olsen, *Constitutional Law: Feminist Critiques of the Public/Private Distinction*, 10 Const. Commentary 327 (1993); Ruth Gavison, *Feminism and the Public/Private Distinction,* 45 Stan. L. Rev. 21 (1992).

[38] Frances Olsen, *The Family and the Market: A Study of Ideology and Legal Reform*, 96 Harv. L. Rev. 1497, 1506 (1983).

CHAPTER 3

PRIVACY AND THE MEDIA

CHAPTER OUTLINE

A. INFORMATION GATHERING
   1. Intrusion upon Seclusion
   2. Paparazzi
   3. Video Voyeurism

B. DISCLOSURE OF TRUTHFUL INFORMATION
   1. Public Disclosure of Private Facts
      (a) Introduction
      (b) Private Matters
      (c) The Newsworthiness Test
   2. First Amendment Limitations

C. DISSEMINATION OF FALSE INFORMATION
   1. Defamation
      (a) Introduction
      (b) Defamation and the Internet
      (c) First Amendment Limitations
   2. False Light
      (a) Introduction
      (b) First Amendment Limitations
   3. Infliction of Emotional Distress

D. APPROPRIATION OF NAME OR LIKENESS
   1. Introduction
   2. Name or Likeness
   3. For One's Own Use or Benefit

In 1890, Samuel Warren and Louis Brandeis wrote about the increasing proliferation of gossip in newspapers.[1] Today, the problems Warren and Brandeis were concerned about are dramatically magnified by the vast expansion of the media. In addition to newspapers, there are magazines, movies, television, and the Internet. From marketers to moviemakers, from tabloids to 24-hour news channels, from talk shows to reality TV, we are witnessing an explosion in the demand for images, video, and stories about the personal lives of individuals, both famous and obscure. Further, anybody with a website can now disseminate information instantly around the world.

Warren and Brandeis were also concerned with photography, a new technology that had the potential to greatly facilitate information gathering by the media. Today, technologies of gathering data are significantly more sophisticated. Video cameras are in widespread use and exist in miniature forms for easy concealment; high-powered telephoto lenses can enable one to film or photograph from large distances. Moreover, almost every cell phone now contains a small built-in camera.

This chapter focuses on legal remedies for the gathering and dissemination of personal information by media entities. "Media" is understood broadly in this chapter to include people and businesses that gather and disseminate information to inform, advertise, or entertain. The chapter then explores four general types of privacy incursion by the media: (1) intrusions and harassment in the course of gathering information; (2) the disclosure of truthful information, (3) the dissemination of misleading or false information; and (4) the appropriation of name or likeness. The principal remedies for media incursions into privacy are the four privacy torts inspired by Warren and Brandeis's article. The privacy torts are not the only remedies for privacy invasions. The tort of defamation, discussed at length in this chapter, is an older remedy for a particular type of privacy intrusion — the dissemination of false information. Another remedy is the tort of infliction of emotional distress, which is discussed briefly in section C. Additionally, a number of states have enacted statutes that protect against particular forms of disclosure.

---

[1] Samuel D. Warren & Louis D. Brandeis, *The Right to Privacy,* 4 Harv. L. Rev. 193 (1890).

A. INFORMATION GATHERING

In order to report the news, journalists must gather information. This task often involves being nosy, inquisitive, and aggressive. Given the vast proliferation of media and the tremendous competition to get breaking information and live video or photographs, there is great potential for media information gathering to become intrusive and harassing, especially when a person becomes the subject of a prominent story. In response to such intrusions by information gatherers, an injured party has available a number of remedies. The primary remedy is the tort of intrusion upon seclusion. Some states, such as California, have passed statutes providing remedies from aggressive photographers, known as "paparazzi." These two types of remedies will be the focus of this section. Other remedies include trespass (if the newsgatherer wrongfully entered one's home or property) and fraud (if the newsgatherer lied or used deceitful methods to obtain information). Additionally, the electronic surveillance laws of many states provide remedies when one records the conversations of others without their consent. In a number of states, consent is required from all participants to a conversation. In some states and under federal electronic surveillance law, consent is only required from one of the parties. As a consequence of such one-party consent statutes, a journalist can secretly record a conversation in which she participates.

1. INTRUSION UPON SECLUSION

INTRUSION UPON SECLUSION

Restatement (Second) of Torts § 652B

One who intentionally intrudes, physically or otherwise, upon the solitude or seclusion of another or his private affairs or concerns, is subject to liability to the other for invasion of his privacy, if the intrusion would be highly offensive to a reasonable person.

NOTES & QUESTIONS

1. ***Intrusion upon Seclusion vs. Public Disclosure of Private Facts.*** The tort of intrusion concerns the way that the information is obtained. In contrast, for the tort of public disclosure of private facts, liability does not depend upon how the information is obtained. Consider the following commentary to the Restatement:

    Comment (a): Intrusion "does not depend upon any publicity given to the person whose interest is invaded or to his affairs."

    Comment (b): "The intrusion itself makes the defendant subject to liability, even though there is no publication or other use of any kind of the photograph or information outlined."

NADER V. GENERAL MOTORS CORP.

255 N.E.2d 765 (N.Y. Ct. App. 1970)

FULD, C.J. . . . The plaintiff [Ralph Nader], an author and lecturer on automotive safety, has, for some years, been an articulate and severe critic of General Motors' products from the standpoint of safety and design. According to the complaint — which, for present purposes, we must assume to be true — the appellant [General Motors Corporation], having learned of the imminent publication of the plaintiff's book "Unsafe at Any Speed," decided to conduct a campaign of intimidation against him in order to "suppress plaintiff's criticism of and prevent his disclosure of information" about its products. To that end, the appellant authorized and directed the other defendants to engage in a series of activities which, the plaintiff claims in his first two causes of action, violated his right to privacy.

Specifically, the plaintiff alleges that the appellant's agents (1) conducted a series of interviews with acquaintances of the plaintiff, "questioning them about, and casting aspersions upon (his) political . . . racial and religious views. . . ; his integrity; his sexual proclivities and inclinations; and his personal habits"; (2) kept him under surveillance in public places for an unreasonable length of time; (3) caused him to be accosted by girls for the purpose of entrapping him into illicit relationships; (4) made threatening, harassing and obnoxious telephone calls to him; (5) tapped his telephone and eavesdropped, by means of mechanical and electronic equipment, on his private conversations with others; and (6) conducted a "continuing" and harassing investigation of him. [Nader's complaint, among other things, contained a cause of action for intrusion.]

. . . It should be emphasized that the mere gathering of information about a particular individual does not give rise to a cause of action under [the intrusion tort]. Privacy is invaded only if the information sought is of a confidential nature and the defendant's conduct was unreasonably intrusive. Just as a common-law copyright is lost when material is published, so, too, there can be no invasion of privacy where the information sought is open to public view or has been voluntarily revealed to others. In order to sustain a cause of action for invasion of privacy, therefore, the plaintiff must show that the appellant's conduct was truly "intrusive" and that it was designed to elicit information which would not be available through normal inquiry or observation. . . .

. . . At most, only two of the activities charged to the appellant are, in our view, actionable as invasions of privacy under the law of the District of Columbia. . . .

Turning, then, to the particular acts charged in the complaint, we cannot find any basis for a claim of invasion of privacy, under District of Columbia law, in the allegations that the appellant, through its agents or employees, interviewed many persons who knew the plaintiff, asking questions about him and casting aspersions on his character. Although those inquiries may have uncovered information of a personal nature, it is difficult to see how they may be said to have invaded the plaintiff's privacy. Information about the plaintiff which was already known to others could hardly be regarded as private to the plaintiff. Presumably, the plaintiff had previously revealed the information to such other persons, and he would necessarily assume the risk that a friend or acquaintance in whom he had confided might breach the confidence. If, as alleged, the questions tended to disparage the plaintiff's character, his remedy would seem to be by way of an action for defamation, not for breach of his right to privacy.

Nor can we find any actionable invasion of privacy in the allegations that the appellant caused the plaintiff to be accosted by girls with illicit proposals, or that it was responsible for the making of a large number of threatening and harassing telephone calls to the plaintiff's home at odd hours. Neither of these activities, howsoever offensive and disturbing, involved intrusion for the purpose of gathering information of a private and confidential nature. . . .

Apart, however, from the foregoing allegations which we find inadequate to spell out a cause of action for invasion of privacy under District of Columbia law, the complaint contains allegations concerning other activities by the appellant or its agents which do satisfy the requirements for such a cause of action. The one which most clearly meets those requirements is the charge that the appellant and its codefendants engaged in unauthorized wiretapping and eavesdropping by mechanical and electronic means. . . .

There are additional allegations that the appellant hired people to shadow the plaintiff and keep him under surveillance. In particular, he claims that, on one occasion, one of its agents followed him into a bank, getting sufficiently close to him to see the denomination of the bills he was withdrawing from his account. From what we have already said, it is manifest that the mere observation of the plaintiff in a public place does not amount to an invasion of his privacy. But, under certain circumstances, surveillance may be so "overzealous" as to render it actionable. Whether or not the surveillance in the present case falls into this latter category will depend on the nature of the proof. A person does not automatically make public everything he does merely by being in a public place, and the mere fact that Nader was in a bank did not give anyone the right to try to discover the amount of money he was withdrawing. On the other hand, if the plaintiff acted in such a way as to reveal that fact to any casual observer, then, it may not be said that the appellant intruded into his private sphere. In any event, though, it is enough for present purposes to say that the surveillance allegation is not insufficient as a matter of law. . . .

BRIETEL, J. concurring in the result. . . . [S]cholars, in trying to define the elusive concept of the right of privacy, have, as of the present, subdivided the common law right into separate classifications, most significantly distinguishing between unreasonable intrusion and unreasonable publicity. This does not mean, however, that the classifications are either frozen or exhausted, or that several of the classifications may not overlap.

Concretely applied to this case, it is suggested, for example, that it is premature to hold that the attempted entrapment of plaintiff in a public place by seemingly promiscuous ladies is no invasion of any of the categories of the right to privacy and is restricted to a much more limited cause of action for intentional infliction of mental distress. Moreover, it does not strain credulity or imagination to conceive of the systematic "public" surveillance of another as being the implementation of a plan to intrude on the privacy of another. Although acts performed in "public," especially if taken singly or in small numbers, may not be confidential, at least arguably a right to privacy may nevertheless be invaded through extensive or exhaustive monitoring and cataloguing of acts normally disconnected and anonymous.

These are but illustrations of the problems raised in attempting to determine issues of relevancy and allocability of evidence in advance of a trial record. The other allegations so treated involve harassing telephone calls, and investigatory interviews. It is just as important that while allegations treated singly may not constitute a cause of action, they may do so in combination, or serve to enhance other violations of the right to privacy.

It is not unimportant that plaintiff contends that a giant corporation had allegedly sought by surreptitious and unusual methods to silence an unusually effective critic. If there was such a plan, and only a trial would show that, it is unduly restrictive of the future trial to allocate the evidence beforehand based only on a pleader's specification of overt acts on the bold assumption that they are not connected causally or do not bear on intent and motive.

It should be observed, too, that the right to privacy, even as thus far developed, does not always refer to that which is not known to the public or is confidential. Indeed, the statutory right of privacy in this State and perhaps the most traditional right of privacy in the "common law sense" relates to the commercialized publicity of one's face or name, perhaps the two most public aspects of an individual. . . .

Accordingly, because of the prematurity of ruling on any other question but the sufficiency of the causes of action, I concur in result only.

NOTES & QUESTIONS

1. ***Postscript.*** General Motors eventually settled the case with Nader for $425,000. It also made a public apology to Nader.[2]
2. ***Intrusion Liability Only for Confidential Information?*** The *Nader* court finds that mere information gathering is not actionable under the intrusion tort. It states: "Privacy is invaded only if the information sought is of a confidential nature and the defendant's conduct was unreasonably intrusive." Hence, GM's interviewing of Nader's acquaintances, harassing phone calls, and use of "girls with illicit proposals" did not constitute an intrusion on his privacy. Note, however, the text of Restatement (Second) Torts, § 652B. Does this text require the court's holding in this regard? Is the text consistent with this holding?
3. ***Surveillance in Public Places.*** The Restatement of Torts adopts a similar approach to the majority in *Nader*:

> The defendant is subject to liability under the rule stated in this Section only when he has intruded into a private place, or has otherwise invaded a private seclusion that the plaintiff has thrown about his person or affairs. Thus there is no liability for the examination of a public record concerning the plaintiff, or of documents that the plaintiff is required to keep and make available for public inspection. Nor is there liability for observing him or even taking his

[2] For more background about case, see Stuart M. Speiser, *Lawsuit* (1980).

> photograph while he is walking on the public highway, since he is not then in seclusion, and his appearance is public and open to the public eye. Even in a public place, however, there may be some matters about the plaintiff, such as his underwear or lack of it, that are not exhibited to the public gaze; and there may still be invasion of privacy when there is intrusion upon these matters. Restatement (Second) of Torts § 652B comment (c).

Judge Breitel's concurrence goes even further than the majority: "Although acts performed in 'public,' especially if taken singly or in small numbers, may not be confidential, at least arguably a right to privacy may nevertheless be invaded through extensive or exhaustive monitoring and cataloguing of acts normally disconnected and anonymous." How does Breitel's approach differ from the majority's approach and that of the Restatement?

Also consider *Summers v. Bailey*, 55 F.3d 1564 (11th Cir. 1995), where the court held:

> Traditionally, watching or observing a person in a public place is not an intrusion upon one's privacy. However, Georgia courts have held that surveillance of an individual on public thoroughfares, where such surveillance aims to frighten or torment a person, is an unreasonable intrusion upon a person's privacy.

4. ***Harassing Phone Calls.*** *Nader* holds that there is no actionable invasion of privacy caused by a "large number of threatening and harassing telephone calls . . . at odd hours." The Restatement of Torts (Second) takes a different view. It first concedes that "there is no liability for knocking at the plaintiff's door, or calling him to the telephone on one occasion or even two or three, to demand payment of a debt." But the Restatement then states: "It is only when the telephone calls are repeated with such persistence and frequency as to amount to a course of hounding the plaintiff, that becomes a substantial burden to his existence, that his privacy is invaded." Restatement (Second) of Torts § 652B comment (d).

   Courts have also found that harassing a person by telephone can support a tort privacy claim. In *Donnel v. Lara*, 703 S.W.2d 257 (Tex. App. 1985), the court held that excessive telephone harassment "by placing repeated phone calls to [a person's] residence at unreasonable hours" can be actionable. In *Harms v. Miami Daily News, Inc.*, 127 So. 2d 715 (Fla. App. 1961), the defendant published in the newspaper the following statement: "Wanna hear a sexy telephone voice? Call [number] and ask for Louise." As a result, the plaintiff was "flooded with hundreds of telephone calls by various and sundry persons." The court concluded that the plaintiff had an actionable claim against the defendant, and that there was sufficient evidence for the jury to decide whether it was highly offensive.

5. ***Wiretapping and Electronic Surveillance.*** In *Hamberger v. Eastman*, 206 A.2d 239 (N.H. 1964), a husband and wife brought an intrusion action against their landlord for installing a secret recording device in their bedroom. The device had wires going into the landlord's residence. The court sided with the plaintiffs:

> The defendant contends that the right of privacy should not be recognized on the facts of the present case as they appear in the pleadings because there are no allegations that anyone listened or overheard any sounds or voices originating from the plaintiffs' bedroom. The tort of intrusion on the plaintiffs' solitude or seclusion does not require publicity and communication to third persons although this would affect the amount of damages, as Prosser makes clear. The defendant also contends that the right of privacy is not violated unless something has been published, written or printed and that oral publicity is not sufficient. Recent cases make it clear that this is not a requirement.
>
> If the peeping Tom, the big ear and the electronic eavesdropper (whether ingenious or ingenuous) have a place in the hierarchy of social values, it ought not to be at the expense of a married couple minding their own business in the seclusion of their bedroom who have never asked for or by their conduct deserved a potential projection of their private conversations and actions to their landlord or to others. Whether actual or potential such "publicity with respect to private matters of purely personal concern is an injury to personality. It impairs the mental peace and comfort of the individual and may produce suffering more acute than that produced by a mere bodily injury." III Pound, Jurisprudence 58 (1959). The use of parabolic microphones and sonic wave devices designed to pick up conversations in a room without entering it and at a considerable distance away makes the problem far from fanciful.

6. ***The Highly Offensive Requirement.*** What intrusions are "highly offensive to a reasonable person" as required by the tort? Courts have held that trespasses into places where people have reasonable expectations of privacy are actionable, as are unjustified searches. *See, e.g., Gerard v. Parish of Jefferson,* 424 So. 2d 440 (La. App. 1982) (dog catcher entered plaintiff's property without authorization); *K-Mart Corp. v. Trotti,* 677 S.W.2d 632 (Tex. App. 1984) (unauthorized search of employee's personal locker). In *Klebanoff v. McMongale,* 552 A.2d 677 (Pa. Super. 1988), about 20 to 30 pro-life demonstrators picketed noisily on the public street directly outside of an abortion doctor's home. This had a "devastating effect . . . on the [doctor and his family's] quiet enjoyment of their home," and the family was "figuratively, and perhaps literally, trapped within the home, and held captive." The court held that the protestors could be enjoined.

   As illustrated by *Hamberger* and *Nader,* non-physical activities such as wiretapping and overzealous surveillance can amount to highly offensive intrusions. Peering into a person's home windows can be actionable according to the court in *Pinkerton Nat'l Detective Agency, Inc. v. Stevens,* 132 S.E.2d 119 (Ga. App. 1963). In *Pulla v. Amoco Oil Co.,* 882 F. Supp. 836 (S.D. Iowa 1994), the court held that it was actionable when the defendant illegally accessed the plaintiff's credit card records to determine if he abused his sick leave at work.

DIETEMANN V. TIME, INC.

449 F.2d 245 (9th Cir. 1971)

HUFSTEDLER, C.J. . . . Plaintiff, a disabled veteran with little education, was engaged in the practice of healing with clay, minerals, and herbs — as practiced, simple quackery.

Defendant, Time, Incorporated, a New York corporation, publishes Life Magazine. Its November 1, 1963 edition carried an article entitled "Crackdown on Quackery." The article depicted plaintiff as a quack and included two pictures of him. One picture was taken at plaintiff's home on September 20, 1963, previous to his arrest on a charge of practicing medicine without a license, and the other taken at the time of his arrest.

Life Magazine entered into an arrangement with the District Attorney's Office of Los Angeles County whereby Life's employees would visit plaintiff and obtain facts and pictures concerning his activities. Two employees of Life, Mrs. Jackie Metcalf and Mr. William Ray, went to plaintiff's home on September 20, 1963. When they arrived at a locked gate, they rang a bell and plaintiff came out of his house and was told by Mrs. Metcalf and Ray that they had been sent there by a friend, a Mr. Johnson. The use of Johnson's name was a ruse to gain entrance. Plaintiff admitted them and all three went into the house and into plaintiff's den.

The plaintiff had some equipment which could at best be described as gadgets, not equipment which had anything to do with the practice of medicine. Plaintiff, while examining Mrs. Metcalf, was photographed by Ray with a hidden camera without the consent of plaintiff. One of the pictures taken by him appeared in Life Magazine showing plaintiff with his hand on the upper portion of Mrs. Metcalf's breast while he was looking at some gadgets and holding what appeared to be a wand in his right hand. Mrs. Metcalf had told plaintiff that she had a lump in her breast. Plaintiff concluded that she had eaten some rancid butter 11 years, 9 months, and 7 days prior to that time. Other persons were seated in the room during this time.

The conversation between Mrs. Metcalf and plaintiff was transmitted by radio transmitter hidden in Mrs. Metcalf's purse to a tape recorder in a parked automobile occupied by Joseph Bride, Life employee, John Miner of the District Attorney's Office, and Grant Leake, an investigator of the State Department of Public Health. While the recorded conversation was not quoted in the article in Life, it was mentioned that Life correspondent Bride was making notes of what was being received via the radio transmitter, and such information was at least referred to in the article.

The foregoing events were photographed and recorded by an arrangement among Miner of the District Attorney's Office, Leake of the State Department of Public Health, and Bride, a representative of Life. It had been agreed that Life would obtain pictures and information for use as evidence, and later could be used by Life for publication. . . .

Plaintiff, although a journeyman plumber, claims to be a scientist. Plaintiff had no listings and his home had no sign of any kind. He did not advertise, nor did he have a telephone. He made no charges when he attempted to diagnose or to prescribe herbs and minerals. He did accept contributions.

[The plaintiff was arrested at his home on a charge of practicing medicine without a license. After the plaintiff entered a plea of nolo contendere to the charges, *Life*'s article was published. The plaintiff sued *Life* in federal district court. The district court concluded that the defendant had invaded the plaintiff's privacy and awarded $1,000 in damages.]

. . . In jurisdictions other than California in which a common law tort for invasion of privacy is recognized, it has been consistently held that surreptitious electronic recording of a plaintiff's conversation causing him emotional distress is actionable. Despite some variations in the description and the labels applied to the tort, there is agreement that publication is not a necessary element of the tort, that the existence of a technical trespass is immaterial, and that proof of special damages is not required. . . .[3]

. . . [W]e have little difficulty in concluding that clandestine photography of the plaintiff in his den and the recordation and transmission of his conversation without his consent resulting in his emotional distress warrants recovery for invasion of privacy in California. . . .

Plaintiff's den was a sphere from which he could reasonably expect to exclude eavesdropping newsmen. He invited two of defendant's employees to the den. One who invites another to his home or office takes a risk that the visitor may not be what he seems, and that the visitor may repeat all he hears and observes when he leaves. But he does not and should not be required to take the risk that what is heard and seen will be transmitted by photograph or recording, or in our modern world, in full living color and hi-fi to the public at large or to any segment of it that the visitor may select. A different rule could have a most pernicious effect upon the dignity of man and it would surely lead to guarded conversations and conduct where candor is most valued, e.g., in the case of doctors and lawyers.

The defendant claims that the First Amendment immunizes it from liability for invading plaintiff's den with a hidden camera and its concealed electronic instruments because its employees were gathering news and its instrumentalities "are indispensable tools of investigative reporting." We agree that newsgathering is an integral part of news dissemination. We strongly disagree, however, that the hidden mechanical contrivances are "indispensable tools" of newsgathering. Investigative reporting is an ancient art; its successful practice long antecedes the invention of miniature cameras and electronic devices. The First Amendment has never been construed to accord newsmen immunity from torts or crimes committed during the course of newsgathering. The First Amendment is not a license to trespass, to steal, or to intrude by electronic means into the precincts of another's home or office. It does not become such a license simply because the person subjected to the intrusion is reasonably suspected of committing a crime.

Defendant relies upon the line of cases commencing with *New York Times Co. v. Sullivan* and extending through *Rosenbloom v. Metromedia, Inc.* to sustain

---

[3] Editors' Note: Special damages, or "consequential" damages, are damages that follow from the initial harm. They include lost profits and other diminishments of the plaintiff's income, such as increased expenses.

its contentions that (1) publication of news, however tortiously gathered, insulates defendant from liability for the antecedent tort, and (2) even if it is not thus shielded from liability, those cases prevent consideration of publication as an element in computing damages. . . .

No interest protected by the First Amendment is adversely affected by permitting damages for intrusion to be enhanced by the fact of later publication of the information that the publisher improperly acquired. Assessing damages for the additional emotional distress suffered by a plaintiff when the wrongfully acquired data are purveyed to the multitude chills intrusive acts. It does not chill freedom of expression guaranteed by the First Amendment. A rule forbidding the use of publication as an ingredient of damages would deny to the injured plaintiff recovery for real harm done to him without any countervailing benefit to the legitimate interest of the public in being informed. The same rule would encourage conduct by news media that grossly offends ordinary men. . . .

DESNICK V. AMERICAN BROADCASTING CO., INC.

44 F.3d 1345 (7th Cir. 1995)

[Dr. Desnick owned an ophthalmic clinic known as the Desnick Eye Center. The Eye Center had 25 offices in four states and performed over 10,000 cataract operations each year, mainly on elderly persons under Medicare. In 1993, Entine, the producer of ABC's news program *Primetime Live*, telephoned Dr. Desnick and told him that the show wanted to do a segment on cataract practices. Entine told Desnick that the segment would be "fair and balanced" and that it would not include undercover surveillance. Desnick permitted an ABC crew to videotape the Eye Center's Chicago office, to film a cataract operation, and to interview doctors and patients. However, unknown to Desnick, Entine sent seven people with concealed cameras to the Eye Center's Wisconsin and Indiana offices. These seven people posed as patients and requested eye operations. Glazer and Simon are among the employees who were secretly videotaped examining these "test patients."

When the program aired, it was introduced by Sam Donaldson, who began by stating: "We begin tonight with the story of a so-called 'big cutter,' Dr. James Desnick. . . . [I]n our undercover investigation of the big cutter you'll meet tonight, we turned up evidence that he may also be a big charger, doing unnecessary cataract surgery for the money." As part of the segment, brief interviews with four patients of the Desnick Eye Center were shown. While one of the patients was satisfied ("I was blessed"), the other three were not. Indeed, one of them commented, "If you got three eyes, he'll get three eyes." Donaldson then reported on the experiences of the seven test patients. The two who were under 65 and therefore ineligible for Medicare reimbursement were found by the clinic not to need cataract surgery. The Desnick eye clinic told four of the other five that they did need this operation.

Donaldson told the viewer that *Primetime Live* hired a professor of ophthalmology to examine the test patients who had been told they needed cataract surgery. The professor not only said that these patients did not need it, but with regard to one, he stated, "I think it would be near malpractice to do surgery on him." Later in the segment he denies that this could just be an honest difference of opinion between professionals. The show also mentioned that the Illinois Medical Board had charged Dr. Desnick with malpractice and deception. Additionally, the show contained an "ambush interview" of Dr. Desnick while he was at an airport, with Donaldson shouting out allegations of fraud to Desnick.

Among a number of causes of action raised by the plaintiffs, who included the Desnick Eye Clinic, and Simon and Glazer as individual plaintiffs, is an action for intrusion upon seclusion.]

POSNER, C.J. . . . To enter upon another's land without consent is a trespass. The force of this rule has, it is true, been diluted somewhat by concepts of privilege and of implied consent. But there is no journalists' privilege to trespass. And there can be no implied consent in any nonfictitious sense of the term when express consent is procured by a misrepresentation or a misleading omission. The Desnick Eye Center would not have agreed to the entry of the test patients into its offices had it known they wanted eye examinations only in order to gather material for a television expose of the Center and that they were going to make secret videotapes of the examinations. Yet some cases, illustrated by *Martin v. Fidelity & Casualty Co.*, 421 So. 2d 109, 111 (Ala. 1982), deem consent effective even though it was procured by fraud. There must be *something* to this surprising result. Without it a restaurant critic could not conceal his identity when he ordered a meal, or a browser pretend to be interested in merchandise that he could not afford to buy. Dinner guests would be trespassers if they were false friends who never would have been invited had the host known their true character, and a consumer who in an effort to bargain down an automobile dealer falsely claimed to be able to buy the same car elsewhere at a lower price would be a trespasser in the dealer's showroom. Some of these might be classified as privileged trespasses, designed to promote competition. Others might be thought justified by some kind of implied consent — the restaurant critic for example might point by way of analogy to the use of the "fair use" defense by book reviewers charged with copyright infringement and argue that the restaurant industry as a whole would be injured if restaurants could exclude critics. But most such efforts at rationalization would be little better than evasions. The fact is that consent to an entry is often given legal effect even though the entrant has intentions that if known to the owner of the property would cause him for perfectly understandable and generally ethical or at least lawful reasons to revoke his consent.

The law's willingness to give effect to consent procured by fraud is not limited to the tort of trespass. The *Restatement* gives the example of a man who obtains consent to sexual intercourse by promising a woman $100, yet (unbeknownst to her, of course) he pays her with a counterfeit bill and intended to do so from the start. The man is not guilty of battery, even though unconsented-to sexual intercourse is a battery. Yet we know that to conceal the fact that one has a venereal disease transforms "consensual" intercourse into battery. Seduction, standardly effected by false promises of love, is not rape; intercourse under the pretense of rendering medical or psychiatric treatment is, at least in most states. It certainly is battery. Trespass presents close parallels. If a homeowner opens his door to a purported meter reader who is in fact nothing of the sort — just a busybody curious about the interior of the home — the homeowner's consent to his entry is not a defense to a suit for trespass. And likewise if a competitor gained entry to a business firm's premises posing as a customer but in fact hoping to steal the firm's trade secrets.

How to distinguish the two classes of case — the seducer from the medical impersonator, the restaurant critic from the meter-reader impersonator? The answer can have nothing to do with fraud; there is fraud in all the cases. It has to do with the interest that the torts in question, battery and trespass, protect. The one protects the inviolability of the person, the other the inviolability of the person's property. The woman who is seduced wants to have sex with her seducer, and the restaurant owner wants to have customers. The woman who is victimized by the medical impersonator has no desire to have sex with her doctor; she wants medical treatment. And the homeowner victimized by the phony meter reader does not want strangers in his house unless they have authorized service functions. The dealer's objection to the customer who claims falsely to have a lower price from a competing dealer is not to the physical presence of the customer, but to the fraud that he is trying to perpetuate. The lines are not bright — they are not even inevitable. They are the traces of the old forms of action, which have resulted in a multitude of artificial distinctions in modern law. But that is nothing new.

There was no invasion in the present case of any of the specific interests that the tort of trespass seeks to protect. The test patients entered offices that were open to anyone expressing a desire for ophthalmic services and videotaped physicians engaged in professional, not personal, communications with strangers (the testers themselves). The activities of the offices were not disrupted. . . . Nor was there any "inva[sion of] a person's private space," as in our hypothetical meter-reader case, as in the famous case of *De May v. Roberts*, 9 N.W. 146 (Mich. 1881) (where a doctor, called to the plaintiff's home to deliver her baby, brought along with him a friend who was curious to see a birth but was not a medical doctor, and represented the friend to be his medical assistant), as in one of its numerous modern counterparts, . . . and as in *Dietemann v. Time, Inc.*, 449 F.2d 245 (9th Cir. 1971), on which the plaintiffs in our case rely. *Dietemann* involved a home. True, the portion invaded was an office, where the plaintiff performed quack healing of nonexistent ailments. The parallel to this case is plain enough, but there is a difference. Dietemann was not in business, and did not advertise his services or charge for them. His quackery was private.

No embarrassingly intimate details of anybody's life were publicized in the present case. There was no eavesdropping on a private conversation; the testers recorded their own conversations with the Desnick Eye Center's physicians. There was no violation of the doctor-patient privilege. There was no theft, or intent to steal, trade secrets; no disruption of decorum, of peace and quiet; no noisy or distracting demonstrations. Had the testers been undercover FBI agents, there would have been no violation of the Fourth Amendment, because there would have been no invasion of a legally protected interest in property or privacy. . . .

What we have said largely disposes of [the claim of] infringement of the right of privacy. . . . The right of privacy embraces several distinct interests, but the only ones conceivably involved here are the closely related interests in concealing intimate personal facts and in preventing intrusion into legitimately private activities, such as phone conversations. As we have said already, no intimate personal facts concerning the two individual plaintiffs . . . were revealed; and the only conversations that were recorded were conversations with the testers themselves.

NOTES & QUESTIONS

1. ***Investigative Reporting.*** As is illustrated by *Dietemann* and *Desnick*, investigative reporting often depends upon deception. Those cases are split on the issue of whether such investigative techniques can give rise to intrusion. Recall the *Dietemann* court's statement:

   > Investigative reporting is an ancient art; its successful practice long antecedes the invention of miniature cameras and electronic devices. The First Amendment has never been construed to accord newsmen immunity from torts or crimes committed during the course of newsgathering. The First Amendment is not a license to trespass, to steal, or to intrude by electronic means into the precincts of another's home or office. It does not become such a license simply because the person subjected to the intrusion is reasonably suspected of committing a crime.

   However, investigative reporting has served an important function throughout history. In 1887, a reporter named Nellie Bly pretended to be mentally ill to gain access to a mental asylum. Her portrayal of the brutal conditions led to significant reforms. Upton Sinclair went undercover as a meatpacker to expose conditions in slaughterhouses for his book *The Jungle* in 1904. C. Thomas Dienes argues:

   > . . . Undercover journalism often serves the public interest. In the public sector, it allows the media to perform its role as the eyes and ears of the people, to perform a checking function on government. Especially at a time when citizens are often unable or unwilling to supervise government, this media role is critical to self-government. In the private sector, when the government fails in its responsibility to protect the public against fraudulent and unethical business and professional practices, whether because of lack of resources or unwillingness, media exposure of such practices can and often does provide the spur forcing government action.[4]

2. ***Posner's Analogies in* Desnick.** Judge Posner draws an analogy between (1) seduction with false promises of love in order to have sexual intercourse and (2) the deceitful trespass in *Desnick.* Are these situations really analogous?
3. ***Trespass: The* Food Lion *Case.*** The tort of trespass is related to the tort of intrusion. To commit a trespass, one must enter upon another's land without consent. To what extent does trespass overlap with intrusion? In many respects, it has fewer requirements — no requirement that solitude or seclusion be invaded, that a private matter be involved, or that the invasion be

[4] C. Thomas Dienes, *Protecting Investigative Journalism*, 67 Geo. Wash. L. Rev. 1139, 1141, 1143 (1999). For further background about investigative journalism and the use of deception, see Bernard W. Bell, *Secrets and Lies: News Media and Law Enforcement Use of Deception as an Investigative Tool*, 60 U. Pitt. L. Rev. 745 (1999).

highly offensive. On the other hand, intrusion can be committed without entering upon another's land.

Can one trespass if one obtains consent through deception? And can a person trespass if she is present upon another's land with consent but secretly engages in activities that the landowner would likely not authorize? Consider *Food Lion, Inc. v. ABC*, 194 F.3d 505 (4th Cir. 2001). ABC reporters investigated allegations of unsanitary food-handling practices at supermarkets operated by Food Lion, Inc. According to the allegations, "Food Lion employees ground out-of-date beef together with new beef, bleached rank meat to remove its odor, and re-dated (and offered for sale) products not sold before their printed expiration date." Two reporters submitted fake resumes to obtain jobs at Food Lion supermarkets. The reporters secretly videotaped the food-handling practices at the stores. The reporters quit their jobs within a few weeks. The video was broadcast on the show *Primetime Live*. "The broadcast included, for example, videotape that appeared to show Food Lion employees repackaging and redating fish that had passed the expiration date, grinding expired beef with fresh beef, and applying barbeque sauce to chicken past its expiration date in order to mask the smell and sell it as fresh in the gourmet food section." Food Lion sued for fraud, breach of duty of loyalty, trespass, and unfair trade practices. Food Lion won at trial — $1,400 on the fraud claim, $1 each for the duty of loyalty and trespass claims, and $1,500 on the unfair trade practices claim. The jury awarded approximately $5.5 million in punitive damages on the fraud claim, which the court reduced to $315,000.

On appeal, the court dismissed the fraud and unfair trade practices claims but affirmed the duty of loyalty and trespass claims.

Regarding the trespass claim, the court reasoned:

> [I]t is a trespass to enter upon another's land without consent. Accordingly, consent is a defense to a claim of trespass. Even consent gained by misrepresentation is sometimes sufficient. *See Desnick v. American Broad. Cos.*, 44 F.3d 1345 (7th Cir. 1995). The consent to enter is canceled out, however, "if a wrongful act is done in excess of and in abuse of authorized entry." . . .
>
> [W]e have not found any case suggesting that consent based on a resume misrepresentation turns a successful job applicant into a trespasser the moment she enters the employer's premises to begin work. . . .
>
> There is a problem, however, with what Dale and Barnett did after they entered Food Lion's property. The jury also found that the reporters committed trespass by breaching their duty of loyalty to Food Lion "as a result of pursuing [their] investigation for ABC." We affirm the finding of trespass on this ground because the breach of duty of loyalty — triggered by the filming in non-public areas, which was adverse to Food Lion — was a wrongful act in excess of Dale and Barnett's authority to enter Food Lion's premises as employees. . . .
>
> [S]ecretly installing a video camera in someone's private home can be a wrongful act in excess of consent given to enter. In the trespass case of *Miller v. Brooks* the (defendant) wife, who claimed she had consent to enter her estranged husband's (the plaintiff's) house, had a private detective place a video camera in the ceiling of her husband's bedroom. The court noted that "[e]ven an authorized entry can be trespass if a wrongful act is done in excess

> of and in abuse of authorized entry." . . . We recognize that *Miller* involved a private home, not a grocery store, and that it involved some physical alteration to the plaintiff's property (installation of a camera). Still, we believe the general principle is applicable here, at least in the case of Dale, who worked in a Food Lion store in North Carolina. Although Food Lion consented to Dale's entry to do her job, she exceeded that consent when she videotaped in non-public areas of the store and worked against the interests of her second employer, Food Lion, in doing so. . . .

The court only affirmed the duty of loyalty and trespass claims. As a result, Food Lion could only collect $2 in damages because the punitive damages were based on the fraud claim. Although *Food Lion* did not involve the tort of intrusion, to what extent is its holding regarding the tort of trespass applicable to intrusion cases? Is its holding consistent with *Dietemann* and *Desnick*?

4. ***Intrusion Liability for the Receipt of Data Obtained by Intrusion.*** In *Pearson v. Dodd*, 410 F.2d 701 (D.C. Cir. 1969), two former employees of Senator Thomas Dodd of Connecticut, with the assistance of two of Dodd's active staff members, entered Dodd's office without authorization and surreptitiously made copies of many documents in his files. These documents related to Dodd's relationship to lobbyists for foreign interests. Newspaper columnists Drew Pearson and Jack Anderson published articles containing information from these documents. Pearson and Anderson did not participate in or order the illegal copying; they only received copies of the documents knowing that they had been copied without authorization. Dodd sued Pearson and Anderson for invasion of privacy. The court held that intrusion could not extend to those who merely received the information:

> If we were to hold appellants liable for invasion of privacy on these facts, we would establish the proposition that one who receives information from an intruder, knowing it has been obtained by improper intrusion, is guilty of a tort. In an untried and developing area of tort law, we are not prepared to go so far. A person approached by an eavesdropper with an offer to share in the information gathered through the eavesdropping would perhaps play the nobler part should he spurn the offer and shut his ears. However, it seems to us that at this point it would place too great a strain on human weakness to hold one liable in damages who merely succumbs to temptation and listens.

SHULMAN V. GROUP W PRODUCTIONS, INC.

955 P.2d 469 (Cal. 1998)

WERDEGAR, J. . . . On June 24, 1990, plaintiffs Ruth and Wayne Shulman, mother and son, were injured when the car in which they and two other family members were riding on interstate 10 in Riverside County flew off the highway and tumbled down an embankment into a drainage ditch on state-owned property, coming to rest upside down. Ruth, the most seriously injured of the two, was pinned under the car. Ruth and Wayne both had to be cut free from the vehicle by the device known as "the jaws of life."

A rescue helicopter operated by Mercy Air was dispatched to the scene. The flight nurse, who would perform the medical care at the scene and on the way to the hospital, was Laura Carnahan. Also on board were the pilot, a medic and Joel Cooke, a video camera operator employed by defendants Group W Productions, Inc., and 4MN Productions. Cooke was recording the rescue operation for later broadcast.

Cooke roamed the accident scene, videotaping the rescue. Nurse Carnahan wore a wireless microphone that picked up her conversations with both Ruth and the other rescue personnel. Cooke's tape was edited into a piece approximately nine minutes long, which, with the addition of narrative voice-over, was broadcast on September 29, 1990, as a segment of *On Scene: Emergency Response*.

The segment begins with the Mercy Air helicopter shown on its way to the accident site. The narrator's voice is heard in the background, setting the scene and describing in general terms what has happened. . . .

The videotape shows only a glimpse of Wayne, and his voice is never heard. Ruth is shown several times, either by brief shots of a limb or her torso, or with her features blocked by others or obscured by an oxygen mask. She is also heard speaking several times. Carnahan calls her "Ruth" and her last name is not mentioned on the broadcast.

While Ruth is still trapped under the car, Carnahan asks Ruth's age. Ruth responds, "I'm old." On further questioning, Ruth reveals she is 47, and Carnahan observes that "it's all relative. You're not that old." During her extrication from the car, Ruth asks at least twice if she is dreaming. At one point she asks Carnahan, who has told her she will be taken to the hospital in a helicopter: "Are you teasing?" At another point she says: "This is terrible. Am I dreaming?" She also asks what happened and where the rest of her family is, repeating the questions even after being told she was in an accident and the other family members are being cared for. While being loaded into the helicopter on a stretcher, Ruth says: "I just want to die." Carnahan reassures her that she is "going to do real well," but Ruth repeats: "I just want to die. I don't want to go through this."

Ruth and Wayne are placed in the helicopter, and its door is closed. The narrator states: "Once airborne, Laura and [the flight medic] will update their patients' vital signs and establish communications with the waiting trauma teams at Loma Linda." Carnahan, speaking into what appears to be a radio microphone, transmits some of Ruth's vital signs and states that Ruth cannot move her feet and has no sensation. The video footage during the helicopter ride includes a few seconds of Ruth's face, covered by an oxygen mask. Wayne is neither shown nor heard.

The helicopter lands on the hospital roof. With the door open, Ruth states while being taken out: "My upper back hurts." Carnahan replies: "Your upper back hurts. That's what you were saying up there." Ruth states: "I don't feel that great." Carnahan responds: "You probably don't."

Finally, Ruth is shown being moved from the helicopter into the hospital. . . .

The accident left Ruth a paraplegic. When the segment was broadcast, Wayne phoned Ruth in her hospital room and told her to turn on the television because "Channel 4 is showing our accident now." Shortly afterward, several hospital workers came into the room to mention that a videotaped segment of her accident was being shown. Ruth was "shocked, so to speak, that this would be run and I would be exploited, have my privacy invaded, which is what I felt had happened." She did not know her rescue had been recorded in this manner and had never consented to the recording or broadcast. Ruth had the impression from the broadcast "that I was kind of talking non-stop, and I remember hearing some of the things I said, which were not very pleasant." Asked at deposition what part of the broadcast material she considered private, Ruth explained: "I think the whole scene was pretty private. It was pretty gruesome, the parts that I saw, my knee sticking out of the car. I certainly did not look my best, and I don't feel it's for the public to see. I was not at my best in what I was thinking and what I was saying and what was being shown, and it's not for the public to see this trauma that I was going through."

Ruth and Wayne sued the producers of *On Scene: Emergency Response*, as well as others. The first amended complaint included two causes of action for invasion of privacy, one based on defendants' unlawful intrusion by videotaping the rescue in the first instance and the other based on the public disclosure of private facts, i.e., the broadcast. . . .

The trial court granted the media defendants' summary judgment motion, basing its ruling on plaintiffs' admissions that the accident and rescue were matters of public interest and public affairs. Those admissions, in the trial court's view, showed as a matter of law that the broadcast material was newsworthy, thereby vesting the media defendants' conduct with First Amendment protection. The court entered judgment for defendants on all causes of action. . . .

[T]he action for intrusion has two elements: (1) intrusion into a private place, conversation or matter, (2) in a manner highly offensive to a reasonable person. We consider the elements in that order.

We ask first whether defendants "intentionally intrude[d], physically or otherwise, upon the solitude or seclusion of another," that is, into a place or conversation private to Wayne or Ruth. . . .

Cameraman Cooke's mere presence at the accident scene and filming of the events occurring there cannot be deemed either a physical or sensory intrusion on plaintiffs' seclusion. Plaintiffs had no right of ownership or possession of the property where the rescue took place, nor any actual control of the premises. Nor could they have had a reasonable expectation that members of the media would be excluded or prevented from photographing the scene; for journalists to attend and record the scenes of accidents and rescues is in no way unusual or unexpected.

Two aspects of defendants' conduct, however, raise triable issues of intrusion on seclusion. First, a triable issue exists as to whether both plaintiffs had an objectively reasonable expectation of privacy in the interior of the rescue helicopter, which served as an ambulance. Although the attendance of reporters and photographers at the scene of an accident is to be expected, we are aware of no law or custom permitting the press to ride in ambulances or enter hospital rooms during treatment without the patient's consent. Other than the two patients and Cooke, only three people were present in the helicopter, all Mercy Air staff. As the Court of Appeal observed, "[i]t is neither the custom nor the habit of our society that any member of the public at large or its media representatives may hitch a ride in an ambulance and ogle as paramedics care for an injured stranger."

Second, Ruth was entitled to a degree of privacy in her conversations with Carnahan and other medical rescuers at the accident scene, and in Carnahan's conversations conveying medical information regarding Ruth to the hospital base. Cooke, perhaps, did not intrude into that zone of privacy merely by being present at a place where he could hear such conversations with unaided ears. But by placing a microphone on Carnahan's person, amplifying and recording what she said and heard, defendants may have listened in on conversations the parties could reasonably have expected to be private. . . .

We turn to the second element of the intrusion tort, offensiveness. . . .

On this summary judgment record, we believe a jury could find defendants' recording of Ruth's communications to Carnahan and other rescuers, and filming in the air ambulance, to be "'highly offensive to a reasonable person.'" With regard to the depth of the intrusion, a reasonable jury could find highly offensive the placement of a microphone on a medical rescuer in order to intercept what would otherwise be private conversations with an injured patient. In that setting, as defendants could and should have foreseen, the patient would not know her words were being recorded and would not have occasion to ask about, and object or consent to, recording. Defendants, it could reasonably be said, took calculated advantage of the patient's "vulnerability and confusion." Arguably, the last thing an injured accident victim should have to worry about while being pried from her wrecked car is that a television producer may be recording everything she says to medical personnel for the possible edification and entertainment of casual television viewers.

For much the same reason, a jury could reasonably regard entering and riding in an ambulance — whether on the ground or in the air — with two seriously injured patients to be an egregious intrusion on a place of expected seclusion. Again, the patients, at least in this case, were hardly in a position to keep careful watch on who was riding with them, or to inquire as to everyone's business and consent or object to their presence. A jury could reasonably believe that fundamental respect for human dignity requires the patients' anxious journey be taken only with those whose care is solely for them and out of sight of the prying eyes (or cameras) of others.

Nor can we say as a matter of law that defendants' motive — to gather usable material for a potentially newsworthy story — necessarily privileged their intrusive conduct as a matter of common law tort liability. A reasonable jury could conclude the producers' desire to get footage that would convey the "feel" of the event — the real sights and sounds of a difficult rescue — did not justify either placing a microphone on Nurse Carnahan or filming inside the rescue helicopter. Although defendants' purposes could scarcely be regarded as evil or malicious (in the colloquial sense), their behavior could, even in light of their motives, be thought to show a highly offensive lack of sensitivity and respect for plaintiffs' privacy. A reasonable jury could find that defendants, in placing a microphone on an emergency treatment nurse and recording her conversation with a distressed, disoriented and severely injured patient, without the patient's knowledge or consent, acted with highly offensive disrespect for the patient's personal privacy. . . .

Turning to the question of constitutional protection for newsgathering, one finds the decisional law reflects a general rule of *nonprotection*: the press in its newsgathering activities enjoys no immunity or exemption from generally applicable laws. . . .

As should be apparent from the above discussion, the constitutional protection accorded newsgathering, if any, is far narrower than the protection surrounding the publication of truthful material; consequently, the fact that a reporter may be seeking "newsworthy" material does not in itself privilege the investigatory activity. The reason for the difference is simple: the intrusion tort, unlike that for publication of private facts, does not subject the press to liability for the contents of its publications. Newsworthiness . . . is a complete bar to liability for publication of private facts and is evaluated with a high degree of deference to editorial judgment. The same deference is not due, however, when the issue is not the media's right to publish or broadcast what they choose, but their right to intrude into secluded areas or conversations in pursuit of publishable material. At most, the Constitution may preclude tort liability that would "place an impermissible burden on newsgatherers" by depriving them of their " 'indispensable tools' " . . . .

NOTES & QUESTIONS

1. ***Intrusion in Public Places.*** Consider *Sanders v. ABC*, 978 P.2d 67 (Cal. 1999), decided by the same court one year after *Shulman*. In *Sanders*, a reporter obtained a job with a telephone psychics company that gave "readings" to callers for a fee. The psychics worked in a large room with rows of cubicles. The reporter secretly videotaped conversations of the plaintiff, an employee, with others at his cubicle or other cubicles. The plaintiff sued for intrusion upon seclusion. The defendants argued that the employee lacked a reasonable expectation of privacy in his conversations because they could be seen and overheard by co-workers. The court sided with the plaintiff:

> . . . [W]e adhere to the view suggested in *Shulman*: privacy, for purposes of the intrusion tort, is not a binary, all-or-nothing characteristic. There are degrees and nuances to societal recognition of our expectations of privacy: the fact that the privacy one expects in a given setting is not complete or absolute does not render the expectation unreasonable as a matter of law. Although the intrusion tort is often defined in terms of "seclusion" the seclusion referred to need not be absolute. "Like 'privacy,' the concept of 'seclusion' is relative. The mere fact that a person can be seen by someone does not automatically mean that he or she can legally be forced to be subject to being seen by everyone."

2. PAPARAZZI

Paparazzi are aggressive photographers who often harass celebrities to take candid photographs to sell to newspapers, tabloids, and magazines. Fueling the behavior of the paparazzi are the exorbitant prices that photographs of celebrities command. For example, a photo of Princess Diana embracing Dodi Al-Fayed was sold for over $3 million. According to the *New York Times*, "A growing constellation of Web sites, magazines and television programs serve [gossip] up minute by minute, creating a river of cash for secrets of the stars, or near stars."[5] It estimated the revenue stream of the "new world of round-the-clock" gossip at $3 billion annually.

Paparazzi have a reputation for being very invasive into the privacy of celebrities. For example, paparazzi flew over Michael J. Fox's wedding in helicopters to take photographs. Disguised photographers took photographs of Paul Reiser's baby in the hospital. Paparazzi also camped outside Reiser's backyard taking photographs with telephoto lenses. Paparazzi chased Arnold Schwarzenegger and Maria Shriver off the road to take the first photos of him leaving the hospital after heart surgery. In 2005, paparazzi followed Lindsey Lohan as she drove onto a dead end street. When she tried to make a U-turn, one photographer drove his automobile into her vehicle. Lohan suffered cuts and bruises from the accident. To what extent does the law of privacy restrict the behavior of paparazzi?

GALELLA V. ONASSIS

487 F.2d 986 (2d Cir. 1973)

SMITH, J. . . . Galella is a free-lance photographer specializing in the making and sale of photographs of well-known persons. Defendant Onassis is the widow of the late President, John F. Kennedy, mother of the two Kennedy children, John and Caroline, and is the wife of Aristotle Onassis, widely known shipping figure and reputed multimillionaire. John Walsh, James Kalafatis and John Connelly are U.S. Secret Service agents assigned to the duty of protecting the Kennedy children under 18 U.S.C. § 3056, which provides for protection of the children of deceased presidents up to the age of 16.

Galella fancies himself as a "paparazzo" (literally a kind of annoying insect, perhaps roughly equivalent to the English "gadfly.") Paparazzi make themselves as visible to the public and obnoxious to their photographic subjects as possible to aid in the advertisement and wide sale of their works.[6]

Some examples of Galella's conduct brought out at trial are illustrative. Galella took pictures of John Kennedy riding his bicycle in Central Park across the way from his home. He jumped out into the boy's path, causing the agents concern for John's safety. The agents' reaction and interrogation of Galella led to Galella's arrest and his action against the agents; Galella on other occasions interrupted Caroline at tennis, and invaded the children's private schools. At one time he came uncomfortably close in a power boat to Mrs. Onassis swimming. He often jumped and postured around while taking pictures of her party notably at a theater opening but also on numerous other occasions. He followed a practice of bribing apartment house, restaurant and nightclub doormen as well as romancing a family servant to keep him advised of the movements of the family.

---

[5] Jim Rutenberg, *The Gossip Machine, Churning Out Cash*, N.Y. Times, May 22, 2011.

[6] The newspapers report a recent incident in which one Marlon Brando, annoyed by Galella, punched Galella, breaking Galella's jaw and infecting Brando's hand.

After detention and arrest following complaint by the Secret Service agents protecting Mrs. Onassis' son and his acquittal in the state court, Galella filed suit in state court against the agents and Mrs. Onassis. Galella claimed that under orders from Mrs. Onassis, the three agents had falsely arrested and maliciously prosecuted him, and that this incident in addition to several others described in the complaint constituted an unlawful interference with his trade.

Mrs. Onassis answered denying any role in the arrest or any part in the claimed interference with his attempts to photograph her, and counterclaimed for damages and injunctive relief, charging that Galella had invaded her privacy, assaulted and battered her, intentionally inflicted emotional distress and engaged in a campaign of harassment. . . .

After a six-week trial the court dismissed Galella's claim and granted relief to both the defendant and the intervenor. Galella was enjoined from (1) keeping the defendant and her children under surveillance or following any of them; (2) approaching within 100 yards of the home of defendant or her children, or within 100 yards of either child's school or within 75 yards of either child or 50 yards of defendant; (3) using the name, portrait or picture of defendant or her children for advertising; (4) attempting to communicate with defendant or her children except through her attorney.

We conclude that grant of summary judgment and dismissal of Galella's claim against the Secret Service agents was proper. . . .

Evidence offered by the defense showed that Galella had on occasion intentionally physically touched Mrs. Onassis and her daughter, caused fear of physical contact in his frenzied attempts to get their pictures, followed defendant and her children too closely in an automobile, endangered the safety of the children while they were swimming, water skiing and horseback riding. Galella cannot successfully challenge the court's finding of tortious conduct.

Finding that Galella had "insinuated himself into the very fabric of Mrs. Onassis' life . . ." the court framed its relief in part on the need to prevent further invasion of the defendant's privacy. Whether or not this accords with present New York law, there is no doubt that it is sustainable under New York's proscription of harassment.

Of course legitimate countervailing social needs may warrant some intrusion despite an individual's reasonable expectation of privacy and freedom from harassment. However the interference allowed may be no greater than that necessary to protect the overriding public interest. Mrs. Onassis was properly found to be a public figure and thus subject to news coverage. Nonetheless, Galella's action went far beyond the reasonable bounds of news gathering. When weighed against the de minimis public importance of the daily activities of the defendant, Galella's constant surveillance, his obtrusive and intruding presence, was unwarranted and unreasonable. If there were any doubt in our minds, Galella's inexcusable conduct toward defendant's minor children would resolve it.

Galella does not seriously dispute the court's finding of tortious conduct. Rather, he sets up the First Amendment as a wall of immunity protecting newsmen from any liability for their conduct while gathering news. There is no such scope to the First Amendment right. Crimes and torts committed in news gathering are not protected. There is no threat to a free press in requiring its agents to act within the law. . . .

California Anti-Paparazzi Act

Cal. Civ. Code § 1708.8

Princess Diana's death in 1997 precipitated calls for anti-paparazzi legislation in the United States. On the evening of August 30, Princess Diana and Dodi Al-Fayed were being chauffeured in a Mercedes from the Ritz Hotel in Paris. Paparazzi followed the Mercedes on motorcycles and in cars. A chase developed, and according to eyewitnesses, the motorcycles were swarming around the Mercedes as it entered a tunnel. The Mercedes crashed in the tunnel, killing both Princess Diana and Dodi Al-Fayed. About 10 to 15 photographers gathered around the Mercedes after the crash and continued to take pictures at the scene of the accident.

In the United States, anti-paparazzi legislation was introduced in Congress but failed to be passed. In 1998, California became the first state to adopt anti-paparazzi legislation. In 2005, California amended the existing statute to add enhanced penalties for violations of the statute by paparazzi who engage in an "assault" to capture a photograph. Further amendments to the statute followed in 2009 and 2010.

California's Anti-Paparazzi Act does not supplant the state's existing privacy torts. Rather, it provides rights and remedies "in addition to any other rights and remedies provided by law." § 1708.8(h).

The Act recognizes two forms of invasion of privacy. First, it defines liability for "physical invasion of privacy":

> (a) A person is liable for physical invasion of privacy when the defendant knowingly enters onto the land of another without permission or otherwise committed a trespass, in order to physically invade the privacy of the plaintiff with the intent to capture any type of visual image, sound recording, or other physical impression of the plaintiff engaging in a personal or familial activity and the physical invasion occurs in a manner that is offensive to a reasonable person.

"Personal or familial activity" is defined as including but not limited to "intimate details of the plaintiff's personal life, interactions with the plaintiff's family or significant others, or other aspects of plaintiff's private affairs or concerns." § 1708.8(k).

Second, the Act defines liability for "constructive invasion of privacy":

> (b) A person is liable for constructive invasion of privacy when the defendant attempts to capture, in a manner that is offensive to a reasonable person, any type of visual image, sound recording, or other physical impression of the plaintiff engaging in a personal or familial activity under circumstances in which the plaintiff had a reasonable expectation of privacy, through the use of a visual or auditory enhancing device, regardless of whether there is a physical trespass, if this image, sound recording, or other physical impression could not have been achieved without a trespass unless the visual or auditory enhancing device was used.

The Act provides for increased damages for the two types of privacy violations defined above:

> (c) A person who commits physical invasion of privacy or constructive invasion of privacy, or both, is liable for up to three times the amount of any general and special damages that are proximately caused by the violation of this section. This person may also be liable for punitive damages, subject to proof according to Section 3294. If the plaintiff proves that the invasion of privacy was committed for a commercial purpose, the defendant shall also be subject to disgorgement to the plaintiff of any proceeds or other consideration obtained as a result of the violation of this section.

Equitable relief is also available. § 1708.8(g).

Further, the Act punishes a person who "directs, solicits, actually induces, or actually causes" a person to violate the law. § 1708.8(d). However, the Act does not punish the sale or dissemination of images or recordings in violation of the Act. § 1708.8(e).

Since the Act is aimed at limiting the intrusive activities of paparazzi, not merely the invasion of privacy caused by having one's photograph taken or voice recorded, the Act applies even if no image or recording is ever captured or sold. § 1708.8(i).

NOTES & QUESTIONS

1. ***"Papa Paparazzo": Ron Galella Post-*Onassis.** According to the *New Yorker*, Galella repeatedly violated the terms of the court order in the *Onassis* litigation, which led to a settlement in which he agreed to stop photographing Onassis.[7] Nonetheless, Galella lost little time in publishing a volume, *Jacqueline* (1978), containing his Onassis photographs. Remaining productive, Galella has published numerous other volumes of his candid photographs. He is considered as the father of the modern celebrity industry as well as a celebrity himself.[8] In 2010, Galella was the subject of a documentary, *Smash His Camera*.
2. ***Collective Actions by Different Journalists.*** Suppose a person is accosted by throngs of reporters. At any moment, there is always one or more reporters on her trail. Groups of reporters camp outside her home. The impact from the collective actions of all the reporters is extremely disruptive to the person's life. Can she sue the reporters collectively? Bruce Sanford argues that each reporter should only be liable for his or her own behavior: "A stake-out by a group of unrelated reporters should be viewed as no more than the sum of its separate parts."[9]
3. ***The Anti-Paparazzi Act vs. the Intrusion Tort.*** How does California's Anti-Paparazzi Act differ from the ordinary intrusion upon seclusion tort?

---

[7] Tad Friend, *No Pictures!*, 86 The New Yorker 24-25 (May 31, 2010). The article described the photographer as "a tireless stalker with an Elmer Fudd laugh."

[8] Jacqueline Mroz, *Papa Paparazzo*, New Jersey Monthly (June 15, 2010).

[9] Bruce W. Sanford, *Libel and Privacy* § 11.2, at 541 (2d ed. 1991).

4. ***The Anti-Paparazzi Act and the First Amendment.*** Is California's Anti-Paparazzi Act constitutional?

Erwin Chemerinsky contends that newsgathering, although currently not protected by the First Amendment, should be protected by intermediate scrutiny because the "very notion of a marketplace of ideas rests on the availability of information. Aggressive newsgathering, such as by undercover reporters, is often the key to gathering the information." However, Chemerinsky goes on to argue that the California Anti-Paparazzi Act would survive intermediate scrutiny:

> Despite strongly believing in First Amendment protection for newsgathering, I believe that this law is constitutional. The government has an important interest in protecting the privacy of the home. Fourth Amendment cases have recognized the special privacy interests surrounding the home. . . .
>
> The California Privacy Protection Act says that people, no matter how famous, should be able to shut their door and close out the media and the world. If the image could not have been gained except through a trespass, the media should not be able to obtain it through technological enhancement equipment. Simply put, the law is constitutional because it substantially advances the government's interest in safeguarding privacy in the home.[10]

Consider the following argument by C. Thomas Dienes:

> The antipaparazzi laws, by focusing only on taking photographs and making sound recordings when done for commercial purposes and on the defendant photographer's profits, clearly target the press. Liability for photographing or recording the same event will depend on whether the photographer is a private individual or a for-profit photojournalist whose work is intended for public distribution. Statements made at legislative hearings by proponents of these laws leave no doubt that the press is the focus of the antipaparazzi legislation.
>
> The taking of photographs or the making of sound recordings is not itself speech. . . . [T]he sale or trade of a photo or recording is probably not a form of expression. . . .
>
> Nevertheless the antipaparazzi legislation singles out press photography and sound recording for significant and discriminatory burdens. Even if such acts do not themselves constitute speech, they are protected means of newsgathering vital to press publication. If the photographs and sound recordings cannot be made, they cannot be published. As the Supreme Court said in *Arcara v. Cloud Books, Inc.*, laws are subject to heightened scrutiny "although directed at activity with no expressive component, [if they] impose a disproportionate burden upon those engaged in protected First Amendment activities." Because media speech-related activity is significantly and disproportionately burdened, the antipaparazzi laws should be treated as presumptively unconstitutional, subject to strict scrutiny review.[11]

---

[10] Erwin Chemerinsky, *Protect the Press: A First Amendment Standard for Safeguarding Aggressive Newsgathering*, 33 U. Rich. L. Rev. 1143, 1159, 1163-64 (2000).

[11] C. Thomas Dienes, *Protecting Investigative Journalism,* 67 Geo. Wash. L. Rev. 1139 (1999).

3. VIDEO VOYEURISM

Cameras are everywhere today. Warren and Brandeis wrote about the perils of small accessible cameras; one wonders what they would have thought about the proliferation of cell phone cameras, which millions of people now carry around with them at all times. Some people are posting their cell phone snapshots on the Web. The dark underbelly of these practices is the rise of what is referred to as "video voyeurism," the use of video or photography to capture people naked without their consent. Websites have been popping up with "upskirt" photos — pictures taken up women's skirts. There are more than 100 websites with images of unsuspecting people who are caught in the act of showering or undressing.[12] Indeed, it is relatively easy to snap photos in locker rooms with a cell phone camera. Several states have passed video voyeurism laws, some with criminal penalties. *See, e.g.,* La. Rev. Stat. Ann. § 14:283; N.J. Stat. Ann. § 2C:18-3; N.Y. Penal Law § 250.45.

The state of Washington passed a video voyeurism law that provided that

> [a] person commits the crime of voyeurism if, for the purpose of arousing or gratifying the sexual desire of any person, he or she knowingly views, photographs, or films another person, without that person's knowledge and consent, while the person being viewed, photographed, or filmed is in a place where he or she would have a reasonable expectation of privacy.

RCW 9A.44.115. The statute defined the place where people have a reasonable expectation of privacy as:

> (i) A place where a reasonable person would believe that he or she could disrobe in privacy, without being concerned that his or her undressing was being photographed or filmed by another; *or*
>
> (ii) A place where one may reasonably expect to be safe from casual or hostile intrusion or surveillance. . . .

In *Washington v. Glas,* 54 P.3d 147 (Wash. 2002), Sean Glas was convicted under the statute for taking photos up women's skirts in a shopping mall without their consent. The court dismissed Glas's conviction because "although the Legislature may have intended to cover intrusions of privacy in public places, the plain language of the statute does not accomplish this goal." The court reasoned that "[c]asual surveillance frequently occurs in public. Therefore, public places could not logically constitute locations where a person could reasonably expect to be safe from casual or hostile intrusion or surveillance."

Shortly after this opinion, in 2003, Washington revised its statute to include "intimate areas of another person without that person's knowledge and consent and under circumstances where the person has a reasonable expectation of privacy, whether in a public or private place." RCW 9A.44.115.

Consider the following law enacted by the U.S. Congress in 2004:

---

[12] Clay Calvert, *Voyeur Nation: Media, Privacy, and Peering in Modern Culture* (2000).

VIDEO VOYEURISM PREVENTION ACT

18 U.S.C. § 1801

(a) Whoever, in the special maritime and territorial jurisdiction of the United States, having the intent to capture an improper image of an individual, knowingly does so and that individual's naked or undergarment clad genitals, pubic area, buttocks, or female breast is depicted in the improper image under circumstances in which that individual has a reasonable expectation of privacy regarding such body part or parts, shall be fined under this title or imprisoned not more than one year, or both.

(b) In this section —

(1) the term "captures," with respect to an image, means videotapes, photographs, films, or records by any means or broadcasts;

(2) the term "female breast" means any portion of the female breast below the top of the areola;

(3) the term "improper image," with respect to an individual, means an image, captured without the consent of that individual, of the naked or undergarment clad genitals, pubic area, buttocks, or female breast of that individual; and

(4) the term "under circumstances in which that individual has a reasonable expectation of privacy" means —

(A) circumstances in which a reasonable person would believe that he or she could disrobe in privacy, without being concerned that his or her image was being videotaped, photographed, filmed, broadcast, or otherwise recorded by any means; or

(B) circumstances in which a reasonable person would believe that his or her naked or undergarment-clad pubic area, buttocks, genitals, or female breast would not be visible to the public, regardless of whether that person is in a public or private area.

(c) This section shall not apply to any person engaged in lawful law enforcement or intelligence activities.

NOTES & QUESTIONS

1. ***The Washington Statute vs. the Video Voyeurism Protection Act.*** How does the federal statute compare with the Washington statute? Does the federal statute violate the First Amendment?
2. ***Privacy in Public.*** Clay Calvert contends that because the Act "applies in public areas, not merely those that are private . . . [t]his would be a radical change for the legal system's conception of privacy, but surely one that is necessary to preserve human dignity from offensive intrusions."[13] Consider again *Nader v. General Motors,* where the court held that "a person does not

[13] Clay Calvert, *Revisiting the Voyeurism Value in the First Amendment: From the Sexually Sordid to the Details of Death,* 27 Seattle U. L. Rev. 721, 731 (2004); *see also* Helen Nissenbaum, *Protecting Privacy in the Information Age: The Problem of Privacy in Public*, 17 Law & Phil. 559 (1998) (arguing that being in public should not eliminate one's privacy interest).

automatically make public everything he does merely by being in a public place." In what circumstances might a person have an expectation of privacy in a public place?

3. ***The Burning Man Festival Video.*** The Burning Man Festival, held annually in the Nevada desert, has nearly 25,000 participants, including a large contingent of technology professionals. There is significant nudity at the festival, as people are encouraged to engage in "radical self-expression." Videos for personal use are permitted with prior approval by the festival organizers. In 2002, 12 videos of nude participants at the festival appeared for sale on a pornographic website called Video Voyeur. Video Voyeur had sought permission to videotape the event, but was denied.[14] Does Video Voyeur's videotaping, which captures naked people, including breasts and genitals, violate the Video Voyeurism Prevention Act?

B. DISCLOSURE OF TRUTHFUL INFORMATION

In certain circumstances, the law provides remedies for individuals who suffer harm as a result of the disclosure of their personal information. One of the primary remedies is the tort of public disclosure of private facts. Other remedies include statutes passed by states and the federal government that restrict the disclosure of specific information. For example, a number of states have laws prohibiting the disclosure of the identities of sexual offense victims. *See, e.g.*, N.Y. Civ. Rights L. § 50-b; 42 Pa. Comp. Stat. § 5988. States have also provided statutory remedies for the disclosure that a person has AIDS. *See, e.g.*, 410 Ill. Comp. Stat. 305/9; Fla. Stat. § 381.004. Federal wiretap law prohibits the disclosure of a communication that one has reason to know was obtained through an illegal wiretap. *See* 18 U.S.C. § 2511(1)(c). This provision of federal wiretap law is the subject of *Bartnicki v. Vopper*, discussed below. What types of disclosures of personal information can and should give rise to civil liability? How can liability for the disclosure of true information coexist with the First Amendment's protection of free speech?

---

[14] Evelyn Nieves, *A Festival With Nudity Sues a Sex Web Site,* N.Y. Times, July 5, 2002. The Burning Man Festival's suit was filed prior to the Video Voyeurism Prevention Act. Among the claims were intrusion, appropriation, public disclosure, breach of contract, and trespass. The suit was settled when Video Voyeur agreed to stop selling the videos, to turn them over to the festival organizers, and to cease from videotaping the event in the future.

1. PUBLIC DISCLOSURE OF PRIVATE FACTS

(a) Introduction

PUBLICITY GIVEN TO PRIVATE LIFE

Restatement (Second) of Torts § 652D

One who gives publicity to a matter concerning the private life of another is subject to liability to the other for invasion of his privacy, if the matter publicized is of a kind that

(a) would be highly offensive to a reasonable person, and

(b) is not of legitimate concern to the public

NOTES & QUESTIONS

1. ***Publicity.*** "Publicity" means that the matter is communicated to the "public at large" or "to so many persons that the matter must be regarded as substantially certain to become one of public knowledge." The Restatement (comment b) notes that communicating "a fact concerning the plaintiff's private life to a single person or even to a small group of persons" is not sufficient to establish publicity. The Restatement commentary goes on to explain:

   > On the other hand, any publication in a newspaper or a magazine, even of small circulation, or in a handbill distributed to a large number of persons, or any broadcast over the radio, or statement made in an address to a large audience, is sufficient to give publicity within the meaning of the term as it is used in this Section. The distinction, in other words, is one between private and public communication.

   Most courts have followed the Restatement and concluded that disclosure to a small group of individuals does not constitute publicity. For example, in *Yoder v. Smith*, 112 N.W.2d 862 (Iowa 1962), the court held that the publicity element was not satisfied when the defendant disclosed the plaintiff's debts to the plaintiff's employer. In *Wells v. Thomas*, 569 F. Supp. 426 (E.D. Pa. 1983), the court held that disclosure to a plaintiff's co-workers at a hospital was not sufficient to establish the publicity element.

   In contrast, posting information in public places constitutes sufficient publicity. In *Brents v. Morgan*, 299 S.W. 967 (Ky. 1927), the court held that there was sufficient publicity when the owner of an automobile garage posted a large sign on a show window of his garage stating that the plaintiff owed him a debt. In *Biederman's of Springfield, Inc. v. Wright*, 322 S.W.2d 892 (Mo. 1959), the court concluded that making loaded comments to a person "in a public restaurant with numerous customers present satisfies any reasonable requirement as to publicity."

   However, consider *Miller v. Motorola, Inc.*, 560 N.E2d 900 (Ill. App. 1990). The plaintiff shared information that with her employer's nurse that she was undergoing a mastectomy and reconstructive surgeries. The information was disclosed to other employees. The court held that although the information was made to a small group, "in circumstances where a special relationship exists between the plaintiff and the 'public' to whom the information has been disclosed, the disclosure may be just as devastating to the person even though the disclosure was made to a limited number of people." The court in *Miller* followed an earlier case, *Beaumont v. Brown*, 257 N.W.2d 522 (Mich. 1977), which explained: "An invasion of a plaintiff's right to privacy is important if it exposes private facts to a public whose knowledge of those facts would be embarrassing to the plaintiff."

Which approach to publicity do you agree with? Consider Jonathan Mintz:

> A person loses some sense of privacy the moment a second person divulges a private fact to a third person, particularly when the third person is a member of the same community as the first person. Thus, the degree of publicity, and the corresponding degree of injury to a person's dignity, is a factor better addressed in damage calculations than in summary judgments or motions to dismiss.[15]

Why does the publicity requirement exist? As one court observed, the requirement of widespread publicity "singles out the print, film, and broadcast media for legal restraints that will not be applied to gossip-mongers in neighborhood taverns or card-parties, to letter writers or telephone tattlers." *Anderson v. Fisher Broadcasting Co.*, 712 P.2d 803, 805 (Or. 1986). A major function of the publicity requirement is to prevent lawsuits for a wide array of gossip, which often occurs between just a few people. The publicity requirement attempts to exclude mere gossip from the tort. Would the public disclosure tort apply too widely without the publicity requirement?

2. ***Highly Offensive.*** The disclosure must be highly offensive. According to the Restatement (comment c):

> Complete privacy does not exist in this world except in a desert, and anyone who is not a hermit must expect and endure the ordinary incidents of the community life of which he is a part. Thus he must expect the more or less casual observation of his neighbors as to what he does, and that his comings and goings and his ordinary daily activities, will be described in the press as a matter of casual interest to others. The ordinary reasonable man does not take offense at a report in a newspaper that he has returned from a visit, gone camping in the woods or given a party at his house for his friends. Even minor and moderate annoyance, as for example through public disclosure of the fact that the plaintiff has clumsily fallen downstairs and broken his ankle, is not sufficient to give him a cause of action under the rule stated in this Section. It is only when the publicity given to him is such that a reasonable person would feel justified in feeling seriously aggrieved by it, that the cause of action arises.

Note the irony. The Restatement commentary suggests that the ordinary person does not take offense of a newspaper report that he has "given a party at his house for his friends." Indeed, it was such a newspaper report that some

---

[15] Jonathan B. Mintz, *The Remains of Privacy's Disclosure Tort: An Exploration of the Private Domain*, 55 Md. L. Rev. 425, 438 (1996).

suggest inspired Samuel Warren to write the law review article with Louis Brandeis that gave rise to this very tort.

3. ***Newsworthiness.*** As stated by Restatement (comment f): "When the subject-matter of the publicity is of legitimate public concern, there is no invasion of privacy." Recall that the first exception to the right to privacy proposed by Brandeis and Warren was for "any publication of matter which is of general public interest."
4. ***Recognition of the Tort by the States.*** Most states recognize the public disclosure tort.[16] There are some states that have not recognized the tort: Nebraska, New York, North Carolina, North Dakota, Rhode Island, Utah, and Virginia.[17] As you read in *Lake v. Wal-Mart*, Minnesota, a long time holdout on recognizing the public disclosure tort, finally recognized the tort in 1998.

(b) Private Matters

GILL V. HEARST PUBLISHING CO.

253 P.2d 441 (Cal. 1953)

SPENCE, J. . . . [P]laintiffs, husband and wife, sought damages for an alleged invasion of their right of privacy. . . . Plaintiffs' original complaint was predicated solely on the charge that in the October, 1947, issue of Harper's Bazaar, a magazine published and distributed by the corporate defendants, there appeared an unauthorized photograph of plaintiffs taken by defendants' employee while plaintiffs were seated in an affectionate pose at their place of business, a confectionery and ice cream concession in the Farmers' Market in Los Angeles. This photograph was used to illustrate an article entitled "And So the World Goes Round," a short commentary reaffirming "the poet's conviction that the world could not revolve without love," despite "vulgarization" of the sentiment by some, and that ballads may still be written about everyday people in love. . . .

Plaintiffs . . . amended their complaint to allege that the same photograph was republished with defendants' consent in the May, 1949, issue of the Ladies' Home Journal, a monthly magazine published and distributed by the Curtis Publishing Company. . . . Specifically, it is here alleged that the "picture" was republished with the "knowledge, permission and consent" of defendants and that "credit" for the publication was given to and required by defendants; that the published photograph depicts plaintiffs in an "uncomplimentary" pose; that

---

[16] For more background about the public disclosure tort, see Jonathan B. Mintz, *The Remains of Privacy's Disclosure Tort: An Exploration of the Private Domain,* 55 Md. L. Rev. 425 (1996); Robert C. Post, *The Social Foundations of Privacy: Community and Self in the Common Law Tort,* 77 Cal. L. Rev. 957 (1989); Peter L. Felcher & Edward L. Rubin, *Privacy, Publicity, and the Portrayal of Real People by the Media,* 88 Yale L.J. 1577 (1979); Dorsey D. Ellis, Jr., *Damages and the Privacy Tort: Sketching a "Legal Profile,"* 64 Iowa L. Rev. 1111 (1979); Randall Bezanson, *Public Disclosure as News: Injunctive Relief and Newsworthiness in Privacy Actions Involving the Press*, 64 Iowa L. Rev. 1061 (1979); John W. Wade, *Defamation and the Right to Privacy*, 15 Vand. L. Rev. 1093 (1962).

[17] *See* Geoff Dendy, Note, *The Newsworthiness Defense to the Public Disclosure Tort*, 85 Ky. L.J. 147, 158 (1997).

plaintiffs' right of privacy was thereby invaded and plaintiffs were subjected to humiliation and annoyance to their damage in the sum of $25,000. . . .

. . . [M]ere publication of the photograph standing alone does not constitute an actionable invasion of plaintiffs' right of privacy. The right "to be let alone" and to be protected from undesired publicity is not absolute but must be balanced against the public interest in the dissemination of news and information consistent with the democratic processes under the constitutional guaranties of freedom of speech and of the press. The right of privacy may not be extended to prohibit any publication of matter which may be of public or general interest, but rather the "general object in view is to protect the privacy of private life, and to whatever degree and in whatever connection a man's life has ceased to be private, before the publication under consideration has been made, to that extent the protection is to be withdrawn." Brandeis-Warren Essay, 4 Harvard Law Rev., 193, 215. Moreover, the right of privacy is determined by the norm of the ordinary man; that is to say, the alleged objectionable publication must appear offensive in the light of "ordinary sensibilities." . . .

The picture allegedly was taken at plaintiffs' "place of business," a confectionery and ice cream concession in the Farmers' Market, Los Angeles. It shows plaintiffs, a young man and young woman, seated at a counter near a cash register, the young woman apparently in intent thought, with a notebook and pencil in her hands, which rest on the counter. Plaintiffs are dressed informally and are in a romantic pose, the young man having one arm about the young woman. There are at least five other persons plainly visible in the photograph in positions in close proximity to plaintiffs as the central figures. Apparently the picture has no particular news value but is designed to serve the function of entertainment as a matter of legitimate public interest. However, the constitution guaranties of freedom of expression apply with equal force to the publication whether it be a news report or an entertainment feature, and defendants' liability accrues only in the event that it can be said that there has been a wrongful invasion of plaintiffs' right of privacy.

In considering the nature of the picture in question, it is significant that it was not surreptitiously snapped on private grounds, but rather was taken of plaintiffs in a pose voluntarily assumed in a public market place. . . . Here plaintiffs, photographed at their concession allegedly "well known to persons and travelers throughout the world" as conducted for "many years" in the "world-famed" Farmers' Market, had voluntarily exposed themselves to public gaze in a pose open to the view of any persons who might then be at or near their place of business. By their own voluntary action plaintiffs waived their right of privacy so far as this particular public pose was assumed, for "There can be no privacy in that which is already public." *Melvin v. Reid*, 297 P. 91, 93. The photograph of plaintiffs merely permitted other members of the public, who were not at plaintiffs' place of business at the time it was taken, to see them as they had voluntarily exhibited themselves. Consistent which their own voluntary assumption of this particular pose in a public place, plaintiffs' right to privacy as to this photographed incident ceased and it in effect became a part of the public domain, as to which they could not later rescind their waiver in an attempt to assert a right of privacy. In short, the photograph did not disclose anything which until then had been private, but rather only extended knowledge of the particular incident to a somewhat larger public then had actually witnessed it at the time of occurrence.

Nor does there appear to be anything "uncomplimentary" or discreditable in the photograph itself, so that its publication might be objectionable as going "beyond the limits of decency" and reasonably indicate defendants' conduct to be such that they "should have realized it would be offensive to persons of ordinary sensibilities." Here the picture of plaintiffs, sitting romantically close to one another, the man with his arm around the woman, depicts no more than a portrayal of an incident which may be seen almost daily in ordinary life couples in a sentimental mood on public park benches, in railroad depots or hotel lobbies, at public games, the beaches, the theatres. Such situation is readily distinguishable from cases where the right of privacy has been enforced with regard to the publication of a picture which was shocking, revolting or indecent in its portrayal of the human body. In fact, here the photograph may very well be said to be complimentary and pleasing in its pictorial representation of plaintiffs.

Plaintiffs have failed to cite, and independent research has failed to reveal, any case where the publication of a mere photograph under the circumstances here prevailing a picture (1) taken in a pose voluntarily assumed in a public place and (2) portraying nothing to shock the ordinary sense of decency or propriety has been held an actionable invasion of the right of privacy. To so hold would mean that plaintiffs "under all conceivable circumstances had an absolute legal right to (prevent publication of) any photograph of them taken without their permission. If every person has such a right, no (periodical) could lawfully publish a photograph of a parade or a street scene. We are not prepared to sustain the assertion of such a right." . . .

CARTER, J. dissenting. I dissent, however, from the holding that the publication of the photograph alone did not violate plaintiffs' right of privacy. . . .

[F]irst, it should be quite obvious that there is no news or educational value whatsoever in the photograph alone. It depicts two persons (plaintiffs) in an amorous pose. There is nothing to show whether they are or are not married. While some remote news significance might be attached to persons in such a pose on the theory that the public likes and is entitled to see persons in such a pose, there is no reason why the publisher need invade the privacy of John and Jane Doe for his purpose. He can employ models for that purpose and the portion of the public interested will never know the difference but its maudlin curiosity will be appeased.

For the same reasons the discussion in the majority opinion to the effect that plaintiffs consented to the publication because they assumed the pose in a public place is fallacious. But in addition, such a theory is completely at odds with the violation of the right of privacy. By plaintiffs doing what they did in view of a tiny fraction of the public, does not mean that they consented to observation by the millions of readers of the defendant's magazine. In effect, the majority holding means that anything anyone does outside of his own home is with consent to the publication thereof, because, under those circumstances he waives his right of privacy even though there is no news value in the event. If such were the case, the blameless exposure of a portion of the naked body of a man or woman in a public place as the result of inefficient buttons, hooks or other clothes-holding devices could be freely photographed and widely published with complete immunity. The majority opinion confuses the situation, as have some of the other cases, with the question of newsworthiness. It has been said that when a person is involved in either a public or private event, voluntarily or involuntarily, of news value, that he has waived his right of privacy. Plainly such is not the case where the event is involuntary such as the victim of a holdup. . . . There is no basis for the conclusion that the second a person leaves the portals of his home he consents to have his photograph taken under all circumstances thereafter. There being no legitimate public interest, there is no excuse for the publication.

The [argument] that the picture would not offend the senses of an ordinary person is equally untenable. It is alleged in plaintiffs' complaint, and admitted by the demurrer that it so offended them. It is then a matter of proof at the trial. Certainly reasonable men could view the picture as showing plaintiffs in a sultry or sensual pose. For this Court to say as a matter of law that such portrayal would not seriously offend the feelings of an ordinary man is to take an extreme view to say the least. The question is one for the trier of fact. If it is in part a question of law it is so only to the extent that the right does not extend to "supersensitiveness or agoraphobia." An examination of the photograph shows that it would offend the feelings of persons other than oversensitive ones. . . .

In announcing a rule of law defining the right of a private citizen to be left alone, and not have his photograph published to the four winds, especially when he is depicted in an uncomplimentary pose, courts should consider the effect of such publication upon the sensibility of the ordinary private citizen, and not upon the sensibility of those persons who seek and enjoy publicity and notoriety and seeing their pictures on public display, or those who are in the "public eye" such as public officials, clergymen, lecturers, actors and others whose professional career brings them in constant contact with the public and in whom the public or some segment thereof is interested. Obviously anything the latter group may do or say has news or educational value such cannot be said of the persons engaged in private business or employment who constitute more that 90% of our population. These private citizens, who desire to be left alone, should have and enjoy a right of privacy so long as they do nothing which can reasonably be said to have news value. Certainly this right is entitled to protection. It seems to me that the law should be so molded as to protect the right of the 90% who do not desire publicity or notoriety and who may be offended by publications such as that here involved. . . .

NOTES & QUESTIONS

1. ***Privacy in Public.*** Similar to *Gill,* many courts hold that matters cease to be "private" when occurring in public. Appearing in public "necessarily involves doffing the cloak of privacy which the law protects." *Cefalu v. Globe Newspaper Co.*, 391 N.E.2d 935, 939 (Mass. App. 1979). In *Penwell v. Taft Broadcasting*, 469 N.E.2d 1025 (Ohio App. 1984), a husband and wife were arrested in a bar, handcuffed, and taken to the police station, where it was discovered that they had been arrested due to mistaken identity. A television film crew that arrived at the bar with the police filmed the plaintiff's arrest

and removal from the bar, and the footage was later broadcast by the television station. The court dismissed the plaintiff's public disclosure action because the arrest was filmed in public and was "left open to the public eye." Does appearing in public extinguish a person's claim to privacy?

2. ***Google Street View.*** Google Street View allows Web surfers to see images of each street at street level. In the United States, Google provides an opt-out option for individuals who do not wish to have an image of their residence included in the Street View database. The Borings, who live on a private road outside of Pittsburgh, sued Google for taking Street View pictures without their permission. In an unpublished opinion, the Third Circuit affirmed a lower court's granting of Google's motion to dismiss. *Boring v. Google*, 38 Media L. Rep. 1306 (2010). On the intrusion upon seclusion claim, the Third Circuit declared, "No person of ordinary sensibility would be shamed, humiliated, or have suffered mentally as a result of a vehicle entering into his or her ungated driveway and photographing the view from there." As for publicity given to private life, it also found that the Borings failed to establish that the publicity would be highly offensive to a reasonable person. As an international comparison, protests in Germany against Google's introduction of this same service led the company to permit individuals, including persons who live in apartment buildings, to opt out their residence from the database *before* it went live. Which version of opt-out is preferable?
3. ***Photography of Public Scenes.*** Judge Carter, in dissent, argues that there is a difference between engaging in public displays of affection "in view of a tiny fraction of the public" and being observed by millions of magazine readers. Thus, the prior public exposure of the plaintiffs did not extinguish their privacy claim. How is the law to draw the appropriate line? At what point does the public exposure of the plaintiff's activities become too great to sustain a claim that the activities are private? Suppose, for example, a photographer is taking photos of people in the park. How is that photographer to know if she can publish the photos? Should she obtain the consent of everyone captured in the photos? According to the majority opinion, if Judge Carter's view were the law, this "would mean that plaintiffs under all conceivable circumstances had an absolute legal right to (prevent publication of) any photograph of them taken without their permission. If every person has such a right, no (periodical) could lawfully publish a photograph of a parade or a street scene." How would Judge Carter respond?
4. ***Take Me Out to the Ball Game.*** In July 2014, a Yankees fan sued Major League Baseball, the Yankees, and ESPN after announcers made allegedly disparaging comments about him as he slept soundly through a baseball game.[18] Among his claims was that Major League Baseball was responsible for "vituperative utterances" about him after it posted a clip of him sleeping on its website. For example, Twitter users inserted the sleeping fan's picture

[18] James C. McKinley, Jr., *Fan Sues After Untimely Nap Brings Unwanted Attention*, N.Y. Times (July 8, 2014).

in various situations, including one that featured him in "Sleeping Beauty." Should the rise of social media and the ability of video clips and photography to "go viral" necessarily alter the analysis regarding photography and broadcasting of images captured in public? Does it matter for the analysis that the Yankees fan attended a publicly broadcast game?

DAILY TIMES DEMOCRAT V. GRAHAM

162 So. 2d 474 (Ala. 1964)

HARWOOD, J. This is an appeal from a judgment in favor of the plaintiff in an action charging an invasion by the defendant of the plaintiff's right of privacy. Damages were assessed by the jury at $4,166.00. . . .

Appellee is a woman 44 years of age who has lived in Cullman County, Alabama her entire life. She is married and has two sons, ages 10 and 8. The family resides in a rural community where her husband is engaged in the business of raising chickens. . . .

On 9 October 1961, the Cullman County Fair was in progress. On that day the appellee took her two children to the Fair. After going on some of the rides, the boys expressed a wish to go through what is called in the record the "Fun House." The boys were afraid to enter alone so the appellee accompanied them. She testified she had never been through a Fun House before and had no knowledge that there was a device that blew jets of air up from the platform of the Fun House upon which one exited therefrom.

The appellee entered the Fun House with her two boys and as she was leaving her dress was blown up by the air jets and her body was exposed from the waist down, with the exception of that portion covered by her "panties."

At this moment the appellant's photographer snapped a picture of the appellee in this situation. This was done without the appellee's knowledge or consent. Four days later the appellant published this picture on the front page of its newspaper.

The appellant publishes about five thousand newspapers daily which are delivered to homes, mailed to subscribers, and displayed on racks in various locations in the city of Cullman and elsewhere.

On the Sunday following the publication of the picture, the appellee went into the city of Cullman. There she saw the appellant's newspaper display with her picture on the front page in one of the appellant's newspaper racks, and she also saw copies of the said newspaper in other places.

While the appellee's back was largely towards the camera in the picture, her two sons are in the picture, and the photograph was recognized as being of her by other people with whom she was acquainted. The matter of her photograph was mentioned to the appellee by others on several occasions. Evidence offered by the appellee during the trial tended to show that the appellee, as a result of the publication of the picture, became embarrassed, self-conscious, upset and was known to cry on occasions. . . .

. . . Counsel contends that as a matter of law the publication of the photograph was a matter of legitimate news of interest to the public; that the publishing of the picture was in connection with a write-up of the Fair, which was a matter of legitimate news. If this be so, then of course the appellant would have been privileged to have published the picture.

Counsel has quoted from an array of cases as to what constitutes news. We see no need to refer to these cases in that their applicability to the facts now before us is negligible. We can see nothing of legitimate news value in the photograph. Certainly it discloses nothing as to which the public is entitled to be informed. . . .

Not only was this photograph embarrassing to one of normal sensibilities, we think it could properly be classified as obscene, in that "obscene" means "offensive to modesty or decency"; or expressing to the mind or view something which delicacy, purity, or decency forbid to be expressed.

The appellant's insistence of error in this aspect is therefore without merit.

Counsel further argues that the court erred in refusal of appellant's requested affirmative charges in that appellee's picture was taken at the time she was a part of a public scene, and the publication of the photograph could not therefore be deemed an invasion of her privacy as a matter of law.

The proposition for which appellant contends is probably best illustrated by the following quotation from *Forster v. Manchester*, 410 Pa. 192, 189 A.2d 147:

> On the public street, or in any other public place, the plaintiff has no right to be alone, and it is no invasion of his privacy to do no more than follow him about. Neither is it such an invasion to take his photograph in such a place, since this amounts to nothing more than making a record, not differing essentially from a full written description of a public sight which anyone present would be free to see.

Admittedly this principle is established by the cases. As well stated in *Hinish v. Meir & Frank Co., Inc.*, 113 P.2d 438:

> When a legal principle is pushed to an absurdity, the principle is not abandoned, but the absurdity avoided.

In other words, a purely mechanical application of legal principles should not be permitted to create an illogical conclusion.

To hold that one who is involuntarily and instantaneously enmeshed in an embarrassing pose forfeits her right of privacy merely because she happened at the moment to be part of a public scene would be illogical, wrong, and unjust.

One who is a part of a public scene may be lawfully photographed as an incidental part of that scene in his ordinary status. Where the status he expects to occupy is changed without his volition to a status embarrassing to an ordinary person of reasonable sensitivity, then he should not be deemed to have forfeited his right to be protected from an indecent and vulgar intrusion of his right of privacy merely because misfortune overtakes him in a public place. . . .

NOTES & QUESTIONS

1. ***The Focus of the News Article.*** Would a change in the focus of the news article change the outcome? What if the article appeared in a journal devoted to amusement parks, the (hypothetical) *Fun House Journal*?
2. ***Voluntary vs. Involuntary Exposure.*** The court holds that although Graham was in public, the exposure of her body was involuntary, and hence a private matter. Does whether a matter is public or private depend upon voluntary or involuntary disclosure or upon one's expectation? Is *Graham* consistent with *Gill v. Hearst Publishing Co.*? Can these cases be reconciled?

   Also consider *McNamara v. Freedom Newspapers, Inc.*, 802 S.W.2d 901 (Tex. Ct. App. 1991). A newspaper published a photo of a high school soccer player's inadvertently exposed genitalia while running on a soccer field. The plaintiff, McNamara, relied on *Daily Times Democrat v. Graham*, but the court found *Graham* unpersuasive and concluded:

   > The uncontroverted facts in this case establish that the photograph of McNamara was taken by a newspaper photographer for media purposes. The picture accurately depicted a public event and was published as part of a newspaper article describing the game. At the time the photograph was taken, McNamara was voluntarily participating in a spectator sport at a public place. None of the persons involved in the publishing procedure actually noticed that McNamara's genitals were exposed.

   Can *McNamara* be reconciled with *Graham*?
3. ***Retracting Statements Made to the Media.*** In *Virgil v. Time, Inc.*, 527 F.2d 1122 (9th Cir. 1975), a well-known body surfer was interviewed by *Sports Illustrated*, and photographs of the surfer were taken for the story. The surfer revoked his consent to publishing the story when he discovered that the article was not going to be exclusively about his surfing but was also going to discuss some of his personal eccentricities and incidents about his life in order to explain the psychological profile of those who engage in such a dangerous sport. The story was published, and the surfer sued for public disclosure. The court held that the information about the surfer's life was private:

   > It is not the manner in which information has been obtained that determines whether it is public or private. Here it is undisputed that the information was obtained without commission of a tort and in a manner wholly unobjectionable. However, that is not determinative as to this particular tort. The offense with which we are here involved is not the intrusion by means of which information is obtained; it is the publicizing of that which is private in character. The question, then, is whether the information disclosed was public rather than private — whether it was generally known and, if not, whether the disclosure by appellant can be said to have been to the public at large.
   >
   > Talking freely to someone is not in itself . . . making public the substance of the talk. There is an obvious and substantial difference between the disclosure of private facts to an individual — a disclosure that is selective and based on a judgment as to whether knowledge by that person would be felt to be objectionable — and the disclosure of the same facts to the public at large. . . .

> Talking freely to a member of the press, knowing the listener to be a member of the press, is not then in itself making public. Such communication can be said to anticipate that what is said will be made public since making public is the function of the press, and accordingly such communication can be construed as a consent to publicize. Thus if publicity results it can be said to have been consented to. However, if consent is withdrawn prior to the act of publicizing, the consequent publicity is without consent. . . .

4. *Privacy and Communication to Other People.* Generally, a fact widely known about a person is not considered private; however, certain limited disclosures of information do not destroy its private nature. In *Times Mirror Co. v. Superior Court*, 244 Cal. Rptr. 556 (Cal. Ct. App. 1988), the plaintiff (Doe) discovered the murdered body of her roommate lying on the floor of her apartment and saw the perpetrator before she fled the apartment. Doe's identity was withheld from the public by the police to protect her safety (since the murderer was still at large), but her identity was leaked to a reporter and published in a newspaper article about the incident. Doe sued for public disclosure, and the newspaper argued that the matter was not private because Doe revealed it to certain neighbors, friends, family members, and investigating officials. The court, however, concluded that Doe had not "rendered otherwise private information public by cooperating in the criminal investigation and seeking solace from friends and relatives."

How many people must a person tell a secret to before it ceases to become private? In *Y.G. v. Jewish Hospital,* 795 S.W.2d 488 (Mo. Ct. App. 1990), a couple used in vitro fertilization at a hospital to become pregnant. While people at the hospital knew about their use of in vitro fertilization, the couple kept this hidden from others because it was against the teachings of their church. At a party in this hospital for in vitro couples, a camera crew from a television station filmed the plaintiffs (despite their making reasonable efforts to not be filmed). The court held that the plaintiffs retained an expectation of privacy because "attending this limited gathering . . . did not waive their right to keep their condition and the process of in vitro private, in respect to the general public." In *Multimedia WMAZ, Inc. v. Kubach*, 443 S.E.2d 491 (Ga. 1994), an HIV-positive plaintiff disclosed that he had the disease to about 60 people — family, friends, doctors, and members of an HIV support group. The plaintiff agreed to appear on a television show with his face obscured, but the obscuring process was botched, and the plaintiff was identifiable. He sued, and the court concluded that his telling his HIV-positive status to 60 people did not extinguish his privacy interest because these people "cared about him . . . or because they also had AIDS."

In contrast, consider *Duran v. Detroit News, Inc.,* 504 N.W.2d 715 (Mich. Ct. App. 1993). A Colombian judge, who indicted the violent drug lord Pablo Escobar, fled to Detroit after receiving death threats. She told a few people about her identity. Reporters, however, revealed her address and discussed the million-dollar bounty on her head. The court rejected Duran's public disclosure claim because she had exposed her identity "to the public eye." In *Fisher v. Ohio Dep't of Rehabilitation and Correction,* 578 N.E.2d 901 (Ohio Ct. Cl. 1988), the plaintiff told just four co-workers about encounters with her child that had "sexual overtones." The court concluded that the information was no longer private because the plaintiff "publicly and openly" told it to her co-workers.

Can you articulate a coherent approach to guide courts when analyzing how sharing information with other people affects the privacy of that information?

5. ***Social Networks and Boundaries of Information Flow***. Lior Strahilevitz concludes that "courts are not being terribly explicit or precise about why particular disclosures waive privacy expectations and others do not. Certainly, a simple head-counting approach does not reconcile the precedents. After all, Kubach's disclosure of facts to sixty people did not render them public, but Fisher's disclosure to three people did." Strahilevitz suggests that looking to the number of people who are exposed to a secret is not the right approach. Instead, he uses social network theory.

Network theory describes how information flows between people. In particular, network theory seeks to assess the probability that information disclosed to one member of a particular group or community will be disseminated to others outside of that realm. According to Strahilevitz, the analysis should not focus on how many people already know a person's secret but how likely the secret is to be widely disseminated beyond the group of people who already know it. Information should be deemed private so long as it remains within a confined group — even if that group is rather large. The law should recognize that a particular person expects information to stay within these boundaries.

Strahilevitz identifies three key factors that affect the likelihood of data staying within a particular group: (1) how interesting the information is (the more interesting, the more likely it is to spread beyond the group); (2) the norms that a particular group has with regard to spreading the kind of information at issue; and (3) the way the group is structured and how information generally flows within and beyond the group. Strahilevtiz agrees with the *Kubach* court's decision that the plaintiff still retained a privacy interest in his HIV-positive status even though 60 others knew about it:

> [An empirical] study of HIV disclosure suggests that information about HIV status is frequently shared with some parts of an individual's social network, while other members, who might know the HIV positive person well and be interested in her health status, remain in the dark. Information about HIV status, therefore, seems not to flow through social networks readily, at least in the case of private figures. . . . Kubach had a reasonable expectation that his disclosure to some people who knew him would not result in the information being revealed to others who knew him, let alone thousands of people in his local community.

Strahilevitz argues that the holding in *Duran* is inconsistent with social network theory:

> According to the court, Duran used her real name when shopping in stores or eating in restaurants, which waived an expectation of privacy in her identity. Under a network theory approach, these acts, combined with her notoriety in

> Colombia, would not have eliminated her reasonable expectation of privacy in her identity. . . . [When shopping or at a restaurant, at] most, Duran would have come into fleeting contact with other customers or service sector employees. There was nothing interesting about Duran's shopping or eating out. In order to generate interest in the story, the defendant had to connect Duran's presence in Detroit to her past notoriety in Colombia and the bounty that had been placed on her head. Such information was quite unlikely to be aggregated through the kinds of weak ties that Duran established in Detroit's public spaces. Perhaps a Colombian waiter put two-and-two together, but this would have been a highly improbable turn of events. Duran's general obscurity in Detroit properly engendered a reasonable expectation of privacy with respect to her shopping and visiting restaurants.[19]

6. ***Closed Communities.*** Woodrow Hartzog notes that there are certain closed communities where a strong expectation of confidentiality has developed, such as Alcoholics Anonymous. Closed communities also exist online — indeed, Alcoholics Anonymous has an online group. Hartzog contends: "Members of these closed communities have not disclosed their personal information to the world. Rather, they have revealed their information to other members of the community based on that community's norms and expectations of confidentiality."[20]

   Suppose a person shares information with a group of 300 Facebook friends on her profile, which is set to be seen by "friends only." One of that person's friends reveals the information on a publicly accessible media site. In a lawsuit for public disclosure of private facts, the friend argues that the person's information was not private because it was available to 300 individuals on Facebook. How should a court rule on whether the information was private?

7. ***Further Dissemination of Previously Disclosed Information.*** Media entities that further disseminate information already disclosed by another media entity are not liable for public disclosure. *Ritzmann v. Weekly World News*, 614 F. Supp. 1336 (N.D. Tex. 1985) (giving further publicity to information contained in news stories already published is not actionable because the information is no longer private); *Heath v. Playboy Enterprises, Inc.*, 732 F. Supp. 1145 (S.D. Fla. 1990) ("Republication of facts already publicized elsewhere cannot provide a basis for an invasion of privacy claim.").

   However, when only partial facts are revealed, the disclosure of more information can give rise to a viable action for public disclosure. For example, in *Michaels v. Internet Entertainment Group, Inc.*, 5 F. Supp. 2d 823 (C.D. Cal. 1998), Bret Michaels, the former lead singer for the rock band Poison, and Pamela Anderson Lee, a celebrity, sought a preliminary injunction to prevent the defendant from making a videotape of the two having sex available on the Internet. The defendant argued that the plaintiffs lacked a privacy

---

[19] Lior Jacob Strahilevitz, *A Social Networks Theory of Privacy,* 72 U. Chi. L. Rev. 919 (2005).

[20] Woodrow Hartzog, *Promises and Privacy: Promissory Estoppel and Confidential Disclosures in Online Communities*, 82 Temple L. Rev. 891 (2009).

interest in the tape because a part of the tape had already been released by a foreign Internet source. The court, however, concluded that "plaintiffs' privacy interest in the unreleased portions of the Tape is undiminished." Further, another videotape depicting Lee having sex with her husband, Tommy Lee, had been widely distributed, and the defendant contended that this negated Lee's privacy interest. The court rejected the defendant's argument: "The Court is not prepared to conclude that public exposure of one sexual encounter forever removes a person's privacy interest in all subsequent and previous sexual encounters." The defendant also contended that Lee lacked a privacy interest because she had previously appeared nude in magazines and on video, but the court concluded that the defendant's "contention unreasonably blurs the line between fiction and reality. Lee is a professional actor. She has played roles involving sex and sexual appeal. The fact that she has performed a role involving sex does not, however, make her real sex life open to the public."

8. ***Obscurity.*** Woodrow Hartzog and Fred Stutzman argue that the law often fails to grasp the concept of obscurity and that the law should better integrate obscurity into its fabric. They contend:

> Perhaps more than anything else, Internet users rely on obscurity for protection of their online information. Obscurity allows Internet users to be genuine by disclosing information that they would not otherwise share in "public." Yet this concept, which is at the very heart of the social web, is largely undeveloped in privacy law. . .
>
> Obscurity could serve as a continuum when courts are asked to determine if information is eligible for privacy protections. Obscurity could be used as a benefit or protection—instead of forcing websites to remove information, a compromise could be some form of mandated obscurity. Finally, obscurity could serve as a metric for the boundary of allowable disclosure by information recipients. Internet users who were bound to a "duty to maintain obscurity" would be allowed to further disclose information, so long as they kept the information as generally obscure as they received it.[21]

Could locating a publicly available yet obscure piece of information about a person and writing about it in a widely read media outlet constitute a violation of privacy? Suppose a reporter finds information online in a blog that has only a handful of readers. The reporter writes about it on a major news media website. Is this a violation of privacy? If not, is anything appearing online and accessible to the public no longer able to be deemed private?

---

[21] Woodrow Hartzog & Fred Stutzman, *The Case for Online Obscurity,* 101 Cal. L. Rev. 1, 48 (2013).

(c) The Newsworthiness Test

SIPPLE V. CHRONICLE PUBLISHING CO.

201 Cal. Rptr. 665 (Cal. Ct. App. 1984)

CALDECOTT, J. On September 22, 1975, Sara Jane Moore attempted to assassinate President Gerald R. Ford while the latter was visiting San Francisco, California. Plaintiff Oliver W. Sipple (hereafter appellant or Sipple) who was in the crowd at Union Square, San Francisco, grabbed or struck Moore's arm as the latter was about to fire the gun and shoot at the President. Although no one can be certain whether or not Sipple actually saved the President's life, the assassination attempt did not succeed and Sipple was considered a hero for his selfless action and was subject to significant publicity throughout the nation following the assassination attempt.

Among the many articles concerning the event was a column, written by Herb Caen and published by the San Francisco Chronicle on September 24, 1975. The article read in part as follows: "One of the heroes of the day, Oliver 'Bill' Sipple, the ex-Marine who grabbed Sara Jane Moore's arm just as her gun was fired and thereby may have saved the President's life, was the center of midnight attention at the Red Lantern, a Golden Gate Ave. bar he favors. The Rev. Ray Broshears, head of Helping Hands, and Gay Politico, Harvey Milk, who claim to be among Sipple's close friends, describe themselves as 'proud — maybe this will help break the stereotype.' Sipple is among the workers in Milk's campaign for Supervisor."

Thereafter, the Los Angeles Times and numerous out-of-state newspapers published articles which referring to the primary source, (i.e., the story published in the San Francisco Chronicle) mentioned both the heroic act shown by Sipple and the fact that he was a prominent member of the San Francisco gay community. Some of those articles speculated that President Ford's failure to promptly thank Sipple for his heroic act was a result of Sipple's sexual orientation.[22]

. . . Sipple filed an action against the [newspapers]. The complaint was predicated upon the theory of invasion of privacy and alleged in essence that defendants without authorization and consent published private facts about plaintiff's life by disclosing that plaintiff was homosexual in his personal and private sexual orientation; that said publications were highly offensive to plaintiff inasmuch as his parents, brothers and sisters learned for the first time of his homosexual orientation; and that as a consequence of disclosure of private facts

---

[22] For example, the September 25, 1975, issue of the *Los Angeles Times* wrote inter alia as follows: "A husky ex-marine who was a hero in the attempted assassination of President Ford emerged Wednesday as a prominent figure in the gay community. And questions were raised in the gay community if Oliver (Bill) Sipple, 32, was being shunned by the White House because of his associations. Sipple, who lunged at Sara Jane Moore and deflected her revolver as she fired at the President, conceded that he is a member of the 'court' of Mike Caringi, who was elected 'emperor of San Francisco' by the gay community. A column item in a morning newspaper here strongly implied Wednesday that Sipple is gay. . . . Harvey Milk, a prominent member of this city's large homosexual community and a longtime friend of Sipple, speculated Wednesday that the absence of a phone call or telegram of gratitude from the White House might not be just an oversight."

about his life plaintiff was abandoned by his family, exposed to contempt and ridicule causing him great mental anguish, embarrassment and humiliation. Plaintiff finally alleged that defendants' conduct amounted to malice and oppression calling for both compensatory and punitive damages.

Appellant's principal contention on appeal is that the trial court prejudicially erred in granting summary judgment in favor of respondents. More precisely, appellant argues that the individual elements of the invasion of privacy (i.e., public disclosure of private facts; the offensiveness of the public disclosure; and the newsworthiness of the publication as an exception to tort liability) constituted a factual determination which could not be resolved or adjudicated by way of summary procedure.

Before discussing appellant's contentions on the merits, as an initial matter we set out the legal principles governing the case. It is well settled that there are three elements of a cause of action predicated on tortious invasion of privacy. First, the disclosure of the private facts must be a public disclosure. Second, the facts disclosed must be private facts, and not public ones. Third, the matter made public must be one which would be offensive and objectionable to a reasonable person of ordinary sensibilities. It is likewise recognized, however, that due to the supreme mandate of the constitutional protection of freedom of the press even a tortious invasion of one's privacy is exempt from liability if the publication of private facts is truthful and newsworthy. . . .

When viewed in light of the aforegoing principles, the summary judgment in this case must be upheld on two grounds. First, as appears from the record properly considered for the purposes of summary judgment, the facts disclosed by the articles were not private facts within the meaning of the law. Second, the record likewise reveals on its face that the publications in dispute were newsworthy and thus constituted a protective shield from liability based upon invasion of privacy. . . .

[Regarding the first ground,] the cases explain that there can be no privacy with respect to a matter which is already public or which has previously become part of the "public domain." Moreover, it is equally underlined that there is no liability when the defendant merely gives further publicity to information about the plaintiff which is already public or when the further publicity relates to matters which the plaintiff leaves open to the public eye.

The case at bench falls within the aforestated rules. The undisputed facts reveal that prior to the publication of the newspaper articles in question appellant's homosexual orientation and participation in gay community activities had been known by hundreds of people in a variety of cities, including New York, Dallas, Houston, San Diego, Los Angeles and San Francisco. Thus, appellant's deposition shows that prior to the assassination attempt appellant spent a lot of time in "Tenderloin" and "Castro," the well-known gay sections of San Francisco; that he frequented gay bars and other homosexual gatherings in both San Francisco and other cities; that he marched in gay parades on several occasions; that he supported the campaign of Mike Caringi for the election of "Emperor"; that he participated in the coronation of the "Emperor" and sat at Caringi's table on that occasion; that his friendship with Harvey Milk, another prominent gay, was well-known and publicized in gay newspapers; and that his homosexual association and name had been reported in gay magazines (such as

Data Boy, Pacific Coast Times, Male Express, etc.) several times before the publications in question. In fact, appellant quite candidly conceded that he did not make a secret of his being a homosexual and that if anyone would ask, he would frankly admit that he was gay. In short, since appellant's sexual orientation was already in public domain and since the articles in question did no more than to give further publicity to matters which appellant left open to the eye of the public, a vital element of the tort was missing rendering it vulnerable to summary disposal. . . .

[Turning to the second ground — newsworthiness,] our courts have recognized a broad privilege cloaking the truthful publication of all newsworthy matters. . . . [T]he cases and authorities further explain that the paramount test of newsworthiness is whether the matter is of legitimate public interest which in turn must be determined according to the community mores. As pointed out in *Virgil v. Time, Inc.*, "In determining what is a matter of legitimate public interest, account must be taken of the customs and conventions of the community; and in the last analysis what is proper becomes a matter of the community mores. The line is to be drawn when the publicity ceases to be the giving of information to which the public is entitled, and becomes a morbid and sensational prying into private lives for its own sake, with which a reasonable member of the public, with decent standards, would say that he had no concern."

In the case at bench the publication of appellant's homosexual orientation which had already been widely known by many people in a number of communities was not so offensive even at the time of the publication as to shock the community notions of decency. Moreover, and perhaps even more to the point, the record shows that the publications were not motivated by a morbid and sensational prying into appellant's private life but rather were prompted by legitimate political considerations, i.e., to dispel the false public opinion that gays were timid, weak and unheroic figures and to raise the equally important political question whether the President of the United States entertained a discriminatory attitude or bias against a minority group such as homosexuals. . . .

Appellant's contention that by saving the President's life he did not intend to enter into the limelight and become a public figure, can be easily answered. In elaborating on involuntary public figures, Restatement Second of Torts section 625D, comment f, sets out in part as follows: "There are other individuals who have not sought publicity or consented to it, but through their own conduct or otherwise have become a legitimate subject of public interest. They have, in other words, become 'news.' "

NOTES & QUESTIONS

1. ***The Sad Fate of a Hero.*** Sipple passed away in January 1989, alone in a cluttered apartment with half-gallon bottles of bourbon within reach of his bed. A story in the *Los Angeles Times* almost a month after he passed away detailed the sad circumstances of his death and filled in some details of his life. Sipple had been wounded twice in Vietnam, lived on a veteran's disability pension, and, despite his lack of funds and poor health, was

remembered by friends as a generous person who would readily give money to charity or to help a derelict.

The *L.A. Times* also noted that a framed letter hung in the apartment where Sipple had died — it was a letter of "heartfelt appreciation," signed "Jerry Ford," which thanked Sipple for his "selfless actions" in acting quickly and without fear and averting danger to the President and the crowd. The letter was sent three days after Sipple had knocked away the gun of the would-be assassin in San Francisco.

The *L.A. Times* article also stressed how much Sipple had suffered after the press outed him. It quoted George Sipple, Bill's brother: "His personal life never should have made it back to Detroit" (his hometown). Sipple's parents were shocked by the revelation of their son's sexual orientation; as the *L.A. Times* states: "The estrangement between Sipple and his father was so deep that when his mother died in 1979, his father made it clear that he was not welcome."[23] Sipple remained in San Francisco and did not attend his mother's funeral.

Taking a break from cleaning his brother's apartment, George Sipple noted that his brother was pleased that he left a mark and remembered that his brother once said that long after he died, "somebody will pick up a book and see Oliver Sipple saved President Ford's life."

2. ***Group Privacy.*** The court rejects Sipple's claim in part because Sipple's homosexuality and participation in the gay community were known by hundreds of people in many cities. But Sipple's argument is that he wanted to keep his homosexuality a secret from certain people — namely his parents and siblings. Can Sipple legitimately claim that something known widely to many people can still remain private?
3. ***President Ford's Prejudice.*** In *Sipple*, the newsworthiness of the story did not just turn on exposing the background of a hero who prevented an assassination. The story also exposed President Ford's possible prejudice against homosexuals. Does this fact alone establish that the story was newsworthy?
4. ***Outing.*** There has been extensive debate about the propriety of outing gays. Is the fact that a prominent individual is gay newsworthy? John Elwood observes that there are three rationales advanced for outing gays:

> According to its advocates, outing serves three basic purposes: (1) to expose the illogic of governmental policies that discriminate against homosexuals and of the hypocrisy of gay public officials who publicly support such policies; (2) to provide positive examples of gays, as role models to other gays and as ambassadors to mainstream America; and (3) to break down the stigma surrounding homosexuality by making it commonplace.

Elwood contends: "Even under the best of circumstances, the relationship between outing a particular figure and effecting a societal change is simply too attenuated to override the outing target's privacy rights." However, "a

[23] Dean Morain, *Sorrow Trailed a Veteran Who Saved a President's Life and Then Was Cast in an Unwanted Spotlight*, L.A. Times, Feb. 13, 1989, at Part 5, 1.

closeted government official who made disparaging public remarks about homosexuals or who enforced discriminatory programs might be a valid target for outing. Her hypocrisy calls into question her honesty and motivation, and thus information about her sexuality is relevant to the question of her fitness for office."[24] How would this argument apply in the *Sipple* case?

In contrast to Elwood, Kathleen Guzman disagrees with the hypocrisy justification for outing:

> . . . [T]his justification presupposes two potentially invalid assumptions. Presuming that the outers are even correct in asserting someone's orientation, one wonders whether there is such a thing as a "gay viewpoint." While abstract generalization may be made regarding the tendency of a group member to sympathize with in-group concerns, it is absurd to attribute to an individual a pre-packaged set of opinions merely because that individual is gay. One's views should no more be determined by sexual orientation than by being Caucasian or agnostic or underweight or female. . . .
>
> Second, what is orientation hypocrisy and at what level of conduct should it be penalized? Hypocrisy is a broad term which can encompass a range of activity: merely keeping same-sex orientation a secret; actively asserting heterosexuality; failing to vote for or affirmatively and publicly support pro-gay legislation; actively opposing similar legislation. The (non)actor whose conduct contravenes the mythical "gay viewpoint" need not necessarily be driven by "hypocrisy," but is equally likely to act through privacy, self-preservation, cowardice, or merely a different belief. A smoker who supports legislation restricting cigarette sales to minors is no more a hypocrite than a non-smoker who does so. A woman who votes against equal rights legislation is no more a hypocrite than a man who does so. To assert that she or he must be a hypocrite anathematizes individuality and accords insufficient weight to the myriad reasons that impel behavior or decision making.[25]

After Sipple's death, Fred Friendly, a journalism professor and former head of CBS News, wrote that journalists did not act fairly in Sipple's case and should not have written about his sexuality.[26] Friendly argued that the right to privacy should prevail unless the "individual's private conduct becomes relevant in assessing his integrity or validity in a public role." Do you agree with this approach? Does it resolve the *Sipple* case?

5. ***Newsworthiness Tests.*** Courts use at least three newsworthiness tests.[27] First is the "leave it to the press" approach, where courts defer to editorial judgment and do not attempt to distinguish between what is news and what is entertainment. Second, the Restatement looks to the "customs and conventions of the community" and draws a line between the "giving of

---

[24] John P. Elwood, Note, *Outing, Privacy, and the First Amendment*, 102 Yale L.J. 747, 748-49, 773-74 (1992).

[25] Kathleen Guzman, *About Outing: Public Discourse, Private Lives*, 73 Wash. U. L.Q. 1531, 1536-37, 1555-56 (1995). For further arguments against outing, see Jean L. Cohen, *Is Privacy a Legal Duty?*, in *Public and Private: Legal, Political, and Philosophical Perspectives* 117, 125 (Maurizio Passerin d'Entreves & Ursula Vogel eds., 2000).

[26] Fred W. Friendly, *Gays, Privacy and a Free Press*, Wash. Post, Apr. 8, 1990, at B7.

[27] *See* Geoff Dendy, Note, *The Newsworthiness Defense to the Public Disclosure Tort*, 85 Ky. L.J. 147 (1997).

information to which the public is entitled" and "morbid and sensational prying into private lives for its own sake." A third approach is the "nexus test," which involves the Restatement approach but also requires a "logical nexus (or relationship) . . . between the complaining individual and the matter of legitimate public interest." Which test do you find most appropriate?

6. ***What Is Newsworthy?*** Many of the cases applying the newsworthiness test do so to avoid First Amendment problems. Keep in mind that the newsworthiness test is an element of the tort of public disclosure. Applications of the tort — involving possibly even non-newsworthy facts — can still be subject to an independent First Amendment challenge. This issue will be discussed later in this chapter.

   How are courts to determine what is newsworthy? According to the Restatement of Torts § 652D (comment h), adopting language from *Virgil v. Time*, 527 F.2d 1122, 1129 (9th Cir. 1975), courts are to look to the "customs and conventions of the community."

   Consider the case of *Diaz v. Oakland Tribune*, 188 Cal. Rptr. 762 (Ct. App. 1983). Diaz was the first woman student body president elected at a community college. The *Oakland Tribune* published the fact that Diaz was a transsexual. Diaz sued for public disclosure, and the court held that the suit could proceed to the jury, which would determine whether the fact that Diaz was a transsexual was newsworthy. The court noted: "[W]e find little if any connection between the information disclosed and Diaz's fitness for office. The fact that she is a transsexual does not adversely reflect on her honesty or judgment." Eugene Volokh, who opposes the tort of public disclosure altogether, argues:

   > Now I agree with the [*Diaz*] court's factual conclusion; people's gender identity strikes me as irrelevant to their fitness for office. But other voters take a different view. Transsexuality, in their opinion, may say various things about politicians (even student body politicians): It may say that they lack attachment to traditional values, that they are morally corrupt, or even just that they have undergone an unnatural procedure and therefore are somehow tainted by it. These views may be wrong and even immoral, but surely it is not for government agents — whether judges or jurors — to dictate the relevant criteria for people's political choices, and to use the coercive force of law to keep others from informing them of things that they may consider relevant to those choices. I may disagree with what you base your vote on, but I must defend your right to base your vote on it, and the right of others to tell you about it.[28]

   If Volokh is right, then what isn't relevant for fitness for office? Do public figures have any claim to privacy, or is everything about them newsworthy?

   In *Neff v. Time, Inc.*, 406 F. Supp. 858 (W.D. Pa. 1976), a *Sports Illustrated* photographer printed a photograph of John W. Neff, a teacher, with the front zipper of his pants open in *Sports Illustrated*. The photograph was used in a story about Pittsburgh Steelers fans, and the article was entitled: "A Strange Kind of Love." The photograph was taken while Neff was with a

---

[28] Eugene Volokh, *Freedom of Speech and Information Privacy: The Troubling Implications of a Right to Stop People from Speaking About You*, 52 Stan. L. Rev. 1049, 1090 (2000).

group of fans at a football game between the Cleveland Browns and Pittsburgh Steelers. The fans were waving Steeler banners, drinking beer, and appeared slightly intoxicated. When the *Sports Illustrated* photographer approached them and the group found out that the photographer was covering the game for *Sports Illustrated*, the group "hammed it up" while the photographer snapped the pictures. Of the 30 pictures of the group that were taken, a committee of five employees at *Sports Illustrated* selected the photograph of Neff with his fly open for inclusion in the issue. According to the court, "[a]lthough Neff's fly was not open to the point of being revealing, the selection was deliberate and surely in utmost bad taste; subjectively, as to Neff, the published picture could have been embarrassing, humiliating and offensive to his sensibilities." According to Neff, the photograph implied "that he is a 'crazy, drunken slob,' and combined with the title of the article, 'a sexual deviate.'" Neff asserted that the article invaded his right to privacy, caused him reputational injury, subjected him to public ridicule, destroyed his peace of mind, and caused him severe emotional distress. The court, however, rejected Neff's claim:

> . . . It seems to us that art directors and editors should hesitate to deliberately publish a picture which most likely would be offensive and cause embarrassment to the subject when many other pictures of the same variety are available. Notwithstanding, "(t)he courts are not concerned with establishing canons of good taste for the press or the public." . . .
>
> The article about Pittsburgh Steeler fans was of legitimate public interest; the football game in Cleveland was of legitimate public interest; Neff's picture was taken in a public place with his knowledge and with his encouragement; he was catapulted into the news by his own actions; nothing was falsified; a photograph taken at a public event which everyone present could see, with the knowledge and implied consent of the subject, is not a matter concerning a private fact. A factually accurate public disclosure is not tortious when connected with a newsworthy event even though offensive to ordinary sensibilities. The constitutional privilege protects all truthful publications relevant to matters of public interest. . . .

Graham involved a photograph taken of a woman who was in an embarrassing position in public. How does the situation in *Neff* differ from that in *Graham*? *Graham* did not focus much on newsworthiness, but suppose that the case were being decided by the *Neff* court — would the photograph in *Graham* be newsworthy?

7. ***The Privacy of Public Figures.*** To what extent can a public figure's life be private? Consider the Restatement of Torts (Second) § 652D (comment h):

> The extent of the authority to make public private facts is not, however, unlimited. There may be some intimate details of [a celebrity actress's] life, such as sexual relations, which even the actress is entitled to keep to herself. In determining what is a matter of legitimate public interest, account must be taken of the customs and conventions of the community; and in the last analysis what is proper becomes a matter of the community mores. The line is to be drawn when the publicity ceases to be the giving of information to which the public is entitled, and becomes a morbid and sensational prying into private lives for its own sake, with which a reasonable member of the public,

> with decent standards, would say that he had no concern. The limitations, in other words, are those of common decency, having due regard to the freedom of the press and its reasonable leeway to choose what it will tell the public, but also due regard to the feelings of the individual and the harm that will be done to him by the exposure. Some reasonable proportion is also to be maintained between the event or activity that makes the individual a public figure and the private facts to which publicity is given.

J.M. Balkin argues that by creating media events that show the politician "with his or her family, participating in casual activities or in a seemingly unguarded and intimate moment," politicians have been "willing accomplices in the creation of a new political culture that sees private aspects of a person's life as politically relevant, that collapses older boundaries between public and private." Moreover, Balkin argues, the media plays a role in shaping the boundaries between public and private: "Journalists do not simply respect the existing boundaries of the public and the private but actively reshape them: Merely by talking about sexual scandal and encouraging others to do so journalists make these topics part of public discourse and public comment."[29]

8. ***The Disclosure of Identifying Information.*** In *Barber v. Time, Inc.*, 159 S.W.2d 291 (Mo. 1942), the plaintiff's photograph taken in a hospital was published in a *Time* magazine article about the plaintiff's unusual disease. The article, "Starving Glutton," described the plaintiff's rare disorder where no matter how much she ate, she continued to lose weight. The photograph showed the plaintiff in her hospital bed. The court held that "[w]hile plaintiff's ailment may have been a matter of some public interest because unusual, certainly the identity of the person who suffered this ailment was not." In other words, the matter about the rare disorder was newsworthy, but the plaintiff's identity was not of public concern.

In contrast, consider *Haynes v. Alfred A. Knopf, Inc.*, 8 F.3d 1222 (7th Cir. 1993). In 1991, Alfred A. Knopf, Inc. published Nicholas Lemann's best-selling historical book entitled *The Promised Land: The Great Black Migration and How It Changed America.* The book chronicled the migration of 5 million African Americans from the rural areas in the South to urban areas in the North from 1940 to 1970. The book focuses centrally around the story of one individual, Ruby Lee Daniels. The book recounts Ruby's troubled marriage to Luther Haynes. Luther had a well-paying factory job but began to drink too much, waste money, and get into bitter fights with Ruby. The book recounts the couple's financial struggles, Luther's squandering of their money, their spiral into poverty, and their difficulties in providing for their children. When the couple was finally able to buy a home, Luther purchased a new car, and as a result, they couldn't meet their house payments and lost the home. Luther would frequently lose jobs and would often fail to come home. Luther then began to have an affair with their neighbor Dorothy

[29] J.M. Balkin, *How Mass Media Stimulate Political Transparency*, 3 Cultural Values 393 (1999). For a discussion of when public figures should be entitled to privacy, see Anita L. Allen, *Lying to Protect Privacy*, 44 Vill. L. Rev. 161, 177 (1999); Anita L. Allen, *Privacy and the Public Official: Talking About Sex as a Dilemma for Democracy*, 67 Geo. Wash. L. Rev. 1165 (1999).

Johnson, which was discovered by the children. Ruby and Luther got a divorce.

Subsequently, Luther married Dorothy. He turned his life around and began acting more responsibly. In their new community, nobody knew of Luther's past behavior toward Ruby. As Luther stated: "I know I haven't been no angel, but since almost 30 years ago I have turned my life completely around. I stopped the drinking and all this bad habits and stuff like that. . . . I look good in the eyes of my church members and my community. Now . . . all this is going to go down the drain. And I worked like a son of a gun to build myself up in a good reputation and he has torn it down."

Luther and Dorothy Haynes sued Lemann and his publisher Knopf under the public disclosure tort. Judge Posner, writing for the Seventh Circuit, rejected their claim: "No detail in the book claimed to invade the Hayneses' privacy is not germane to the story that the author wanted to tell, a story not only of legitimate but of transcendent public interest."

Was Luther Haynes's actual name really necessary for telling the story? The court concluded:

> The details of the Hayneses' lives recounted in the book would identify them unmistakably to anyone who has known the Hayneses well for a long time (members of their families, for example), or who knew them before they got married; and no more is required for liability either in defamation law or in privacy law. Lemann would have had to change some, perhaps many, of the details. But then he would no longer have been writing history. He would have been writing fiction. The nonquantitative study of living persons would be abolished as a category of scholarship, to be replaced by the sociological novel. That is a genre with a distinguished history punctuated by famous names, such as Dickens, Zola, Stowe, Dreiser, Sinclair, Steinbeck, and Wolfe, but we do not think that the law of privacy makes it (or that the First Amendment would permit the law of privacy to make it) the exclusive format for a social history of living persons that tells their story rather than treating them as data points in a statistical study. Reporting the true facts about real people is necessary to "obviate any impression that the problems raised in the [book] are remote or hypothetical."

Also consider *Gilbert v. Medical Economics Co.*, 665 F.2d 305 (10th Cir. 1981). An article describing a doctor's malpractice and arguing that hospitals and other physicians were not adequately self-policing included the doctor's name and photograph and discussed her psychiatric and marital problems. The doctor sued, contending that her photo, name, and personal life "add[ed] nothing to the concededly newsworthy topic of policing failures in the medical profession." The court disagreed, concluding:

> . . . [T]hese truthful representations are substantially relevant to a newsworthy topic because they strengthen the impact and credibility of the article. They obviate any impression that the problems raised in the article are remote or hypothetical, thus providing an aura of immediacy and even urgency that might not exist had plaintiff's name and photograph been suppressed. Similarly, we find the publication of plaintiff's psychiatric and marital problems to be substantially relevant to the newsworthy topic [because] . . . they are connected to the newsworthy topic by the rational inference that

plaintiff's personal problems were the underlying cause of the acts of alleged malpractice.

In *Howard v. Des Moines Register & Tribune Co.*, 870 F.2d 271 (5th Cir. 1989), the identities of victims of involuntary sterilization were disclosed in a report about abuses by a mental institution. The court rejected the argument that the identities were unnecessarily disclosed because they were needed to "strengthen the accuracy of the public perception of the merits of the controversy." In *Ross v. Midwest Communications, Inc.*, 870 F.2d 271 (5th Cir. 1989), the court held that the disclosure of a rape victim's name in an article about the potential innocence of the man convicted of the rape was of "unique importance to the credibility and persuasive force of the story."

Daniel Solove argues in favor of the approach taken in *Barber.* He contends that the use of initials or pseudonyms is a workable compromise between the interests of reporting the news and of protecting privacy: "Journalists generally do not include the names of rape victims or whistleblowers in their stories. On television, the media sometimes obscures the faces of particular people in video footage. With minimal effort, the media can report stories and also protect privacy."[30] In response to arguments about the importance of identifying people to help make the story more verifiable, Solove argues:

> [S]tories of paramount importance have not identified the critical parties; for example, in exposing Watergate, Bob Woodward and Carl Bernstein relied on the well-known pseudonymous source "Deep Throat." Certainly, it affects verifiability when a story does not identify a party. However, when the journalists protect confidential sources, they engage in a balancing determination, sacrificing the public's ability to verity for the importance of protecting confidentiality. Public verifiability is not sacrosanct, but can be outweighed by privacy interests.[31]

9. ***Who Decides What Is Newsworthy?*** Who ought to determine the proper subject for news? Courts? Journalists? The market? Juries? A number of courts defer to the judgment of the press for newsworthiness: "[W]hat is newsworthy is primarily a function of the publisher, not the courts." *Heath v. Playboy Enterprises, Inc.*, 732 F. Supp. 1145, 1149 (S.D. Fla. 1990); *see also Jenkins v. Dell Publishing Co.*, 251 F.2d 447, 451-52 (3d Cir. 1958); *Wagner v. Fawcett Publications*, 307 F.2d 409, 410 (7th Cir. 1962). If courts are not to second guess the judgment of the press, how are courts to determine newsworthiness? Is anything not newsworthy?

Daniel Solove contends that the deference to the media approach is a poor one. He argues that although the media might be a capable decision maker for assessing public interest in a story, "[w]hat is of interest to most of society is not the same question as what is of legitimate public concern. . . . [Public] interest can stem from a desire for entertainment or sexual pleasure just as much as it can from wanting to learn about the news and current events."

---

[30] Daniel J. Solove, *The Virtues of Knowing Less: Justifying Privacy Protections Against Disclosure*, 53 Duke L.J. 967, 1018-19 (2003).

[31] *Id.* at 1018.

Therefore, Solove concludes, "the media should not have a monopoly on determining what is of public concern."[32] In contrast, consider Eugene Volokh, who contends: "Under the First Amendment, it's generally not the government's job to decide what subjects speakers and listeners should concern themselves with."[33]

10. ***Is the Newsworthiness Test Necessary or Desirable?*** Lior Strahilevitz argues that the newsworthiness test is not the best way to reconcile the public disclosure tort with free speech. He contends that the First Amendment already provides a sufficient constraint on the tort and a newsworthiness test is not needed:

> The fact that the First Amendment may constrain the state's ability to impose damages on those who publish private facts does not mean that the underlying tort causes of action need to look any different. Rather, it simply means that once tort liability is found, the courts should conduct an independent inquiry as to whether imposing liability on that defendant (or class of defendants) will undermine fundamental expressive or self-governance interests. Indeed, such a textured inquiry better coheres with First Amendment doctrine than does the public disclosure tort's binary newsworthiness/non-newsworthiness distinction.[34]

If the newsworthiness test is merely designed to protect First Amendment interests, then why not just have the First Amendment provide the protection? Is there a good reason to keep the newsworthiness test?

SHULMAN V. GROUP W PRODUCTIONS, INC.

955 P.2d 469 (Cal. 1998)

[Recall the facts of this case earlier in this chapter. The plaintiffs, Ruth and Wayne Shulman, mother and son, were injured in a car accident. A medical transport and rescue helicopter crew came to their assistance along with a video camera operator, who filmed the plaintiffs' rescue from the car, the flight nurse and medic's medical aid during the rescue, as well as their medical aid in the helicopter en route to the hospital. The flight nurse wore a small microphone that picked up her conversations with Ruth and other rescue workers. The segment was broadcast on a television show called *On Scene: Emergency Response*. Ruth, a paraplegic from the accident, watched the episode in her hospital room in shock. Neither Ruth nor Wayne Shulman consented to the filming or broadcasting. They sued the producers of the show, and their complaint included causes of action for public disclosure of private facts and intrusion upon seclusion. The trial court granted the defendants' motion for summary judgment on all causes of action.

---

[32] Daniel J. Solove, *The Virtues of Knowing Less: Justifying Privacy Protections Against Disclosure*, 53 Duke L.J. 967, 1001, 1006 (2003).

[33] Eugene Volokh, *Freedom of Speech and Information Privacy: The Troubling Implications of a Right to Stop People from Speaking About You,* 52 Stan. L. Rev. 1049, 1089 (2000).

[34] Lior Strahilevitz, *Reunifying Privacy Law,* 98 Cal. L. Rev. 2007, 2033 (2010).

On the intrusion claim, the California Supreme Court held that the activities of the defendants in recording the events in the helicopter constituted a valid cause of action for intrusion upon seclusion. The court's decision on the public disclosure claim is excerpted below.]

WERDEGAR, J. . . . [U]nder California common law the dissemination of truthful, newsworthy material is not actionable as a publication of private facts. If the contents of a broadcast or publication are of legitimate public concern, the plaintiff cannot establish a necessary element of the tort action, the lack of newsworthiness. . . .

Although we speak of the lack of newsworthiness as an element of the private facts tort, newsworthiness is at the same time a constitutional defense to, or privilege against, liability for publication of truthful information. . . . Tort liability, obviously, can extend no further than the First Amendment allows; conversely, we see no reason or authority for fashioning the newsworthiness element of the private facts tort to *preclude* liability where the Constitution would allow it. . . .

Newsworthiness — constitutional or common law — is also difficult to define because it may be used as either a descriptive or a normative term. "Is the term 'newsworthy' a descriptive predicate, intended to refer to the fact there is widespread public interest? Or is it a value predicate, intended to indicate that the publication is a meritorious contribution and that the public's interest is praiseworthy?" A position at either extreme has unpalatable consequences. If "newsworthiness" is completely descriptive — if all coverage that sells papers or boosts ratings is deemed newsworthy — it would seem to swallow the publication of private facts tort, for "it would be difficult to suppose that publishers were in the habit of reporting occurrences of little interest." At the other extreme, if newsworthiness is viewed as a purely normative concept, the courts could become to an unacceptable degree editors of the news and self-appointed guardians of public taste. . . .

Courts balancing these interests in cases similar to this have recognized that, when a person is involuntarily involved in a newsworthy incident, not all aspects of the person's life, and not everything the person says or does, is thereby rendered newsworthy. . . . This principle is illustrated in the decisions holding that, while a particular event was newsworthy, identification of the plaintiff as the person involved, or use of the plaintiff's identifiable image, added nothing of significance to the story and was therefore an unnecessary invasion of privacy. . .

Consistent with the above, courts have generally protected the privacy of otherwise private individuals involved in events of public interest "by requiring that a logical nexus exist between the complaining individual and the matter of legitimate public interest." . . .

Intensely personal or intimate revelations might not, in a given case, be considered newsworthy, especially where they bear only slight relevance to a topic of legitimate public concern. . . .

Turning now to the case at bar, we consider whether the possibly private facts complained of here — broadly speaking, Ruth's appearance and words during the rescue and evacuation — were of legitimate public interest. If so, summary judgment was properly entered. . . .

We agree at the outset with defendants that the subject matter of the broadcast as a whole was of legitimate public concern. Automobile accidents are by their nature of interest to that great portion of the public that travels frequently by automobile. The rescue and medical treatment of accident victims is also of legitimate concern to much of the public, involving as it does a critical service that any member of the public may someday need. The story of Ruth's difficult extrication from the crushed car, the medical attention given her at the scene, and her evacuation by helicopter was of particular interest because it highlighted some of the challenges facing emergency workers dealing with serious accidents.

The more difficult question is whether Ruth's appearance and words as she was extricated from the overturned car, placed in the helicopter and transported to the hospital were of legitimate public concern. Pursuant to the analysis outlined earlier, we conclude the disputed material was newsworthy as a matter of law. One of the dramatic and interesting aspects of the story as a whole is its focus on flight nurse Carnahan, who appears to be in charge of communications with other emergency workers, the hospital base and Ruth, and who leads the medical assistance to Ruth at the scene. Her work is portrayed as demanding and important and as involving a measure of personal risk (e.g., in crawling under the car to aid Ruth despite warnings that gasoline may be dripping from the car). The broadcast segment makes apparent that this type of emergency care requires not only medical knowledge, concentration and courage, but an ability to talk and listen to severely traumatized patients. One of the challenges Carnahan faces in assisting Ruth is the confusion, pain and fear that Ruth understandably feels in the aftermath of the accident. For that reason the broadcast video depicting Ruth's injured physical state (which was not luridly shown) and audio showing her disorientation and despair were substantially relevant to the segment's newsworthy subject matter.

Plaintiffs argue that showing Ruth's "intimate private, medical facts and her suffering was not *necessary* to enable the public to understand the significance of the accident or the rescue as a public event." The standard, however, is not necessity. That the broadcast *could* have been edited to exclude some of Ruth's words and images and still excite a minimum degree of viewer interest is not determinative. Nor is the possibility that the members of this or another court, or a jury, might find a differently edited broadcast more to their taste or even more interesting. The courts do not, and constitutionally could not, sit as superior editors of the press. . . .

BROWN, J. concurring and dissenting. . . . I respectfully dissent . . . from the conclusion that summary judgment was proper as to plaintiff Ruth Shulman's cause of action for publication of private facts. . . .

. . . The private facts broadcast had little, if any, social value. The public has no legitimate interest in witnessing Ruth's disorientation and despair. Nor does it have any legitimate interest in knowing Ruth's personal and innermost thoughts immediately after sustaining injuries that rendered her a paraplegic and left her hospitalized for months — "I just want to die. I don't want to go through this." The depth of the broadcast's intrusion into ostensibly private affairs was substantial. . . . There was nothing voluntary about Ruth's position of public notoriety. She was involuntarily caught up in events of public interest, all the more so because defendants appear to have surreptitiously and unlawfully recorded her private conversations with nurse Laura Carnahan. . . .

NOTES & QUESTIONS

1. ***Voluntariness and Public Exposure.*** Is this case consistent with *Graham*?
2. ***Grief and Newsworthiness.*** Reality television shows and "caught on film" docudramas frequently capture people in moments of profound trauma and grief. Is it newsworthy to display footage of grieving relatives after a disaster or personal tragedy occurs?
3. ***Post-Mortem Privacy Rights?*** Generally, privacy rights are said to expire when the subject of this interest dies. The traditional exception to this doctrine is the right of publicity. Another exception is that courts recognize actions for privacy torts such as public disclosure and intrusion upon seclusion for family members of a decedent in autopsy or death-scene photos. In *Catsouras v. Department of the California Highway Patrol (CHP)*, 104 Cal. Rptr. 3d 352 (2010), 18-year-old Nicole Catsouras "was decapitated in an automobile accident." Police officers took multiple photographs of her corpse. According to allegations in a lawsuit filed by her family, the photos were e-mailed by these police officers to some members of the public.

   The *Catsouras* court found that the decedent's family had a cognizable claim for an invasion of privacy based on the public disclosure tort. The court reasoned that "family members do have their own privacy rights in death images." The court noted that the images were "allegedly disseminated out of sheer morbidity or gossip, as opposed to any official law enforcement purpose or genuine public interest."

   Would it be significant if the Catsouras family had attempted to sue the media and not the police? Would it matter to the outcome of this litigation if the leaked photographs accompanied an article on driving safety?

BONOME V. KAYSEN

17 Mass. L. Rptr. 695 (Mass. Supp. 2004)

MUSE, J. Joseph Bonome filed this action alleging invasion of privacy against Susana Kaysen, the author of a memoir at the center of this case, and Random House, Inc., the publisher. . . .

In the early 1990s, Bonome owned and operated a tree surgery and landscaping business primarily in the Cambridge, Massachusetts area. At the time, he was living in New Hampshire and was married with step-children. Kaysen was an author living in Cambridge. She had gained success and notoriety for her book *Girl, Interrupted* which was made into what has been described to be a critically acclaimed film. In 1994, Bonome met Kaysen and the two began having an affair, including a physical relationship. Kaysen pressured Bonome to leave his wife, and Bonome ultimately succumbed to that pressure. Bonome divorced his wife in 1996 and shortly thereafter moved into Kaysen's home, where they continued the relationship.

Within six months or a year into the relationship, Kaysen began to experience severe vaginal pain. She began to regularly see doctors for her problem, but over the course of several years was unable to receive sufficient curative treatment. During this time period, she began working on a new book, which book is the subject of this case. Despite Bonome's inquiries, Kaysen would not reveal the subject of the book to him.

The fact of their relationship was well-known to Bonome's family, friends, and clientele. However, the details of their physical relationship were private. Bonome's parents and three brothers all spent time, including some holidays, with the couple. However, in July 1998, the relationship "ended" when Kaysen asked Bonome to move out, which he did. Despite the breakup, their physical relationship continued for at least three months longer.

In 2001, Random House published the book [*The Camera My Mother Gave Me*]. The book only refers to Bonome as Kaysen's "boyfriend" and alters details about his life — such as where he was from, and his occupation. The book is an autobiographical memoir chronicling the effects of Kaysen's seemingly undiagnosable vaginal pain in a series of ruminations about the condition's effects on many aspects of her life, including her overall physical and emotional state, friendships, and her relationship with her boyfriend. It details her intense pain and discomfort and her many fruitless attempts to obtain an accurate medical diagnosis and effective treatment.

One of the central themes of the book concerns the impact of her chronic pain on the emotional and physical relationship with Kaysen's boyfriend. To that end, the book details, graphically on a few occasions, several sexual encounters between them. It portrays the boyfriend as becoming increasingly frustrated and impatient with Kaysen's condition and her reluctance and/or refusal to engage in physical intimacy. The boyfriend is described as "always bugging [her] for sex" and "whining and pleading" for sex, as well as being ignorant and insensitive to her emotional and physical state. In this vein, it attributes many aggressive and overtly offensive sexual quotes to him. Ultimately, the development of this theme culminates in a scene where the boyfriend is physically forceful in an attempt to engage her in sex. This scene is followed by ruminations about whether the relationship had exceeded the bounds of consensual sexual relations into the realm of coerced non-consensual sex. . . .

After publication of the book, Bonome learned that many local friends and family had read the book and understood the portrayal of the "boyfriend" to be a depiction of him. In addition, Bonome's business clientele included friends of Kaysen who also understood that Bonome was the "boyfriend." As a result of the publication, Bonome has suffered severe personal humiliation, and his reputation has been severely damaged among a substantial percentage of his clients and acquaintances. . . .

General Laws chapter 214 Section 1B provides that: "[a] person shall have a right against unreasonable, substantial or serious interference with his privacy." Section 1B has been interpreted to include the common-law tort of "public disclosure of private facts" as articulated in the Restatement (Second) of Torts. . . .

[T]his case presents an additional challenge in that it pits Kaysen's right of publicity — her own right to disclose intimate facts about herself — directly in conflict Bonome's right to control the dissemination of private information about himself. . . .

Undoubtedly, the information revealed was of an intensely intimate and personal nature. Indeed, commentators and courts have almost universally recognized one's sexual affairs as falling squarely within the sphere of private life. . . .

[O]therwise private information may properly be published when it is sufficiently related to a broader topic of legitimate public concern. In this case, a critical issue is whether the personal information concerning Bonome is in the book for its relevance to issues of legitimate public concern or is merely "morbid and sensational plying into [Bonome's] private [life] for its own sake."

After examining the statements concerning the boyfriend and their relevance to the broader themes of the book, it is clear that the details are included to develop and explore those themes. Specifically, the book explores the way in which Kaysen's undiagnosed physical condition impacted her physical and emotional relationship with "her boyfriend." Moreover, it explores the issue of when undesired physical intimacy crosses the line into non-consensual sexual relations in the context of her condition. These broader topics are all matters of legitimate public concern, and it is within this specific context that the explicit and highly personal details of the relationship are discussed. Thus, the defendants had a legitimate and protected interest to publish these facts.

As noted above, there is an additional interest in this case: Kaysen's right to disclose her own intimate affairs. In this case, it is critical that Kaysen was not a disinterested third party telling Bonome's personal story in order to develop the themes in her book. Rather, she is telling *her own* personal story — which inextricably involves Bonome in an intimate way. In this regard, several courts have held that where an autobiographical account related to a matter of legitimate public interest reveals private information concerning a third party, the disclosure is protected so long as there is a sufficient nexus between those private details and the issue of public concern.

Where one's own personal story involves issues of legitimate public concern, it is often difficult, if not impossible, to separate one's intimate and personal experiences from the people with whom those experiences are shared. Thus, it is within the context of Bonome and Kaysen's lives being inextricably bound together by their intimate relationship that the disclosures in this case must be viewed. Because the First Amendment protects Kaysen's ability to contribute *her own* personal experiences to the public discourse on important and legitimate issues of public concern, disclosing Bonome's involvement in those experiences is a necessary incident thereto.

. . . [T]he privilege to disclose private information is limited by the requirement that the disclosure bear the necessary nexus (both logical and proportional) to the issue of legitimate public concern. In this regard, it is of importance that Kaysen did not use Bonome's name in the book. The defendants did not subject Bonome to unnecessary publicity or attention. The realm of people that could identify Bonome as the boyfriend are those close personal friends, family, and business clients that knew of the relationship. This is not to overlook or discount the impact this disclosure may have had on Bonome, or his substantial claim that Kaysen breached a fundamental trust of their relationship. However arguably odious, the defendants did not exercise the right of disclosure in a manner offensive to the balance of those interests. See Restatement (Second) Torts § 652D, comment a ("Publicity . . . means that the matter is made public, by communicating it to the public at large, or to so many persons that the matter must be regarded as substantially certain to become one of public knowledge"). . . .

This court is not unmindful of the injury claimed by Bonome, who alleges to have suffered personal humiliation within his familial circle, as well as with friends and business clientele as a result of the book's publication. Nonetheless, Kaysen's own personal story — insofar as it relates to matters of legitimate public concern — is hers to contribute to the public discourse. This right is protected by the First Amendment. Inasmuch as the book does not exceed the bounds of that constitutional privilege, Bonome's claim for invasion of privacy under G.L.c. 214, § 1B is *DISMISSED.*

NOTES & QUESTIONS

1. ***The Right to Tell One's Story.*** The newsworthiness test examines whether a disclosure is of "legitimate concern to the public." It does not matter who is making the disclosure for the purposes of the test. However, the court suggests that "there is an additional interest in this case: Kaysen's right to disclose her own intimate affairs." The court states that "it is critical that Kaysen was not a disinterested third party telling Bonome's personal story in order to develop the themes in her book. Rather, she is telling *her own* personal story — which inextricably involves Bonome in an intimate way." Does the autobiographical nature of the disclosure change the newsworthiness analysis? Should it?

   Sonja West contends that when autobiographical speech is involved, courts should not look to whether it is of legitimate public interest: "The power to decide what is of consequence in a person's life story should ultimately lie with that person alone. As long as the content and intention of the speech is truly autobiographical, its perceived importance by others should not affect its constitutional protection."[35] Should a person have increased latitude when revealing private information about others when it also involves her own autobiographical details?

   Suppose Kaysen told her story to a journalist, who wrote about it in an article. Should the journalist receive less protection for making the disclosure than Kaysen would receive for revealing the same facts?

2. ***Blogs, Social Network Websites, and Gossip.*** In *Steinbuch v. Cutler*, 463 F. Supp. 2d 1 (D.D.C. 2006), Jessica Cutler, a staff member for a U.S. senator, wrote a blog about her relationships with several men, including a man she was dating who also worked for the senator. In her blog, The Washingtonienne, she recounted in vivid detail their budding romance.

[35] Sonja West, *The Story of Me: The Underprotection of Autobiographical Speech,* 84 Wash. U. L. Rev. 905, 966 (2006).

Specifically, Cutler described their sexual practices, personal conversations, and other intimate details. Cutler did not identify Steinbuch directly, but she used his real initials and disclosed other personally identifiable information that made it possible for him to be identified. For a few weeks, only a handful of people knew about Cutler's blog. Then Wonkette, a very popular political gossip blog, linked to her blog and tens of thousands began flocking to the site. The story was written about in many major newspapers. Steinbuch sued Cutler for violating his privacy. The case never proceeded to trial because Cutler declared bankruptcy.

One of Cutler's arguments was that the blog was only read by a handful of her friends until Wonkette linked to it. Cutler contended that she never gave widespread publicity to the information — Wonkette did. When information is disclosed on the Internet, but only a few people read it, is disclosure sufficiently widespread for the publicity element to be satisfied?

Cutler also argued that her account of her relationships was newsworthy. According to her motion to dismiss: "Cutler's Blog makes a shocking and disturbing portrayal of casual and even reckless sexual encounters between young, entry-level Capitol Hill staffers like Cutler and more senior staffers like Steinbuch. . . . The interrelationship between youth, beauty, sex, money, and power in Washington has long been a matter of legitimate and sometimes *pressing* public interest." Is Cutler's blog newsworthy? What are the best arguments on each side of the issue?

In his book, *The Future of Reputation,* Daniel Solove observes that people are increasingly expressing themselves in blogs and social network websites. People are revealing information about their private lives as well as gossip and rumors about their friends, family, co-workers, and others. Solove notes:

> The Internet is transforming the nature and effects of gossip. It is making gossip more permanent and widespread, but less discriminating in the appropriateness of audience. . . . The problem with Internet gossip is that it can so readily be untethered from its context.

More broadly, Solove observes, the transformation of gossip from the fleeting and forgettable to the permanent and searchable might have significant social effects:

> We may find it increasingly difficult to have a fresh start, a second chance, or a clean slate. We might find it harder to engage in self-exploration if every false step and foolish act is chronicled forever in a permanent record. This record will affect our ability to define our identities, to obtain jobs, to participate in public life, and more. Ironically, the unconstrained flow of information on the Internet might impede our freedom.[36]

Are the privacy torts a viable way to protect people from having their personal lives written about online?

---

[36] Daniel J. Solove, *The Future of Reputation: Gossip, Rumor, and Privacy on the Internet* (2007). For more background about applying the privacy torts to blogs and social network sites, see Patricia Sánchez Abril, *Recasting Privacy Torts in a Spaceless World,* 21 Harv. J.L. & Tech. 1 (2007).

3. *The Breach of Confidentiality Tort.* The breach of confidentiality tort protects against the nonconsensual disclosures of confidential information. To establish liability under the tort, a plaintiff must prove that the defendant owed the plaintiff a duty of confidentiality and that the defendant breached that duty.[37] Unlike the tort of public disclosure, the breach of confidentiality tort does not have the elements of highly offensive, publicity, or the newsworthiness test. In America, the breach of confidentiality tort has been applied to doctors and other professionals. In contrast, in England, which rejects the Warren and Brandeis privacy torts, including the public disclosure tort, has a robust breach of confidentiality tort. As Neil Richards and Daniel Solove observe:

> The law of confidentiality in England also has attributes that the American privacy torts lack. In America, the prevailing belief is that people assume the risk of betrayal when they share secrets with each other. But in England, spouses, ex-spouses, friends, and nearly anyone else can be liable for divulging confidences. As one English court noted: "The fact is that when people kiss and later one of them tells, that second person is almost certainly breaking a confidential arrangement." Confidentiality thus recognizes that nondisclosure expectations emerge not just from norms of individual dignity, but also from norms of relationships, trust, and reliance on promises. American privacy law has never fully embraced privacy within relationships; it typically views information exposed to others as no longer private. Although a tort remedying breach of confidence would emerge later on in American law, it has developed slowly in comparison to the Warren and Brandeis privacy torts.[38]

Should a person accept the risk of betrayal when sharing confidential information with another?

Suppose the breach of confidentiality tort were applied more broadly to situations where friends, spouses, and others disclosed the secrets of others. Andrew McClurg notes that the First Amendment implications of the breach of confidentiality tort are different from those of the public disclosure tort:

> If one accepts the proposition that a party to an intimate relationship impliedly agrees not the breach the other party's confidence by publishing private, embarrassing information about them via an instrument of mass communication, the speech restriction is one that is self-imposed, rather than state-imposed.[39]

How might a broader application of the breach of confidentiality tort impact bloggers like Jessica Cutler who write about their sexual activities

---

[37] For more background about the tort, see Alan B. Vickery, Note, *Breach of Confidence: An Emerging Tort,* 82 Colum. L. Rev. 1426 (1982); G. Michael Harvey, Comment, *Confidentiality: A Measured Response to the Failure of Privacy,* 140 U. Pa. L. Rev. 2385 (1992); Susan M. Gilles, *Promises Betrayed: Breach of Confidence as a Remedy for Invasion of Privacy,* 43 Buff. L. Rev. 1 (1995).

[38] Neil M. Richards & Daniel J. Solove, *Privacy's Other Path: Recovering the Law of Confidentiality,* 96 Geo. L.J. 123 (2007).

[39] Andrew J. McClurg, *Kiss and Tell: Protecting Intimate Relationship Privacy Through Implied Contracts of Confidentiality*, 74 U. Cin. L. Rev. 887, 938 (2006).

with others? Would the tort impair free speech too much? Note that there is no newsworthiness test under the tort, so information of public concern is not protected. On the other hand, as McClurg notes, the breach of confidentiality tort understands that parties have made an implicit contract of confidentiality. Is it a violation of free speech to enforce a person's explicit or implicit promise not to speak about something?

4. ***Reputation-Tracking Technologies.*** Lior Strahilevitz argues that reputation-tracking technologies can yield beneficial results. He points to programs such as "How's My Driving?" (HMD) programs in which some commercial vehicles have stickers with a number to call to complain about bad driving. Insurance company statistics reveal significant reductions in crash costs and accidents (declines of well over 30 percent) following the implementation of HMD programs. Strahilevitz argues that the reason for the effectiveness of HMD programs is that they reduce driver anonymity:

   > The problems associated with urban and suburban driving are, by and large, creatures of motorist anonymity. That statement may seem too bold to readers accustomed to hearing about drunken driving, drowsy driving, and road rage. But a review of the literature on driving suggests that these problems largely stem from roadway anonymity. If society were able to monitor its roadways around the clock and to analyze this data immediately to identify and punish problematic motorists, many of the traffic accident deaths that occur every year would be averted. A dangerous driving environment is the almost inevitable consequence of sporadic traffic law enforcement by the police combined with rare traffic norm enforcement by motorists.[40]

   Strahilevitz points out that various websites such as Amazon.com, Tripadvisor.com, and eBay.com harness user feedback, where people can leave comments about a particular merchant or individual: "Though eBay's reputation system is admittedly imperfect, it has been extraordinarily successful at preventing fraud among auction participants." He proposes that more measures like HMD programs in other contexts might be beneficial. In what other situations would reputation-tracking technologies be useful? What are the potential problems with such technologies? Is there a way to implement these technologies that minimize these problems?

5. ***Practical Limitations on the Public Disclosure Tort.*** Consider Jacqueline Lipton:

   > Individuals who have faced shame, humiliation, or embarrassment as a result of the public dissemination of truthful information may have a variety of practical reasons for declining to bring a legal action, even if a cause of action is technically available. Many individual plaintiffs may not have the financial wherewithal or the time to litigate to protect their privacy. More worrisome, the private individual would have to relive the shame and embarrassment of the damaging information being entered into the public record during the course of court proceedings. On top of this, bringing a privacy-based action is effectively an admission by the plaintiff that the information in question is

[40] Lior Strahilevitz, *"How's* My *Driving?" For Everyone (and Everything?),* 81 N.Y.U. L. Rev. 1699, 1706 (2006).

> true. . . . [A] privacy action — unlike a defamation suit, which can have a restorative nature by publicly disclaiming the information in question and by imposing a monetary penalty for the disclosure — emphasizes the truth of the information.[41]

Are there ways to reduce these impediments to plaintiffs who desire to vindicate their privacy rights in court?

2. FIRST AMENDMENT LIMITATIONS

The First Amendment has a complex relationship to privacy. In many instances, the First Amendment and privacy are mutually reinforcing. Privacy is often essential to freedom of assembly. The Supreme Court has noted that there is a "vital relationship between freedom to associate and privacy in one's associations." *NAACP v. Alabama*, 357 U.S. 449 (1958). Privacy is also essential for freedom of speech, as the Supreme Court has recognized the importance of protecting the anonymity of speakers. *See McIntyre v. Ohio Elections Commission*, 514 U.S. 334 (1995).

However, privacy can come into conflict with the First Amendment. The privacy torts exist in an uneasy tension with the First Amendment. Indeed, Warren and Brandeis's article was aimed at the excesses of the press. Recall the authors' strong criticism of the press: "The press is overstepping in every direction the obvious bounds of propriety and of decency. Gossip is no longer the resource of the idle and of the vicious, but has become a trade, which is pursued with industry as well as effrontery."[42]

Although Brandeis was interested in privacy and skeptical of the press's trade in gossip, as a Supreme Court Justice, Brandeis was one of the champions of free speech.[43] Consider Brandeis's concurrence in *Whitney v. California*, 274 U.S. 357, 375 (1927):

> Those who won our independence believed that the final end of the state was to make men free to develop their faculties, and that in its government the deliberative forces should prevail over the arbitrary. They valued liberty both as an end and as a means. They believed liberty to be the secret of happiness and courage to be the secret of liberty. They believed that freedom to think as you will and to speak as you think are means indispensable to the discovery and spread of political truth; that without free speech and assembly discussion would be futile; that with them, discussion affords ordinarily adequate protection against the dissemination of noxious doctrine; that the greatest menace to freedom is an inert people; that public discussion is a political duty; and that this should be a fundamental principle of the American government. They recognized the risks to which all human institutions are subject. But they knew that order cannot be secured merely through fear of punishment for its

---

[41] Jacqueline D. Lipton, *Mapping Online Privacy,* 104 Nw. U. L. Rev. 477, 505-06 (2010).

[42] Samuel D. Warren & Louis D. Brandeis, *The Right to Privacy*, 4 Harv. L. Rev. 193 (1890).

[43] Neil Richards contends that Brandeis actually changed his views on privacy and free speech: "Although he never repudiated tort privacy, by the end of his life, Brandeis had moved to a position on publicity and free speech that was inconsistent with a broad reading of the tort theory of *The Right to Privacy*." Neil M. Richards, *The Puzzle of Brandeis, Privacy, and Speech,* 63 Vand. L. Rev. 1295, 1298 (2010).

> infraction; that it is hazardous to discourage thought, hope and imagination; that fear breeds repression; that repression breeds hate; that hate menaces stable government; that the path of safety lies in the opportunity to discuss freely supposed grievances and proposed remedies; and that the fitting remedy for evil counsels is good ones. Believing in the power of reason as applied through public discussion, they eschewed silence coerced by law — the argument of force in its worst form. Recognizing the occasional tyrannies of governing majorities, they amended the Constitution so that free speech and assembly should be guaranteed.

Although the privacy torts are litigated by private parties, they employ the machinery of the state (its tort law and legal system) to impose costs on the press for gathering, producing, and disseminating news. The danger is that the threat of lawsuits will chill the press from running certain stories. Further, the threat of lawsuits alone might chill the press, because even if the press ultimately prevails in such suits, the lawsuits cost money to defend.

The public disclosure tort raises complicated tensions with the First Amendment, for it permits liability for the publication of truthful information. Built into the tort, however, is the newsworthiness test, which a number of courts have stated is required to square the tort with the First Amendment. The newsworthiness test, however, is a limitation *within* the tort. Does the First Amendment provide any additional limitations upon the tort?[44] The cases in this section address this question. In order to understand the cases, some basic background about First Amendment analysis is necessary.

Unprotected Forms of Expression. The Court has held that certain forms of expression receive no First Amendment protection. Such categories include obscenity, *Miller v. California,* 413 U.S. 15 (1973); fighting words, *Chaplinsky v. New Hampshire,* 315 U.S. 568 (1942); and child pornography, *New York v. Ferber,* 458 U.S. 747 (1982).

Strict and Intermediate Scrutiny. Most restrictions on speech are reviewed under either strict or intermediate scrutiny. Under strict scrutiny, a law must be the "least restrictive means" to achieve a "compelling" government interest. *Sable Communications, Inc. v. FCC,* 492 U.S. 115, 116 (1989). Strict scrutiny is very difficult to withstand, and most laws subject to it are struck down. In contrast, under intermediate scrutiny, a law must be narrowly tailored to a "substantial government interest." *United States v. O'Brien,* 391 U.S. 467, 377 (1968).

---

[44] For more background on the First Amendment and the privacy torts, see Peter B. Edelman, *Free Press v. Privacy: Haunted by the Ghost of Justice Black*, 68 Tex. L. Rev. 1195 (1990); Thomas I. Emerson, *The Right of Privacy and Freedom of Press*, 14 Harv. CR-CL L. Rev. 329 (1979); Edward Bloustein, *The First Amendment and Privacy: The Supreme Court Justice and the Philosopher*, 28 Rutgers L. Rev. 41 (1974); Melville B. Nimmer, *The Right to Speak from Times to Time: First Amendment Theory Applied to Libel and Misapplied to Privacy*, 56 Cal. L. Rev. 935 (1968); Harry Kalven, Jr., *Privacy in Tort Law — Were Warren and Brandeis Wrong?*, 31 Law & Contemp. Probs. 326 (1966); Marc A. Franklin, *A Constitutional Problem in Privacy Protection: Legal Inhibitions on Reporting of Fact*, 16 Stan. L. Rev. 107 (1963; Rodney A. Smolla, *Accounting for the Slow Growth of American Privacy Law,* 27 Nova L. Rev. 289 (2002).

Content-Based vs. Content-Neutral Regulation. Under First Amendment analysis, the Court first analyzes whether a speech restriction is content-based or content-neutral. A content-based regulation targets particular messages. Content-neutral regulation restricts speech regardless of its message, such as regulating the time, place, or manner of the speech. If a speech restriction is content-based, then strict scrutiny is generally applied. There are some exceptions. For example, the Court has held that the government may single out content if the purpose is to prevent certain secondary effects caused by such speech. In *City of Renton v. Playtime Theatres,* 475 U.S. 41 (1986), the Court did not apply strict scrutiny to an ordinance restricting the location of adult movie theaters because the purpose was to prevent crime — a secondary effect. Content-neutral speech regulation is generally subject to intermediate scrutiny.

In *R.A.V. v. City of St. Paul,* 505 U.S. 377 (1992), the Court held that a content-based regulation of expression that falls in an unprotected category will be subject to strict scrutiny. The Court struck down a hate speech law because it regulated the content of "fighting words" — it applied to fighting words based on "race, color, creed, religion, or gender." Unprotected categories of expression, such as fighting words, may be regulated so long as they are not "made the vehicle for content discrimination unrelated to their distinctively proscribable content. Thus, the government may proscribe libel; but it may not make the further content discrimination of proscribing only libel critical of the government." Content-based regulation on an unprotected category of expression is permissible if "based on the very reasons why the particular class of speech . . . is proscribable."

COX BROADCASTING CORP. V. COHN

420 U.S. 469 (1975)

WHITE, J. . . . In August 1971, appellee's 17-year-old daughter was the victim of a rape and did not survive the incident. Six youths were soon indicted for murder and rape. Although there was substantial press coverage of the crime and of subsequent developments, the identity of the victim was not disclosed pending trial, perhaps because of Ga. Code Ann. § 26-9901 (1972),[45] which makes it a misdemeanor to publish or broadcast the name or identity of a rape victim. In April 1972, some eight months later, the six defendants appeared in court. Five pleaded guilty to rape or attempted rape, the charge of murder having been dropped. The guilty pleas were accepted by the court, and the trial of the defendant pleading not guilty was set for a later date.

In the course of the proceedings that day, appellant Wasell, a reporter covering the incident for his employer, learned the name of the victim from an

[45] "It shall be unlawful for any news media or any other person to print and publish, broadcast, televise, or disseminate through any other medium of public dissemination or cause to be printed and published, broadcast, televised, or disseminated in any newspaper, magazine, periodical or other publication published in this State or through any radio or television broadcast originating in the State the name or identity of any female who may have been raped or upon whom an assault with intent to commit rape may have been made. Any person or corporation violating the provisions of this section shall, upon conviction, be punished as for a misdemeanor." Three other States have similar statutes. . . .

examination of the indictments which were made available for his inspection in the courtroom. That the name of the victim appears in the indictments and that the indictments were public records available for inspection are not disputed. Later that day, Wassell broadcast over the facilities of station WSB-TV, a television station owned by appellant Cox Broadcasting Corp., a news report concerning the court proceedings. The report named the victim of the crime and was repeated the following day.

In May 1972, appellee brought an action for money damages against appellants, relying on § 26-9901 and claiming that his right to privacy had been invaded by the television broadcasts giving the name of his deceased daughter. . . .

Georgia stoutly defends both § 26-9901 and the State's common-law privacy action challenged here. Its claims are not without force, for powerful arguments can be made, and have been made, that however it may be ultimately defined, there is a zone of privacy surrounding every individual, a zone within which the State may protect him from intrusion by the press, with all its attendant publicity. Indeed, the central thesis of the root article by Warren and Brandeis, *The Right to Privacy*, 4 Harv. L. Rev. 193 (1890), was that the press was overstepping its prerogatives by publishing essentially private information and that there should be a remedy for the alleged abuses.

More compellingly, the century has experienced a strong tide running in favor of the so-called right of privacy. In 1967, we noted that "[it] has been said that a 'right of privacy' has been recognized at common law in 30 States plus the District of Columbia and by statute in four States." *Time, Inc. v. Hill*, 385 U.S. 374, 383 n.7. We there cited the 1964 edition of Prosser's *Law of Torts*. The 1971 edition of that same source states that "[in] one form or another, the right of privacy is by this time recognized and accepted in all but a very few jurisdictions." . . .

These are impressive credentials for a right of privacy, but we should recognize that we do not have at issue here an action for the invasion of privacy involving the appropriation of one's name or photograph, a physical or other tangible intrusion into a private area, or a publication of otherwise private information that is also false although perhaps not defamatory. The version of the privacy tort now before us — termed in Georgia "the tort of public disclosure," — is that in which the plaintiff claims the right to be free from unwanted publicity about his private affairs, which, although wholly true, would be offensive to a person of ordinary sensibilities. Because the gravamen of the claimed injury is the publication of information, whether true or not, the dissemination of which is embarrassing or otherwise painful to an individual, it is here that claims of privacy most directly confront the constitutional freedoms of speech and press. The face-off is apparent, and the appellants urge upon us the broad holding that the press may not be made criminally or civilly liable for publishing information that is neither false nor misleading but absolutely accurate, however damaging it may be to reputation or individual sensibilities. . . .

It is true that in defamation actions, where the protected interest is personal reputation, the prevailing view is that truth is a defense. . . .

The Court has nevertheless carefully left open the question whether the First and Fourteenth Amendments require that truth be recognized as a defense in a defamation action brought by a private person as distinguished from a public official or public figure. . . . In similar fashion, *Time, Inc. v. Hill*, expressly saved the question whether truthful publication of very private matters unrelated to public affairs could be constitutionally proscribed. . . .

Those precedents, as well as other considerations, counsel similar caution here. In this sphere of collision between claims of privacy and those of the free press, the interests on both sides are plainly rooted in the traditions and significant concerns of our society. Rather than address the broader question whether truthful publications may ever be subjected to civil or criminal liability consistently with the First and Fourteenth Amendments, or to put it another way, whether the State may ever define and protect an area of privacy free from unwanted publicity in the press, it is appropriate to focus on the narrower interface between press and privacy that this case presents, namely, whether the State may impose sanctions on the accurate publication of the name of a rape victim obtained from public records — more specifically, from judicial records which are maintained in connection with a public prosecution and which themselves are open to public inspection. We are convinced that the State may not do so.

In the first place, in a society in which each individual has but limited time and resources with which to observe at first hand the operations of his government, he relies necessarily upon the press to bring to him in convenient form the facts of those operations. Great responsibility is accordingly placed upon the news media to report fully and accurately the proceedings of government, and official records and documents open to the public are the basic data of governmental operations. Without the information provided by the press most of us and many of our representatives would be unable to vote intelligently or to register opinions on the administration of government generally. With respect to judicial proceedings in particular, the function of the press serves to guarantee the fairness of trials and to bring to bear the beneficial effects of public scrutiny upon the administration of justice. . . .

. . . By placing the information in the public domain on official court records, the State must be presumed to have concluded that the public interest was thereby being served. Public records by their very nature are of interest to those concerned with the administration of government, and a public benefit is performed by the reporting of the true contents of the records by the media. The freedom of the press to publish that information appears to us to be of critical importance to our type of government in which the citizenry is the final judge of the proper conduct of public business. In preserving that form of government the First and Fourteenth Amendments command nothing less than that the States may not impose sanctions on the publication of truthful information contained in official court records open to public inspection.

We are reluctant to embark on a course that would make public records generally available to the media but forbid their publication if offensive to the sensibilities of the supposed reasonable man. Such a rule would make it very difficult for the media to inform citizens about the public business and yet stay within the law. The rule would invite timidity and self-censorship and very likely lead to the suppression of many items that would otherwise be published and that should be made available to the public. At the very least, the First and Fourteenth Amendments will not allow exposing the press to liability for truthfully publishing information released to the public in official court records. If there are privacy interests to be protected in judicial proceedings, the States must respond by means which avoid public documentation or other exposure of private information. Their political institutions must weigh the interests in privacy with the interests of the public to know and of the press to publish. Once true information is disclosed in public court documents open to public inspection, the press cannot be sanctioned for publishing it. In this instance as in others reliance must rest upon the judgment of those who decide what to publish or broadcast.

NOTES & QUESTIONS

1. ***Justifications for the* Cox *Holding.*** There are two potential justifications for the rule in *Cox*. The first is that the information in public records is not private because it is in the public domain, and once that information falls into the public domain, the First Amendment prohibits restrictions on speaking about it. The other justification is that the press must be able to report on public records dealing with the criminal justice system to permit greater accountability and transparency in government. Which justification does the Court's opinion rely upon most heavily? Under the second justification, would the state be permitted to keep rape victims' names confidential?
2. ***The* Oklahoma Publishing *and* Daily Mail *Cases.*** After *Cox*, the Supreme Court held in *Oklahoma Publishing Co. v. Oklahoma County District Court*, 430 U.S. 308 (1977), that a state court violated the First Amendment by prohibiting the media from publishing the name or photograph of an 11-year-old boy in a juvenile proceeding which members of the media attended. A few years later, the Court confronted the issue of whether a state could prohibit the press from publishing the name of a juvenile offender. In *Smith v. Daily Mail Publishing Co.*, 443 U.S. 97 (1979), two newspapers published the name and photograph of a 15-year-old who had shot and killed his 14-year-old classmate. The newspapers were indicted with the misdemeanor offense of publishing the name of a juvenile offender without a court order. The Court stated: "At issue is simply the power of a state to punish the truthful publication of an alleged juvenile delinquent's name lawfully obtained by a newspaper. The asserted state interest [to protect the anonymity of juvenile offenders] cannot justify the statute's imposition of criminal sanctions on this type of publication."
3. **Melvin v. Reid.** One of the earliest cases to recognize the tort of public disclosure is *Melvin v. Reid,* 297 P. 91 (Cal. 1931). Gabrielle Darley was a prostitute who was tried for murder but was acquitted. She abandoned her life as a prostitute, married Bernard Melvin, and became a housewife. In 1925, *The Red Kimono,* a motion picture based on her past life, was released. The film used her maiden name of Darley. As a result, some of her friends learned

"for the first time of the unsavory incidents of her early life." Gabrielle sued. The California Supreme Court concluded that she had a cause of action:

> One of the major objectives of society as it is now constituted, and of the administration of our penal system, is the rehabilitation of the fallen and the reformation of the criminal. Under these theories of sociology, it is our object to lift up and sustain the unfortunate rather than tear him down. Where a person has by his own efforts rehabilitated himself, we, as right-thinking members of society, should permit him to continue in the path of rectitude rather than throw him back into a life of shame or crime. Even the thief on the cross was permitted to repent during the hours of his final agony.

According to Lawrence Friedman, who has examined the history of the case, the facts surrounding Gabrielle's murder trial were sensational. Gabrielle was on trial for murdering her lover, who was also her pimp. Gabrielle had given him money to buy her a wedding ring, but instead he used the money to buy a ring to wed another woman. Gabrielle confronted him in the street with a gun and shot him dead. Gabrielle was charged with murder. Gabrielle was acquitted. But the lurid details surrounding the incident attracted attention:

> Rogers's daughter, Adela Rogers St. John, a writer, covered the trial. Later, she wrote a short story based on the case and called it "The Red Kimono." It used incidents from Gabrielle's life, and it used her actual name. Dorothy Reid bought the story and produced a movie based on it. The film also was called *The Red Kimono*. It was shown in theaters in 1927. The movie identified the heroine as Gabrielle Darley. The next year, Gabrielle, now calling herself Gabrielle Darley Melvin, brought suit against Reid and Reid's motion picture company.

Friedman believes that Gabrielle's claim that she had reformed herself was fake:

> There is good evidence that she was, in fact, as phony as a three dollar bill. A journalist in Arizona argues that she was still working as a prostitute and madam at the time of the trial in a town in Arizona. During her lifetime she had several husbands, but they had the distressing habit of turning up dead.[46]

After Gabrielle won in the California Supreme Court, she moved to dismiss the case in 1933 prior to trial. Evidence suggests that she settled the case, which caused Reid to lose her home in West Hollywood. Today, Reid is considered as an important pioneering woman producer and director. The film, *The Red Kimono*, is available on DVD in a series devoted to "Early Women Filmmakers." Paul Schwartz has noted that the film itself "is a protofeminist account, a morality play, regarding the difficulty faced by a former prostitute in finding a life free of shame notoriety."[47] In this regard, as Friedman also notes, the film makes a point similar to the *Melvin* court.

---

[46] Lawrence M. Friedman, *Guarding Life's Dark Secrets: Legal and Social Controls over Reputation, Propriety, and Privacy* 216-18 (2007).

[47] Paul M. Schwartz, *From Victorian Secrets to Cyberspace Shaming*, 76 U. Chi. L. Rev. 1407, 1416 (2009).

Are the facts about Gabrielle in *The Red Kimono* newsworthy? Should the interest in allowing people like Gabrielle to start a new life trump people like Reid's right to make her movie or the public's right to know about a person's past?

4. ***Information About Past Crimes.*** In *Briscoe v. Reader's Digest*, 483 P.2d 34 (Cal. 1971), a magazine article about hijacking discussed the plaintiff's hijacking of a truck 11 years earlier. Since then, the plaintiff had rehabilitated himself, and many people did not know of his previous crime. Similar to *Melvin v. Reid*, the court held that the article was newsworthy, but that the use of the plaintiff's real name had no relevance to the article.

> We have no doubt that reports of the facts of past crimes are newsworthy. . . . However, identification of the Actor in reports of long past crimes usually serves little independent public purpose. Once legal proceedings have terminated, and a suspect or offender has been released, identification of the individual will not usually aid the administration of justice. Identification will no longer serve to bring forth witnesses or obtain succor for victims. Unless the individual has reattracted the public eye to himself in some independent fashion, the only public "interest" that would usually be served is that of curiosity. . . .
>
> Another factor militating in favor of protecting the individual's privacy here is the state's interest in the integrity of the rehabilitative process. . . .
>
> One of the premises of the rehabilitative process is that the rehabilitated offender can rejoin that great bulk of the community from which he has been ostracized for his anti-social acts. In return for becoming a "new man," he is allowed to melt into the shadows of obscurity. . . .
>
> Plaintiff is a man whose last offense took place 11 years before, who has paid his debt to society, who has friends and an 11-year-old daughter who were unaware of his early life—a man who assumed a position in "respectable" society. Ideally, his neighbors should recognize his present worth and forget his past life of shame. But men are not so divine as to forgive the past trespasses of others, and plaintiff therefore endeavored to reveal as little as possible of his past life. Yet, as if in some bizarre canyon of echoes, petitioner's past life pursues him through the pages of Reader's Digest, now published in 13 languages and distributed in 100 nations, with a circulation in California alone of almost 2,000,000 copies. . . .

Consider Eugene Volokh's criticism of the *Briscoe* case:

> [S]ome people do take a view that differs from that of the *Briscoe* judges: While criminals can change their character, this view asserts, they often don't. Someone who was willing to fight a gun battle with the police eleven years ago may be more willing than the average person to do something bad today, even if he has led a blameless life since then. . . .
>
> Under this ideology, it's perfectly proper to keep this possibility in mind in one's dealings with the supposedly "reformed" felon. While the government may want to give him a second chance by releasing him from prison, restoring his right to vote and possess firearms, and even erasing its publicly accessible records related to the conviction, his friends, acquaintances, and business associates are entitled to adopt a different attitude. Most presumably wouldn't treat him as a total pariah, but they might use extra caution in dealing with

> him, especially when it comes to trusting their business welfare or even their physical safety (or that of their children) to his care. . . .[48]

According to Richard Posner, the *Briscoe* case improperly assumes that people will behave irrationally toward rehabilitated people:

> Remote past criminal activity is less relevant to a prediction of future misconduct than recent — and those who learn of it will discount it accordingly — but such information is hardly irrelevant to people considering whether to enter into or continue social or business relations with the individual; if it were irrelevant, publicizing it would not injure the individual. People conceal past criminal acts not out of bashfulness but because potential acquaintances quite sensibly regard a criminal past as negative evidence of the value of associating with a person.[49]

In *Gates v. Discovery Communications, Inc.,* 101 P.3d 552 (Cal. 2004), the California Supreme Court held that the U.S. Supreme Court's "decision in *Cox* and its subsequent pronouncements . . . have fatally undermined *Briscoe*'s holding that a media defendant may be held liable in tort for recklessly publishing true but not newsworthy facts concerning a rehabilitated former criminal, insofar as that holding applies to facts obtained from public official court records."

To what extent does *Gates* overturn *Melvin* or *Briscoe*? In both cases, the information about them was available in public records. But do *Cox* and its progeny turn on the *availability* of the information in public records or whether the media actually *obtained* the information from public records? In other words, if the information was obtained elsewhere, would plaintiffs in *Melvin* and *Briscoe* still have a cause of action?

5. ***The Right to Be Forgotten.*** In 2014, a Spanish man requested that Google search results stop including links to a 1998 article in a newspaper about an auction for his foreclosed house. The EU Court of Justice (ECJ) ruled in favor of the plaintiff. Under what has become known as the "right to be forgotten," EU citizens have a right to the deletion of certain personal data under the EU Data Protection Directive. The ECJ concluded that "the operator of a search engine is obliged to remove from the list of results displayed following a search made on the basis of a person's name links to web pages, published by third parties and containing information relating to that person, also in a case where that name or information is not erased beforehand or simultaneously from those web pages, and even, as the case may be, when its publication in itself on those pages is lawful." *Google Spain, S.L., Google Inc. y Agencia Española de Protección de Datos (AEPD)*, European Court of Justice, EU:C:2014:317. This case is excerpted and covered in more detail in Chapter 13.

---

[48] Eugene Volokh, *Freedom of Speech and Information Privacy: The Troubling Implications of a Right to Stop People from Speaking About You*, 52 Stan. L. Rev. 1049, 1091-92 (2000). For another critique, see T. Markus Funk, *The Dangers of Hiding Criminal Pasts*, 66 Tenn. L. Rev. 287 (1998).

[49] Richard A. Posner, *The Economics of Justice* 260-61 (1983).

The ECJ noted that the invasion of privacy search engines create for individuals "cannot be justified by merely the economic interest which the operator of such an engine has in that processing." Moreover, the court noted that "the removal of links from the list of results could, depending on the information at issue, have effects upon the legitimate interest of internet users potentially interested in having access to that information." Thus, the court stated, "a fair balance should be sought in particular between that interest and the data subject's fundamental [privacy] rights." The court went on to state: "Whilst it is true that the data subject's rights protected by those articles also override, as a general rule, that interest of internet users, that balance may however depend, in specific cases, on the nature of the information in question and its sensitivity for the data subject's private life and on the interest of the public in having that information, an interest which may vary, in particular, according to the role played by the data subject in public life."

Although the ECJ decision was referred to as enforcing the right to be forgotten, the ECJ did not technically require forgetting. Instead, the information remained online in the original articles. Google just could not show these articles in search results. Should Google be forced to remove search results when the newspapers can continue to keep the information on their websites?

As Evan Selinger and Woodrow Hartzog note, the use of the word "forgetting" is misleading: "This debate is not and should not be about forgetting or disappearing in the traditional sense. Instead, let's recognize that the talk about forgetting and disappearing is really concern about the concept of obscurity in the protection of our personal information."[50]

In the United States, the First Amendment would very likely restrict any attempt to force the newspapers to remove the personal data from their websites. But to what extent does the First Amendment protect linking to information, especially when those links are generated by a computer algorithm?

6. ***Anti-SLAPP.*** When lawsuits implicate a defendant's speech, 30 states and the District of Columbia provide special anti-SLAPP protections. A SLAPP lawsuit — or a "strategic lawsuit against public participation" — is a lawsuit designed to censor or retaliate against a person for their speech. Fearing significant legal defense costs, defendants might retract their speech or stop engaging in new speech about a matter. SLAPP suits can successfully silence people engaging in protected speech even when the suit is without merit because the costs of getting the suit dismissed can still be significant.

   Nearly all anti-SLAPP legislation shares important common elements, which include: (1) requirements that the plaintiff demonstrate early that the case has merit; (2) provisions that allow the defendant to seek an expedited hearing; (3) limits on long costly discovery; (4) the right of a prevailing defendant to recover attorney fees and costs.

---

[50] Evan Seligner & Woodrow Hartzog, *Google Can't Forget You, But It Should Make You Hard to Find,* Wired, May 20, 2014,http://www.wired.com/2014/05/google-cant-forget-you-but-it-should-make-you-hard-to-find/.

THE FLORIDA STAR V. B.J.F.

491 U.S. 524 (1989)

MARSHALL, J. Florida Stat. § 794.03 (1987) makes it unlawful to "print, publish, or broadcast . . . in any instrument of mass communication" the name of the victim of a sexual offense. Pursuant to this statute, appellant The Florida Star was found civilly liable for publishing the name of a rape victim which it had obtained from a publicly released police report. The issue presented here is whether this result comports with the First Amendment. We hold that it does not. . . .

The Florida Star is a weekly newspaper which serves the community of Jacksonville, Florida, and which has an average circulation of approximately 18,000 copies. A regular feature of the newspaper is its "Police Reports" section. That section, typically two to three pages in length, contains brief articles describing local criminal incidents under police investigation.

On October 20, 1983, appellee B.J.F.[51] reported to the Duval County, Florida, Sheriff's Department (Department) that she had been robbed and sexually assaulted by an unknown assailant. The Department prepared a report on the incident which identified B.J.F. by her full name. The Department then placed the report in its pressroom. The Department does not restrict access either to the pressroom or to the reports made available therein.

A Florida Star reporter-trainee sent to the pressroom copied the police report verbatim, including B.J.F.'s full name, on a blank duplicate of the Department's forms. A Florida Star reporter then prepared a one-paragraph article about the crime, derived entirely from the trainee's copy of the police report. The article included B.J.F.'s full name. It appeared in the "Robberies" subsection of the "Police Reports" section on October 29, 1983, one of 54 police blotter stories in that day's edition. . . .

In printing B.J.F.'s full name, The Florida Star violated its internal policy of not publishing the names of sexual offense victims.

On September 26, 1984, B.J.F. filed suit in the Circuit Court of Duval County against the Department and The Florida Star, alleging that these parties negligently violated § 794.03. Before trial, the Department settled with B.J.F. for $2,500. The Florida Star moved to dismiss, claiming, inter alia, that imposing civil sanctions on the newspaper pursuant to § 794.03 violated the First Amendment. The trial judge rejected the motion.

At the ensuing daylong trial, B.J.F. testified that she had suffered emotional distress from the publication of her name. She stated that she had heard about the article from fellow workers and acquaintances; that her mother had received several threatening phone calls from a man who stated that he would rape B.J.F. again; and that these events had forced B.J.F. to change her phone number and residence, to seek police protection, and to obtain mental health counseling. In defense, The Florida Star put forth evidence indicating that the newspaper had

---

[51] In filing this lawsuit, appellee used her full name in the caption of the case. On appeal, the Florida District Court of Appeal sua sponte revised the caption, stating that it would refer to the appellee by her initials, "in order to preserve [her] privacy interests." Respecting those interests, we, too, refer to appellee by her initials, both in the caption and in our discussion.

learned B.J.F.'s name from the incident report released by the Department, and that the newspaper's violation of its internal rule against publishing the names of sexual offense victims was inadvertent.

At the close of B.J.F.'s case, and again at the close of its defense, The Florida Star moved for a directed verdict. On both occasions, the trial judge denied these motions. He ruled from the bench that § 794.03 was constitutional because it reflected a proper balance between the First Amendment and privacy rights, as it applied only to a narrow set of "rather sensitive . . . criminal offenses." . . . The jury awarded B.J.F. $75,000 in compensatory damages and $25,000 in punitive damages. . . .

Appellant takes the position that this case is indistinguishable from *Cox Broadcasting*. Alternatively, it urges that our decisions . . . can be distilled to yield a broader First Amendment principle that the press may never be punished, civilly or criminally, for publishing the truth. . . .

We conclude that imposing damages on appellant for publishing B.J.F.'s name violates the First Amendment, although not for either of the reasons appellant urges. Despite the strong resemblance this case bears to *Cox Broadcasting*, that case cannot fairly be read as controlling here. The name of the rape victim in that case was obtained from courthouse records that were open to public inspection. . . . Significantly, one of the reasons we gave in *Cox Broadcasting* for invalidating the challenged damages award was the important role the press plays in subjecting trials to public scrutiny and thereby helping guarantee their fairness. That role is not directly compromised where, as here, the information in question comes from a police report prepared and disseminated at a time at which not only had no adversarial criminal proceedings begun, but no suspect had been identified.

Nor need we accept appellant's invitation to hold broadly that truthful publication may never be punished consistent with the First Amendment. Our cases have carefully eschewed reaching this ultimate question, mindful that the future may bring scenarios which prudence counsels our not resolving anticipatorily. . . . We continue to believe that the sensitivity and significance of the interests presented in clashes between First Amendment and privacy rights counsel relying on limited principles that sweep no more broadly than the appropriate context of the instant case.

In our view, this case is appropriately analyzed with reference to such a limited First Amendment principle. It is the one, in fact, which we articulated in *Daily Mail* in our synthesis of prior cases involving attempts to punish truthful publication: "[I]f a newspaper lawfully obtains truthful information about a matter of public significance then state officials may not constitutionally punish publication of the information, absent a need to further a state interest of the highest order." According the press the ample protection provided by that principle is supported by at least three separate considerations, in addition to, of course, the overarching "'public interest, secured by the Constitution, in the dissemination of truth.'" . . .

First, because the *Daily Mail* formulation only protects the publication of information which a newspaper has "lawfully obtain[ed]," the government retains ample means of safeguarding significant interests upon which publication may impinge, including protecting a rape victim's anonymity. . . . Where information is entrusted to the government, a less drastic means than punishing truthful publication almost always exists for guarding against the dissemination of private facts.[52]

A second consideration undergirding the *Daily Mail* principle is the fact that punishing the press for its dissemination of information which is already publicly available is relatively unlikely to advance the interests in the service of which the State seeks to act. . . . [W]here the government has made certain information publicly available, it is highly anomalous to sanction persons other than the source of its release. . . . As *Daily Mail* observed in its summary of Oklahoma Publishing, "once the truthful information was 'publicly revealed' or 'in the public domain' the court could not constitutionally restrain its dissemination."

A third and final consideration is the "timidity and self-censorship" which may result from allowing the media to be punished for publishing certain truthful information. . . . A contrary rule, depriving protection to those who rely on the government's implied representations of the lawfulness of dissemination, would force upon the media the onerous obligation of sifting through government press releases, reports, and pronouncements to prune out material arguably unlawful for publication. . . .

Applied to the instant case, the *Daily Mail* principle clearly commands reversal. The first inquiry is whether the newspaper "lawfully obtain[ed] truthful information about a matter of public significance." It is undisputed that the news article describing the assault on B.J.F. was accurate. In addition, appellant lawfully obtained B.J.F.'s name. Appellee's argument to the contrary is based on the fact that under Florida law, police reports which reveal the identity of the victim of a sexual offense are not among the matters of "public record" which the public, by law, is entitled to inspect. But the fact that state officials are not required to disclose such reports does not make it unlawful for a newspaper to receive them when furnished by the government. . . . It is, clear, furthermore, that the news article concerned "a matter of public significance," in the sense in which the *Daily Mail* synthesis of prior cases used that term. That is, the article generally, as opposed to the specific identity contained within it, involved a matter of paramount public import: the commission, and investigation, of a violent crime which had been reported to authorities.

The second inquiry is whether imposing liability on appellant pursuant to § 794.03 serves "a need to further a state interest of the highest order." Appellee argues that a rule punishing publication furthers three closely related interests: the privacy of victims of sexual offenses; the physical safety of such victims, who may be targeted for retaliation if their names become known to their assailants; and the goal of encouraging victims of such crimes to report these offenses without fear of exposure.

At a time in which we are daily reminded of the tragic reality of rape, it is undeniable that these are highly significant interests. . . . For three independent reasons, however, imposing liability for publication under the circumstances of

---

[52] The *Daily Mail* principle does not settle the issue whether, in cases where information has been acquired unlawfully by a newspaper or by a source, government may ever punish not only the unlawful acquisition, but the ensuing publication as well. This issue was raised but not definitively resolved in *New York Times Co. v. United States*, 403 U.S. 713 (1971), and reserved in *Landmark Communications*, 435 U.S., at 837. We have no occasion to address it here.

this case is too precipitous a means of advancing these interests to convince us that there is a "need" within the meaning of the *Daily Mail* formulation for Florida to take this extreme step.

First is the manner in which appellant obtained the identifying information in question. As we have noted, where the government itself provides information to the media, it is most appropriate to assume that the government had, but failed to utilize, far more limited means of guarding against dissemination than the extreme step of punishing truthful speech. That assumption is richly borne out in this case. B.J.F.'s identity would never have come to light were it not for the erroneous, if inadvertent, inclusion by the Department of her full name in an incident report made available in a pressroom open to the public. Florida's policy against disclosure of rape victims' identities, reflected in § 794.03, was undercut by the Department's failure to abide by this policy. Where, as here, the government has failed to police itself in disseminating information, it is clear under *Cox Broadcasting*, *Oklahoma Publishing*, and *Landmark Communications* that the imposition of damages against the press for its subsequent publication can hardly be said to be a narrowly tailored means of safeguarding anonymity. . . .

A second problem with Florida's imposition of liability for publication is the broad sweep of the negligence per se standard applied under the civil cause of action implied from § 794.03. Unlike claims based on the common law tort of invasion of privacy, civil actions based on § 794.03 require no case-by-case findings that the disclosure of a fact about a person's private life was one that a reasonable person would find highly offensive. On the contrary, under the per se theory of negligence adopted by the courts below, liability follows automatically from publication. This is so regardless of whether the identity of the victim is already known throughout the community; whether the victim has voluntarily called public attention to the offense; or whether the identity of the victim has otherwise become a reasonable subject of public concern — because, perhaps, questions have arisen whether the victim fabricated an assault by a particular person. Nor is there a scienter requirement of any kind under § 794.03, engendering the perverse result that truthful publications challenged pursuant to this cause of action are less protected by the First Amendment than even the least protected defamatory falsehoods. . . .

Third, and finally, the facial underinclusiveness of § 794.03 raises serious doubts about whether Florida is, in fact, serving, with this statute, the significant interests which appellee invokes in support of affirmance. Section 794.03 prohibits the publication of identifying information only if this information appears in an "instrument of mass communication," a term the statute does not define. Section 794.03 does not prohibit the spread by other means of the identities of victims of sexual offenses. An individual who maliciously spreads word of the identity of a rape victim is thus not covered, despite the fact that the communication of such information to persons who live near, or work with, the victim may have consequences as devastating as the exposure of her name to large numbers of strangers.

When a State attempts the extraordinary measure of punishing truthful publication in the name of privacy, it must demonstrate its commitment to advancing this interest by applying its prohibition evenhandedly, to the smalltime disseminator as well as the media giant. Where important First Amendment interests are at stake, the mass scope of disclosure is not an acceptable surrogate for injury. . . .

Our holding today is limited. We do not hold that truthful publication is automatically constitutionally protected, or that there is no zone of personal privacy within which the State may protect the individual from intrusion by the press, or even that a State may never punish publication of the name of a victim of a sexual offense. We hold only that where a newspaper publishes truthful information which it has lawfully obtained, punishment may lawfully be imposed, if at all, only when narrowly tailored to a state interest of the highest order, and that no such interest is satisfactorily served by imposing liability under § 794.03 to appellant under the facts of this case. . . .

WHITE, J. joined by REHNQUIST, C.J. and O'CONNOR, J. dissenting. . . . *Cox Broadcasting* reversed a damages award entered against a television station, which had obtained a rape victim's name from public records maintained in connection with the judicial proceedings brought against her assailants. While there are similarities, critical aspects of that case make it wholly distinguishable from this one. First, in *Cox Broadcasting*, the victim's name had been disclosed in the hearing where her assailants pleaded guilty; and, as we recognized, judicial records have always been considered public information in this country. . . . Second, unlike the incident report at issue here, which was meant by state law to be withheld from public release, the judicial proceedings at issue in *Cox Broadcasting* were open as a matter of state law. . . .

Cox Broadcasting stands for the proposition that the State cannot make the press its first line of defense in withholding private information from the public — it cannot ask the press to secrete private facts that the State makes no effort to safeguard in the first place. In this case, however, the State has undertaken "means which avoid [but obviously, not altogether prevent] public documentation or other exposure of private information." . . .

More importantly, at issue in *Daily Mail* was the disclosure of the name of the perpetrator of an infamous murder of a 15-year-old student. Surely the rights of those accused of crimes and those who are their victims must differ with respect to privacy concerns. That is, whatever rights alleged criminals have to maintain their anonymity pending an adjudication of guilt — and after *Daily Mail*, those rights would seem to be minimal — the rights of crime victims to stay shielded from public view must be infinitely more substantial. . . .

Consequently, I cannot agree that *Cox Broadcasting*, or *Oklahoma Publishing*, or *Daily Mail* requires — or even substantially supports — the result reached by the Court today. . . .

We are left, then, to wonder whether the . . . "independent reasons" the Court cites for reversing the judgment for B.J.F. support its result.

The first of these reasons relied on by the Court is the fact "appellant gained access to [B.J.F.'s name] through a government news release." "The government's issuance of such a release, without qualification, can only convey to recipients that the government considered dissemination lawful," the Court suggests. So described, this case begins to look like the situation in *Oklahoma Publishing*, where a judge invited reporters into his courtroom, but then tried to prohibit them from reporting on the proceedings they observed. But this case is profoundly different. Here, the "release" of information provided by the government was not, as the Court says, "without qualification." As the Star's own reporter conceded at trial, the crime incident report that inadvertently included B.J.F.'s name was posted in a room that contained signs making it clear that the names of rape victims were not matters of public record, and were not to be published. The Star's reporter indicated that she understood that she "[was not] allowed to take down that information" (i.e., B.J.F.'s name) and that she "[was] not supposed to take the information from the police department." Thus, by her own admission the posting of the incident report did not convey to the Star's reporter the idea that "the government considered dissemination lawful"; the Court's suggestion to the contrary is inapt. . . .

. . . By amending its public records statute to exempt rape victims names from disclosure, and forbidding its officials to release such information, the State has taken virtually every step imaginable to prevent what happened here. This case presents a far cry, then, from *Cox Broadcasting* or *Oklahoma Publishing*, where the State asked the news media not to publish information it had made generally available to the public: here, the State is not asking the media to do the State's job in the first instance. Unfortunately, as this case illustrates, mistakes happen: even when States take measures to "avoid" disclosure, sometimes rape victims' names are found out. As I see it, it is not too much to ask the press, in instances such as this, to respect simple standards of decency and refrain from publishing a victims' name, address, and/or phone number. . . .

. . . By holding that only "a state interest of the highest order" permits the State to penalize the publication of truthful information, and by holding that protecting a rape victim's right to privacy is not among those state interests of the highest order, the Court accepts appellant's invitation to obliterate one of the most noteworthy legal inventions of the 20th century: the tort of the publication of private facts. Even if the Court's opinion does not say as much today, such obliteration will follow inevitably from the Court's conclusion here. . . .

NOTES & QUESTIONS

1. ***The Government's Responsibility for Leaking the Information.*** What more could the state have done to protect the information? Florida made it a crime to disseminate the information. The state recognized that the police might make a mistake in certain cases and accidentally fail to redact a rape victim's name from the report. To protect against this, signs were put up outside the room notifying the press not to record a rape victim's name that was inadvertently left on the report. The Court did not dispute that the government could refuse to divulge the rape victim's name. If the government is not required to divulge the name, what is the problem with the government making it available and then punishing its further disclosure?
2. ***The Legality of How the Information Was Obtained.*** The Court relies in part on the fact that the information was "legally available." If the journalist had stolen a confidential police report and published the information, would the Court's holding have been different? Since the Florida law proscribed both

the government dissemination of the information and the press publication of it, was the information "legally available"?

3. ***The Future of the Public Disclosure Tort After* Florida Star.** What effect does *Florida Star* have on the public disclosure tort? Rodney Smolla writes that the public disclosure tort exists "more 'in the books' than in practice."[53] Commentators describe the tort as "alive, but on life support"[54] and as "a phantom tort."[55] According to Jacqueline Rolfs: "Given the narrow class of information that fulfills the *Florida Star* requirements, the tort can no longer be an effective tool for protecting individual privacy."[56] Peter Edelman contends: "The Court paid lip service to the possibility that a private fact plaintiff may recover in some cases, but its decisions leave little hope for vindication of such a plaintiff's rights."[57] Do you agree with these characterizations?

   Consider Daniel Solove:

   > Many have read *Florida Star* as a broad indication that restrictions on the disclosure of true information are unconstitutional. Nevertheless, this case can be read very narrowly. The Court suggested that the Florida statute was far too broad. The statute applied "regardless of whether the identity of the victim is already known throughout the community; whether the victim has voluntarily called public attention to the offense; or whether the identity of the victim [had] otherwise become a reasonable subject of public concern." The law focused only on the nature of the information, rather than on whether each particular use of a rape victim's name in a specific context would be of public or private concern. *Florida Star* can be construed to suggest that a law adopting a less categorical approach—by addressing the use of the identifying data more contextually—might not be subject to strict scrutiny under the First Amendment.[58]

   Under this analysis, how could the Florida statute be rewritten to pass constitutional muster?

4. ***Free Speech and Privacy: Weighing the Values.*** Eugene Volokh argues that both normatively and doctrinally, free speech considerations outweigh privacy:

   > . . . [T]he speech vs. privacy and speech vs. speech tensions are not tensions between constitutional rights on both sides. The Constitution presumptively prohibits government restrictions on speech and perhaps some government re-

---

[53] Rodney A. Smolla, *Privacy and the First Amendment Right to Gather News*, 67 Geo. Wash. L. Rev. 1097 (1999).

[54] Richard S. Murphy, *Property Rights in Personal Information: An Economic Defense of Privacy*, 84 Geo. L.J. 2381, 2388 (1996). *But see* John A. Jurata, Jr., *Comment, The Tort That Refuses to Go Away: The Subtle Reemergence of Public Disclosure of Private Facts*, 36 San Diego L. Rev. 489 (1999).

[55] Phillip E. DeLaTorre, *Resurrecting a Sunken Ship: An Analysis of Current Judicial Attitudes Toward Public Disclosure Claims*, 38 Sw. L.J. 1151, 1184 (1985).

[56] Jacqueline K. Rolfs, The Florida Star v. B.J.F.: *The Beginning of the End for the Tort of Public Disclosure*, 1990 Wis. L. Rev. 1107, 1128.

[57] Peter B. Edelman, *Free Press v. Privacy: Haunted by the Ghost of Justice Black*, 68 Tex. L. Rev. 1195, 1207 (1990).

[58] Solove, *Virtues of Knowing Less, supra.*

> velation of personal information, but it says nothing about interference with speech or revelation of personal information by nongovernmental speakers. . .
>
> [I]s it constitutional for the government to suppress certain kinds of speech in order to protect dignity, prevent disrespectful behavior, prevent emotional distress, or to protect a supposed civil right not to be talked about? Under current constitutional doctrine, the answer seems to be no. . . . Even offensive, outrageous, disrespectful, and dignity-assaulting speech is constitutionally protected.
>
> And there is good reason for this approach. All of us can imagine some speech that is so offensive and at the same time so valueless that we would feel no loss if it were restricted, but the trouble is that each of us has a somewhat different vision of which speech should qualify. . . .
>
> . . . [A] good deal of speech that reveals information about people, including speech that some describe as being of merely "private concern," is actually of eminently legitimate interest. Some of it is directly relevant to the formation of general social and political opinions; most of it is of interest to people deciding how to behave in their daily lives, whether daily business or daily personal lives — whom to approach to do business, whom to trust with their money, and the like.[59]

In contrast to Volokh, Daniel Solove argues that privacy fares quite well when balanced against free speech. Solove argues that "speech of private concern does not strongly further the interests justifying free speech. If society wants to promote the interests justifying free speech, a vigorous protection of speech at the expense of privacy can, in fact, impair these interests." Free speech is often justified as essential for individual autonomy, but Solove contends that "[t]here is no clear reason why the autonomy of speakers or listeners should prevail over that of the harmed individuals." Regarding the theory that free speech is valued because it promotes democratic self-governance, Solove argues:

> [S]peech of private concern often does not promote democratic self-governance. For example, it is difficult to justify how the sale from one company to another of mailing lists about people's hobbies and incomes promotes democratic self-governance. Additionally, the reporting of one's personal secrets often does not illuminate the sphere of politics. In fact, privacy protections against disclosure strongly promote democratic self-governance. . . .
>
> Privacy encourages uninhibited speech by enabling individuals to direct frank communication to those people they trust and who will not cause them harm because of what they say. Important discourse, especially communication essential for democratic participation, often takes place in microlevel contexts (between two people or in small groups) rather than in macrolevel contexts (public rallies or nationwide television broadcasts).

---

[59] Eugene Volokh, *Freedom of Speech and Information Privacy: The Troubling Implications of a Right to Stop People from Speaking About You,* 52 Stan. L. Rev. 1049, 1089, 1092-93, 1107, 1112-15 (2000). For other free speech critiques of privacy protections, see Thomas I. Emerson, *The System of Freedom of Expression* (1970); Solveig Singleton, *Privacy Versus the First Amendment: A Skeptical Approach,* 11 Fordham Intell. Prop. Media & Ent. L.J. 97 (2000); Harry Kalven, Jr., *Privacy in Tort Law — Were Warren and Brandeis Wrong?*, 31 Law & Contemp. Probs. 326 (1966); Diane L. Zimmerman, *Requiem for a Heavyweight: A Farewell to Warren and Brandeis's Privacy Tort*, 68 Cornell L. Rev. 291 (1983).

> Indeed, a significant amount of political discussion occurs not on soapboxes or street corners, but within private conversations. . . . Therefore, privacy protections do not just inhibit free speech; they can promote it as well.

Solove argues that the value of speech of private concern is significantly less than that of public concern: "Privacy regulations that promote speech should not simply be viewed in terms of their speech-restrictive elements; they should be understood holistically, in terms of their overall purpose in the protection of free speech. We protect free speech to promote certain ends. Volokh loses sight of the ends of the First Amendment by focusing too heavily on the means."[60]

5. ***The First Amendment and Threats to People's Private Lives.*** In *Planned Parenthood v. American Coalition of Life Activists*, 290 F.3d 1058 (9th Cir. 2002) (en banc), the American Coalition of Life Activists (ACLA), an antiabortion advocacy group, provided a series of dossiers it assembled on doctors, clinic employees, politicians, judges, and other abortion rights supporters to Neal Horsley, an antiabortion activist, who posted the information on his website entitled the "Nuremberg Files." The "Nuremberg Files" dossiers included doctors' names, photos, Social Security numbers, home addresses, descriptions of their cars, and information about their families. The website marked the names of doctors who had been killed with a black line through them and the names of wounded doctors shaded in gray. The website did not contain any explicit threats against the doctors. The website caused the doctors great fear, and several protected themselves by wearing bulletproof vests, closing all the curtains to the windows of their homes, and even asking for the protection of the U.S. Marshals. Some of the doctors sued ACLA alleging a variety of causes of action including the Freedom of Access to Clinic Entrances Act of 1994 (FACE), 18 U.S.C. § 248.

   A jury awarded the doctors $107 million in actual and punitive damages. The Ninth Circuit, en banc, affirmed the actual damages and reversed on punitive damages. The court held that the "Nuremberg Files" (in combination with "wanted" posters of various doctors) constituted a "true threat" to the doctors' lives under FACE, and such true threats were not protected under the First Amendment. Although speech advocating violence is protected, speech "directed to inciting or producing imminent lawless action" is not. "Violence is not a protected value. Nor is a *true threat* of violence *with intent to intimidate*. . . . ACLA was not staking out a position of debate but of threatened demise." According to a dissent by Judge Kozinski: "The Nuremberg Files website is clearly an expression of a political point of view. . . . [S]peech, including the intimidating message, does not constitute a direct threat because there is no evidence other than the speech itself that the speakers intend to resort to physical violence if their threat is not heeded." Would the doctors have a cause of action for public disclosure of private facts? Would the First Amendment prohibit liability on this basis?

---

[60] Daniel J. Solove, *The Virtues of Knowing Less: Justifying Privacy Protections Against Disclosure*, 53 Duke L.J. 967, 988-98 (2003).

Recently, antiabortion protesters have begun to photograph individuals entering abortion clinics. A loose network of activists across the country photographs women and places the photos on websites. Sometimes personal information, such as license plate numbers or medical records, is posted next to the photograph. Should these activities be actionable? What does the Restatement suggest? Based on the *American Coalition of Life Activists* case above, would liability for this activity run afoul of the First Amendment?

6. ***Restricting Speech to Protect Speech: Cyber Civil Rights.*** Danielle Citron argues that online attacks, especially those against women, can have the effect of silencing them. In one incident, a group of anonymous people engaged in extensive online harassment of blogger Kathy Sierra. They threatened to rape and strangle her, and posted doctored photos of her with a noose near her neck. She stopped blogging and canceled public speaking appearances out of fear. Citron argues:

> One of free speech's most important functions is promoting individual autonomy. This view urges that people be free to choose their own path. Free speech facilitates self-mastery, allowing people to author their own narratives. . . .
>
> Restraining a mob's most destructive assaults is essential to defending the expressive autonomy and equality of its victims. Preventing mobs from driving vulnerable people offline would "advance the reasons why we protect free speech in the first place," even though it would inevitably chill some speech of online mobs. Free from mob attacks, victims might continue to blog, join online discussions, and generally express themselves on public issues. Protecting them from grotesque defamation, threats, invasions of privacy, and technological attacks would allow them to be candid about their ideas.
>
> Although online mobs express themselves and their autonomy through their assaults, their actions also implicate their victims' autonomy and ability to participate in political and social discourse. Self-expression should receive no protection if its sole purpose is to extinguish the self-expression of another. . . . Rarely is that more true than when one group of voices consciously exploits the Internet's aggregating power to silence others and its disaggregative power to escape social responsibility for the group's actions.

Citron argues that civil rights law should apply in this context:

> Online assaults motivated by race discrimination that interfere with an individual's ability to make a living can support civil and criminal actions. Title 42 U.S.C. § 1981 guarantees members of racial minorities "the same right in every State . . . to make and enforce contracts . . . as is enjoyed by white citizens . . . ." A plaintiff must show that the defendant intended to discriminate on the basis of race and that the discrimination concerned the "making and enforcing" of contracts. Courts have upheld § 1981 damages in cases where masked mob members used tactics of intimidation to prevent members of racial minorities from "making a living" in their chosen field. Section 1981 remedies "purely private" acts of racial discrimination and thus does not require state action.
>
> Similarly, 18 U.S.C. § 245(b)(2)(C), a provision of the Civil Rights Act of 1968, criminalizes "force or threat[s] of force" designed to intimidate or

> interfere with a person's private employment due to that person's race, religion, or national origin. . . .
>
> Gender discrimination that interferes with a person's ability to make a living can be pursued under Title VII of the Civil Rights Act of 1964, which sanctions those who intimidate, threaten, or coerce, or attempt to intimidate, threaten, or coerce someone with the purpose of interfering with employment opportunities due to their gender. The Attorney General can file civil suits for injunctive relief. . . .
>
> Because the Internet fuses our public and private lives and is a workplace for many, online attacks on vulnerable individuals often interfere with their equal right to pursue work. For instance, women who stop blogging in the face of an online mob's attack lose advertising revenue and opportunities for advancement. . . .
>
> Online mob attacks also implicate state laws penalizing those who harass or stalk another by communicating words, images, or language through electronic mail or the Internet, directed to a specific person, which would cause a reasonable person substantial emotional distress or fear of bodily harm. Some states explicitly criminalize posting messages with the intent to urge or incite others to harass a particular individual.[61]

Is the "sole purpose" of those who engage in online attacks of others to silence them? How can we draw the line between harassment triggering civil rights laws and mere crude speech, which is common online? To what extent should individuals be responsible for the actions of the mob? Suppose each individual said one or two nasty things, but collectively, the impact was severe. How should the law handle such an instance? Should the First Amendment look not just to the extent to which the law is restricting speech but also to the extent to which the law's restrictions are promoting speech?

7. ***The Value of Gossip.*** Diane Zimmerman questions the very existence of the public disclosure tort. She argues that the tort should be "scuttled" as inconsistent with the First Amendment. According to Zimmerman, the "idle gossip" Warren and Brandeis complained about is highly valuable speech, entitled to no less protection than any other form of speech:

> . . . [F]rom the perspective of the anthropologist and sociologist, gossip is a basic form of information exchange that teaches about other lifestyles and attitudes, and through which community values are changed or reinforced. This description is a far cry from that of Warren and Brandeis, which characterized gossip as a trivializing influence that destroys "robustness of thought and delicacy of feeling" and serves the interests primarily of the "prurient" and the "indolent."
>
> Gossip thus appears to be a normal and necessary part of life for all but the rare hermit among us. Perceived in this way, gossip contributes directly to the first amendment "marketplace of ideas," and the comparative weight assigned to an interest in its limitation merits careful consideration.[62]

---

[61] Danielle Keats Citron, *Cyber Civil Rights,* 89 B.U. L. Rev. 61, 92-93, 97-98 (2009); *see also* Danielle Keats Citron, *Law's Expressive Value in Combating Cyber Gender Harassment,* 108 Mich. L. Rev. 373 (2009).

[62] Diane L. Zimmerman, *Requiem for a Heavyweight: A Farewell to Warren and Brandeis's Privacy Tort*, 68 Cornell L. Rev. 291, 333-34, 340 (1983). Katherine Strandburg contends that society does not exalt unfettered gossip and that it is regulated by norms of restraint (which she

Do you agree with Zimmerman about the high value of gossip? Does the value of gossip outweigh the harms it causes?

8. ***Revenge Porn.*** A growing privacy invasion is nonconsensual pornography (known as "revenge porn") — the nonconsensual disclosure of a sexually explicit image or video of a person. For example, an ex-boyfriend may have a nude photo of his ex-girlfriend and post it online to seek revenge by embarrassing her. Some websites have emerged that solicit and distribute revenge porn.

To what extent can victims use the privacy torts and other laws discussed in this chapter to obtain a remedy? Which torts would be most suitable? How strong a case would a plaintiff have under these torts? One practical difficulty is that defendants often lack much money to pay if a plaintiff prevails, and thus lawyers do not want to take these cases on a contingent fee basis.

If victims took the photos or videos themselves, they could bring civil copyright claims against the people who posted them. A person who creates the photo or video has common law copyright in the material, and this branch of intellectual property law provides strong protections.

A movement has begun to criminalize revenge porn. California Attorney General Kamala Harris brought extortion and identity theft charges against Kevin Bolleart who operated a website called UGotPosted. Bolleart urged users to post revenge porn and then charged a fee to victims to have the material removed.

The federal cyber stalking statute has been invoked to pursue defendants. *See* 18 U.S.C. § 2261A. For example in *United States v. Petrovic*, 701 F.3d 849 (8th Cir. 2012), a defendant was convicted of cyber stalking because he posted revenge porn of his ex-wife online and then tried to extort money from her to remove it. In *United States v. Shepard,* 2012 WL 113027 (D. Ariz. Jan. 13, 2012), a defendant was convicted of cyber stalking for posting his ex-girlfriend's nude photos online in porn advertisements. According to Danielle Citron, however, the federal cyber stalking statute has rarely been invoked, with just ten cases from 2010 to 2013.[63]

Seven states have criminalized revenge porn. In 2004, New Jersey adopted the first criminal invasion of privacy statute prohibiting the disclosure of someone's sexually explicit images without that person's consent. *See* N.J. Stat. Ann. § 2C:14-9. Under New Jersey law, a person commits criminal invasion of privacy if, "knowing that he is not licensed or privileged to do so, he discloses any photograph, film, videotape, recording or any other reproduction of the image of another person whose intimate parts are exposed or who is engaged in an act of sexual penetration or sexual contact, unless that person has consented to such disclosure." The crime carries a prison sentence of between three and five years and monetary penalties of up to $30,000.

In 2010, a Rutgers University student, Dahrun Ravi, was charged under the New Jersey statute after he set up a webcam to capture his roommate, Tyler Clementi, having sex with a man. He then streamed it online to watch with

calls "willpower norms"). Katherine J. Strandburg, *Privacy, Rationality, and Temptation: A Theory of Willpower Norms*, 57 Rutgers L. Rev. 1235 (2005).

[63] *See* Danielle Keats Citron, *Hate Crimes in Cyberspace* (2014).

several others. When he learned about what happened, Clementi committed suicide. Among other things, Ravi was convicted of two crimes: (1) the nonconsensual observation of Clementi having sex; and (2) the nonconsensual disclosure of the sex video. *See State v. Parsons*, 2011 WL 6089210 (N.J. Super. Ct. App. Div. 2011).

Six other states have criminalized revenge porn: Alaska, Arizona, California, Idaho, Maryland, and Utah. These laws vary in their effectiveness and scope. For example, California's revenge porn law requires that the defendant have the intent to cause the victim substantial emotional distress and does not cover images that victims take of themselves. However, a study revealed that 80 percent of revenge porn cases involve images that victims themselves took and then shared with their partners with the understanding that they would be kept private. Revenge porn bills are pending in many other states.

Should revenge porn be criminalized? Some contend that civil lawsuits are the more appropriate way to address the problem. On the other hand, consider the following argument by Mary Anne Franks, a law professor who has helped states draft revenge porn laws, writing with Citron:

> At a fundamental level, nonconsensual pornography is an extreme invasion of privacy, one that causes serious and often irreversible harm to a person's physical and emotional well-being, damage to their reputations, and can even threaten their financial security. As modern societies, we impose criminal punishments for far less. We punish theft, drug possession and destruction of property. So why don't we punish revenge porn?[64]

Do revenge porn laws violate the First Amendment? Consider Citron's argument:

> Maintaining the confidentiality of someone's sexually explicit images has little impact on a poster's expression of ideas. Revenge porn does not promote civic character or educate us about cultural, religious, or political issues. On the other hand, the nonconsensual disclosure of a person's nude images would assuredly chill private expression. Without any expectation of privacy, victims would not share their naked images. With an expectation of privacy, victims would be more inclined to engage in communications of a sexual nature. Such sharing may enhance intimacy among couples and the willingness to be forthright in other aspects of relationships.[65]

Some have challenged revenge porn laws as not being sufficiently narrow and clear and thus raising concerns of overbreadth and vagueness. In defense of these statutes, Citron has argued that they can avoid these problems if they make clear that (1) the "images do not concern matters of public importance"; (2) the defendant shared the revenge porn intentionally; and (3) the defendant knew that sharing the revenge porn would violate the victim's reasonable expectation of privacy or reasonable expectation that the image or video

---

[64] Mary Anne Franks & Danielle Citron, *It's Simple: Criminalize Revenge Porn, or Let Men Punish Women They Don't Like*, The Guardian, Apr. 17, 2014, http://www.theguardian.com/commentisfree/2014/apr/17/revenge-porn-must-be-criminalized-laws.

[65] Citron, *Hate Crimes in Cyberspace, supra.*

would remain confidential.[66] Would these requirements cure overbreadth and vagueness concerns?

Revenge porn often does not fall into unprotected categories of speech such as obscenity or true threats. Does this mean that it cannot be criminalized? Revenge porn would constitute a violation of one or more of the privacy torts, but should criminalization be treated differently?

Lee Rowland, a lawyer with the ACLU, argues that "revenge porn laws tend to criminalize the sharing of nude images that people lawfully own."[67] Rowland also raises concerns that such laws could potentially criminalize the activities of many teenagers.

Free speech proponents also raise concerns of a slippery slope if revenge porn is a crime. What if all violations of the public disclosure of private facts tort were criminalized?

Citron pushes back against any slippery slope, arguing that "[n]ude photos and sex tapes are amongst the most private and intimate facts; the public has no legitimate interest in seeing someone's nude images without that person's consent."[68] Are images and videos different from other things? Could merely writing about the private sexual activities of another person be criminalized?

Citron also defends revenge porn criminalization because a breach of confidentiality is involved, and "confidentiality regulations are less troubling from a First Amendment perspective because they penalize the breach of an assumed or implied duty rather than the injury caused by the publication of words. Instead of prohibiting a certain kind of speech, confidentiality law enforces express or implied promises and shared expectations."[69] Is revenge porn sufficiently distinct to warrant criminal penalties? Are Citron's defenses sufficient to address the slippery slope concerns?

9. ***Contracts, Promises, and the First Amendment.*** Does the enforcement of a contract of confidentiality against a media entity trigger First Amendment scrutiny? In *Cohen v. Cowles Media Co.*, 501 U.S. 663 (1991), a journalist had promised a source confidentiality but nevertheless published the source's name. The source sued and obtained a promissory estoppel damage award. According to the Court, *Florida Star* did not control because "generally applicable laws do not offend the First Amendment simply because their enforcement against the press has incidental effects on its ability to gather and report the news." Why is a suit under contract or promissory estoppel different from a suit under tort, such as public disclosure of private facts?

After *Cohen,* the courts apply two dramatically different rules when it comes to free speech and civil liability. As Daniel Solove and Neil Richards explain:

---

[66] Danielle Citron, *How to Make Revenge Porn a Crime* Slate, Nov. 7, 2013, http://www.slate.com/articles/news_and_politics/jurisprudence/2013/11/making_revenge_porn_a_crime_without_trampling_free_speech.html. For more background, see Danielle Keats Citron and Mary Anne Franks, *Criminalizing Revenge Porn*, forthcoming Wake Forest L. Rev.

[67] Liz Halloran, *Race To Stop 'Revenge Porn' Raises Free Speech Worries*, NPR, Mar. 6, 2014, http://www.npr.org/blogs/itsallpolitics/2014/03/06/286388840/race-to-stop-revenge-porn-raises-free-speech-worries.

[68] See Franks & Citron, *Criminalizing Revenge Porn, supra.*

[69] *Id.*

> For a panoply of torts for harms caused by speech, the well-settled rule is that the First Amendment provides full protection. There are, however, many instances where the Supreme Court applies virtually no First Amendment scrutiny when civil liability implicates speech. In particular, many lawsuits involving the enforcement of contracts or property rights do not trigger any significant First Amendment scrutiny. Thus, there are two radically different ways that the First Amendment addresses civil liability involving speech — either full First Amendment protection or virtually none at all. . . .
>
> Suppose a newspaper obtains the name of a rape victim from a police report and publishes it. The rape victim sues the newspaper under the privacy tort of public disclosure of private facts. Does the First Amendment protect the newspaper? If the story is newsworthy, then the answer is yes. . . .
>
> Now suppose that a rape victim speaks anonymously to a newspaper, which promises not to publish her name. The newspaper publishes a highly newsworthy story about the rape victim, and it decides to break its promise and reveal her identity. She sues for promissory estoppel and breach of implied contract. Does the First Amendment protect the newspaper? The answer is no. . . .
>
> Why do these cases have such different outcomes under the First Amendment? Both involve civil liability, free speech, and newsworthy information.

Solove and Richards point out that contract and tort are often not distinct categories but bleed into one another. Certain torts, such as the breach of confidentiality tort, are premised on notions of implied contractual duties. They propose a new way to determine which First Amendment rule should apply to certain forms of civil liability:

> We suggest that when government power is used to dictate the terms of civil duties not to speak (what we call the "duty-defining power"), the special dangers of this power warrant application of the First Amendment. In contrast, when private parties create the content of speech-restrictive rules, the First Amendment should not apply.[70]

Should a distinction be made in free speech protection for various forms of civil liability? Does focusing on government power serve as a coherent way to make the distinction? If not, what approach would work better?

BARTNICKI V. VOPPER

532 U.S. 514 (2001)

STEVENS, J. These cases raise an important question concerning what degree of protection, if any, the First Amendment provides to speech that discloses the contents of an illegally intercepted communication. That question is both novel and narrow. Despite the fact that federal law has prohibited such disclosures since 1934, this is the first time that we have confronted such an issue. . . .

---

[70] Daniel J. Solove & Neil M. Richards, *Rethinking Free Speech and Civil Liability*, 109 Colum. L. Rev. 1650, 1651-52, 1686 (2009).

During 1992 and most of 1993, the Pennsylvania State Education Association, a union representing the teachers at the Wyoming Valley West High School, engaged in collective-bargaining negotiations with the school board. Petitioner Kane, then the president of the local union, testified that the negotiations were "'contentious'" and received "a lot of media attention." In May 1993, petitioner Bartnicki, who was acting as the union's "chief negotiator," used the cellular phone in her car to call Kane and engage in a lengthy conversation about the status of the negotiations. An unidentified person intercepted and recorded that call.

In their conversation, Kane and Bartnicki discussed the timing of a proposed strike, difficulties created by public comment on the negotiations, and the need for a dramatic response to the board's intransigence. At one point, Kane said: "'If they're not gonna move for three percent, we're gonna have to go to their, their homes. . . . To blow off their front porches, we'll have to do some work on some of those guys. (PAUSES). Really, uh, really and truthfully because this is, you know, this is bad news. (UNDECIPHERABLE).'"

In the early fall of 1993, the parties accepted a non-binding arbitration proposal that was generally favorable to the teachers. In connection with news reports about the settlement, respondent Vopper, a radio commentator who had been critical of the union in the past, played a tape of the intercepted conversation on his public affairs talk show. Another station also broadcast the tape, and local newspapers published its contents. After filing suit against Vopper and other representatives of the media, Bartnicki and Kane (hereinafter petitioners) learned through discovery that Vopper had obtained the tape from Jack Yocum, the head of a local taxpayers' organization that had opposed the union's demands throughout the negotiations. Yocum, who was added as a defendant, testified that he had found the tape in his mailbox shortly after the interception and recognized the voices of Bartnicki and Kane. Yocum played the tape for some members of the school board, and later delivered the tape itself to Vopper. . . .

In their amended complaint, petitioners alleged that their telephone conversation had been surreptitiously intercepted by an unknown person using an electronic device, that Yocum had obtained a tape of that conversation, and that he intentionally disclosed it to Vopper, as well as other individuals and media representatives. Thereafter, Vopper and other members of the media repeatedly published the contents of that conversation. The amended complaint alleged that each of the defendants "knew or had reason to know" that the recording of the private telephone conversation had been obtained by means of an illegal interception. Relying on both federal and Pennsylvania statutory provisions, petitioners sought actual damages, statutory damages, punitive damages, and attorney's fees and costs. . . .

[Title 18 U.S.C. § 2511(1)(c) provides that any person who "intentionally discloses, or endeavors to disclose, to any other person the contents of any wire, oral, or electronic communication, knowing or having reason to know that the information was obtained through the interception of a wire, oral, or electronic communication in violation of this subsection; . . . shall be punished. . . ." The Pennsylvania Act contains a similar provision.]

. . . [W]e accept respondents' submission on three factual matters that serve to distinguish most of the cases that have arisen under § 2511. First, respondents played no part in the illegal interception. Rather, they found out about the interception only after it occurred, and in fact never learned the identity of the person or persons who made the interception. Second, their access to the information on the tapes was obtained lawfully, even though the information itself was intercepted unlawfully by someone else. Third, the subject matter of the conversation was a matter of public concern. If the statements about the labor negotiations had been made in a public arena — during a bargaining session, for example — they would have been newsworthy. This would also be true if a third party had inadvertently overheard Bartnicki making the same statements to Kane when the two thought they were alone.

We agree with petitioners that § 2511(1)(c), as well as its Pennsylvania analog, is in fact a content-neutral law of general applicability. . . . In this case, the basic purpose of the statute at issue is to "protec[t] the privacy of wire[, electronic,] and oral communications." S. Rep. No. 1097, 90th Cong., 2d Sess., 66 (1968). The statute does not distinguish based on the content of the intercepted conversations, nor is it justified by reference to the content of those conversations. Rather, the communications at issue are singled out by virtue of the fact that they were illegally intercepted — by virtue of the source, rather than the subject matter.

On the other hand, the naked prohibition against disclosures is fairly characterized as a regulation of pure speech. . . .

As a general matter, "state action to punish the publication of truthful information seldom can satisfy constitutional standards." *Smith v. Daily Mail Publishing Co.*, 443 U.S. 97, 102 (1979). More specifically, this Court has repeatedly held that "if a newspaper lawfully obtains truthful information about a matter of public significance then state officials may not constitutionally punish publication of the information, absent a need . . . of the highest order." *Id.*, at 103; *see also Florida Star v. B.J.F.*; *Landmark Communications, Inc. v. Virginia*. . . .

. . . [T]he issue here is this: "Where the punished publisher of information has obtained the information in question in a manner lawful in itself but from a source who has obtained it unlawfully, may the government punish the ensuing publication of that information based on the defect in a chain?" . . .

The Government identifies two interests served by the statute — first, the interest in removing an incentive for parties to intercept private conversations, and second, the interest in minimizing the harm to persons whose conversations have been illegally intercepted. . . .

The normal method of deterring unlawful conduct is to impose an appropriate punishment on the person who engages in it. If the sanctions that presently attach to a violation of § 2511(1)(a) do not provide sufficient deterrence, perhaps those sanctions should be made more severe. But it would be quite remarkable to hold that speech by a law-abiding possessor of information can be suppressed in order to deter conduct by a non-law-abiding third party. . . .

The Government's second argument, however, is considerably stronger. Privacy of communication is an important interest, and Title III's restrictions are intended to protect that interest, thereby "encouraging the uninhibited exchange of ideas and information among private parties. . . ." Moreover, the fear of public disclosure of private conversations might well have a chilling effect on private speech. . . .

Accordingly, it seems to us that there are important interests to be considered on both sides of the constitutional calculus. . . .

In this case, privacy concerns give way when balanced against the interest in publishing matters of public importance. As Warren and Brandeis stated in their classic law review article: "The right of privacy does not prohibit any publication of matter which is of public or general interest." *The Right to Privacy*, 4 Harv. L. Rev. 193, 214 (1890). One of the costs associated with participation in public affairs is an attendant loss of privacy. . . .

Our opinion in *New York Times Co. v. Sullivan*, 376 U.S. 254 (1964), reviewed many of the decisions that settled the "general proposition that freedom of expression upon public questions is secured by the First Amendment." . . .

We think it clear that parallel reasoning requires the conclusion that a stranger's illegal conduct does not suffice to remove the First Amendment shield from speech about a matter of public concern. The months of negotiations over the proper level of compensation for teachers at the Wyoming Valley West High School were unquestionably a matter of public concern, and respondents were clearly engaged in debate about that concern. . . .

BREYER, J. joined by O'CONNOR, J. concurring. I join the Court's opinion because I agree with its "narrow" holding, limited to the special circumstances present here: (1) the radio broadcasters acted lawfully (up to the time of final public disclosure); and (2) the information publicized involved a matter of unusual public concern, namely a threat of potential physical harm to others. I write separately to explain why, in my view, the Court's holding does not imply a significantly broader constitutional immunity for the media. . . .

As the Court recognizes, the question before us—a question of immunity from statutorily imposed civil liability—implicates competing constitutional concerns. The statutes directly interfere with free expression in that they prevent the media from publishing information. At the same time, they help to protect personal privacy—an interest here that includes not only the "right to be let alone." Given these competing interests "on both sides of the equation, the key question becomes one of proper fit."

I would ask whether the statutes strike a reasonable balance between their speech-restricting and speech-enhancing consequences. Or do they instead impose restrictions on speech that are disproportionate when measured against their corresponding privacy and speech-related benefits, taking into account the kind, the importance, and the extent of these benefits, as well as the need for the restrictions in order to secure those benefits? What this Court has called "strict scrutiny"—with its strong presumption against constitutionality—is normally out of place where, as here, important competing constitutional interests are implicated. The statutory restrictions before us directly enhance private speech. The statutes ensure the privacy of telephone conversations much as a trespass statute ensures privacy within the home. That assurance of privacy helps to overcome our natural reluctance to discuss private matters when we fear that our private conversations may become public. And the statutory restrictions consequently encourage conversations that otherwise might not take place.

At the same time, these statutes restrict public speech directly, deliberately, and of necessity. They include media publication within their scope not simply as a means, say, to deter interception, but also as an end. Media dissemination of an intimate conversation to an entire community will often cause the speakers serious harm over and above the harm caused by an initial disclosure to the person who intercepted the phone call. . . .

As a general matter, despite the statutes' direct restrictions on speech, the Federal Constitution must tolerate laws of this kind because of the importance of these privacy and speech-related objectives. . . . Rather than broadly forbid this kind of legislative enactment, the Constitution demands legislative efforts to tailor the laws in order reasonably to reconcile media freedom with personal, speech-related privacy.

Nonetheless, looked at more specifically, the statutes, as applied in these circumstances, do not reasonably reconcile the competing constitutional objectives. Rather, they disproportionately interfere with media freedom. For one thing, the broadcasters here engaged in no unlawful activity other than the ultimate publication of the information another had previously obtained. They "neither encouraged nor participated directly or indirectly in the interception." No one claims that they ordered, counselled, encouraged, or otherwise aided or abetted the interception, the later delivery of the tape by the interceptor to an intermediary, or the tape's still later delivery by the intermediary to the media. . . .

For another thing, the speakers had little or no *legitimate* interest in maintaining the privacy of the particular conversation. That conversation involved a suggestion about "blow[ing] off . . . front porches" and "do[ing] some work on some of those guys," thereby raising a significant concern for the safety of others. Where publication of private information constitutes a wrongful act, the law recognizes a privilege allowing the reporting of threats to public safety. . . .

Further, the speakers themselves, the president of a teacher's union and the union's chief negotiator, were "limited public figures," for they voluntarily engaged in a public controversy. They thereby subjected themselves to somewhat greater public scrutiny and had a lesser interest in privacy than an individual engaged in purely private affairs. . . .

Here, the speakers' legitimate privacy expectations are unusually low, and the public interest in defeating those expectations is unusually high. Given these circumstances, along with the lawful nature of respondents' behavior, the statutes' enforcement would disproportionately harm media freedom.

REHNQUIST, C.J., joined by SCALIA and THOMAS, JJ., dissenting. Technology now permits millions of important and confidential conversations to occur through a vast system of electronic networks. These advances, however, raise significant privacy concerns. We are placed in the uncomfortable position of not knowing who might have access to our personal and business e-mails, our medical and financial records, or our cordless and cellular telephone conversations. In an attempt to prevent some of the most egregious violations of privacy, the United States, the District of Columbia, and 40 States have enacted laws prohibiting the intentional interception and knowing disclosure of electronic communications. The Court holds that all of these statutes violate the First Amendment insofar as the illegally intercepted conversation touches upon a matter of "public concern," an amorphous concept that the Court does not even attempt to define. But the Court's decision diminishes, rather than enhances, the purposes of the First Amendment: chilling the speech of the millions of Americans who rely upon electronic technology to communicate each day. . . .

The Court correctly observes that these are "content-neutral law[s] of general applicability" which serve recognized interests of the "highest order": "the interest in individual privacy and . . . in fostering private speech." It nonetheless subjects these laws to the strict scrutiny normally reserved for governmental attempts to censor different viewpoints or ideas. There is scant support, either in precedent or in reason, for the Court's tacit application of strict scrutiny.

A content-neutral regulation will be sustained if

> "'it furthers an important or substantial governmental interest; if the governmental interest is unrelated to the suppression of free expression; and if the incidental restriction on alleged First Amendment freedoms is no greater than is essential to the furtherance of that interest.'" *Turner Broadcasting System, Inc. v. FCC*, 512 U.S. 622, 662 (1994). . . .

The Court's attempt to avoid these precedents by reliance upon the *Daily Mail* string of newspaper cases is unpersuasive. In these cases, we held that statutes prohibiting the media from publishing certain truthful information — the name of a rape victim, *Florida Star v. B. J. F.*; *Cox Broadcasting Corp. v. Cohn*, the confidential proceedings before a state judicial review commission, *Landmark Communications, Inc. v. Virginia*, and the name of a juvenile defendant, *Daily Mail* — violated the First Amendment. In so doing, we stated that "if a newspaper lawfully obtains truthful information about a matter of public significance then state officials may not constitutionally punish publication of the information, absent a need to further a state interest of the highest order." *Daily Mail*. Neither this *Daily Mail* principle nor any other aspect of these cases, however, justifies the Court's imposition of strict scrutiny here. . . .

These laws are content neutral; they only regulate information that was illegally obtained; they do not restrict republication of what is already in the public domain; they impose no special burdens upon the media; they have a scienter requirement to provide fair warning; and they promote the privacy and free speech of those using cellular telephones. It is hard to imagine a more narrowly tailored prohibition of the disclosure of illegally intercepted communications, and it distorts our precedents to review these statutes under the often fatal standard of strict scrutiny. These laws therefore should be upheld if they further a substantial governmental interest unrelated to the suppression of free speech, and they do. . .

The "dry up the market" theory, which posits that it is possible to deter an illegal act that is difficult to police by preventing the wrongdoer from enjoying the fruits of the crime, is neither novel nor implausible. It is a time-tested theory that undergirds numerous laws, such as the prohibition of the knowing possession of stolen goods. We ourselves adopted the exclusionary rule based upon similar reasoning, believing that it would "deter unreasonable searches," by removing an officer's "incentive to disregard [the Fourth Amendment]."

The same logic applies here and demonstrates that the incidental restriction on alleged First Amendment freedoms is no greater than essential to further the interest of protecting the privacy of individual communications. Were there no prohibition on disclosure, an unlawful eavesdropper who wanted to disclose the conversation could anonymously launder the interception through a third party and thereby avoid detection. Indeed, demand for illegally obtained private information would only increase if it could be disclosed without repercussion. The law against interceptions, which the Court agrees is valid, would be utterly ineffectual without these antidisclosure provisions. . . .

These statutes undeniably protect this venerable right of privacy. Concomitantly, they further the First Amendment rights of the parties to the conversation. . . . The chilling effect of the Court's decision upon these private conversations will surely be great. . . .

Although public persons may have forgone the right to live their lives screened from public scrutiny in some areas, it does not and should not follow that they also have abandoned their right to have a private conversation without fear of it being intentionally intercepted and knowingly disclosed. . . .

NOTES & QUESTIONS

1. ***Privacy and Free Speech.*** The concurrence and dissent both recognize that the statutory provisions of federal wiretap law serve to protect, rather than merely infringe, First Amendment values. According to the concurrence, the statutory provisions "directly enhance private speech," and in the words of the dissent, the statutory provisions serve to protect against "chilling the speech of millions of Americans who rely upon electronic technology to communicate each day." How should the Court analyze statutes that restrict some speech in order to promote more speech? Should such statutes be treated like laws that exclusively restrict speech?

   Consider Paul Gewirtz's critique of the majority opinion in *Bartnicki*:

   > But there is a more basic problem with Justice Stevens's approach: He looks to the content of the broadcast communication to decide whether the Constitution protects it, rather than to the circumstances under which the conversation took place. . . . [Instead, o]ne could look to whether the original communication takes place within a protected zone. If a zone is deemed a protected private zone — which can be either a place or a kind of situation — then the content of what is communicated within that zone would be irrelevant in deciding whether the First Amendment protects the media in reporting on it. The press could be sanctioned for publishing information about conversations within that zone, regardless of content. In Title III, Congress sought to protect privacy by creating such a protected zone, and made intrusions on that zone illegal. . . . Put another way, speech acts must be understood in terms of audiences as well as content. In our daily narrative transactions, we are always negotiating our relationship to an audience. Privacy is ultimately about our power to choose our audience. When privacy is invaded, we are compelled to have an audience we do not want. The Court in *Bartnicki* says that publishing the intercepted conversation contributed to public debate — but the two people speaking on their cell phones did not wish to contribute to a public debate before a public audience. Their words were taken from them by stealth and put into public debate against their will. If every private statement on a

> public subject may be forcibly disclosed because it contributes to public debate, then privacy is a dead letter. We cannot have it both ways.[71]

Would this hold true no matter what was said or who was saying it? In *Bartnicki,* it is safe to assume the comment about the bomb was not meant literally. Suppose the conversation was between two terrorists who were really planning to set off a bomb. Or suppose the conversation was the President talking to a chief advisor about covering up major corruption. Should these conversations also be protected because they are within the "protected private zone"?

2. ***The Effect of* Bartnicki *on the Public Disclosure Tort.*** According to Rodney Smolla, "*Bartnicki* accepted the premise that the conflict posed between speech and privacy is a conflict between two rights of constitutional stature. By this important measure, all nine Justices in *Bartnicki* were in agreement." Smolla reads *Bartnicki* to be "inviting the importation into First Amendment jurisprudence of the 'newsworthiness' analysis as it has developed so far in common-law cases."[72] The Court has yet to confront whether the tort of public disclosure is constitutional. As Daniel Solove observes:

> In numerous cases, the Court has articulated a public and private concern distinction, and it has applied the First Amendment to curtail restrictions on speech of public concern without answering questions about limiting speech of private concern. . . . The Court appears to view the public and private concern distinction as having significance because it has used this distinction to limit the application of heightened scrutiny to restrictions on speech of public concern. Although it has yet to address the private concern side of the distinction, the Court appears to be heading in the direction [of requiring less First Amendment protection to speech of private concern].[73]

Eugene Volokh takes issue with this conclusion:

> Though the Court has often said in dictum that political speech or public-issue speech is on the "highest rung" of constitutional protection, it has never held that there's any general exception for speech on matters of "private concern." Political speech, scientific speech, art, entertainment, consumer product reviews, and speech on matters of private concern are thus all doctrinally entitled to the same level of high constitutional protection, restrictable only through laws that pass strict scrutiny.[74]

---

[71] Paul Gewirtz, *Privacy and Speech,* 2001 Sup. Ct. Rev. 139, 154-55 (2001).

[72] Rodney A. Smolla, *Information as Contraband: The First Amendment and Liability for Trafficking in Speech,* 96 Nw. U. L. Rev. 1099, 1150, 1153 (2002).

[73] Solove, *Virtues of Knowing Less, supra,* at 987.

[74] Eugene Volokh, *Freedom of Speech and Information Privacy: The Troubling Implications of a Right to Stop People from Speaking About You,* 52 Stan. L. Rev. 1049, 1089, 1092-95 (2000). For other free speech critiques of privacy protections, see Thomas I. Emerson, *The System of Freedom of Expression* (1970); Solveig Singleton, *Privacy Versus the First Amendment: A Skeptical Approach,* 11 Fordham Intell. Prop. Media & Ent. L.J. 97 (2000); Harry Kalven, Jr., *Privacy in Tort Law — Were Warren and Brandeis Wrong?*, 31 Law & Contemp. Probs. 326 (1966); Diane L. Zimmerman, *Requiem for a Heavyweight: A Farewell to Warren and Brandeis's Privacy Tort*, 68 Cornell L. Rev. 291 (1983).

Does the newsworthiness test adequately deal with the First Amendment concerns of the public disclosure tort?

Consider Neil Richards:

> But crafting tort privacy as a remedy for press disclosures of embarrassing information brought privacy directly into tension with the First Amendment. Warren and Brandeis recognized the tension in 1890, but as First Amendment law became more robust over the course of the twentieth century (aided of course by Brandeis), the conflict between the First Amendment and tort privacy's core case against the press only increased. The hallmark of modern American First Amendment jurisprudence is that hurt feelings alone cannot justify the suppression of truthful information or opinion. And under the modern, post-*New York Times v. Sullivan* First Amendment regulation of speech (even by tort) on the grounds that it causes emotional injury is highly disfavored. It should thus be unsurprising that in a series of Supreme Court cases in which psychological privacy harms have been balanced against free press rights, the First Amendment has always prevailed. . . .
>
> In extraordinary cases, perhaps involving sexually-themed disclosures such as sex tapes, tort privacy can survive a direct clash with the First Amendment protections given to the press. A few such cases impose liability for psychological injuries over free press challenges. But such cases are likely to remain outliers, and appropriately so. As Brandeis himself implicitly recognized later in life, a tort-based conception of privacy protecting against purely emotional harm must remain exceptional in a constitutional regime dedicated to speech, publicity, and disclosure.
>
> This is not to say that information can never be regulated or that all information nondisclosure rules create constitutional problems. I have argued elsewhere that a wide variety of restrictions can be placed on commercial databases consistent with the First Amendment, a conclusion with which courts have agreed. And in some contexts, the concept of confidentiality has great promise to regulate information disclosure in the context of relationships. But these are not tort privacy rules, as they do not apply to all speakers and they remedy injuries other than emotional injury. As currently understood, tort privacy in the Warren and Brandeis tradition seems too crude an instrument to effectively resolve these problems, particularly because tort remedies based upon emotional harm conflict directly with the post-*New York Times v. Sullivan* First Amendment.[75]

3. ***Protections Against the Disclosure of Leaked Information.*** In *Landmark Communications v. Virginia*, 435 U.S. 829 (1978), a newspaper was indicted for violating a Virginia law making it a misdemeanor to disclose the identity of a state judge whose conduct was being investigated by the Virginia Judicial Inquiry and Review Commission. The law was designed to ensure that judicial disciplinary proceedings would remain confidential (until such proceedings were concluded) to protect judges from the publication of frivolous and unwarranted complaints. The newspaper did not challenge the requirement of confidentiality, only the prohibition of disclosing the identities of judges if the newspaper happened to find out that a judge was the subject of

[75] Neil M. Richards, *The Puzzle of Brandeis, Privacy, and Speech,* 63 Vand. L. Rev. 1295, 1345-47 (2010).

a disciplinary proceeding. The Supreme Court held that such prohibition violated the First Amendment. Although the interest in confidentiality of disciplinary proceedings was legitimate, it was not sufficient to justify the encroachment on the First Amendment because "[t]he operations of the courts and the judicial conduct of judges are matters of utmost public concern." Further, the statutory scheme could remain effective by restricting the improper leaking of such information rather than criminalizing the disclosure of that information by parties that did not participate in the illegal obtaining of such information.

4. ***Interpreting the Scope of* Bartnicki.** In *Boehner v. McDermott*, 484 F.3d 573 (D.C. Cir. 2007), U.S. Representative James McDermott was provided with a tape of a conference call between U.S. Representative John Boehner, then-Speaker of the House Newt Gingrich, and other Republican Party members. Boehner participated via a cell phone, and John and Alice Martin intercepted the call with a police radio scanner. They gave the tape to another member of the U.S. House, and the tape was eventually forwarded on to McDermott, the ranking Democrat on the Ethics Committee. Along with the tape was a letter from the Martins stating that the call was "heard over a scanner" and that they understood that they would be granted immunity. McDermott contacted reporters at the *Atlanta Journal-Constitution* and the *New York Times.* He played the tape to the *New York Times* reporter, who wrote a story about the tape. The Martins were prosecuted for a violation of the Wiretap Act, 18 U.S.C. § 2511(1)(a), prohibiting the interception of wire, oral, or electronic communications. They pled guilty and paid a $500 fine.

   Boehner sued McDermott for violating 18 U.S.C. § 2511(1)(c), which prohibits disclosing a communication that one knows or has reason to know is acquired in violation of the Wiretap Act. The D.C. Circuit, en banc, concluded that *Bartnicki* could be distinguished:

   > Whatever the *Bartnicki* majority meant by "lawfully obtain," the decision does not stand for the proposition that anyone who has lawfully obtained truthful information of public importance has a First Amendment right to disclose that information. *Bartnicki* avoided laying down such a broad rule of law, and for good reason. There are many federal provisions that forbid individuals from disclosing information they have lawfully obtained. The validity of these provisions has long been assumed. Grand jurors, court reporters, and prosecutors, for instance, may "not disclose a matter occurring before the grand jury." Fed. R. Crim. P. 6(e)(2)(B). The Privacy Act imposes criminal penalties on government employees who disclose agency records containing information about identifiable individuals to unauthorized persons. *See* 5 U.S.C. § 552a(i)(1). The Espionage Act punishes officials who willfully disclose sensitive national defense information to persons not entitled to receive it. *See* 18 U.S.C. § 793(d). The Intelligence Identities Protection Act prohibits the disclosure of a covert intelligence agent's identity. *See* 50 U.S.C. § 421. Employees of the Internal Revenue Service, among others, may not disclose tax return information. *See* 26 U.S.C. § 6103(a). State motor vehicle department employees may not make public information about an individual's driver's license or registration. *See* 18 U.S.C. § 2721. Employees of the Social Security Administration,

as well as other government employees, may not reveal social security numbers or records. *See* 42 U.S.C. § 405(c)(2)(C)(viii)(I), (III). Judicial employees may not reveal confidential information received in the course of their official duties. *See* Code of Conduct for Judicial Employees Canon 3D. And so forth.

In analogous contexts the Supreme Court has sustained restrictions on disclosure of information even though the information was lawfully obtained. The First Amendment did not shield a television station from liability under the common law right of publicity when it filmed a plaintiff's "human cannonball" act and broadcast the film without his permission. *Zacchini v. Scripps-Howard Broad. Co.,* 433 U.S. 562 (1977). When a newspaper divulged the identity of an individual who provided information to it under a promise of confidentiality, the First Amendment did not provide the paper with a defense to a breach of contract claim. *Cohen v. Cowles Media Co.,* 501 U.S. 663 (1991). The First Amendment did not prevent the government from enforcing reasonable confidentiality restrictions on former employees of the CIA. *See Snepp v. United States,* 444 U.S. 507 (1980). Parties to civil litigation did not "have a First Amendment right to disseminate, in advance of trial, information gained through the pretrial discovery process." *Seattle Times Co. v. Rhinehart,* 467 U.S. 20 (1984).

In *United States v. Aguilar,* 515 U.S. 593 (1995), a case closely analogous to this one, the Supreme Court held that the First Amendment did not give a federal judge, who obtained information about an investigative wiretap from another judge, the right to disclose that information to the subject of the wiretap. The judge challenged his conviction for violating 18 U.S.C. § 2232(c), which prohibits the improper disclosure of an investigative wiretap. In rejecting his First Amendment claim, the Court wrote that the judge was not "simply a member of the general public who happened to lawfully acquire possession of information about the wiretap; he was a Federal District Court Judge who learned of a confidential wiretap application from the judge who had authorized the interception, and who wished to preserve the integrity of the court. Government officials in sensitive confidential positions may have special duties of non-disclosure."

Aguilar stands for the principle that those who accept positions of trust involving a duty not to disclose information they lawfully acquire while performing their responsibilities have no First Amendment right to disclose that information. The question thus becomes whether, in the words of *Aguilar,* Representative McDermott's position on the Ethics Committee imposed a "special" duty on him not to disclose this tape in these circumstances. *Bartnicki* has little to say about that issue. The individuals who disclosed the tape in that case were private citizens who did not occupy positions of trust.

All members of the Ethics Committee, including Representative McDermott, were subject to Committee Rule 9, which stated that "Committee members and staff shall not disclose any evidence relating to an investigation to any person or organization outside the Committee unless authorized by the Committee." . . .

There is no question that the rules themselves are reasonable and raise no First Amendment concerns. . . .

When Representative McDermott became a member of the Ethics Committee, he voluntarily accepted a duty of confidentiality that covered his receipt and handling of the Martins' illegal recording. He therefore had no First Amendment right to disclose the tape to the media.

C. DISSEMINATION OF FALSE INFORMATION

1. DEFAMATION

(a) Introduction

At the most practical level, an understanding of defamation law is essential to understanding some of the aspects and issues related to the privacy torts. While the privacy torts are a relatively recent invention, a remedy for defamation extends far back in history. Since ancient times, one's reputation and character have been viewed as indispensable to one's ability to engage in public life. Accordingly, the importance of permitting people to protect their reputations has given rise to the law of defamation.[76]

Defamation goes way back to pre-Norman times. "Defamation" (*diffamatus*) was a technical term in church law. It signified a reputation bad enough to be put on trial in ecclesiastical court. Money awards for defamation were a way to prevent people from engaging in duels. Defamation law also served as a popular tool of the monarchy to prosecute its critics.[77]

According to modern defamation law:

> To create liability for defamation there must be:
>
> (a) a false and defamatory statement concerning another;
> (b) an unprivileged publication to a third party;
> (c) fault amounting at least to negligence on the part of the publisher; and
> (d) either actionability of the statement irrespective of special harm or the existence of special harm caused by the publication. Restatement (Second) of Torts § 558.

A "defamatory" statement "tends so to harm the reputation of another as to lower him in the estimation of the community or to deter third persons from associating or dealing with him." Restatement § 559.

A defamatory statement must also be "false." Therefore, a true statement that harms the reputation of another cannot give rise to liability for defamation.

"Publication" means that a defamatory statement is communicated "intentionally or by a negligent act to one other than the person defamed." Restatement § 577. If a person intentionally and unreasonably fails to remove defamatory matter that she knows is under her control, then that person is subject to liability for its continued publication. *See* Restatement § 577. Further "one who repeats or otherwise republishes defamatory matter is subject to liability as if he had originally published it." Restatement § 578.

One who distributes, transmits, or broadcasts on television or radio defamatory material is also liable if she knows or would have reason to know of its defamatory character. *See* Restatement § 581.

---

[76] For an excellent discussion of the rationales behind defamation law, see Robert C. Post, *The Social Foundations of Defamation Law: Reputation and the Constitution*, 74 Cal. L. Rev. 691 (1986).

[77] *See generally* Theodore F.T. Plucknett, *A Concise History of the Common Law* 484-87 (5th ed. 1956).

Libel vs. Slander. There are two forms of defamation: libel, which consists of written defamatory statements, and slander, which consists of spoken defamatory statements. According to the Restatement:

> (1) Libel consists of the publication of defamatory matter by written or printed words, by its embodiment in physical form or by any other form of communication that has the potentially harmful qualities characteristic of written or printed words.
>
> (2) Slander consists of the publication of defamatory matter by spoken words, transitory gestures or by any form of communication other than those stated in Subsection (1). Restatement § 568.

As is demonstrated by the above definitions, the Restatement takes a rather broad view of what constitutes libel.

The classification of certain types of statements as either libel or slander has proven difficult. One example is a statement made over the radio or on television. According to the Restatement, all broadcasting is libel, see Restatement § 568A, but some states take a contrary view.

The distinction between libel and slander is important for the purposes of proving harm. To establish libel, a plaintiff does not need to show "special harm" (i.e., a particular harm or injury); damages are presumed. In contrast, for slander, a plaintiff must show actual pecuniary harm, with the exception of four types of slander known as "slander per se" for which damages are presumed. Slander per se consists of defamatory statements imputing to another (1) a criminal offense; (2) a loathsome disease; (3) a matter incompatible with one's business, trade, profession, or office; or (4) serious sexual misconduct. *See* Restatement §§ 570-574. The distinction between libel and slander is less important today, since, in the cases you will read below, the Supreme Court curtailed the availability of presumed damages in defamation law.

Why is libel treated more severely than slander? As then Judge Cardozo put it:

> The schism in the law of defamation between the older wrong of slander and the newer one of libel is not the product of mere accident. It has its genesis in evils which the years have not erased. Many things that are defamatory may be said with impunity through the medium of speech. Not so, however, when speech is caught upon the wing and transmuted into print. What gives the sting to writing is its permanence in form. The spoken word dissolves, but the written one abides and perpetuates the scandal. *Ostrowe v. Lee*, 175 N.E. 505, 506 (N.Y. Ct. App. 1931).

Defamation and Privacy. It might strike you that defamation does not have much to do with privacy. After all, defamation involves false information about individuals, whereas privacy seems to be about true information. This, however, is a limited view of privacy. Privacy involves more than finding out true things about individuals. If privacy is understood as an individual's ability to have some control over the self-image she projects to society, then the ability to prevent the spread of false information about oneself is essential for this sort of control. Indeed, one of the cornerstone principles of privacy law is the ability to correct errors in one's records.

(b) Defamation and the Internet

The Internet presents interesting problems for the application of defamation law and the privacy torts because the Internet enables the widespread publication of information by any individual. Typically, it was through the news media that defamatory or private information about individuals was communicated. As a result, it would be viable to sue such entities, since they would be able to pay any judgment a plaintiff might obtain. With the Internet, however, suppose an individual posts defamatory information about another person on her website. Most likely, that individual isn't wealthy enough to be sued. Further, information is sometimes posted anonymously. As a result of this difficulty, plaintiffs have attempted to advance theories upon which Internet Service Providers (ISPs) would be liable.

In defamation law, in addition to the one who makes a libelous statement, other parties who disseminate the libelous statement can also be found liable. Repeating or publishing the libelous statements of others can give rise to "publisher" liability. A newspaper is an example of a publisher because it exercises editorial control over its content. Merely disseminating a libelous statement can give rise to "distributor" liability. In contrast to a publisher, a distributor cannot be found liable unless it is found to be at fault — if it knew or had reason to know about the defamatory statement. Bookstores and libraries are examples of distributors. When a person posts a statement on an ISP's electronic bulletin board or other online forum, is the ISP a "publisher," "distributor," or neither?

The first two courts to reach this issue reached contrary conclusions. In *Cubby, Inc. v. CompuServe, Inc.*, 776 F. Supp. 135 (S.D.N.Y. 1991), CompuServe, an Internet Service Provider, was held not liable for the statements because it didn't have knowledge or reason to know of the statements. The court held that CompuServe was a distributor rather than a publisher: "CompuServe has no more editorial control over such a publication than does a public library, book store, or newsstand, and it would be no more feasible for CompuServe to examine every publication it carries for potentially defamatory statements than it would be for any other distributor to do so."

In *Stratton Oakmont, Inc. v. Prodigy Services Co.*, 23 Media L. Rep. 1794 (N.Y. Sup. 1995), the plaintiff brought a defamation action against Prodigy, the operator of the computer network. An unidentified user posted allegedly defamatory statements on one of Prodigy's electronic bulletin boards. The plaintiffs contended that Prodigy should be considered the "publisher" of the statements. Under Prodigy's stated policy, it was a family-oriented computer network and would screen posts for offensive content. The court concluded that Prodigy was liable as a publisher because "Prodigy held itself out to the public and its members as controlling the content of its computer bulletin boards."

In response to *Stratton Oakmont,* Congress passed § 230 of the Communications Decency Act (CDA) of 1996, which provides in relevant part: "No provider or user of an interactive computer service shall be treated as the publisher or speaker of any information provided by another information content provider." 47 U.S.C. § 230(c)(1). Based on this provision, will ISPs that provide forums where defamatory statements are posted be treated as publishers, distributors, or neither?

ZERAN V. AMERICA ONLINE, INC.

129 F.3d 327 (4th Cir. 1997)

WILKINSON, C.J. . . . On April 25, 1995, an unidentified person posted a message on an [America Online (AOL)] bulletin board advertising "Naughty Oklahoma T-Shirts." The posting described the sale of shirts featuring offensive and tasteless slogans related to the April 19, 1995, bombing of the Alfred P. Murrah Federal Building in Oklahoma City. Those interested in purchasing the shirts were instructed to call "Ken" at [Kenneth] Zeran's home phone number in Seattle, Washington. As a result of this anonymously perpetrated prank, Zeran received a high volume of calls, comprised primarily of angry and derogatory messages, but also including death threats. Zeran could not change his phone number because he relied on its availability to the public in running his business out of his home. Later that day, Zeran called AOL and informed a company representative of his predicament. The employee assured Zeran that the posting would be removed from AOL's bulletin board but explained that as a matter of policy AOL would not post a retraction. The parties dispute the date that AOL removed this original posting from its bulletin board.

On April 26, the next day, an unknown person posted another message advertising additional shirts with new tasteless slogans related to the Oklahoma City bombing. Again, interested buyers were told to call Zeran's phone number, to ask for "Ken," and to "please call back if busy" due to high demand. The angry, threatening phone calls intensified. Over the next four days, an unidentified party continued to post messages on AOL's bulletin board, advertising additional items including bumper stickers and key chains with still more offensive slogans. During this time period, Zeran called AOL repeatedly and was told by company representatives that the individual account from which the messages were posted would soon be closed. Zeran also reported his case to Seattle FBI agents. By April 30, Zeran was receiving an abusive phone call approximately every two minutes.

Meanwhile, an announcer for Oklahoma City radio station KRXO received a copy of the first AOL posting. On May 1, the announcer related the message's contents on the air, attributed them to "Ken" at Zeran's phone number, and urged the listening audience to call the number. After this radio broadcast, Zeran was inundated with death threats and other violent calls from Oklahoma City residents. Over the next few days, Zeran talked to both KRXO and AOL representatives. He also spoke to his local police, who subsequently surveilled his home to protect his safety. By May 14, after an Oklahoma City newspaper published a story exposing the shirt advertisements as a hoax and after KRXO made an on-air apology, the number of calls to Zeran's residence finally subsided to fifteen per day.

Zeran first filed suit on January 4, 1996, against radio station KRXO in the United States District Court for the Western District of Oklahoma. On April 23, 1996, he filed this separate suit against AOL in the same court. Zeran did not bring any action against the party who posted the offensive messages.[78] . . . AOL answered Zeran's complaint and interposed [the Communications Decency Act,] 47 U.S.C. § 230 as an affirmative defense. AOL then moved for judgment on the pleadings pursuant to Fed. R. Civ. P. 12(c). The district court granted AOL's motion, and Zeran filed this appeal.

Because § 230 was successfully advanced by AOL in the district court as a defense to Zeran's claims, we shall briefly examine its operation here. Zeran seeks to hold AOL liable for defamatory speech initiated by a third party. He argued to the district court that once he notified AOL of the unidentified third party's hoax, AOL had a duty to remove the defamatory posting promptly, to notify its subscribers of the message's false nature, and to effectively screen future defamatory material. Section 230 entered this litigation as an affirmative defense pled by AOL. The company claimed that Congress immunized interactive computer service providers from claims based on information posted by a third party.

The relevant portion of § 230 states: "No provider or user of an interactive computer service shall be treated as the publisher or speaker of any information provided by another information content provider." 47 U.S.C. § 230(c)(1). By its plain language, § 230 creates a federal immunity to any cause of action that would make service providers liable for information originating with a third-party user of the service. Specifically, § 230 precludes courts from entertaining claims that would place a computer service provider in a publisher's role. Thus, lawsuits seeking to hold a service provider liable for its exercise of a publisher's traditional editorial functions — such as deciding whether to publish, withdraw, postpone or alter content — are barred.

The purpose of this statutory immunity is not difficult to discern. Congress recognized the threat that tort-based lawsuits pose to freedom of speech in the new and burgeoning Internet medium. The imposition of tort liability on service providers for the communications of others represented, for Congress, simply another form of intrusive government regulation of speech. . . .

. . . Interactive computer services have millions of users. The amount of information communicated via interactive computer services is therefore staggering. The specter of tort liability in an area of such prolific speech would have an obvious chilling effect. It would be impossible for service providers to screen each of their millions of postings for possible problems. Faced with potential liability for each message republished by their services, interactive computer service providers might choose to severely restrict the number and type of messages posted. Congress considered the weight of the speech interests implicated and chose to immunize service providers to avoid any such restrictive effect.

Another important purpose of § 230 was to encourage service providers to self-regulate the dissemination of offensive material over their services. In this respect, § 230 responded to a New York state court decision, *Stratton Oakmont, Inc. v. Prodigy Servs. Co.* . . .

---

[78] Zeran maintains that AOL made it impossible to identify the original party by failing to maintain adequate records of its users. The issue of AOL's recordkeeping practices, however, is not presented by this appeal.

Congress enacted § 230 to remove the disincentives to self-regulation created by the *Stratton Oakmont* decision. Under that court's holding, computer service providers who regulated the dissemination of offensive material on their services risked subjecting themselves to liability, because such regulation cast the service provider in the role of a publisher. Fearing that the specter of liability would therefore deter service providers from blocking and screening offensive material, Congress enacted § 230's broad immunity "to remove disincentives for the development and utilization of blocking and filtering technologies that empower parents to restrict their children's access to objectionable or inappropriate online material." 47 U.S.C. § 230(b)(4). In line with this purpose, § 230 forbids the imposition of publisher liability on a service provider for the exercise of its editorial and self-regulatory functions.

Zeran argues, however, that the § 230 immunity eliminates only publisher liability, leaving distributor liability intact. Publishers can be held liable for defamatory statements contained in their works even absent proof that they had specific knowledge of the statement's inclusion. According to Zeran, interactive computer service providers like AOL are normally considered instead to be distributors, like traditional news vendors or book sellers. Distributors cannot be held liable for defamatory statements contained in the materials they distribute unless it is proven at a minimum that they have actual knowledge of the defamatory statements upon which liability is predicated. Zeran contends that he provided AOL with sufficient notice of the defamatory statements appearing on the company's bulletin board. This notice is significant, says Zeran, because AOL could be held liable as a distributor only if it acquired knowledge of the defamatory statements' existence.

Because of the difference between these two forms of liability, Zeran contends that the term "distributor" carries a legally distinct meaning from the term "publisher." Accordingly, he asserts that Congress' use of only the term "publisher" in § 230 indicates a purpose to immunize service providers only from publisher liability. He argues that distributors are left unprotected by § 230 and, therefore, his suit should be permitted to proceed against AOL. We disagree. Assuming arguendo that Zeran has satisfied the requirements for imposition of distributor liability, this theory of liability is merely a subset, or a species, of publisher liability, and is therefore also foreclosed by § 230. . . .

AOL falls squarely within this traditional definition of a publisher and, therefore, is clearly protected by § 230's immunity. . . .

Zeran simply attaches too much importance to the presence of the distinct notice element in distributor liability. The simple fact of notice surely cannot transform one from an original publisher to a distributor in the eyes of the law. . . .

If computer service providers were subject to distributor liability, they would face potential liability each time they receive notice of a potentially defamatory statement — from any party, concerning any message. Each notification would require a careful yet rapid investigation of the circumstances surrounding the posted information, a legal judgment concerning the information's defamatory character, and an on-the-spot editorial decision whether to risk liability by allowing the continued publication of that information. Although this might be feasible for the traditional print publisher, the sheer number of postings on interactive computer services would create an impossible burden in the Internet context. Because service providers would be subject to liability only for the publication of information, and not for its removal, they would have a natural incentive simply to remove messages upon notification, whether the contents were defamatory or not. Thus, like strict liability, liability upon notice has a chilling effect on the freedom of Internet speech. . . .

More generally, notice-based liability for interactive computer service providers would provide third parties with a no-cost means to create the basis for future lawsuits. Whenever one was displeased with the speech of another party conducted over an interactive computer service, the offended party could simply "notify" the relevant service provider, claiming the information to be legally defamatory. In light of the vast amount of speech communicated through interactive computer services, these notices could produce an impossible burden for service providers, who would be faced with ceaseless choices of suppressing controversial speech or sustaining prohibitive liability. Because the probable effects of distributor liability on the vigor of Internet speech and on service provider self-regulation are directly contrary to § 230's statutory purposes, we will not assume that Congress intended to leave liability upon notice intact. . . .

NOTES & QUESTIONS

1. ***The Applicability of the CDA § 230 to the Privacy Torts.*** Is § 230 of the CDA applicable to the privacy torts? In *Barnes v. Yahoo!, Inc.*, 570 F.3d 1096 (9th Cir. 2009), a woman alleged that her former boyfriend created fake profiles under her name on Yahoo. He posted nude photos of her in the profiles and provided contact information for her. She also claimed that he was impersonating her in chatrooms and directing people to the profiles. She contacted Yahoo and asked them several times to try to put a stop to the boyfriend's misuse of Yahoo's services. She alleged that although Yahoo employees promised they would help her, they failed to stop the boyfriend's conduct. The court held that Yahoo was immune under § 230. However, the court held that Yahoo could be held liable on a promissory estoppel theory because it promised to take down the content.
2. ***Anonymity and Accountability for Harmful Internet Speech.*** Shouldn't plaintiffs sue the people who post defamatory or privacy-invasive statements rather than the ISPs or websites on which the statements appear? Recall in *Zeran* that the anonymous poster of the information could not be identified. Should the website be forced to maintain records of the identities of the individuals who post so that people can sue those individuals? What are the benefits and costs of such a solution?
3. ***Critiques of* Zeran.** Consider the following argument against *Zeran* from *Barrett v. Rosenthal*, 5 Cal. Rptr. 3d 416 (Cal. Ct. App. 2003):

   > . . . [W]e . . . think it debatable whether notice liability would actually have an unduly chilling effect on cyberspeech. Neither the record before us nor any other information brought to our attention provides an answer to that question. Moreover, the speculative conclusion of the *Zeran* court that exposing Internet

intermediaries to knowledge-based liability would significantly chill online speech is disputed by the speculations of other authorities. . . .

It is also asserted that by ignoring how difficult it is for a plaintiff to prevail on a defamation claim or receive significant money damages, the *Zeran* court overstated the danger such claims present to Internet intermediaries, and therefore also exaggerated the danger they would engage in excessive self-censorship.

The California Supreme Court reversed the court of appeals in *Barrett v. Rosenthal*, 146 P.3d 510 (Cal. 2006):

> We agree with the *Zeran* court, and others considering the question, that subjecting Internet service providers and users to defamation liability would tend to chill online speech. . . .
>
> We reject the argument that the difficulty of prevailing on a defamation claim mitigates the deterrent effect of potential liability. Defamation law is complex, requiring consideration of multiple factors. These include whether the statement at issue is true or false, factual or figurative, privileged or unprivileged, whether the matter is of public or private concern, and whether the plaintiff is a public or private figure. Any investigation of a potentially defamatory Internet posting is thus a daunting and expensive challenge. For that reason, we have observed that even when a defamation claim is "clearly nonmeritorious," the threat of liability "ultimately chills the free exercise of expression."
>
> Nor are we convinced by the observation that a "distributor" faces no liability without notice. Distributors are liable not merely upon receiving notice from a third party, but also if they independently "knew or had reason to know" of the defamatory statement. Thus, as the *Zeran* court pointed out, this aspect of distributor liability would discourage active monitoring of Internet postings. It could also motivate providers to insulate themselves from receiving complaints. Such responses would frustrate the goal of self-regulation.
>
> The third practical implication noted in *Zeran* is no less compelling, and went unaddressed by the Court of Appeal. Notice-based liability for service providers would allow complaining parties to impose substantial burdens on the freedom of Internet speech by lodging complaints whenever they were displeased by an online posting. . . .
>
> Requiring providers, users, and courts to account for the nuances of common law defamation, and all the various ways they might play out in the Internet environment, is a Herculean assignment that we are reluctant to impose. We conclude the *Zeran* court accurately diagnosed the problems that would attend notice-based liability for service providers.

Which opinion has the better argument as to the meaning and purpose of § 230?

Consider Daniel Solove:

> Unfortunately, courts are interpreting Section 230 so broadly as to provide too much immunity, eliminating the incentive to foster a balance between speech and privacy. The way courts are using Section 230 exalts free speech to the detriment of privacy and reputation. As a result, a host of websites have arisen

> that encourage others to post gossip and rumors as well as to engage in online shaming. These websites thrive under Section 230's broad immunity.[79]

Solove contends that a notice and take-down system is preferable to a broader immunity that eliminates distributor liability. What are the benefits and problems of a notice and take-down regime? In copyright law, "one who distributes a device with the object of promoting its use to infringe copyright, as shown by clear expression or other affirmative steps taken to foster infringement, is liable for the resulting acts of infringement by third parties." *MGM Studios, Inc. v. Grokster, Ltd.*, 545 U.S. 913 (2005). Examine the pros and cons of such a rule for defamation or privacy tort liability.

4. ***Who Is the Content Provider?*** In *Batzel v. Smith*, 333 F.3d 1018 (9th Cir. 2003), a handyman (Robert Smith) who worked at Ellen Batzel's home e-mailed Ton Cremers, the director of security at a museum in Amsterdam, who maintained an e-mail listserv about looted art. Smith said that several of Batzel's paintings were stolen from the Jews by the Nazis during World War II. Cremers made a few small changes to the text of Smith's e-mail and sent it out to his listserv. The paintings were not looted art from the Nazis, and Batzel sued both Smith and Cremers. The court concluded that since Cremers was not the originator of the information, he was immune under § 230:

> Obviously, Cremers did not create Smith's e-mail. Smith composed the e-mail entirely on his own. . . . [T]he exclusion of "publisher" liability necessarily precludes liability for exercising the usual prerogative of publishers to choose among proffered material and to edit the material published while retaining its basic form and message.
>
> Because Cremers did no more than select and make minor alterations to Smith's e-mail, Cremers cannot be considered the content provider of Smith's e-mail for purposes of § 230. . . .
>
> We therefore hold that a service provider or user is immune from liability under § 230(c)(1) when a third person or entity that created or developed the information in question furnished it to the provider or user under circumstances in which a reasonable person in the position of the service provider or user would conclude that the information was provided for publication on the Internet or other "interactive computer service."

In dissent, Judge Gould wrote:

> Congress wanted to ensure that excessive government regulation did not slow America's expansion into the exciting new frontier of the Internet. But Congress did not want this new frontier to be like the Old West: a lawless zone governed by retribution and mob justice. The CDA does not license anarchy. A person's decision to disseminate the rankest rumor or most blatant falsehood should not escape legal redress merely because the person chose to disseminate it through the Internet rather than through some other medium. . . .
>
> In this case, I would hold that Cremers is *not* entitled to CDA immunity because Cremers actively selected Smith's e-mail message for publication.

---

[79] Daniel J. Solove, *The Future of Reputation: Gossip, Rumor, and Privacy on the Internet* 159 (2007).

Batzel demonstrates the difficulties in certain situations of determining whether a person is providing content or is merely disseminating the content of another. If a person is deemed the content provider, then § 230 immunity does not apply, as § 230 is designed to immunize a person from being liable for disseminating the content of others. In *Batzel,* is Cremers the content provider because he decided to forward the e-mail? Or is Smith the content provider because he wrote the e-mail? *Batzel* holds that if a person receives a communication sent by another for the purpose of having the person publish it online, then the person is immune under § 230 for publishing it. Few courts have adopted a rule like that in *Batzel* because few have explored situations where it is unclear who precisely is the content provider.

Suppose Cremers has a blog about stolen art. Smith is interested in spreading the rumor about the stolen art on Cremers's blog. Consider the following situations and examine whether Cremers would have § 230 immunity under the majority's rule and also under Judge Gould's:

(a) Cremers's blog allows anybody to post comments. Smith posts a comment about the rumor on Cremers's blog. Batzel wants Cremers to delete the comment, but Cremers refuses to do so.

(b) Cremers has a comment moderation system on his blog where he must approve comments before they are published on his blog. Smith posts the stolen art comment and Cremers approves it, whereupon it is published on the blog.

(c) Smith e-mails Cremers and tells him about the stolen art rumor. Instead of posting the e-mail itself, Cremers writes a blog post about the rumor in his own words and posts it.

(d) Smith calls Cremers and tells him the rumor about the stolen art. Cremers writes a post about the rumor.

Is there any meaningful difference between the above situations and the way that Cremers disseminated Smith's e-mail to the listserv? As a normative matter, should Cremers's liability be different in any of the above situations? How should the law determine when a person should be deemed the content provider and when a person should be deemed to merely be relaying the content of another?

5. ***Wikipedia.*** Wikipedia is an online encyclopedia that anybody can edit. It has millions of entries and is widely used and cited. What are the legal consequences when a Wikipedia entry is defamatory?

A notable case occurred in 2005 involving John Seigenthaler, a former assistant to Attorney General Bobby Kennedy during the Kennedy Administration. His Wikipedia entry falsely accused him of being involved in President John F. Kennedy's assassination. In an article in *USA Today,* Seigenthaler wrote:

> I have no idea whose sick mind conceived the false, malicious "biography" that appeared under my name for 132 days on Wikipedia, the popular, online, free encyclopedia whose authors are unknown and virtually untraceable.[80]

Eventually, the anonymous person who wrote the defamatory statement was identified, and he apologized. If Seigenthaler sued Wikipedia for defamation, would § 230 provide Wikipedia with immunity? Consider the views of Ken Myers on this topic:

> Because of the unique relationship between Wikipedia and its user-community, the question of whether an individual user-poster is a separate "information content provider," as opposed to somehow being a representative of Wikipedia, is unclear. If Wikipedia is determined to be the relevant "information content provider" then there is no immunity under § 230(c)(1), as Wikipedia itself will be held responsible for the defamatory content. Thus, the definition of "information content provider" raises an important threshold question in this case: what counts as the "person or entity" whose actions the court should analyze in determining whether Wikipedia is the "information content provider" under the third prong? . . .
>
> The Wikipedia community is self-consciously inclusive, designating all of its contributors as "Wikipedians." Presumably, this inclusiveness fosters the cooperative atmosphere critical to Wikipedia's success. However, if *all* members of the Wikipedia community — that is, all contributors — are considered part of the Wikipedia "entity," then it would, by definition and by operation of the third prong, not be eligible for § 230(c)(1) immunity because Wikipedia would be the site's only contributor — there could be no "[]other information content provider." . . .
>
> Wikipedia would argue that, for purposes of § 230(f)(3), only employees of the Wikimedia Foundation should be considered as part of the Wikipedia "entity." However, "the fact that work is performed gratuitously does not relieve a principal of liability."[81]

To the extent that websites like Wikipedia create hierarchies of users, with some having greater editorial powers, does this alter immunity for the actions of the users at the top of the hierarchy?

(c) First Amendment Limitations

NEW YORK TIMES CO. V. SULLIVAN

376 U.S. 254 (1964)

[L.B. Sullivan, one of the three elected Commissioners of Montgomery, Alabama, sued four African-American clergymen and the *New York Times* for libel. Sullivan claimed that a full-page advertisement in the *New York Times* on March 29, 1960, entitled "Heed Their Rising Voices" defamed him. The advertisement discussed the civil rights movement and the wave of terror against

---

[80] John Seigenthaler, *A False Wikipedia "Biography,"* USA Today, Nov. 29, 2005.

[81] Ken S. Myers, *Wikimmunity: Fitting the Communications Decency Act to Wikipedia,* 20 Harv. J.L. & Tech. 163, 188-90 (2006).

the nonviolent protest. It was signed by various clergymen in Southern cities, including the four clergymen named in the lawsuit.

Two paragraphs of the ten in the advertisement were the basis of Sullivan's libel claim.

> . . . In Montgomery, Alabama, after students sang "My Country, 'Tis of Thee" on the State Capitol steps, their leaders were expelled from school, and truckloads of police armed with shotguns and tear-gas ringed the Alabama State College Campus. When the entire student body protested to state authorities by refusing to re-register, their dining hall was padlocked in an attempt to starve them into submission. . . .
>
> Again and again the Southern violators have answered Dr. King's peaceful protests with intimidation and violence. They have bombed his home almost killing his wife and child. They have assaulted his person. They have arrested him seven times — for "speeding," "loitering" and similar "offenses." And now they have charged him with "perjury" — a felony under which they could imprison him for ten years. . . .

Although Sullivan was never mentioned by name, he claimed that the word "police" implicated him because he supervised the police department. Although Sullivan made no effort to prove he suffered actual pecuniary loss as a result of the alleged libel, a Montgomery County jury awarded Sullivan damages of $500,000, the full amount claimed against all the petitioners, and the Supreme Court of Alabama affirmed.]

BRENNAN, J. . . . Under Alabama law as applied in this case, a publication is "libelous per se" if the words "tend to injure a person . . . in his reputation" or to "bring (him) into public contempt"; the trial court stated that the standard was met if the words are such as to "injure him in his public office, or impute misconduct to him in his office, or want of official integrity, or want of fidelity to a public trust. . . ." The jury must find that the words were published "of and concerning" the plaintiff, but where the plaintiff is a public official his place in the governmental hierarchy is sufficient evidence to support a finding that his reputation has been affected by statements that reflect upon the agency of which he is in charge. Once "libel per se" has been established, the defendant has no defense as to stated facts unless he can persuade the jury that they were true in all their particulars. His privilege of "fair comment" for expressions of opinion depends on the truth of the facts upon which the comment is based. Unless he can discharge the burden of proving truth, general damages are presumed, and may be awarded without proof of pecuniary injury. A showing of actual malice is apparently a prerequisite to recovery of punitive damages, and the defendant may in any event forestall a punitive award by a retraction meeting the statutory requirements. Good motives and belief in truth do not negate an inference of malice, but are relevant only in mitigation of punitive damages if the jury chooses to accord them weight.

The question before us is whether this rule of liability, as applied to an action brought by a public official against critics of his official conduct, abridges the freedom of speech and of the press that is guaranteed by the First and Fourteenth Amendments.

Respondent relies heavily, as did the Alabama courts, on statements of this Court to the effect that the Constitution does not protect libelous publications. . . . Like insurrection, contempt, advocacy of unlawful acts, breach of the peace, obscenity, solicitation of legal business, and the various other formulae for the repression of expression that have been challenged in this Court, libel can claim no talismanic immunity from constitutional limitations. It must be measured by standards that satisfy the First Amendment.

The general proposition that freedom of expression upon public questions is secured by the First Amendment has long been settled by our decisions. . . .

. . . [W]e consider this case against the background of a profound national commitment to the principle that debate on public issues should be uninhibited, robust, and wide-open, and that it may well include vehement, caustic, and sometimes unpleasantly sharp attacks on government and public officials. The present advertisement, as an expression of grievance and protest on one of the major public issues of our time, would seem clearly to qualify for the constitutional protection. The question is whether it forfeits that protection by the falsity of some of its factual statements and by its alleged defamation of respondent.

Authoritative interpretations of the First Amendment guarantees have consistently refused to recognize an exception for any test of truth — whether administered by judges, juries, or administrative officials — and especially one that puts the burden of proving truth on the speaker. The constitutional protection does not turn upon "the truth, popularity, or social utility of the ideas and beliefs which are offered." . . .

That erroneous statement is inevitable in free debate, and that it must be protected if the freedoms of expression are to have the "breathing space" that they "need to survive." . . .

A rule compelling the critic of official conduct to guarantee the truth of all his factual assertions — and to do so on pain of libel judgments virtually unlimited in amount — leads to a comparable "self-censorship." . . . Under such a rule, would-be critics of official conduct may be deterred from voicing their criticism, even though it is believed to be true and even though it is in fact true, because of doubt whether it can be proved in court or fear of the expense of having to do so. They tend to make only statements which "steer far wider of the unlawful zone." The rule thus dampens the vigor and limits the variety of public debate. It is inconsistent with the First and Fourteenth Amendments.

The constitutional guarantees require, we think, a federal rule that prohibits a public official from recovering damages for a defamatory falsehood relating to his official conduct unless he proves that the statement was made with "actual malice" — that is, with knowledge that it was false or with reckless disregard of whether it was false or not. . . .

We hold today that the Constitution delimits a State's power to award damages for libel in actions brought by public officials against critics of their official conduct. Since this is such an action, the rule requiring proof of actual malice is applicable. While Alabama law apparently requires proof of actual malice for an award of punitive damages, where general damages are concerned malice is "presumed." Such a presumption is inconsistent with the federal rule. Since the trial judge did not instruct the jury to differentiate between general and punitive damages, it may be that the verdict was wholly an award of one or the other. But it is impossible to know, in view of the general verdict returned. Because of this uncertainty, the judgment must be reversed and the case remanded. . . .

NOTES & QUESTIONS

1. ***Should Defamation Have Survived?*** Justices Black, Douglas, and Goldberg would have gone further, eliminating all defamation liability for public officials. In other words, public officials could not sue for defamation even if the defamatory statement were made with actual malice. As Justice Goldberg explained, the right to criticize public officials is unconditional and "should not depend upon a probing by the jury of the motivation of the citizen or press." Does Justice Brennan's logic lead to this result? Why not just bar all libel actions by public officials? Consider Justice Holmes's dissent in *Abrams v. United States*, 250 U.S. 616, 630 (1919):

   > But when men have realized that time has upset many fighting faiths, they may come to believe even more than they believe the very foundations of their own conduct that the ultimate good desired is better reached by free trade in ideas — that the best test of truth is the power of the thought to get itself accepted in the competition of the market, and that truth is the only ground upon which their wishes safely can be carried out. That at any rate is the theory of our Constitution.

   If Holmes is right, and the marketplace of ideas will result in the truth eventually winning out, then is defamation law even necessary?[82]
2. ***Actual Malice.*** The actual malice standard is a subjective one. As Randall Bezanson describes it:

   > The actual malice inquiry is avowedly focused on the subjective state of mind of the publisher at the time of publication. It asks only whether falsity was calculated or whether the publisher's decision was sufficiently indifferent to likely falsity that the publication decision should not be respected under the First Amendment. Actual malice, in short, reveals a frame of mind, an animating intention for the publication, that belies any significant publisher concern for the audience or for the function being performed in the selection and presentation of information, or news. . . .

   In practice, actual malice is very difficult for plaintiffs to establish. Bezanson observes:

   > In making actual malice determinations, state courts attempt to determine the speaker's subjective state of mind by two primary means. First, courts examine the speaker's observable conduct at the time of the speech act, viewing such outward manifestations as a potential insight into the speaker's state of mind. . . . The second means by which courts attempt to determine the speaker's state of mind is through the personal testimony of the speaker. State courts grant considerable weight to the speaker's own reflective statements

[82] For more background about *New York Times v. Sullivan*, see Anthony Lewis, *Make No Law: The Sullivan Case and the First Amendment* (1991).

> concerning his or her belief as to the truth of the speech at the time the speech judgment was made.[83]

3. ***Public Figures.*** Subsequently, the Court extended the approach in *New York Times* to persons who were not public officials but who were " 'public figures' and involved in issues in which the public has a justified and important interest." *Curtis Publishing Co. v. Butts*, 388 U.S. 130 (1967).

   In *Gertz v. Robert Welch, Inc.*, 418 U.S. 323 (1974), which is excerpted below, the Court turned to the issue of whether the *New York Times* approach should be extended to private figures.

GERTZ V. ROBERT WELCH, INC.

418 U.S. 323 (1974)

[In 1968, Nuccio, a Chicago policeman, shot and killed Nelson, a youth. Nuccio was prosecuted and convicted for murder in the second degree. The Nelson family retained petitioner Elmer Gertz, a reputable attorney, to represent them in civil litigation against Nuccio. Robert Welch, Inc. published *American Opinion*, a monthly magazine representing the views of the John Birch Society. The magazine had been warning of a national conspiracy to discredit local police forces and create a national police force as a step toward establishing a Communist dictatorship. In 1969, the magazine published an article about the murder trial of Officer Nuccio, alleging that he was framed as part of the Communist campaign against the police. Among other things, the article portrayed Gertz as the mastermind of the frame-up. It stated that Gertz was a "Leninist" and a "Communist-fronter," that Gertz belonged to Marxist and Socialist organizations, and that Gertz had a criminal record. All of these statements were false. The managing editor made no effort to verify the charges; in fact, he wrote an editorial introduction stating that the author had conducted extensive research. Gertz sued for libel and won a jury verdict of $50,000. The district court, however, decided that the *New York Times* standard should apply and entered judgment for Robert Welch, Inc.]

POWELL, J. . . . The principal issue in this case is whether a newspaper or broadcaster that publishes defamatory falsehoods about an individual who is neither a public official nor a public figure may claim a constitutional privilege against liability for the injury inflicted by those statements. . . .

The legitimate state interest underlying the law of libel is the compensation of individuals for the harm inflicted on them by defamatory falsehood. We would not lightly require the State to abandon this purpose, for, as Mr. Justice Stewart has reminded us, the individual's right to the protection of his own good name

> reflects no more than our basic concept of the essential dignity and worth of every human being — a concept at the root of any decent system of ordered liberty. The protection of private personality, like the protection of life itself, is

---

[83] Randall P. Bezanson, *The Developing Law of Editorial Judgment,* 78 Neb. L. Rev. 754, 774-75, 763-64 (1999).

> left primarily to the individual States under the Ninth and Tenth Amendments. But this does not mean that the right is entitled to any less recognition by this Court as a basic of our constitutional system. *Rosenblatt v. Baer*, 383 U.S. 75, 92 (1966) (concurring opinion). . . .

. . . [W]e have no difficulty in distinguishing among defamation plaintiffs. The first remedy of any victim of defamation is self-help — using available opportunities to contradict the lie or correct the error and thereby to minimize its adverse impact on reputation. Public officials and public figures usually enjoy significantly greater access to the channels of effective communication and hence have a more realistic opportunity to counteract false statements then private individuals normally enjoy. Private individuals are therefore more vulnerable to injury, and the state interest in protecting them is correspondingly greater.

More important than the likelihood that private individuals will lack effective opportunities for rebuttal, there is a compelling normative consideration underlying the distinction between public and private defamation plaintiffs. An individual who decides to seek governmental office must accept certain necessary consequences of that involvement in public affairs. He runs the risk of closer public scrutiny than might otherwise be the case. And society's interest in the officers of government is not strictly limited to the formal discharge of official duties. As the Court pointed out in *Garrison v. Louisiana*, the public's interest extends to "anything which might touch on an official's fitness for office. . . . Few personal attributes are more germane to fitness for office than dishonesty, malfeasance, or improper motivation, even though these characteristics may also affect the official's private character."

Those classed as public figures stand in a similar position. Hypothetically, it may be possible for someone to become a public figure through no purposeful action of his own, but the instances of truly involuntary public figures must be exceedingly rare. For the most part those who attain this status have assumed roles of especial prominence in the affairs of society. Some occupy positions of such persuasive power and influence that they are deemed public figures for all purposes. More commonly, those classed as public figures have thrust themselves to the forefront of particular public controversies in order to influence the resolution of the issues involved. In either event, they invite attention and comment.

Even if the foregoing generalities do not obtain in every instance, the communications media are entitled to act on the assumption that public officials and public figures have voluntarily exposed themselves to increased risk of injury from defamatory falsehood concerning them. No such assumption is justified with respect to a private individual. He has not accepted public office or assumed an "influential role in ordering society." He has relinquished no part of his interest in the protection of his own good name, and consequently he has a more compelling call on the courts for redress of injury inflicted by defamatory falsehood. Thus, private individuals are not only more vulnerable to injury than public officials and public figures; they are also more deserving of recovery.

For these reasons we conclude that the States should retain substantial latitude in their efforts to enforce a legal remedy for defamatory falsehood injurious to the reputation of a private individual. The extension of the *New York*

Times test . . . would abridge this legitimate state interest to a degree that we find unacceptable. And it would occasion the additional difficulty of forcing state and federal judges to decide on an ad hoc basis which publications address issues of "general or public interest" and which do not — to determine, in the words of Mr. Justice Marshall, "what information is relevant to self-government." We doubt the wisdom of committing this task to the conscience of judges. . . .

We hold that, so long as they do not impose liability without fault, the States may define for themselves the appropriate standard of liability for a publisher or broadcaster of defamatory falsehood injurious to a private individual. . . .

. . . Under the traditional rules pertaining to actions for libel, the existence of injury is presumed from the fact of publication. Juries may award substantial sums as compensation for supposed damage to reputation without any proof that such harm actually occurred. The largely uncontrolled discretion of juries to award damages where there is no loss unnecessarily compounds the potential of any system of liability for defamatory falsehood to inhibit the vigorous exercise of First Amendment freedoms. Additionally, the doctrine of presumed damages invites juries to punish unpopular opinion rather than to compensate individuals for injury sustained by the publication of a false fact. More to the point, the States have no substantial interest in securing for plaintiffs such as this petitioner gratuitous awards of money damages far in excess of any actual injury. . . .

. . . It is necessary to restrict defamation plaintiffs who do not prove knowledge of falsity or reckless disregard for the truth to compensation for actual injury. . . . Suffice it to say that actual injury is not limited to out-of-pocket loss. Indeed, the more customary types of actual harm inflicted by defamatory falsehood include impairment of reputation and standing in the community, personal humiliation, and mental anguish and suffering. . . .

We also find no justification for allowing awards of punitive damages against publishers and broadcasters held liable under state-defined standards of liability for defamation. In most jurisdictions jury discretion over the amounts awarded is limited only by the gentle rule that they not be excessive. Consequently, juries assess punitive damages in wholly unpredictable amounts bearing no necessary relation to the actual harm caused. And they remain free to use their discretion selectively to punish expressions of unpopular views. Like the doctrine of presumed damages, jury discretion to award punitive damages unnecessarily exacerbates the danger of media self-censorship, but, unlike the former rule, punitive damages are wholly irrelevant to the state interest that justifies a negligence standard for private defamation actions. They are not compensation for injury. Instead, they are private fines levied by civil juries to punish reprehensible conduct and to deter its future occurrence. In short, the private defamation plaintiff who establishes liability under a less demanding standard than that stated by *New York Times* may recover only such damages as are sufficient to compensate him for actual injury.

Notwithstanding our refusal to extend the *New York Times* privilege to defamation of private individuals, respondent contends that we should affirm the judgment below on the ground that petitioner is either a public official or a public figure. . . .

. . . In some instances an individual may achieve such pervasive fame or notoriety that he becomes a public figure for all purposes and in all contexts.

More commonly, an individual voluntarily injects himself or is drawn into a particular public controversy and thereby becomes a public figure for a limited range of issues. In either case such persons assume special prominence in the resolution of public questions.

Petitioner has long been active in community and professional affairs. He has served as an officer of local civic groups and of various professional organizations, and he has published several books and articles on legal subjects. Although petitioner was consequently well known in some circles, he had achieved no general fame or notoriety in the community. None of the prospective jurors called at the trial had ever heard of petitioner prior to this litigation, and respondent offered no proof that this response was atypical of the local population. We would not lightly assume that a citizen's participation in community and professional affairs rendered him a public figure for all purposes. Absent clear evidence of general fame or notoriety in the community, and pervasive involvement in the affairs of society, an individual should not be deemed a public personality for all aspects of his life. It is preferable to reduce the public-figure question to a more meaningful context by looking to the nature and extent of an individual's participation in the particular controversy giving rise to the defamation.

In this context it is plain that petitioner was not a public figure. He played a minimal role at the coroner's inquest, and his participation related solely to his representation of a private client. He took no part in the criminal prosecution of Officer Nuccio. Moreover, he never discussed either the criminal or civil litigation with the press and was never quoted as having done so. He plainly did not thrust himself into the vortex of this public issue, nor did he engage the public's attention in an attempt to influence its outcome. We are persuaded that the trial court did not err in refusing to characterize petitioner as a public figure for the purpose of this litigation. . . .

WHITE, J. dissenting. . . . The press today is vigorous and robust. To me, it is quite incredible to suggest that threats of libel suits from private citizens are causing the press to refrain from publishing the truth. I know of no hard facts to support that proposition, and the Court furnishes none.

The communications industry has increasingly become concentrated in a few powerful hands operating very lucrative businesses reaching across the Nation and into almost every home. Neither the industry as a whole nor its individual components are easily intimidated, and we are fortunate that they are not. Requiring them to pay for the occasional damage they do to private reputation will play no substantial part in their future performance or their existence. . . .

NOTES & QUESTIONS

1. ***Public vs. Private Figures.*** What distinguishes a public from a private figure? In *Time, Inc. v. Firestone*, 424 U.S. 448 (1976), Mary Alice Firestone and her husband had a messy divorce. The court issued a judgment granting the divorce, stating that according to the testimony of the husband, the wife's "extramarital escapades . . . were bizarre and of an amatory nature which

would have made Dr. Freud's hair curl. Other testimony . . . would indicate that [the husband] was guilty of bounding from one bedpartner to another with the erotic zest of a satyr. The court is inclined to discount much of this testimony as unreliable." *Time* magazine published the following article in its "Milestones" section the following week:

> DIVORCED. By Russell A. Firestone Jr., 41, heir to the tire fortune: Mary Alice Sullivan Firestone, 32, his third wife; a onetime Palm Beach schoolteacher; on grounds of extreme cruelty and adultery; after six years of marriage, one son; in West Palm Beach, Fla. The 17-month intermittent trial produced enough testimony of extramarital adventures on both sides, said the judge, "to make Dr. Freud's hair curl."

Mary Firestone sued for libel. When the case ended up in the U.S. Supreme Court, the issue was whether Firestone was a public or private figure. According to the Court:

> Petitioner contends that because the Firestone divorce was characterized by the Florida Supreme Court as a "cause celebre," it must have been a public controversy and respondent must be considered a public figure. But in so doing petitioner seeks to equate "public controversy" with all controversies of interest to the public. . . .
>
> Dissolution of a marriage through judicial proceedings is not the sort of "public controversy" referred to in *Gertz*, even though the marital difficulties of extremely wealthy individuals may be of interest to some portion of the reading public. Nor did respondent freely choose to publicize issues as to the propriety of her married life. She was compelled to go to court by the State in order to obtain legal release from the bonds of matrimony. We have said that in such an instance "(r)esort to the judicial process . . . is no more voluntary in a realistic sense than that of the defendant called upon to defend his interests in court." . . . She assumed no "special prominence in the resolution of public questions." *Gertz*, 418 U.S., at 351. We hold respondent was not a "public figure" for the purpose of determining the constitutional protection afforded petitioner's report of the factual and legal basis for her divorce.

In *Wolston v. Readers Digest Ass'n, Inc.*, 443 U.S. 157 (1979), the plaintiff was summoned to appear before a grand jury in connection with an investigation into his aunt and uncle's spying for the Soviet Union in 1958. Due to mental depression, the plaintiff failed to appear before the grand jury and was held in contempt. In 1984, a book about Soviet agents stated that the plaintiff had been indicted for being such an agent. The district court and court of appeals held that the plaintiff was a limited-purpose public figure (regarding Soviet espionage) — those who, under the language of *Gertz*, "thrust themselves to the forefront of particular public controversies in order to influence the resolution of the issues involved." The Supreme Court disagreed:

> . . . [T]he undisputed facts do not justify the conclusion of the District Court and Court of Appeals that petitioner "voluntarily thrust" or "injected" himself into the forefront of the public controversy surrounding the investigation of Soviet espionage in the United States. It would be more accurate to say that petitioner was dragged unwillingly into the controversy. The Government

> pursued him in its investigation. Petitioner did fail to respond to a grand jury subpoena, and this failure, as well as his subsequent citation for contempt, did attract media attention. But the mere fact that petitioner voluntarily chose not to appear before the grand jury, knowing that his action might be attended by publicity, is not decisive on the question of public-figure status. . . . It is clear that petitioner played only a minor role in whatever public controversy there may have been concerning the investigation of Soviet espionage. We decline to hold that his mere citation for contempt rendered him a public figure for purposes of comment on the investigation of Soviet espionage.
>
> Petitioner's failure to appear before the grand jury and citation for contempt no doubt were "newsworthy," but the simple fact that these events attracted media attention also is not conclusive of the public-figure issue. A private individual is not automatically transformed into a public figure just by becoming involved in or associated with a matter that attracts public attention. . . . A libel defendant must show more than mere newsworthiness to justify application of the demanding burden of *New York Times*. . . .

If being involved in newsworthy events is not the appropriate test for whether a person is a public figure, then what are the dispositive factors?

Consider *Atlanta Journal-Constitution v. Jewell,* 555 S.E.2d 175 (Ga. Ct. App. 2001). Richard Jewell, a security guard in Olympic Park during the 1996 Olympics in Atlanta, spotted a suspicious unattended package and helped to evacuate the area. The package contained a bomb, and Jewell was initially recognized as a hero for helping prevent the terrorist attack. The FBI, however, believed that Jewell might have planted the bomb to make himself into a hero, and the FBI's suspicions of Jewell were leaked to the press. The *Atlanta Journal-Constitution* published an article entitled "FBI Suspects 'Hero' Guard May Have Planted Bomb." The FBI investigation eventually cleared Jewell. However, during the interim, Jewell's life was turned upside down, and he could not seek employment or even go out in public without being mobbed by reporters. Jewell sued the *Journal-Constitution* for defamation. The trial court held that Jewell was a "voluntary limited-purpose public figure." Jewell appealed, arguing that "he is not [such a public figure] because he did not assume a role of special prominence in the controversy over the safety of Olympic Park, he did not voluntarily thrust himself to the forefront of the controversy of the safety of Olympic Park, and he did not intentionally seek to influence the resolution or outcome of any public controversy surrounding the safety of Olympic Park." The court concluded that the trial court's designation of Jewell as a voluntary limited-purpose public figure was correct:

> In *Silvester v. American Broadcasting Cos.*, 839 F.2d 1491 (11th Cir. 1988), the Eleventh Circuit adopted a three-prong test to determine whether a person is a limited-purpose public figure. Under this test, the court must isolate the public controversy, examine the plaintiff's involvement in the controversy, and determine whether the alleged defamation was germane to the plaintiff's participation in the controversy. Whether a person is a public figure, general or limited, is a question of law for the court to resolve. . . .
>
> While we can envision situations in which news coverage alone would be insufficient to convert Jewell from private citizen to public figure, we agree with the trial court that Jewell's actions show that he voluntarily assumed a

position of influence in the controversy. Jewell granted ten interviews and one photo shoot in the three days between the bombing and the reopening of the park, mostly to prominent members of the national press. While no magical number of media appearances is required to render a citizen a public figure, Jewell's participation in the public discussion of the bombing exceeds what has been deemed sufficient to render other citizens public figures. . . .

Furthermore, the United States Supreme Court has held the actual malice rule is applicable whenever "an individual voluntarily injects himself *or is drawn into* a particular public controversy." The evidence in this case, at the very least, supports a finding that Jewell was initially drawn into the controversy unwillingly and thereafter assumed a prominent position as to its outcome. Jewell did not reject any role in the public controversy debate, was a prominent figure in the coverage of the controversy, and, whatever his reticence regarding his media appearances, encountered them voluntarily. . . .

The third prong of the *Silvester* test requires the court to ascertain whether the allegedly defamatory statements were germane to Jewell's participation in the controversy. Anything which might touch on the controversy is relevant. Misstatements wholly unrelated to the controversy do not require a showing of actual malice to be actionable. . . .

Certainly, the information reported regarding Jewell's character was germane to Jewell's participation in the controversy over the Olympic Park's safety. A public figure's talents, education, experience, and motives are relevant to the public's decision to listen to him. The articles and the challenged statements within them dealt with Jewell's status as a suspect in the bombing and his law enforcement background. . . .

Whether he liked it or not, Jewell became a central figure in the specific public controversy with respect to which he was allegedly defamed: the controversy over park safety. . . .

2. ***Are Corporate CEOs Public Figures?*** Patricia Sánchez Abril argues that the traditional way courts distinguish between public and private figures unfairly deems many business leaders to be public figures:

> Because contemporary business requires a public face, courts should give businesspeople certain latitude in their public dealings before branding them as public figures. Small-scale promotion, advertising campaigns, and lobbying and networking efforts should be considered part of modern business reality. Even some print and electronic media involvement is commonplace and should not be an automatic marker of larger-scale notoriety.[84]

Although CEOs may be less well known than celebrities, they may have a larger social impact because of the activities of their companies. Perhaps CEOs should be more likely to be deemed public figures than celebrities because of the power and influence they wield. What should entitle the press to have wider latitude in speaking about people? Their fame? Their power? Another factor?

3. ***Matters of Private Concern: The* Dun & Bradstreet *Case.*** Subsequent to *Gertz*, a plurality of the Court examined whether the *Gertz* rule would apply when, in contrast to the situation in *Gertz*, the alleged defamatory statements

---

[84] Patricia Sánchez Abril, The Evolution of Business Celebrity in American Law and Society, 48 Am. Bus. L.J. 177, 223 (2011).

did not involve a matter of public concern. In *Dun & Bradstreet, Inc. v. Greenmoss Builders, Inc.*, 472 U.S. 749 (1985), Dun & Bradstreet, a credit reporting agency, provided an erroneous report about the financial condition of Greenmoss Builders. Upon learning of the defamatory report, the president of Greenmoss called Dun & Bradstreet and asked for a correction and a list of all those to whom Dun & Bradstreet had sent the report. Dun & Bradstreet corrected the report but did not inform Greenmoss of the list of recipients of the report. Greenmoss sued for defamation, winning $50,000 in compensatory or presumed damages and $300,000 in punitive damages. The Court held that this did not involve a matter of public concern and that therefore the *Gertz* rule should not apply:

> The First Amendment interest . . . is less important than the one weighed in Gertz. We have long recognized that not all speech is of equal First Amendment importance. It is speech on "'matters of public concern'" that is "at the heart of the First Amendment's protection." . . .
>
> In contrast, speech on matters of purely private concern is of less First Amendment concern. As a number of state courts, including the court below, have recognized, the role of the Constitution in regulating state libel law is far more limited when the concerns that activated *New York Times* and *Gertz* are absent. . . .
>
> While such speech is not totally unprotected by the First Amendment, its protections are less stringent. In *Gertz*, we found that the state interest in awarding presumed and punitive damages was not "substantial" in view of their effect on speech at the core of First Amendment concern. . . . In light of the reduced constitutional value of speech involving no matters of public concern, we hold that the state interest adequately supports awards of presumed and punitive damages — even absent a showing of "actual malice." . . .

2. FALSE LIGHT

(a) Introduction

PUBLICITY PLACING PERSON IN FALSE LIGHT

Restatement (Second) of Torts § 652E

One who gives publicity to a matter concerning another that places the other before the public in a false light is subject to liability to the other for invasion of his privacy, if

(a) the false light in which the other was placed would be highly offensive to a reasonable person, and

(b) the actor had knowledge of or acted in reckless disregard as to the falsity of the publicized matter and the false light in which the other would be placed.

NOTES & QUESTIONS

1. ***False Light vs. Defamation.*** False light is similar in many respects to defamation. Both torts protect against material false statements. However,

defamation requires some form of reputational injury (although, once shown, one can collect for emotional distress). False light, on the other hand, can compensate exclusively for emotional distress. According to the Restatement: "It is enough that he is given unreasonable and highly objectionable publicity that attributes to him characteristics, conduct or beliefs that are false, and so is placed before the public in a false position. When this is the case and the matter attributed to the plaintiff is not defamatory, the rule here stated affords a different remedy, not available in an action for defamation." Comment (b). Since false light does not require reputational harm, a plaintiff can recover for false light that even improves her reputation.[85] While defamation concerns one's status in the community, false light concerns one's peace of mind. As Bryan Lasswell explains, the "false light tort, to the extent distinct from the tort of defamation . . . rests on an awareness that people who are made to seem pathetic or ridiculous may be shunned, and not just people who are thought to be dishonest or incompetent or immoral."[86]

Another difference between false light and defamation is that false light requires a wider communication of the information. False light requires "publicity," which must be made to the public at large. Defamation requires "publication," which means that the communication merely requires communication to another person.

2. ***Damages for False Light and Defamation.*** In *Braun v. Flynt*, 726 F.2d 245 (5th Cir. 1984), Jeannie Braun worked at an amusement park and performed a routine with "Ralph the Diving Pig." The pig dove into the pool and was fed by Braun from a milk bottle. One of Larry Flynt's publications, *Chic*, a pornographic magazine, obtained a photograph of Braun's act. The picture appeared in a section of the magazine called "Chic Thrills," implying that something kinky was going on. When Braun saw the photograph, she was mortified. She could not return to work and suffered from depression. She sued Flynt for defamation and false light. A jury awarded her actual and punitive damages for both causes of action. Flynt appealed, arguing among other things that liability was barred by the First Amendment. The court, applying the *Gertz* rule, concluded that Braun was not a public figure and that the First Amendment did not bar her recovery. However, the court concluded that she could not recover damages for both false light and defamation. Accordingly, the case was remanded for a new trial on damages.
3. ***Critics of the False Light Tort.*** Diane Zimmerman argues: "Most injuries from untruths will, and should, be handled as defamation actions; of those that cannot be, many will either be too trivial to remedy or will not be actionable because the 'falsity' complained of will be constitutionally-protected opinion or ideas."[87] A number of courts agree. Recall *Lake v. Wal-Mart* from

[85] *See, e.g.*, Nathan E. Ray, *Let There Be False Light: Resisting the Growing Trend Against an Important Tort*, 84 Minn. L. Rev. 713, 735 (2000).

[86] Bryan R. Lasswell, *In Defense of False Light: Why False Light Must Remain a Viable Cause of Action*, 34 S. Tex. L. Rev. 149, 176 (1993).

[87] Diane Leehneer Zimmerman, *False Light Invasion of Privacy: The Light That Failed*, 64 N.Y.U. L. Rev. 364, 452 (1989). For a defense of the false light tort, see Ray, *Let There Be False*

Chapter 1. There, the court recognized three of the four Warren and Brandeis privacy torts, declining to recognize false light: "We are concerned that claims under false light are similar to claims of defamation, and to the extent that false light is more expansive than defamation, tension between this tort and the First Amendment is increased." *See also Renwick v. News and Observer Publishing Co.*, 312 S.E.2d 405 (N.C. 1984) (declining to recognize false light tort). Does the false light tort serve a viable purpose?

4. ***Forms of False Light.*** An illustration of the type of misleading statement that can give rise to a false light action is when a mostly true story is somewhat embellished. *See Varnish v. Best Medium Publishing Co.*, 405 F.2d 608 (2d Cir. 1968) (viable false light action for false facts about the relationship between husband and wife who killed herself and their three children). Another example of a false light claim is when one's photograph is used out of context. *See, e.g., Thompson v. Close-up, Inc.*, 98 N.Y.S.2d 300 (1950) (article on drug dealing using the plaintiff's photo); *Holmes v. Curtis Publishing Co.*, 303 F. Supp. 522 (D.S.C. 1969) (use of plaintiff's photo with caption that plaintiff was a high-stakes gambler); *Morrell v. Forbes, Inc.*, 603 F. Supp. 1305 (D. Mass. 1985) (photo used in connection with article about organized crime). In *Wood v. Hustler Magazine*, 736 F.2d 1084 (5th Cir. 1984), a photograph of LaJuan Wood was stolen by another person, who sent it into *Hustler*, a pornographic magazine, along with a forged consent form. *Hustler* sent a mailgram to the address given on the forged consent form asking the sender to call *Hustler*. The sender did, and again lied that there was consent. *Hustler* published LaJuan's photo in its magazine stating: "LaJuan Wood is a 22-year old housewife and mother from Bryan, Texas, whose hobby is collecting arrowheads. Her fantasy is 'to be screwed by two bikers.'" LaJuan sued *Hustler*, and the court held that *Hustler* could be liable for false light because of the "publication of the false and highly offensive fantasy." The court reasoned that the magazine was negligent in making sure that the consent form was valid.

5. ***Obvious Fictions.*** Suppose a story is deliberately designed to be fictional and is so preposterous that a reasonable person could not possibly believe it to be true. Would there be a viable claim for false light? The answer is no, although it must be clear that the story is pure fiction. In *People's Bank and Trust Co. v. Globe International Publishing, Inc.*, 978 F.2d 1065 (8th Cir. 1992), a tabloid ran a story about a 97-year-old woman who became pregnant. The story used the name of a real person, who sued. The tabloid contended that no reader could reasonably believe that the story was true. The court rejected the contention because the publisher of the tabloid "holds out the publication as factual and true," and it "mingles factual, fictional, and hybrid stories without overtly identifying one from the other."

Light, supra; Lasswell, *In Defense of False Light, supra*; Gary T. Schwartz, *Explaining and Justifying a Limited Tort of False Light Invasion of Privacy*, 41 Case W. Res. L. Rev. 885 (1991).

(b) First Amendment Limitations

TIME, INC. V. HILL

385 U.S. 374 (1967)

[In 1952, the Hill family was held prisoner in their home for 19 hours by three escaped convicts. The family escaped unharmed and were treated courteously by the convicts. The convicts were later killed by police during their apprehension. The story made the front page news. The Hill family tried hard to remain out of the spotlight. Nevertheless, the Hill family's experience was written about in a novel by Joseph Hayes called *The Desperate Hours*. In contrast to the actual events, the book depicted the convicts beating the father and son and making a verbal sexual insult to the daughter. A Broadway play and a movie were made based on the book. In 1955, *Life* magazine published an article entitled "True Crime Inspires Tense Play." The article stated that "Americans all over the country read about the desperate ordeal of the James Hill family" and "read about it in Joseph Hayes's novel, *The Desperate Hours*, inspired by the family's experience." The article then stated: "Now they can see the story re-enacted in Hayes's Broadway play based on the book." Pictures accompanying the article displayed scenes from the play depicting the son being beaten and the daughter biting the hand of a convict. The *Life* magazine photographs were taken in the Hills' former home, where they had been held hostage. The Hills sued under §§ 50-51 of the New York Civil Rights Law, contending that the *Life* article gave the false impression that the play accurately depicted the Hills' experience. A jury awarded the Hills $50,000 compensatory and $25,000 punitive damages.]

BRENNAN, J. . . . The question in this case is whether appellant, publisher of Life Magazine, was denied constitutional protections of speech and press by the application by the New York courts of §§ 50-51 of the New York Civil Rights Law to award appellee damages on allegations that Life falsely reported that a new play portrayed an experience suffered by appellee and his family.

. . . In *New York Times Co. v. Sullivan*, we held that the Constitution delimits a State's power to award damages for libel in actions brought by public officials against critics of their official conduct. Factual error, content defamatory of official reputation, or both, are insufficient for an award of damages for false statements unless actual malice — knowledge that the statements are false or in reckless disregard of the truth — is alleged and proved. . . .

. . . We hold that the constitutional protections for speech and press preclude the application of the New York statute to redress false reports of matters of public interest in the absence of proof that the defendant published the report with knowledge of its falsity or in reckless disregard of the truth.

The guarantees for speech and press are not the preserve of political expression or comment upon public affairs, essential as those are to healthy government. One need only pick up any newspaper or magazine to comprehend the vast range of published matter which exposes persons to public view, both private citizens and public officials. Exposure of the self to others in varying degrees is a concomitant of life in a civilized community. The risk of this exposure is an essential incident of life in a society which places a primary value on freedom of speech and of press. "Freedom of discussion, if it would fulfill its historic function in this nation, must embrace all issues about which information is needed or appropriate to enable the members of society to cope with the exigencies of their period." . . . We have no doubt that the subject of the Life article, the opening of a new play linked to an actual incident, is a matter of public interest. "The line between the informing and the entertaining is too elusive for the protection of . . . (freedom of the press)." Erroneous statement is no less inevitable in such a case than in the case of comment upon public affairs, and in both, if innocent or merely negligent, ". . . it must be protected if the freedoms of expression are to have the 'breathing space' that they 'need . . . to survive' . . . ." *New York Times Co. v. Sullivan*. . . . We create a grave risk of serious impairment of the indispensable service of a free press in a free society if we saddle the press with the impossible burden of verifying to a certainty the facts associated in news articles with a person's name, picture or portrait, particularly as related to nondefamatory matter. Even negligence would be a most elusive standard, especially when the content of the speech itself affords no warning of prospective harm to another through falsity. A negligence test would place on the press the intolerable burden of guessing how a jury might assess the reasonableness of steps taken by it to verify the accuracy of every reference to a name, picture or portrait.

In this context, sanctions against either innocent or negligent misstatement would present a grave hazard of discouraging the press from exercising the constitutional guarantees. Those guarantees are not for the benefit of the press so much as for the benefit of all of us. A broadly defined freedom of the press assures the maintenance of our political system and an open society. Fear of large verdicts in damage suits for innocent or merely negligent misstatement, even fear of the expense involved in their defense, must inevitably cause publishers to "steer . . . wider of the unlawful zone," *New York Times Co. v. Sullivan*, and thus "create the danger that the legitimate utterance will be penalized."

But the constitutional guarantees can tolerate sanctions against calculated falsehood without significant impairment of their essential function. We held in *New York Times* that calculated falsehood enjoyed no immunity in the case of alleged defamation of a public official concerning his official conduct. Similarly, calculated falsehood should enjoy no immunity in the situation here presented us. . . .

Turning to the facts of the present case, the proofs reasonably would support either a jury finding of innocent or merely negligent misstatement by Life, or a finding that Life portrayed the play as a reenactment of the Hill family's experience reckless of the truth or with actual knowledge that the portrayal was false. . . . [The jury instructions were thus defective because they did not instruct the jury that liability could only be found against *Life* if *Life* acted in reckless disregard for the truth or with actual knowledge that the play was false.]

The judgment of the Court of Appeals is set aside and the case is remanded for further proceedings not inconsistent with this opinion. . . .

NOTES & QUESTIONS

1. ***An Inside Look at* Time, Inc. v. Hill.** Before the Supreme Court, the Hills were represented by Richard Nixon, the future President, then in private practice. In a memoir, Leonard Garment, a long-time Nixon advisor, writes: "Nixon's main effort [as the Hills' attorney] was to demonstrate that the magazine had consciously presented the fictionalized play as a 're-enacted' account of the Hill incident." This depiction was, however, "a deliberate falsification," a gimmick "to justify the use of the former Hill home as a 'True Crime' site for the magazine's review of the play."

   Garment also observes that Nixon, in his first argument in any appellate court, "sounded like a polished professional of the bar — his footing confident, his language lawyer-like, his organization clear." Originally, the Court voted 6-3 in favor of the Hills, with Justice Abe Fortas to write the majority opinion. But after Fortas's memorandum was circulated, Justice Hugo Black circulated a pro-press memorandum and was able to convince a majority of the Court to join him in finding for Time.

   Elizabeth Hill committed suicide in August 1971. In Garment's opinion, the magazine article did not cause the suicide, but "troubled persons . . . suffer with special acuteness when they are forced into the spotlight of negative community attention."[88]
2. ***The Time Line of Leading Constitutional Law Cases.*** *Time, Inc. v. Hill* was decided after *New York Times v. Sullivan* but before *Gertz*. Do false light actions involving private figures also have to prove actual malice under *New York Times*? Although the Court never explicitly applied the *Gertz* rule to a false light case, courts are split in cases involving private figures as to whether *Gertz* applies to false light or whether all false light claims must satisfy the more stringent *New York Times* standard. *See, e.g., Braun v. Flynt*, 726 F.2d 245 (5th Cir. 1984) (applying *Gertz*); *Dietz v. Wometco West Michigan TV*, 407 N.W.2d 649 (Mich. App. 1987) (applying *Gertz*); *Dodrill v. Arkansas Democrat*, 590 S.W.2d 840 (Ark. 1979) (applying *New York Times*); *Schifano v. Greene County Greyhound Park, Inc.*, 624 So. 2d 178 (Ala. 1993) (applying *New York Times*). Consider Restatement (Second) of Torts § 652E comment d:

   > If *Time v. Hill* is modified along the lines of *Gertz v. Robert Welch*, then the reckless-disregard rule would apparently apply if the plaintiff is a public official or public figure and the negligence rule will apply to other plaintiffs.

3. INFLICTION OF EMOTIONAL DISTRESS

Another tort remedy for the dissemination of false or misleading information is the tort of infliction of emotional distress. This tort may also serve as a remedy to the disclosure of true information. As defined by the Restatement (Second) of Torts § 46, the tort requires:

---

[88] Leonard Garment, *Crazy Rhythm: From Brooklyn and Jazz to Nixon's White House, Watergate, and Beyond* (1997).

> One who by extreme and outrageous conduct intentionally or recklessly causes severe emotional distress to another is subject to liability for such emotional distress, and if bodily harm to the other results from it, for such bodily harm.

The tort has some significant limitations as a remedy for privacy infringements. First, it requires "extreme and outrageous conduct," which is conduct significantly outside the bounds of propriety. This is quite a high bar for a plaintiff to leap over. Second, it requires "severe emotional distress," and many privacy violations may not be viewed by courts as causing such a high level of psychological turmoil. For example, in *DeGregario v. CBS*, 473 N.Y.S.2d 922 (N.Y. Sup. Ct. 1984), a news segment called "Couples in New York" included video of two construction workers, a male and a female, holding hands. Each was married or engaged to another person. After the video was shot, the workers asked the television crew not to include them in the segment, but they were included anyway. The court rejected their infliction of emotional distress claim because "broadcasting a film depicting unnamed couples engaging in romantic conduct on a public street . . . in a news report about romance cannot be said to be unusual conduct transcending the norms tolerated by a decent society."

In a similar fashion to the privacy torts, the tort of infliction of emotional distress is subject to First Amendment restrictions. Consider the following case:

HUSTLER MAGAZINE V. FALWELL

485 U.S. 46 (1988)

[A 1983 issue of *Hustler* magazine featured a parody using nationally known minister Jerry Falwell's name and photo. The parody, entitled "Jerry Falwell Talks About His First Time," was patterned after a series of ads for a brand of liquor which interviewed celebrities about their "first times" trying the liquor (but playing on the sexual double meaning). In a similar layout, *Hustler*'s parody interview with Falwell had him drunk and engaging in incest with his mother. In small print, the parody contained the disclaimer, "ad parody — not to be taken seriously." Falwell sued for, among other things, intentional infliction of emotional distress. This issue made it to the U.S. Supreme Court, where the Court confronted the task of defining whether the First Amendment limitations that applied to defamation and false light should also be applied to intentional infliction of emotional distress.]

REHNQUIST, C.J. . . . "Freedoms of expression require 'breathing space.'" This breathing space is provided by a constitutional rule that allows public figures to recover for libel or defamation only when they can prove *both* that the statement was false and that the statement was made with the requisite level of culpability.

Respondent argues, however, that a different standard should apply in this case because here the State seeks to prevent not reputational damage, but the severe emotional distress suffered by the person who is the subject of an offensive publication. *Cf. Zacchini v. Scripps-Howard Broadcasting Co.*, 433 U.S. 562 (ruling that the "actual malice" standard does not apply to the tort of appropriation of a right of publicity). In respondent's view, and in the view of the Court of Appeals, so long as the utterance was intended to inflict emotional distress, was outrageous, and did in fact inflict serious emotional distress, it is of no constitutional import whether the statement was a fact or an opinion, or whether it was true or false. It is the intent to cause injury that is the gravamen of the tort, and the State's interest in preventing emotional harm simply outweighs whatever interest a speaker may have in speech of this type.

Generally speaking the law does not regard the intent to inflict emotional distress as one which should receive much solicitude, and it is quite understandable that most if not all jurisdictions have chosen to make it civilly culpable where the conduct in question is sufficiently "outrageous." But in the world of debate about public affairs, many things done with motives that are less than admirable are protected by the First Amendment. . . .

Thus while such a bad motive may be deemed controlling for purposes of tort liability in other areas of the law, we think the First Amendment prohibits such a result in the area of public debate about public figures.

Were we to hold otherwise, there can be little doubt that political cartoonists and satirists would be subjected to damages awards without any showing that their work falsely defamed its subject. Webster's defines a caricature as "the deliberately distorted picturing or imitating of a person, literary style, etc. by exaggerating features or mannerisms for satirical effect." Webster's New Unabridged Twentieth Century Dictionary of the English Language 275 (2d ed. 1979). The appeal of the political cartoon or caricature is often based on exploitation of unfortunate physical traits or politically embarrassing events — an exploitation often calculated to injure the feelings of the subject of the portrayal. The art of the cartoonist is often not reasoned or evenhanded, but slashing and one-sided. . . .

Several famous examples of this type of intentionally injurious speech were drawn by Thomas Nast, probably the greatest American cartoonist to date, who was associated for many years during the post-Civil War era with Harper's Weekly. In the pages of that publication Nast conducted a graphic vendetta against William M. "Boss" Tweed and his corrupt associates in New York City's "Tweed Ring." . . .

Despite their sometimes caustic nature, from the early cartoon portraying George Washington as an ass down to the present day, graphic depictions and satirical cartoons have played a prominent role in public and political debate. Nast's castigation of the Tweed Ring, Walt McDougall's characterization of Presidential candidate James G. Blaine's banquet with the millionaires at Delmonico's as "The Royal Feast of Belshazzar," and numerous other efforts have undoubtedly had an effect on the course and outcome of contemporaneous debate. Lincoln's tall, gangling posture, Teddy Roosevelt's glasses and teeth, and Franklin D. Roosevelt's jutting jaw and cigarette holder have been memorialized by political cartoons with an effect that could not have been obtained by the photographer or the portrait artist. From the viewpoint of history it is clear that our political discourse would have been considerably poorer without them. Respondent contends, however, that the caricature in question here was so "outrageous" as to distinguish it from more traditional political cartoons. There is no doubt that the caricature of respondent and his mother published in Hustler is at best a distant cousin of the political cartoons described above, and a rather poor relation at that. If it were possible by laying down a principled standard to separate the one from the other, public discourse would probably suffer little or no harm. But we doubt that there is any such standard, and we are quite sure that the pejorative description "outrageous" does not supply one. "Outrageousness" in the area of political and social discourse has an inherent subjectiveness about it which would allow a jury to impose liability on the basis of the jurors' tastes or views, or perhaps on the basis of their dislike of a particular expression. An "outrageousness" standard thus runs afoul of our longstanding refusal to allow damages to be awarded because the speech in question may have an adverse emotional impact on the audience. . . .

We conclude that public figures and public officials may not recover for the tort of intentional infliction of emotional distress by reason of publications such as the one here at issue without showing in addition that the publication contains a false statement of fact which was made with "actual malice," *i.e.*, with knowledge that the statement was false or with reckless disregard as to whether or not it was true. This is not merely a "blind application" of the *New York Times* standard, see *Time, Inc. v. Hill*, 385 U.S. 374 (1967), it reflects our considered judgment that such a standard is necessary to give adequate "breathing space" to the freedoms protected by the First Amendment.

Here it is clear that respondent Falwell is a "public figure" for purposes of First Amendment law. The jury found against respondent on his libel claim when it decided that the Hustler ad parody could not "reasonably be understood as describing actual facts about [respondent] or actual events in which [he] participated." The Court of Appeals interpreted the jury's finding to be that the ad parody "was not reasonably believable," and in accordance with our custom we accept this finding. Respondent is thus relegated to his claim for damages awarded by the jury for the intentional infliction of emotional distress by "outrageous" conduct. But for reasons heretofore stated this claim cannot, consistently with the First Amendment, form a basis for the award of damages when the conduct in question is the publication of a caricature such as the ad parody involved here. . . .

NOTES & QUESTIONS

1. ***Private Figures and the Intentional Infliction of Emotional Distress Tort.*** The *Hustler* Court focused on public figures and public officials, imposing the *New York Times* standard requiring proof of actual malice. What should the standard be for private figures? The standard in *Gertz*? Under the First Amendment, should the intentional infliction of emotional distress tort be treated the same as the defamation torts? Or differently?
2. ***Is the Intentional Infliction of Emotional Distress Tort Too Subjective?*** The Court states:

> "Outrageousness" in the area of political and social discourse has an inherent subjectiveness about it which would allow a jury to impose liability on the basis of the jurors' tastes or views, or perhaps on the basis of their dislike of a particular expression.

If this is true, does this make the intentional infliction of emotional distress tort too easy a way for juries to penalize speech they find distasteful?

SNYDER V. PHELPS

131 S. Ct. 1207 (2011)

ROBERTS, C.J. A jury held members of the Westboro Baptist Church liable for millions of dollars in damages for picketing near a soldier's funeral service. The picket signs reflected the church's view that the United States is overly tolerant of sin and that God kills American soldiers as punishment. The question presented is whether the First Amendment shields the church members from tort liability for their speech in this case.

Fred Phelps founded the Westboro Baptist Church in Topeka, Kansas, in 1955. The church's congregation believes that God hates and punishes the United States for its tolerance of homosexuality, particularly in America's military. The church frequently communicates its views by picketing, often at military funerals. In the more than 20 years that the members of Westboro Baptist have publicized their message, they have picketed nearly 600 funerals.

Marine Lance Corporal Matthew Snyder was killed in Iraq in the line of duty. Lance Corporal Snyder's father selected the Catholic church in the Snyders' hometown of Westminster, Maryland, as the site for his son's funeral. Local newspapers provided notice of the time and location of the service.

Phelps became aware of Matthew Snyder's funeral and decided to travel to Maryland with six other Westboro Baptist parishioners (two of his daughters and four of his grandchildren) to picket. On the day of the memorial service, the Westboro congregation members picketed on public land adjacent to public streets near the Maryland State House, the United States Naval Academy, and Matthew Snyder's funeral. The Westboro picketers carried signs that were largely the same at all three locations. They stated, for instance: "God Hates the USA/Thank God for 9/11," "America is Doomed," "Don't Pray for the USA," "Thank God for IEDs," "Thank God for Dead Soldiers," "Pope in Hell," "Priests Rape Boys," "God Hates Fags," "You're Going to Hell," and "God Hates You."

The church had notified the authorities in advance of its intent to picket at the time of the funeral, and the picketers complied with police instructions in staging their demonstration. The picketing took place within a 10- by 25-foot plot of public land adjacent to a public street, behind a temporary fence. That plot was approximately 1,000 feet from the church where the funeral was held. Several buildings separated the picket site from the church. The Westboro picketers displayed their signs for about 30 minutes before the funeral began and sang hymns and recited Bible verses. None of the picketers entered church property or went to the cemetery. They did not yell or use profanity, and there was no violence associated with the picketing.

The funeral procession passed within 200 to 300 feet of the picket site. Although Snyder testified that he could see the tops of the picket signs as he drove to the funeral, he did not see what was written on the signs until later that night, while watching a news broadcast covering the event.[89]

Snyder filed suit against Phelps, Phelps's daughters, and the Westboro Baptist Church (collectively Westboro or the church) in the United States District Court for the District of Maryland under that court's diversity jurisdiction. Snyder alleged five state tort law claims: defamation, publicity given to private life, intentional infliction of emotional distress, intrusion upon seclusion, and civil conspiracy. Westboro moved for summary judgment contending, in part, that the church's speech was insulated from liability by the First Amendment.

The District Court awarded Westboro summary judgment on Snyder's claims for defamation and publicity given to private life, concluding that Snyder could not prove the necessary elements of those torts. A trial was held on the remaining claims. . . .

A jury found for Snyder on the intentional infliction of emotional distress, intrusion upon seclusion, and civil conspiracy claims, and held Westboro liable for $2.9 million in compensatory damages and $8 million in punitive damages. Westboro filed several post-trial motions, including a motion contending that the jury verdict was grossly excessive and a motion seeking judgment as a matter of law on all claims on First Amendment grounds. The District Court remitted the punitive damages award to $2.1 million, but left the jury verdict otherwise intact. . . .

To succeed on a claim for intentional infliction of emotional distress in Maryland, a plaintiff must demonstrate that the defendant intentionally or recklessly engaged in extreme and outrageous conduct that caused the plaintiff to suffer severe emotional distress. . . .

Whether the First Amendment prohibits holding Westboro liable for its speech in this case turns largely on whether that speech is of public or private concern, as determined by all the circumstances of the case. "[S]peech on 'matters of public concern' . . . is 'at the heart of the First Amendment's protection.'" . . . .

" '[N]ot all speech is of equal First Amendment importance,' " however, and where matters of purely private significance are at issue, First Amendment protections are often less rigorous. That is because restricting speech on purely private matters does not implicate the same constitutional concerns as limiting speech on matters of public interest: "[T]here is no threat to the free and robust debate of public issues; there is no potential interference with a meaningful dialogue of ideas"; and the "threat of liability" does not pose the risk of "a reaction of self-censorship" on matters of public import. *Dun & Bradstreet*. . . .

Speech deals with matters of public concern when it can "be fairly considered as relating to any matter of political, social, or other concern to the community," or when it "is a subject of legitimate news interest; that is, a subject of general interest and of value and concern to the public." The arguably

---

[89] A few weeks after the funeral, one of the picketers posted a message on Westboro's Web site discussing the picketing and containing religiously oriented denunciations of the Snyders, interspersed among lengthy Bible quotations. Snyder discovered the posting, referred to by the parties as the "epic," during an Internet search for his son's name. The epic is not properly before us and does not factor in our analysis. Although the epic was submitted to the jury and discussed in the courts below, Snyder never mentioned it in his petition for certiorari. . . .

"inappropriate or controversial character of a statement is irrelevant to the question whether it deals with a matter of public concern."

Our opinion in *Dun & Bradstreet,* on the other hand, provides an example of speech of only private concern. In that case we held, as a general matter, that information about a particular individual's credit report "concerns no public issue." The content of the report, we explained, "was speech solely in the individual interest of the speaker and its specific business audience." . . .

The "content" of Westboro's signs plainly relates to broad issues of interest to society at large, rather than matters of "purely private concern." . . . While these messages may fall short of refined social or political commentary, the issues they highlight — the political and moral conduct of the United States and its citizens, the fate of our Nation, homosexuality in the military, and scandals involving the Catholic clergy — are matters of public import. The signs certainly convey Westboro's position on those issues, in a manner designed, unlike the private speech in *Dun & Bradstreet,* to reach as broad a public audience as possible. And even if a few of the signs — such as "You're Going to Hell" and "God Hates You" — were viewed as containing messages related to Matthew Snyder or the Snyders specifically, that would not change the fact that the overall thrust and dominant theme of Westboro's demonstration spoke to broader public issues. . . .

Given that Westboro's speech was at a public place on a matter of public concern, that speech is entitled to "special protection" under the First Amendment. Such speech cannot be restricted simply because it is upsetting or arouses contempt. . . .

The jury here was instructed that it could hold Westboro liable for intentional infliction of emotional distress based on a finding that Westboro's picketing was "outrageous." "Outrageousness," however, is a highly malleable standard with "an inherent subjectiveness about it which would allow a jury to impose liability on the basis of the jurors' tastes or views, or perhaps on the basis of their dislike of a particular expression." . . .

For all these reasons, the jury verdict imposing tort liability on Westboro for intentional infliction of emotional distress must be set aside. . . .

The jury also found Westboro liable for the state law torts of intrusion upon seclusion and civil conspiracy. . . .

Snyder argues that even assuming Westboro's speech is entitled to First Amendment protection generally, the church is not immunized from liability for intrusion upon seclusion because Snyder was a member of a captive audience at his son's funeral. We do not agree. In most circumstances, "the Constitution does not permit the government to decide which types of otherwise protected speech are sufficiently offensive to require protection for the unwilling listener or viewer. Rather, . . . the burden normally falls upon the viewer to avoid further bombardment of [his] sensibilities simply by averting [his] eyes." . . .

As a general matter, we have applied the captive audience doctrine only sparingly to protect unwilling listeners from protected speech. . . .

Here, Westboro stayed well away from the memorial service. Snyder could see no more than the tops of the signs when driving to the funeral. And there is no indication that the picketing in any way interfered with the funeral service itself. We decline to expand the captive audience doctrine to the circumstances presented here. . . .

ALITO, J. dissenting. . . . Respondents and other members of their church have strong opinions on certain moral, religious, and political issues, and the First Amendment ensures that they have almost limitless opportunities to express their views. They may write and distribute books, articles, and other texts; they may create and disseminate video and audio recordings; they may circulate petitions; they may speak to individuals and groups in public forums and in any private venue that wishes to accommodate them; they may picket peacefully in countless locations; they may appear on television and speak on the radio; they may post messages on the Internet and send out e-mails. And they may express their views in terms that are "uninhibited," "vehement," and "caustic."

It does not follow, however, that they may intentionally inflict severe emotional injury on private persons at a time of intense emotional sensitivity by launching vicious verbal attacks that make no contribution to public debate. To protect against such injury, "most if not all jurisdictions" permit recovery in tort for the intentional infliction of emotional distress (or IIED).

This is a very narrow tort with requirements that "are rigorous, and difficult to satisfy." . . .

In this case, respondents brutally attacked Matthew Snyder, and this attack, which was almost certain to inflict injury, was central to respondents' well-practiced strategy for attracting public attention. . . .

After the funeral, the Westboro picketers reaffirmed the meaning of their protest. They posted an online account entitled "The Burden of Marine Lance Cpl. Matthew A. Snyder. The Visit of Westboro Baptist Church to Help the Inhabitants of Maryland Connect the Dots!" Belying any suggestion that they had simply made general comments about homosexuality, the Catholic Church, and the United States military, the "epic" addressed the Snyder family directly:

> "God blessed you, Mr. and Mrs. Snyder, with a resource and his name was Matthew. He was an arrow in your quiver! In thanks to God for the comfort the child could bring you, you had a DUTY to prepare that child to serve the LORD his GOD — PERIOD! You did JUST THE OPPOSITE — you raised him for the devil. . . .
>
> "Albert and Julie RIPPED that body apart and taught Matthew to defy his Creator, to divorce, and to commit adultery. They taught him how to support the largest pedophile machine in the history of the entire world, the Roman Catholic monstrosity. Every dime they gave the Roman Catholic monster they condemned their own souls. They also, in supporting satanic Catholicism, taught Matthew to be an idolater. . . ."

While commentary on the Catholic Church or the United States military constitutes speech on matters of public concern, speech regarding Matthew Snyder's purely private conduct does not. . . .

The Court concludes that respondents' speech was protected by the First Amendment for essentially three reasons, but none is sound.

First — and most important — the Court finds that "the overall thrust and dominant theme of [their] demonstration spoke to" broad public issues. As I have attempted to show, this portrayal is quite inaccurate; respondents' attack on Matthew was of central importance. But in any event, I fail to see why actionable speech should be immunized simply because it is interspersed with speech that is protected. The First Amendment allows recovery for defamatory statements that are interspersed with nondefamatory statements on matters of public concern, and there is no good reason why respondents' attack on Matthew Snyder and his family should be treated differently.

Second, the Court suggests that respondents' personal attack on Matthew Snyder is entitled to First Amendment protection because it was not motivated by a private grudge, but I see no basis for the strange distinction that the Court appears to draw. Respondents' motivation — "to increase publicity for its views," — did not transform their statements attacking the character of a private figure into statements that made a contribution to debate on matters of public concern. . . .

Third, the Court finds it significant that respondents' protest occurred on a public street, but this fact alone should not be enough to preclude IIED liability.

NOTES & QUESTIONS

1. ***Intrusion upon Seclusion.*** On what basis could the jury have found that the defendants were liable for intrusion upon seclusion? Should the claim have been dismissed before it even reached the jury?
2. ***Is Actual Malice the Appropriate Standard?*** Consider Jeffrey Shulman:

> There is no justification for applying the actual malice standard to emotional distress claims outside the public arena (and little enough inside). The literal application of the actual malice standard offers no protection to the plaintiff claiming emotional injury from rhetorically hyperbolic speech. The victim of a libel can show that the statement was false. The victim of rhetorical hyperbole can prove or disprove nothing that will bring judicial redress. This may be the cost of doing business in the public arena, but why should the private plaintiff be left defenseless against emotionally injurious speech that serves no valid communicative purpose?[90]

If the actual malice standard is not appropriate for public figures or matters of public concern, what should the standard be? Consider Shulman's view:

> The *Hustler* Court was concerned that " '[o]utrageousness' in the area of political and social discourse has an inherent subjectiveness about it which would allow a jury to impose liability on the basis of the jurors' tastes or views, or perhaps on the basis of their dislike of a particular expression." Perhaps so, but in the funeral of a private individual we might find "a principled standard" by which to circumscribe emotional distress claims within a safe constitutional perimeter. Where discourse is not, in fact, of public concern, where it is targeted to a private audience unwilling to receive it but unable to avoid it, where its purpose is to injure, then its restriction is little threat to free speech values; where public concern is a mask

---

[90] Jeffrey Shulman, *Free Speech at What Cost?* Snyder v. Phelps *and Speech-Based Tort Liability*, 2010 Cardozo L. Rev. De Novo 312, 315.

> for mere personal abuse, private individuals should have full legal recourse to secure their right to be let alone.

Was Westboro Baptist Church's speech directed at specific people? Set aside the online speech, quoted in Justice Alito's dissent, as the Court did not consider it in its analysis. The picketers used the occasion of the funeral to draw attention to their message, but was Snyder at the center of their message? Was their speech of public concern? Was it "targeted to a private audience unwilling to receive it but unable to avoid it"?

Should the First Amendment condone using a private person as fodder for one's speech when that message could have readily been made without any connection to the private person?

D. APPROPRIATION OF NAME OR LIKENESS

1. INTRODUCTION

APPROPRIATION OF NAME OR LIKENESS

Restatement (Second) of Torts § 652C

One who appropriates to his own use or benefit the name or likeness of another is subject to liability to the other for invasion of his privacy.

NOTES & QUESTIONS

1. ***The Development of the Appropriation Tort.*** The tort of appropriation protects "the interest of the individual in the exclusive use of his own identity, in so far as it is represented by his name or likeness, and in so far as the use may be of benefit to him or to others." Restatement § 652C, comment (a). To be liable for appropriation, "the defendant must have appropriated to his own use or benefit the reputation, prestige, social or commercial standing, public interest or other values of the plaintiff's name or likeness." *Id.*, comment (c).

   Recall from section A that two of the first cases to address the creation of new causes of action in response to the Warren and Brandeis article — *Roberson* and *Pavesich* — both involved appropriation claims.

   One of the most widely discussed state appropriation tort formulations is that of New York. New York's statute, passed in response to *Roberson*, which refused to recognize the tort in the common law, provides criminal and civil remedies for appropriation. Pursuant to New York Civil Rights Law § 50:

   > A person, firm or corporation that uses for advertising purposes, or for the purposes of trade, the name, portrait or picture of any living person without having first obtained the written consent of such person, or if a minor of his or her parent or guardian, is guilty of a misdemeanor.

   New York Civil Rights Law § 51 provides a civil remedy:

> Any person whose name, portrait, picture or voice is used within this state for advertising purposes or for the purposes of trade without the written consent first obtained . . . may maintain an equitable action in the supreme court of this state against the person, firm or corporation so using his name, portrait, picture or voice, to prevent and restrain the use thereof; and may also sue and recover damages for any injuries sustained by reason of such use. . . .

California has a similar statute, which provides: "Any person who knowingly uses another's name, photograph or likeness, in any manner, for purposes of advertising . . . or for purposes of solicitation of purchases of products . . . without . . . prior consent . . . shall be liable for any damages." Cal. Civ. Code § 3344. In many states, the tort of appropriation is recognized through the common law and is not statutory in nature.

2. ***Appropriation and the "Right of Publicity."*** The original rationale for the tort of appropriation was privacy-based, as a protection of one's dignity against the exploitation of her identity. However, another rationale for the tort has emerged, one that is property-based. Many courts and commentators refer to this alternative rationale as the "right of publicity."[91] The "right of publicity" was first referred to as such in *Haelan Laboratories v. Topps Chewing Gum, Inc.*, 202 F.2d 866 (2d Cir. 1953), where Judge Jerome Frank held that New York recognized a common law tort of "publicity" distinct from §§ 50-51's remedy for appropriation:

> We think that, in addition to and independent of that right of privacy (which in New York derives from statute), a man has a right in the publicity value of his photograph, i.e., the right to grant the exclusive privilege of publishing his picture, and that such a grant may validly be made "in gross," i.e., without an accompanying transfer of a business or of anything else. Whether it be labeled a "property" right is immaterial; for here, as often elsewhere, the tag "property" simply symbolizes the fact that courts enforce a claim which has pecuniary worth.
>
> This right might be called a "right of publicity." For it is common knowledge that many prominent persons (especially actors and ball-players), far from having their feelings bruised through public exposure of their likenesses, would feel sorely deprived if they no longer received money for authorizing advertisements, popularizing their countenances, displayed in newspapers, magazines, busses, trains and subways.

Subsequently, courts held that the publicity tort was subsumed under § 51 and was not a common law cause of action. *See Welch v. Group W Productions, Inc.*, 525 N.Y.S.2d 466, 468 n.1 (N.Y. Sup. Ct. 1987) ("In New York State the so-called 'right of publicity' is merely an aspect of the right of privacy and is not an independent common-law right.").

How is the "right of publicity" distinct from the privacy interests involved in appropriation? As one court describes the distinction:

---

[91] J. Thomas McCarthy, *The Rights of Publicity and Privacy* (2d ed. 2011); Melville B. Nimmer, *The Right of Publicity*, 19 Law & Contemp. Probs. 203 (1954); Sheldon Halpern, *The Right of Publicity: Maturation of an Independent Right Protecting the Associative Value of Personality*, 46 Hastings L.J. 853 (1995); Oliver R. Goodenough, *Go Fish: Evaluating the Restatement's Formulation of the Law of Publicity*, 47 S.C. L. Rev. 709 (1996).

> The privacy-based action is designed for individuals who have not placed themselves in the public eye. It shields such people from the embarrassment of having their faces plastered on billboards and cereal boxes without their permission. The interests protected are dignity and peace of mind, and damages are measured in terms of emotional distress. By contrast, a right of publicity action is designed for individuals who have placed themselves in the public eye. It secures for them the exclusive right to exploit the commercial value that attaches to their identities by virtue of their celebrity. The right to publicity protects that value as property, and its infringement is a commercial, rather than a personal tort. Damages stem not from embarrassment but from the unauthorized use of the plaintiffs' property. *Jim Henson Productions, Inc. v. John T. Brady & Associates, Inc.*, 687 F. Supp. 185, 188-89 (S.D.N.Y. 1994).

Thomas McCarthy articulates the distinction most succinctly: "Simplistically put, while the appropriation branch of the right of privacy is invaded by an injury to the psyche, the right of publicity is infringed by an injury to the pocket book."[92]

The Restatement (Third) of the Law of Unfair Competition § 46 provides for a distinct tort of "publicity":

> *Appropriation of the Commercial Value of a Person's Identity: The Right of Publicity.* One who appropriates the commercial value of a person's identity by using without consent the person's name, likeness, or other indicia of identity for purposes of trade is subject to liability for [monetary and injunctive] relief.

The commentary to the Restatement § 46 contrasts the "publicity" right in § 46 with the "appropriation tort" in the Restatement of Torts: "The 'appropriation' tort as described by Prosser and the Restatement, Second, of Torts, subsumes harm to both personal and commercial interests caused by an unauthorized exploitation of the plaintiff's identity." Restatement (Third) of the Law of Unfair Competition § 46, comment (b). A number of jurisdictions recognize a distinct tort of "publicity."

Although there is now a separate "right of publicity" to protect property interests, the tort of appropriation has shifted towards being a property protection similar to the right of publicity. William Prosser, in his 1960 article describing the torts spawned by Warren and Brandeis's article, did not recognize a distinct tort of publicity; it was merely a part of the appropriation tort. Likewise, the Restatement (Second) of Torts did not recognize a distinct tort of publicity. However, according to the Restatement, it appears that the central interest protected by appropriation is property rather than privacy: "Although the protection of [a person's] personal feelings against mental distress is an important factor leading to a recognition of the [appropriation tort], the right created by it is in the nature of a property right. . . ." Restatement (Second) of Torts § 652C, comment (a). A number of jurisdictions follow this approach. *See Ainsworth v. Century Supply Co.*, 693 N.E.2d 510 (Ill. App. 1998); *Candlebat v. Flanagan*, 487 So. 2d 207 (Miss. 1986). According to Jonathan Kahn:

[92] J. Thomas McCarthy, *The Rights of Publicity and Privacy* § 5:63 (2d ed. 2011).

> While publicity is grounded in property rights, appropriation of identity involves the personal right to privacy. Publicity rights implicate monetary interests. In contrast, privacy rights protect and vindicate less tangible personal interests in dignity and integrity of the self. However, both rights are clearly linked and find their common origin in American law around the turn of this century. Yet over the years, the privacy-based tort of appropriation has receded into the background as its flashier cousin, publicity, has risen to prominence. Such is perhaps to be expected in a world where seemingly everything has been turned into a saleable commodity.[93]

Is privacy or property the central interest of appropriation? Or does the tort adequately redress both interests?

2. NAME OR LIKENESS

CARSON V. HERE'S JOHNNY PORTABLE TOILETS, INC.

698 F.2d 831 (6th Cir. 1983)

BROWN, J. . . . Appellant, John W. Carson (Carson), is the host and star of "The Tonight Show," a well-known television program broadcast five nights a week by the National Broadcasting Company. . . . From the time he began hosting "The Tonight Show" in 1962, he has been introduced [by Ed McMahon] on the show each night with the phrase "Here's Johnny." . . . The phrase "Here's Johnny" is generally associated with Carson by a substantial segment of the television viewing public. In 1967, Carson first authorized use of this phrase by an outside business venture, permitting it to be used by a chain of restaurants called "Here's Johnny Restaurants." . . .

. . . The phrase "Here's Johnny" has never been registered by appellants as a trademark or service mark.

Appellee, Here's Johnny Portable Toilets, Inc., is a Michigan corporation engaged in the business of renting and selling "Here's Johnny" portable toilets. Appellee's founder was aware at the time he formed the corporation that "Here's Johnny" was the introductory slogan for Carson on "The Tonight Show." He indicated that he coupled the phrase with a second one, "The World's Foremost Commodian," to make "a good play on a phrase."

[Carson brought an action for, among other things, invasion of privacy and the right to publicity.] . . .

We do not believe that Carson's claim that his right of privacy has been invaded is supported by the law or the facts. Apparently, the gist of this claim is that Carson is embarrassed by and considers it odious to be associated with the appellee's product. Clearly, the association does not appeal to Carson's sense of humor. But the facts here presented do not, it appears to us, amount to an invasion of any of the interests protected by the right of privacy. . . .

---

[93] Jonathan Kahn, *Bringing Dignity Back to Light: Publicity Rights and the Eclipse of the Tort of Appropriation of Identity,* 17 Cardozo Arts & Ent. L.J. 213, 213-14 (1999); *see also* Jonathan Kahn, *What's in a Name? Law's Identity Under the Tort of Appropriation,* 74 Temp. L. Rev. 263 (2001).

The right of publicity has developed to protect the commercial interest of celebrities in their identities. The theory of the right is that a celebrity's identity can be valuable in the promotion of products, and the celebrity has an interest that may be protected from the unauthorized commercial exploitation of that identity. . . .

The district court dismissed appellants' claim based on the right of publicity because appellee does not use Carson's name or likeness. . . . We believe that, on the contrary, the district court's conception of the right of publicity is too narrow. The right of publicity, as we have stated, is that a celebrity has a protected pecuniary interest in the commercial exploitation of his identity. If the celebrity's identity is commercially exploited, there has been an invasion of his right whether or not his "name or likeness" is used. Carson's identity may be exploited even if his name, John W. Carson, or his picture is not used. . . .

In this case, Earl Braxton, president and owner of Here's Johnny Portable Toilets, Inc., admitted that he knew that the phrase "Here's Johnny" had been used for years to introduce Carson. Moreover, in the opening statement in the district court, appellee's counsel stated:

> Now, we've stipulated in this case that the public tends to associate the words "Johnny Carson," the words "Here's Johnny" with plaintiff, John Carson and, Mr. Braxton, in his deposition, admitted that he knew that and probably absent that identification, he would not have chosen it.

That the "Here's Johnny" name was selected by Braxton because of its identification with Carson was the clear inference from Braxton's testimony irrespective of such admission in the opening statement.

We therefore conclude that, applying the correct legal standards, appellants are entitled to judgment. The proof showed without question that appellee had appropriated Carson's identity in connection with its corporate name and its product. . . .

. . . It is not fatal to appellant's claim that appellee did not use his "name." Indeed, there would have been no violation of his right of publicity even if appellee had used his name, such as "J. William Carson Portable Toilet" or the "John William Carson Portable Toilet" or the "J. W. Carson Portable Toilet." The reason is that, though literally using appellant's "name," the appellee would not have appropriated Carson's identity as a celebrity. Here there was an appropriation of Carson's identity without using his "name.". . .

KENNEDY, J. dissenting. . . . The majority's extension of the right of publicity to include phrases or other things which are merely associated with the individual permits a popular entertainer or public figure, by associating himself or herself with a common phrase, to remove those words from the public domain. . . .

. . . [T]he majority is awarding Johnny Carson a windfall, rather than vindicating his economic interests, by protecting the phrase "Here's Johnny" which is merely associated with him. In *Zacchini*, the Supreme Court stated that a mechanism to vindicate an individual's economic rights is indicated where the appropriated thing is "the product of . . . [the individual's] own talents and energy, the end result of much time, effort and expense." There is nothing in the record to suggest that "Here's Johnny" has any nexus to Johnny Carson other than being the introduction to his personal appearances. The phrase is not part of an identity that he created. In its content "Here's Johnny" is a very simple and common introduction. The content of the phrase neither originated with Johnny Carson nor is it confined to the world of entertainment. The phrase is not said by Johnny Carson, but said of him. Its association with him is derived, in large part, by the context in which it is said — generally by Ed McMahon in a drawn out and distinctive voice after the theme music to "The Tonight Show" is played, and immediately prior to Johnny Carson's own entrance. Appellee's use of the content "Here's Johnny," in light of its value as a double entendre, written on its product and corporate name, and therefore outside of the context in which it is associated with Johnny Carson, does little to rob Johnny Carson of something which is unique to him or a product of his own efforts. . . .

Protection under the right of publicity confers a monopoly on the protected individual that is potentially broader, offers fewer protections and potentially competes with federal statutory monopolies. As an essential part of three federal monopoly rights, copyright, trademark and patents, notice to the public is required in the form of filing with the appropriate governmental office and use of an appropriate mark. This apprises members of the public of the nature and extent of what is being removed from the public domain and subject to claims of infringement. The right of publicity provides limited notice to the public of the extent of the monopoly right to be asserted, if one is to be asserted at all. As the right of privacy is expanded beyond protections of name, likeness and actual performances, which provide relatively objective notice to the public of the extent of an individual's rights, to more subjective attributes such as achievements and identifying characteristics, the public's ability to be on notice of a common law monopoly right, if one is even asserted by a given famous individual, is severely diminished. Protecting phrases and other things merely associated with an individual provides virtually no notice to the public at all of what is claimed to be protected. By ensuring the invocation of the adjudicative process whenever the commercial use of a phrase or other associated thing is considered to have been wrongfully appropriated, the public is left to act at their peril. The result is a chilling effect on commercial innovation and opportunity.

Also unlike the federal statutory monopolies, this common law monopoly right offers no protections against the monopoly existing for an indefinite time or even in perpetuity. . . .

NOTES & QUESTIONS

1. ***Privacy or Property?*** In *Carson*, Johnny Carson made two claims. First, he contended that a privacy interest was violated because his identity was being associated with toilets, which he found quite unflattering. The court appears to reject this claim. Carson's other claim is that a property interest was violated by his valuable identity being stolen and used for the commercial purposes of another. What do you think was the real reason Carson brought this suit? To vindicate his privacy interest, his property interest, or both? Suppose Carson were not famous and his name had little value. Would he be likely to succeed under the reasoning of the court?

2. ***No Sense of Humor?*** In 2013, Carson's attorney published a memoir about his late boss. Henry Buskin was critical of the decision to pursue the litigation:

> It even got to the point where it seemed like he couldn't recognize a joke. Somehow we learned of an Ohio company called Here's Johnny Portable Toilets, which advertised its product with the slogan "The World's Foremost Commodian." Carson didn't think that was funny and ordered me to sue the company to make them stop. Ultimately we spent about $500,000 to win less than $40,000 in damages. . . . To me, it didn't matter that we won. I thought it made him look mean and small.[94]

3. ***Post-Mortem Publicity Rights.*** Despite losing the case before the Sixth Circuit in 1987, Earl Braxton, the defendant in the *Carson* case, did not give up his dream. Johnny Carson died in 2005, and in 2006 Braxton sought to trademark the phrase "Here's Johnny." A trademark is a form of intellectual property that identifies the source of a product or service. The Trademark and Trial Appeal Board held that the relevant states in question recognized post-mortem rights of publicity and that these rights had passed to Carson's estate.[95] Thus, the *Carson* decision still prevents Braxton from use of the phrase, "Here's Johnny."

   Concerning post-mortem rights, the overwhelming majority of states in the United States have also recognized a postmortem dimension to the publicity right. The publicity right can be inherited, sold in whole or in part, and otherwise licensed after the subject's death. The question of whether or not these interests were exploited during a party's life is irrelevant. A survey of the duration of the postmortem right in the United States found periods ranging from a potentially unlimited period to 100 years to 20 years.[96]

   In California, the legislature has even extended the applicable statute *backward* in time to protect the interests of those who died as long as 70 years before the state first legislatively acknowledged this right. Publicity rights are also a routine subject in negotiations with prominent individuals and, in the case of deceased celebrities, with their estates.

4. ***First Amendment and Related Limits on Publicity Rights.*** Carson won his case against use of the phrase "Here's Johnny" against a toilet company. He did not, however, sue the Beach Boys for their 1977 song, "Johnny Carson," which used the same phrase in a lyric: "Johnny Carson/Ed McMahon comes on and says 'Here's Johnny'/Every night at 11:30 he's so funny." The use of Johnny Carson's celebrity identity and the famous phrase in a song clearly implicates a wide range of different issues, including the freedom of expression.

   In a case involving commercial use of a charcoal drawing of the Three Stooges, *Comedy III Productions, Inc. v. Gary Saderup, Inc.*, 25 Cal. 4th 387 (2001), the California Supreme Court found that use of the image on a t-shirt

---

[94] Henry Bushkin, *Johnny Carson* 223 (2013).

[95] *The John W. Carson Foundation v. Toilets.com, Inc.*, Opposition No. 91181092 (T.T.A.B. Mar. 25, 2009).

[96] J. Thomas McCarthy, 2 *The Rights of Publicity and Privacy* 435-37, 445-46 (2009).

implicated the First Amendment: "First Amendment doctrine does not disfavor nontraditional media of expression." The *Comedy III* court identified a need to balance the right of publicity against the First Amendment. Its key test was whether a work represented a "transformative" use of the celebrity's identity. According to the California Supreme Court, one way to identify a transformative use of a celebrity image was whether the work is "primarily the defendant's own expression rather than the celebrity's likeness." Another inquiry was whether "the marketability and economic value of the challenged work derive primarily from the fame of the celebrity depicted."

Two years after its *Comedy III* decision, the California Supreme Court found that a comic book with characters that resembled two blues musicians, Johnny and Edgar Winter, was "transformative." *Winter v. DC Comics*, 30 Cal. 4th 881(2003). The comic book featured brothers Johnny and Edgar Autumn, who were evil half-worm, half-human creatures. The California Supreme Court found that there was no triable issue of fact and upheld the trial court's summary judgment decision dismissing the case. There could be no right of publicity claim by the Winter brothers because the comic book's use of their persona was protected by the First Amendment. The court stated:

> Although the fictional characters Johnny and Edgar Autumn are less-than-subtle evocations of Johnny and Edgar Winter, the books do not depict the plaintiff's literally. Instead, the plaintiffs are merely part of the raw materials from which the comic books were synthesized. To the extent the drawings of the Autumn brothers resembled the plaintiffs at all, they are distorted for the purposes of lampoon, parody, or caricature ... in a larger story, which is itself quite expressive.

The *Winter* court also noted that the comic book would not detract from any interest that the brothers had in their image as it would be "unsatisfactory as a substitute for conventional depictions." Does *Winter* rest on an underlying idea that the overall work did not free-ride, or otherwise unfairly exploit, the Winters' celebrity persona because it added its own "expressive" concepts?

5. ***What Constitutes "Name or Likeness"?*** The appropriation tort has been extended far beyond a person's actual name and likeness. Courts have held that the use of well-known nicknames can give rise to an appropriation action. In *Hirsch v. S.C. Johnson & Son, Inc.*, 280 N.W.2d 129 (Wis. 1979), the Supreme Court of Wisconsin found that an unauthorized commercial use of Elroy Hirsch's (a famous football player) nickname "Crazylegs" raised triable issues regarding violation of the appropriation tort. S.C. Johnson had used "Crazylegs" as the product name for a shaving gel for women. The court rejected the argument that an appropriation claim by Hirsch was not possible because Crazylegs was his nickname, not his actual name. It stated that to overcome the lower court's rejection of the cause of action, "[a]ll that is required is that the name clearly identify the wronged person." It also declared that "[t]he question whether Crazylegs identifies Elroy Hirsch, however, is one of fact to be determined by the jury on remand. . . ."

Courts have also held that certain drawings depicting one's profession but otherwise with no distinctive facial characteristics can still give rise to an appropriation claim. In *Ali v. Playgirl, Inc.*, 447 F. Supp. 723 (S.D.N.Y. 1978), Muhammad Ali, former heavyweight boxing champion, sued *Playgirl* magazine for appropriation when the magazine published a drawing of a nude African-American male sitting on a stool in a corner of a boxing ring with hands taped. The drawing did not mention Ali's name and was entitled "Mystery Man," but accompanying text identified the man in the drawing as "The Greatest." Because "The Greatest" was Ali's nickname, the picture was sufficiently identifiable as Ali to constitute his likeness. The court emphasized the offensive nature of the full frontal nude of Ali; the fact that the portrait was clearly one of Ali; and that the publication was for "purposes of trade" within New York Civil Rights Law § 51. It stated, "the picture is a dramatization, an illustration falling somewhere between representational art and cartoon, and is accompanied by a plainly fictional and allegedly libelous bit of doggerel."

Appropriation has even been extended to identifying characteristics. In *Motschenbacher v. R.J. Reynolds Tobacco Co.*, 498 F.2d 821 (9th Cir. 1974), a famous race car driver alleged that a photograph of his distinctive racing car, which did not include a likeness of himself or use his name, was nevertheless an appropriation of his name or likeness. The court agreed. The photograph did use a "likeness" of the plaintiff because the "distinctive decorations" on his car "were not only peculiar to the plaintiff's cars but they caused some persons to think the car in question was plaintiff's and to infer that the person driving the car was the plaintiff."

Further, appropriation can also extend to use of a look-alike model. In *Onassis v. Christian Dior*, 472 N.Y.S. 2d 254 (N.Y. Supp. 1984), Jacqueline Kennedy Onassis won an injunction against use of a look-alike model in an advertisement. The *Onassis* court found a cause of action under the New York Civil Rights Law § 51, so long as the advertisement created an illusion that the plaintiff herself had appeared in the advertisement.

Courts have also recognized appropriation liability for the imitation of one's voice. In *Midler v. Ford Motor Co.*, 849 F.2d 460 (9th Cir. 1988), the Ninth Circuit held that singer Bette Midler had a viable cause of action for appropriation for the use of a singer to imitate her voice in a commercial. When a voice is a sufficient indication of the celebrity's identity, appropriation protects against a company hiring someone to imitate it for commercial purposes without the celebrity's consent.

In a later sound-alike case, the Ninth Circuit found for Tom Waits, a singer with a distinctive sound. *Waits v. Frito Lay*, 978 F. 2d 1093 (9th Cir. 1992). The court noted that Waits had "a distinctive gravelly singing voice, described by one fan as 'like how you'd sound if you drank a quart of bourbon, smoked a pack of cigarettes and swallowed a pack of razor blades. . . . Late at night. After not sleeping for three days.' " The *Waits* court upheld a jury verdict that found the celebrity plaintiff had a voice that was distinctive, widely known, and deliberately imitated by a defendant for a commercial purpose. The Ninth Circuit added that even if Tom Waits was not as well known as Bette Midler, "'[w]ell-known' is a relative term, and differences in the extent of celebrity are adequately reflected in the amount of damages recoverable."

6. ***Property Rights and Creativity.*** Consider the following argument against the propertization of identity by Judge Kozinski dissenting from the denial of a petition for rehearing en banc in *White v. Samsung Electronics America, Inc.*, 989 F.2d 1512 (9th Cir. 1993):

> . . . Saddam Hussein wants to keep advertisers from using his picture in unflattering contexts. Clint Eastwood doesn't want tabloids to write about him. Rudolf Valentino's heirs want to control his film biography. The Girl Scouts don't want their image soiled by association with certain activities. . . . And scads of copyright holders see purple when their creations are made fun of.
>
> Something very dangerous is going on here. . . .
>
> . . . Overprotecting intellectual property is as harmful as underprotecting it. Creativity is impossible without a rich public domain. . . .
>
> . . . Intellectual property rights aren't free. They're imposed at the expense of future creators and of the public at large. Where would we be if Charles Lindbergh had an exclusive right in the concept of a heroic solo aviator? If Arthur Conan Doyle had gotten a copyright in the idea of the detective story, or Albert Einstein had patented the theory of relativity? If every author and celebrity had been given the right to keep people from mocking them or their work? Surely this would have made the world poorer, not richer, culturally as well as economically. . . .

7. ***Property Rights and the Manufacturing of Identity.*** One of the predominant rationales for the right of publicity is that the celebrity, through her labor, creates her persona. But, with regard to celebrities, does this rationale always hold true? According to Michael Madow, the identity of a celebrity is "the product of a complex social process in which the 'labor' of the celebrity is but one ingredient, and not always the main one."[97] In a similar argument, Rosemary Coombe observes: "Star images are authored by studios, the mass media, public relations agencies, fan clubs, gossip columnists, photographers, hairdressers, body-building coaches, athletic trainers, teachers, screenwriters, ghostwriters, directors, lawyers, and doctors."[98] Why should we afford celebrities property rights in their names and likenesses when frequently a celebrity's persona is manufactured by others?

   Madow also argues that individuals and groups participating actively in the process of generating and circulating meanings that constitute "culture." Thus, "against-the-grain readings" of mainstream cultural products are possible. As an example, Madow points to the example of a card showing "John Wayne, wearing cowboy hat and bright red lipstick, above the caption, 'It's such a bitch being butch.' " Wayne's children, among others, objected to the card. Madow comments:

> Against-the-grain readings of John Wayne are also possible. For instance, in a course on how to survive as a prisoner of war, the U.S. Navy uses the term

---

[97] Michael T. Madow, *Private Ownership of Public Image: Popular Culture and Publicity Rights*, 81 Cal. L. Rev. 127, 195 (1993).

[98] Rosemary J. Coombe, *The Cultural Life of Intellectual Properties: Authorship, Appropriation, and the Law* 94 (1998).

"John Wayning it" to mean trying foolishly to hold out against brutal torture. The particular greeting card that Wayne's children and others objected to so strenuously represents an even more subversive inflection of Wayne's image. The card uses his image to interrogate and challenge mainstream conceptions of masculinity and heterosexuality. It recodes Wayne's image so as to make it carry a cultural meaning that presumably works for gay men, among others, but which Wayne's children (and no doubt many of his fans) find deeply offensive. . . .

What it comes down to, then, is that the power to license is the power to suppress. When the law gives a celebrity a right of publicity, it does more than funnel additional income her way. It gives her (or her assignee) a substantial measure of power over the production and circulation of meaning and identity in our society: power, if she so chooses, to suppress readings or appropriations of her persona that depart from, challenge, or subvert the meaning she prefers; power to deny to others the use of her persona in the construction and communication of alternative or oppositional identities and social relations; power, ultimately, to limit the expressive and communicative opportunities of the rest of us. The result is a potentially significant narrowing of the space available for alternative cultural and dialogic practice. Do you agree that the tort of appropriation and right of publicity threaten popular cultural production? Or will social debate about the meaning of John Wayne, Madonna, or Elvis continue, more or less unaffected, in spite of these legal interests?

8. ***Are Privacy and Property Rights Mutually Exclusive?*** According to Robert Post, the right of publicity views one's personality as "commodified," as an object separate from oneself that can be valued by the market. In his view, Warren and Brandeis's right to privacy, in contrast, "attaches personality firmly to the actual identity of a living individual." The right of publicity protects personality as detachable from individuals, as a commodity that can be bought and sold (and can persist after the death of the individual). The right to privacy, in contrast, protects personality as constitutive of the individual. Post suggests that perhaps we need both property rights and privacy rights to protect our personalities: "Personality can so effortlessly be legally embodied by either property or privacy rights precisely because it embraces both these aspects."[99]

3. FOR ONE'S OWN USE OR BENEFIT

The Restatement of Torts recognizes appropriation of another's name or likeness when it is used for the appropriator's "own use or benefit." Consider the Restatement § 652C comment (b):

> The common form of invasion of privacy under the rule here stated is the appropriation and use of the plaintiff's name or likeness to advertise the defendant's business or product, or for some similar commercial purpose. Apart from statute, however, the rule stated is not limited to commercial appropriation.

[99] Robert C. Post, *Rereading Warren and Brandeis: Privacy, Property, and Appropriation*, 41 Case W. Res. L. Rev. 647 (1991).

> It applies also when the defendant makes use of the plaintiff's name or likeness for his own purposes and benefit, even though the use is not a commercial one, and even though the benefit sought to be obtained is not a pecuniary one. Statutes in some states have, however, limited the liability to commercial uses of the name or likeness.

What does "use or benefit" mean? In many jurisdictions, appropriation occurs only when the use or benefit is commercial in nature — i.e., used to promote or endorse a service or product.

RAYMEN V. UNITED SENIOR ASSOCIATION, INC.

409 F. Supp. 2d 15 (D.D.C. 2006)

WALTON, J. On March 9, 2005, the plaintiffs filed this action seeking to prevent the defendants from further using their images in an advertising campaign which challenged various public policy positions taken by the American Association of Retired Persons ("AARP") regarding Social Security reform and the military. Currently before the Court are the defendants' motions to dismiss, and the plaintiffs' opposition thereto. . . .

On March 3, 2004, the plaintiffs were among 300 citizens of Multnomah County, Oregon who were married pursuant to a newly established right to same-sex marriage in that county. While at City Hall awaiting their opportunity to marry, the plaintiffs, Steve Hansen and Richard Raymen, kissed. A photographer from a Portland, Oregon newspaper, the *Tribune,* captured the kiss in a photograph he took. The photograph was subsequently published in both the *Tribune* newspaper on March 4, 2004, and later on the *Tribune*'s website. At some later point in time, the *Tribune*'s website photograph was used without permission as part of an advertisement created by defendant Mark Montini. The advertising campaign was created for a nonprofit organization, United Senior Association, Inc., which does business under the name USA Next. The advertisement, which features the photograph of the plaintiffs kissing, was part of a campaign by USA Next challenging various public policy positions purportedly taken by the AARP. Specifically, the advertisement contains two pictures. The first is a picture of an American soldier, who presumably is in Iraq, with a red "X" superimposed over it, and the second is the photograph of the plaintiffs with a green checkmark superimposed over it. The caption under the advertisement reads: "The Real AARP Agenda," suggesting that the AARP opposes the United States military efforts abroad and supports the gay lifestyle. This advertisement ran on the website of *The American Spectator* magazine from February 15, 2005, to February 21, 2005.

According to the plaintiffs, the purpose of the advertising campaign was "to incite viewer passions against the AARP because of its alleged support of equal marriage rights for same-sex couples and its alleged lack of support of American troops." Moreover, the plaintiffs opine that the "advertisement also conveys the message that the plaintiffs . . . are against American troops . . . and are unpatriotic." The plaintiffs contend that the advertisement attracted media attention, which then caused an even wider distribution of the advertisement throughout the media. The plaintiffs assert that because of the advertisement, they "have suffered embarrassment, extreme emotional distress, and the invasion of their privacy." In addition, the plaintiffs represent that as a result of the false and misleading inference "communicated by the [a]dvertisement about [the] plaintiffs, their reputations as patriotic American citizens has been severely damaged." . . .

"'One who appropriates to his own use or benefit the name or likeness of another is subject to liability to the other for invasion of his privacy.'" *Martinez v. Democrat-Herald Publ'g Co., Inc.,* 669 P.2d 818, 820 (1983) (quoting Restatement (Second) of Torts § 652C (1976)). Under § 652C of the Restatement, plaintiffs can recover "damages when their names, pictures or other likenesses have been used without their consent to advertise a defendant's product, to accompany an article sold, to add luster to the name of a corporation or for some other business purpose." However, there is no actionable appropriation of a person's likeness claim "when a person's picture is used to illustrate a noncommercial, newsworthy article." . . . Whether a communication is commercial or noncommercial is a question of law. . . .

The photograph of the plaintiffs was used as part of USA Next's advertising campaign, which sought, at least in part, to engender opposition to AARP's policy position on social security reform. Presumably, the advertisement sought to vilify the AARP by conveying a message concerning AARP's alleged views on two hot button policy issues — support of same-sex marriage and opposition to the military. While the advertisement itself lacked any substantive discussion of these issues, it did convey AARP's purported position on both subjects. And someone who viewed the advertisement online could then access the USA Next's webpages which described the organization and its position on Social Security reform. Clearly the issues of same-sex marriage and support for the military are issues of public concern and both have been widely discussed in the media. In fact, the plaintiffs contend in their complaint that the purpose of the advertisement was to influence Congress.

The plaintiffs' argument that the advertisement is commercial in nature because it sought contributions and promoted USA Next's lobbying services, is unpersuasive. First, nothing in the advertisement itself seeks donations. Rather, only after using the advertisement (by clicking on it) to access the webpages were viewers exposed to the information about USA Next and the solicitation for financial contributions. This Court cannot conclude that this detached solicitation elevates the advertisement itself to a level where it can be deemed commercial in nature. *See, e.g., Martinez,* 669 P.2d at 820 ("The fact that the defendant is engaged in the business of publication, for example of a newspaper, out of which he makes or seeks to make a profit, is not enough to make the incidental publication of a commercial use of the name or likeness.") (quoting Restatement (Second) Torts § 652C, cmt. D (1976)). Moreover, contrary to the plaintiffs' assertion, this case is not analogous to . . . *Beverley v. Choices Women's Med. Ctr. Inc.,* 587 N.E.2d 275 (N.Y. 1991). . . .

In *Beverley,* the Court concluded that a calendar produced by a for-profit hospital was commercial in nature because it had the hospital's "name, logo, address, and telephone number on each page of the calendar," along with "glowing characterizations and endorsements concerning the services" provided by the hospital, and thus left no doubt that the calendar was created to preserve existing patronage and to solicit new patients. Here, the advertisement does not even associate itself with USA Next through the use of its address, telephone number, logo, or in any other manner. Moreover, the calendar in *Beverley* promoted the use of the hospital's services, while the advertisement here discusses public policy issues that are currently the subject of public debate. . . .

NOTES & QUESTIONS

1. ***The Fuzzy Line Between Commercial and Non-Commercial Uses.*** Is using a person's photograph to solicit donations a commercial use? In *Raymen,* the image of the plaintiffs kissing was used not as a positive endorsement but as a way to spark outrage in their readers and spur them to donate. Isn't this using their image for financial gain? On the other hand, the plaintiffs' anger at the use of their photograph stems from their outrage over the defendants' message. The defendant could argue that the image of the plaintiffs was a popular iconic image representing gay marriage. Should the plaintiffs be able to control that image whenever they dislike the viewpoints of those that use it?
2. ***Girls Gone Wild.*** In *Lane v. MRA Holdings, LLC*, 242 F. Supp. 2d 1205 (M.D. Fla. 2002), the plaintiff was approached by a crew who produced the Girls Gone Wild video series, which featured clips of women stripping at various parties and events, such as spring break or Mardi Gras. The plaintiff claimed that the crew promised that the footage would be for their personal use only, but it was used in a Girls Gone Wild video. Among many claims, the plaintiff argued that the makers of Girls Gone Wild appropriated her likeness. The court, however, rejected her appropriation claim:

> The Defendants first argue that they are not liable under Fla. Stat. § 540.08 because they did not use Lane's image for trade, commercial, or advertising purposes. Under Fla. Stat. § 540.08, the terms "trade", "commercial", or "advertising purpose" mean using a person's name or likeness to directly promote a product or service.
>
> As a matter of law, this Court finds that Lane's image and likeness were not used to directly promote a product or service. In coming to this conclusion, this Court relies upon Section 47 of the Restatement (Third) of Unfair Competition which defines "the purposes of trade" as follows:
>
> > The names, likeness, and other indicia of a person's identity are used "for the purposes of trade" . . . if they are used in advertising the user's goods or services, or are placed on merchandise marketed by the user, or are used in connection with services rendered by the user. However, use "for the purpose of trade" does not ordinarily include the use of a person's identity in news reporting, commentary, entertainment, works of fiction or nonfiction, or in advertising incidental to such uses.
>
> Therefore, under this definition, the "use of another's identity in a novel, play, or motion picture is . . . not ordinarily an infringement . . . [unless] the name or likeness is used solely to attract attention to a work that is not related to the identified person. . . ." *Id.* at comment c.

> In this case, it is irrefutable that the *Girls Gone Wild* video is an expressive work created solely for entertainment purposes. Similarly, it is also irrefutable that while Lane's image and likeness were used to sell copies of *Girls Gone Wild,* her image and likeness were never associated with a product or service unrelated to that work. Indeed, in both the video and its commercial advertisements, Lane is never shown endorsing or promoting a product, but rather, as part of an expressive work in which she voluntarily participated. Consequently, in accordance with Section 47 of the Restatement, the use of Lane's image or likeness in *Girls Gone Wild,* and in the marketing of that video cannot give rise to liability. . . .
>
> Upon reviewing Florida case law, it has come to this Court's attention that only one case has applied the provisions of Fla. Stat. § 540.08 to an expressive work. In *Gritzke v. M.R.A. Holding, LLC,* No. 4:01cv495-RH (N.D. Fla. Mar, 15, 2002), Judge Hinkle of the Northern District of Florida determined that the plaintiff stated a valid claim under § 540.08 by alleging that her half naked image was plastered on the front cover of the videotape *Girls Gone Wild* without her authorization. . . . [T]he plaintiff in *Gritzke* was complaining about the use of her image on the outside cover of a videotape package. In this case, Lane has not alleged that her image was plastered on a billboard or box cover advertising *Girls Gone Wild.* Rather, this cause of action arises from the Defendants truthful and accurate depiction of Lane voluntarily exposing her breasts to a camera, just as she did on Labor Day Weekend in Panama City Beach, Florida. Unlike in *Gritzke,* the Plaintiff's image in this case was never doctored. It has always remained in its original video format. Accordingly, the *Gritzke* case offers Lane little assistance. . . .
>
> Lane's lawsuit arose from an expressive work that has no purpose other than to entertain a segment of the general population. . . . [T]he Plaintiff in this case is not shown endorsing or promoting a product, but rather as participating in an expressive work. . . . [T]his Court finds that the publication of *Girls Gone Wild* is not actionable simply because it is sold for a profit.

The court's definition of commercial use in this case appears to be a use for "endorsing or promoting a product." Is this too limited a definition of commercial use? Would selling posters of a celebrity constitute a commercial use according to the *Lane* court?

4. CONNECTION TO MATTERS OF PUBLIC INTEREST

Unlike the tort of public disclosure, the lack of newsworthiness is not an element of the appropriation tort. However, appropriation protects against the "commercial" exploitation of one's name or likeness, not the use of one's name or likeness for news, art, literature, parody, satire, history, and biography. Otherwise, a newspaper would have to obtain the consent of every person it wrote about or photographed for use in a story. People could prevent others from writing their biographies or from criticizing them, making a parody of them, or using their names in a work of literature. In New York, for example, one's name or likeness must be used for "advertising purposes or for the uses of trade." N.Y. Civ. Rights L. §§ 50-51. Although not employing the same language, other states adopt a similar approach, requiring that the use of one's name or likeness be for "commercial" purposes. Some courts refer to this as a "First Amendment privilege" to use one's name or likeness in matters of legitimate public concern.

The quintessential instance where the use of one's name or likeness is newsworthy and not "commercial" is in connection with the reporting of the news. In *Time Inc. v. Sand Creek Partners*, 825 F. Supp. 210 (S.D. Ind. 1993), country singer Lyle Lovett and actress Julia Roberts were photographed together at a Lovett concert immediately prior to their marriage. Roberts was in her wedding gown. A photographer for *People* magazine snapped several rolls of film, but they were confiscated by security. The magazine's publisher sued to get the photos back, but Lovett claimed that they were his, because he had a property interest in his name or likeness. The court sided with the magazine:

> Lovett and Roberts are widely known celebrities and in that sense are public figures and, in addition, their appearance on stage before thousands of people on the day of their highly-publicized but theretofore unannounced and private wedding ceremony, with Roberts still wearing her wedding dress, was a newsworthy event of widespread public interest.

Beyond news, uses that are "commercial" or "for advertising or trade purposes" generally do not encompass works of fiction or nonfiction or artistic expression. In *Rosemont Enterprises, Inc. v. Random House, Inc.*, 294 N.Y.S.2d 122 (1968), the defendants published an unauthorized biography of the reclusive Howard Hughes. The court concluded that the biography "falls within those 'reports of newsworthy people or events'" and is therefore not subject to liability for appropriation. A sculpture of supermodel Cheryl Tiegs was not appropriation because "[w]orks of art, including sculptures, convey ideas, just as do literature, movies or theater." *Simeonov v. Tiegs*, 602 N.Y.S.2d 1014 (Civ. Ct. 1993). The use of a person's identity in a work of fiction generally cannot give rise to an appropriation action. *See, e.g., Maritote v. Desilu Productions, Inc.*, 345 F.2d 418 (7th Cir. 1965); *Loft v. Fuller*, 408 So. 2d 619 (Fla. Ct. App. 1981).

However, in New York and other states, the right of the media to use one's name or likeness for news purposes is not absolute. There must exist a "legitimate connection between the use of plaintiff's name and picture and the matter of public interest sought to be portrayed." *Delan by Delan v. CBS, Inc.*, 458 N.Y.S.2d 608 (N.Y. Ct. App. 1983). As another court articulated the test:

> A picture illustrating an article on a matter of public interest is not considered used for the purpose of trade or advertising within the prohibition of the statute unless it has no real relationship to the article, or unless the article is an advertisement in disguise. It makes no difference whether the article appears in a newspaper; a magazine; a newsreel; on television; in a motion picture; or in a book. The test of permissible use is not the currency of the publication in which the picture appears but whether it is illustrative of a matter of public interest. *Dallesandro v. Henry Holt & Co.*, 106 N.Y.S.2d 805 (1957).

This test has become known as the "real relationship" test. *See, e.g., Haskell v. Stauffer Communications, Inc.*, 990 P.2d 163 (Kan. App. 1999); *Lane v. Random House*, 985 F. Supp. 141 (D.D.C. 1995).

FINGER V. OMNI PUBLICATIONS INTERNATIONAL, LTD.

566 N.E.2d 141 (N.Y. Ct. App. 1990)

ALEXANDER, J. Plaintiffs Joseph and Ida Finger commenced this action on behalf of themselves and their six children against defendant Omni Publications International, Ltd. seeking damages for the publication, without their consent, of a photograph of plaintiffs in conjunction with an article in Omni magazine discussing a research project relating to caffeine-aided fertilization. . . .

. . . The June 1988 issue of Omni magazine included in its "Continuum" segment an article entitled "Caffeine and Fast Sperm," in which it was indicated that based on research conducted at the University of Pennsylvania School of Medicine, in vitro fertilization rates may be enhanced by exposing sperm to high concentrations of caffeine.

A photograph of plaintiffs depicting two adults surrounded by six attractive and apparently healthy children accompanied the article. The caption beneath the photograph read "Want a big family? Maybe your sperm needs a cup of Java in the morning. Tests reveal that caffeine-spritzed sperm swim faster, which may increase the chances for in vitro fertilization." Neither the article nor the caption mentioned plaintiffs' names or indicated in any fashion that the adult plaintiffs used caffeine or that the children were produced through in vitro fertilization.

Plaintiffs commenced this action alleging only violations of Civil Rights Law §§ 50 and 51. Defendant moved to dismiss the complaint, arguing that its use of the photograph in conjunction with the article did not violate Civil Rights Law §§ 50 and 51 because the picture was not used for trade or advertising but to illustrate a related news article on fertility. Defendant contended that because fertility is a topic of legitimate public interest, its use of the picture fit within the "newsworthiness exception" to the prohibitions of Civil Rights Law § 50. . . .

Plaintiffs contend that defendant violated Civil Rights Law §§ 50 and 51 by using their photograph without their consent "for advertising purposes or for the purposes of trade." . . .

Although the statute does not define "purposes of trade" or "advertising," courts have consistently refused to construe these terms as encompassing publications concerning newsworthy events or matters of public interest. Additionally, it is also well settled that "'[a] picture illustrating an article on a matter of public interest is not considered used for the purpose of trade or advertising within the prohibition of the statute . . . unless it has no real relationship to the article . . . or unless the article is an advertisement in disguise.'"

Plaintiffs do not contest the existence of this "newsworthiness exception" and concede that the discussion of in vitro fertilization and the use of caffeine to enhance sperm velocity and motility are newsworthy topics. They contend, however, that their photograph bears "no real relationship" to the article, that none of plaintiffs' children were conceived by in vitro fertilization or any other artificial means, and that they never participated in the caffeine-enhanced reproductive research conducted at the University of Pennsylvania.

Consequently, according to plaintiffs, there was no "real relationship" between their photograph and the article, and any relationship that may exist is too tenuous to be considered a relationship at all. They argue that there are no "external and objective" criteria . . . that would indicate that plaintiffs have any real or legitimate connection with the subject of caffeine-enhanced in vitro fertilization. . . .

Plaintiffs misperceive the "newsworthy" theme of the article, which is fertility or increased fertility. Indeed, the article, in its opening sentences, observes that caffeine "can increase a man's fertility by boosting the performance of his sperm" and further indicates that "those who are looking for a fertility tonic shouldn't head for the nearest coffee pot" because the concentrations of caffeine used in the experiment "were so high [as to] be toxic."

The theme of fertility is reasonably reflected both in the caption beneath the picture, "Want a big family?", and the images used — six healthy and attractive children with their parents to whom each child bears a striking resemblance. Clearly then, there is a "real relationship" between the fertility theme of the article and the large family depicted in the photograph. That the article also discusses in vitro fertilization as being enhanced by "caffeine-spritzed sperm" does no more than discuss a specific aspect of fertilization and does not detract from the relationship between the photograph and the article.

As we have noted, the "newsworthiness exception" should be liberally applied. . . . [Q]uestions of "newsworthiness" are better left to reasonable editorial judgment and discretion; judicial intervention should occur only in those instances where there is "no real relationship" between a photograph and an article or where the article is an "advertisement in disguise." . . .

NOTES & QUESTIONS

1. ***Levels of Generality in Applying the Real Relationship Test.*** Do you agree with the court's approach to the relationship between the photograph and the article? Does the court properly view the topic of the article broadly as about fertility in general? The Fingers' argument, however, is not that the picture has no relation to the subject matter of the article; rather, they contend that they have nothing to do with the article's specific topic. Is this relevant to the court?
2. ***What Injuries Does the Appropriation Tort Redress?*** What type of interest are the Fingers attempting to protect? Why doesn't the appropriation tort protect that interest?

   Consider *Arrington v. New York Times*, 434 N.E.2d 1319 (N.Y. Ct. App. 1982). The *New York Times Magazine* published an article called "The Black Middle Class: Making It." On the cover of the publication was the photograph of the plaintiff Clarence W. Arrington in a suit. The photograph was taken without Arrington's consent or knowledge as he was walking down the street. Arrington, a young African-American financial analyst, strongly disagreed with the views stated in the article, which criticized how the "expanding black middle/professional class in today's society" was growing more removed from its "less fortunate brethren." Arrington, along with many other readers, found the article to be "insulting, degrading, distorting and disparaging." Others, including his friends and acquaintances, thought that he had shared the ideas in the article because his picture was featured as the exemplar of the "black middle class." Arrington sued the publisher, the freelance photographer who took the picture, and the agency that arranged for the photo to be sold to the *Times* for appropriation and false light. With regard to appropriation, the New York law recognized the importance of protecting free speech values:

> . . . [W]e not too long ago reiterated that "'[a] picture illustrating an article on a matter of public interest is not considered used for the purposes of trade or advertising within the prohibition of the statute . . . unless it has no real relationship to the article . . . or unless the article is an advertisement in disguise.'" And this holds true though the dissemination of news and views is carried on for a profit or that illustrations are added for the very purpose of encouraging sales of the publications.

Arrington contended that his picture had no "real relationship" to the article, but the court disagreed:

> Plaintiff's emphasis . . . is on the fact that, as he reads it, the article depicts the "black middle class" as one peopled by "materialistic, status-conscious and frivolous individuals without any sense of moral obligation to those of their race who are economically less fortunate," a conception of the "class" with which he disclaims any "legitimate connection." While the concededly innocuous title of the article is superimposed over part of the picture (as is the title of another on Christmas pleasures), nothing of the ideas with which he wishes to disassociate himself appear at this point. And, though the article itself gives the names and quotes the statements and opinions of persons whom the author interviewed, as indicated earlier, the plaintiff is neither mentioned, nor are any of the ideas or opinions it expresses attributed to him. The asserted lack of a "real relationship" boils down then, to his conviction that his views are not consonant with those of the author. . . . [However,] it would be unwise for us to assay the dangerous task of passing on value judgments based on the subjective happenstance of whether there is agreement with views expressed on a social issue.
>
> No more persuasive is plaintiff's perfectly understandable preference that his photograph not have been employed in this manner and in this connection. However, other than in the purely commercial setting covered by [New York's appropriation tort], an inability to vindicate a personal predilection for greater privacy may be part of the price every person must be prepared to pay for a society in which information and opinion flow freely.

However, as to the photographer and the agency that sold the photo, the court declared that Arrington's action could proceed because the sale of the photo "commercialized" it, and the other defendants were not protected in the same way by the statute as the publisher. Subsequent to *Arrington*, the New York legislature amended § 51 to protect photographers and agents.

How would you characterize Arrington's injury? Did it involve the commercial use of his photograph? Or did it involve his being associated with an article that he found distasteful? Should a person have legal recourse from having her image associated, without her consent, with views that she disagrees with?

Arrington also raised a false light claim, but the court rejected it because the use of the photo was not "highly offensive." Do you agree?

3. ***The Limits of the Real Relationship Test.*** In *Spahn v. Julian Messner, Inc.*, 233 N.E.2d 840 (N.Y. 1967), the defendants published a book about the famous baseball player, Warren Spahn. The book was largely a work of fiction, with imaginary events and dialogue. The defendants intended to create a fictitious biography, as they did not engage in research or interviews of Spahn or those who knew him. Spahn sued under New York's appropriation law (Civil Rights Law § 51) and won a jury verdict. The verdict was upheld on appeal:

> To hold that this research effort entitles the defendants to publish the kind of knowing fictionalization presented here would amount to granting a literary license which is not only unnecessary to the protection of free speech but destructive of an individual's right — albeit a limited one in the case of a public figure — to be free of the commercial exploitation of his name and personality.

In *Messenger v. Gruner + Jahr Printing and Publishing,* 208 F.3d 122 (2d Cir. 2000), photographs of a young woman were used to illustrate a story called "Love Crisis" in a magazine called *Young and Modern (YM)*:

> The column began with a letter to Sally Lee, *YM*'s editor-in-chief, from a 14-year-old girl identified only as "Mortified." Mortified writes that she got drunk at a party and then had sex with her 18-year-old boyfriend and two of his friends. Lee responds that Mortified should avoid similar situations in the future, and advises her to be tested for pregnancy and sexually transmitted diseases. Above the column, in bold type, is a pull-out quotation stating, "I got trashed and had sex with three guys." Three full-color photographs of plaintiff illustrate the column — one, for example, shows her hiding her face, with three young men gloating in the background. The captions are keyed to Lee's advice: "Wake up and face the facts: You made a pretty big mistake;" "Don't try to hide — just ditch him and his buds;" and "Afraid you're pregnant? See a doctor."

The court applied the real relationship test: "[W]here a photograph illustrates an article on a matter of public interest, the newsworthiness exception bars recovery unless there is no real relationship between the photograph and the article, or the article is an advertisement in disguise." The defendants cited *Finger* and *Arrington.* The plaintiff relied on *Spahn.* The court concluded that *Finger* and *Arrington* controlled, not *Spahn.* Like the photographs in *Young and Modern,* the photos used in *Finger* and *Arrington* were used to "illustrate newsworthy articles." In contrast, "*Spahn* concerned a strikingly different scenario from the onc before us. . . . [D]efendants invented biographies of plaintiffs' lives. The courts concluded that the substantially fictional works at issue were nothing more than attempts to trade on the persona of Warren Spahn." The court also concluded that the tort of false light was not recognized in New York.

In dissent, Judge Bellacosa argued:

> [The holding of this case] justifies a too-facile escape valve from the operation of the [appropriation] statute, one that is also unilaterally within the control of the alleged wrongdoer. The paradigm for editors is a "newsworthy" homily to lovesick adolescents or any other audience; they then just have to use a journalistic conceit of tying the advice to a purported letter to the editor, with an inescapable first person identification of the letter as originating with any adolescent in the photo array. When an aggrieved person like Messenger reaches for the statutory lifeline, the newsworthiness notion dissipates it into a dry mirage. That is not fair or right.

Assess the strength of a potential defamation suit based on *Young and Modern*'s use of the photo.

5. FIRST AMENDMENT LIMITATIONS

ZACCHINI V. SCRIPPS-HOWARD BROADCASTING CO.

433 U.S. 562 (1977)

WHITE, J. Petitioner, Hugo Zacchini, is an entertainer. He performs a "human cannonball" act in which he is shot from a cannon into a net some 200 feet away. Each performance occupies some 15 seconds. In August and September 1972, petitioner was engaged to perform his act on a regular basis at the Geauga County Fair in Burton, Ohio. He performed in a fenced area, surrounded by grandstands, at the fair grounds. Members of the public attending the fair were not charged a separate admission fee to observe his act.

On August 30, a freelance reporter for Scripps-Howard Broadcasting Co., the operator of a television broadcasting station and respondent in this case, attended the fair. He carried a small movie camera. Petitioner noticed the reporter and asked him not to film the performance. The reporter did not do so on that day; but on the instructions of the producer of respondent's daily newscast, he returned the following day and videotaped the entire act. This film clip approximately 15 seconds in length, was shown on the 11 o'clock news program that night, together with favorable commentary.

Petitioner then brought this action for damages, alleging that he is "engaged in the entertainment business," that the act he performs is one "invented by his father and . . . performed only by his family for the last fifty years," that respondent "showed and commercialized the film of his act without his consent," and that such conduct was an "unlawful appropriation of plaintiff's professional property." Respondent answered and moved for summary judgment, which was granted by the trial court.

[The Ohio Supreme Court held that the broadcast was protected by the First Amendment because the press "must be accorded broad latitude in its choice of how much it presents of each story or incident, and of the emphasis to be given to such presentation." The United States Supreme Court granted certiorari to determine whether the First Amendment immunized the media broadcaster from damages under Ohio's "right of publicity" (appropriation tort).]

. . . The Ohio Supreme Court relied heavily on *Time, Inc. v. Hill*, 385 U.S. 374 (1967), but that case does not mandate a media privilege to televise a performer's entire act without his consent. Involved in *Time, Inc. v. Hill* was a claim under the New York "Right of Privacy" statute that Life Magazine, in the course of reviewing a new play, had connected the play with a long-past incident involving petitioner and his family and had falsely described their experience and conduct at that time. The complaint sought damages for humiliation and suffering flowing from these nondefamatory falsehoods that allegedly invaded Hill's privacy. The Court held, however, that the opening of a new play linked to an actual incident was a matter of public interest and that Hill could not recover without showing that the Life report was knowingly false or was published with reckless disregard for the truth the same rigorous standard that had been applied in *New York Times Co. v. Sullivan*.

Time, Inc. v. Hill, which was hotly contested and decided by a divided Court, involved an entirely different tort from the "right of publicity" recognized by the Ohio Supreme Court. As the opinion reveals in *Time, Inc. v. Hill*, the Court was steeped in the literature of privacy law and was aware of the developing distinctions and nuances in this branch of the law. . . . The Court was aware that it was adjudicating a "false light" privacy case involving a matter of public interest, not a case involving "intrusion," "appropriation" of a name or likeness for the purposes of trade, or "private details" about a non-newsworthy person or event. It is also abundantly clear that *Time, Inc. v. Hill* did not involve a performer, a person with a name having commercial value, or any claim to a "right of publicity." This discrete kind of "appropriation" case was plainly identified in the literature cited by the Court and had been adjudicated in the reported cases.

The differences between these two torts are important. First, the State's interests in providing a cause of action in each instance are different. "The interest protected" in permitting recovery for placing the plaintiff in a false light "is clearly that of reputation, with the same overtones of mental distress as in defamation." By contrast, the State's interest in permitting a "right of publicity" is in protecting the proprietary interest of the individual in his act in part to encourage such entertainment. As we later note, the State's interest is closely analogous to the goals of patent and copyright law, focusing on the right of the individual to reap the reward of his endeavors and having little to do with protecting feelings or reputation. Second, the two torts differ in the degree to which they intrude on dissemination of information to the public. In "false light" cases the only way to protect the interests involved is to attempt to minimize publication of the damaging matter, while in "right of publicity" cases the only question is who gets to do the publishing. An entertainer such as petitioner usually has no objection to the widespread publication of his act as long as he gets the commercial benefit of such publication. Indeed, in the present case petitioner did not seek to enjoin the broadcast of his act; he simply sought compensation for the broadcast in the form of damages. . . .

. . . *Time, Inc. v. Hill*, *New York Times*, *Metromedia*, *Gertz*, and *Firestone* all involved the reporting of events; in none of them was there an attempt to broadcast or publish an entire act for which the performer ordinarily gets paid. It is evident, and there is no claim here to the contrary, that petitioner's state-law right of publicity would not serve to prevent respondent from reporting the newsworthy facts about petitioner's act. Wherever the line in particular situations is to be drawn between media reports that are protected and those that are not, we are quite sure that the First and Fourteenth Amendments do not immunize the media when they broadcast a performer's entire act without his consent. The Constitution no more prevents a State from requiring respondent to compensate petitioner for broadcasting his act on television than it would privilege respondent to film and broadcast a copyrighted dramatic work without liability to the copyright owner, or to film and broadcast a prize fight, or a baseball game, where the promoters or the participants had other plans for publicizing the event. . . .

The broadcast of a film of petitioner's entire act poses a substantial threat to the economic value of that performance. . . . The effect of a public broadcast of the performance is similar to preventing petitioner from charging an admission fee. The rationale for (protecting the right of publicity) is the straightforward one of preventing unjust enrichment by the theft of good will. . . .

There is no doubt that entertainment, as well as news, enjoys First Amendment protection. It is also true that entertainment itself can be important news. But it is important to note that neither the public nor respondent will be deprived of the benefit of petitioner's performance as long as his commercial stake in his act is appropriately recognized. Petitioner does not seek to enjoin the broadcast of his performance; he simply wants to be paid for it. . . .

We conclude that although the State of Ohio may as a matter of its own law privilege the press in the circumstances of this case, the First and Fourteenth Amendments do not require it to do so. . . .

NOTES & QUESTIONS

1. ***Different First Amendment Treatment.*** Why does the *Zacchini* Court conclude that the First Amendment impacts the torts of appropriation and publicity differently than the other privacy torts? Do you agree with the distinction the Court makes?
2. ***Newsworthiness.*** Is Zacchini's human cannonball act newsworthy? The media frequently provides news about entertainment, such as sports and movies. If the act is newsworthy, then why shouldn't the First Amendment protect the broadcast of it? If Zacchini suffered an accident while performing his cannonball act, would a broadcast of it be newsworthy? Would this accident justify broadcast of the entire act?

E. PRIVACY PROTECTIONS FOR ANONYMITY AND RECEIPT OF IDEAS

When it comes to the privacy torts, the First Amendment typically has clashed with privacy. But in other contexts, the First Amendment is used as a way to protect privacy. Anonymous speakers have invoked First Amendment rights to protect themselves from being identified. The First Amendment has been used by those who want to explore ideas without being monitored. And the

First Amendment is invoked by journalists seeking to protect themselves from being compelled to reveal their anonymous sources.

1. ANONYMITY

One of the most major such contexts is anonymity. Anonymity (or the use of pseudonyms) involves people's ability to conduct activities without being identified. People may want to speak anonymously because their speech might be unpopular or might be disliked by an employer or others who might retaliate against them. People may also want to read or surf the Internet anonymously because they are concerned about negative reactions toward their intellectual interests. Anonymity promotes freedom to speak or read without fear of reprisal or ostracism. However, when people can engage in anonymous activities, they might cause significant harm to other people and escape from being held accountable because their identities are not known. In a paradoxical way, people might use the cloak of anonymity to violate the privacy of others by revealing their private information.

When should the government be able to remove the cloak of anonymity on a person? When should a private party be able to do so? And to what extent can the government restrict anonymity to prevent fraud, crime, or other problems?

(a) Anonymous Speech

TALLEY V. STATE OF CALIFORNIA

362 U.S. 60 (1960)

BLACK, J. The question presented here is whether the provisions of a Los Angeles City ordinance restricting the distribution of handbills "abridge the freedom of speech and of the press secured against state invasion by the Fourteenth Amendment of the Constitution." The ordinance, § 28.06 of the Municipal Code of the City of Los Angeles, provides:

> No person shall distribute any hand-bill in any place under any circumstances, which does not have printed on the cover, or the face thereof, the name and address of the following:
>
> (a) The person who printed, wrote, compiled or manufactured the same.
>
> (b) The person who caused the same to be distributed; provided, however, that in the case of a fictitious person or club, in addition to such fictitious name, the true names and addresses of the owners, managers or agents of the person sponsoring said hand-bill shall also appear thereon.

The petitioner was arrested and tried in a Los Angeles Municipal Court for violating this ordinance. . . .

Anonymous pamphlets, leaflets, brochures and even books have played an important role in the progress of mankind. Persecuted groups and sects from time to time throughout history have been able to criticize oppressive practices and laws either anonymously or not at all. The obnoxious press licensing law of

England, which was also enforced on the Colonies was due in part to the knowledge that exposure of the names of printers, writers and distributors would lessen the circulation of literature critical of the government. The old seditious libel cases in England show the lengths to which government had to go to find out who was responsible for books that were obnoxious to the rulers. John Lilburne was whipped, pilloried and fined for refusing to answer questions designed to get evidence to convict him or someone else for the secret distribution of books in England. Two Puritan Ministers, John Penry and John Udal, were sentenced to death on charges that they were responsible for writing, printing or publishing books. Before the Revolutionary War colonial patriots frequently had to conceal their authorship or distribution of literature that easily could have brought down on them prosecutions by English-controlled courts. Along about that time the Letters of Junius were written and the identity of their author is unknown to this day. Even the Federalist Papers, written in favor of the adoption of our Constitution, were published under fictitious names. It is plain that anonymity has sometimes been assumed for the most constructive purposes.

We have recently had occasion to hold in two cases that there are times and circumstances when States may not compel members of groups engaged in the dissemination of ideas to be publicly identified. *Bates v. City of Little Rock*, 361 U.S. 516; *N.A.A.C.P. v. State of Alabama*, 357 U.S. 449. The reason for those holdings was that identification and fear of reprisal might deter perfectly peaceful discussions of public matters of importance. This broad Los Angeles ordinance is subject to the same infirmity. We hold that it, like the Griffin, Georgia, ordinance, is void on its face. . . .

McIntyre v. Ohio Elections Commission

514 U.S. 334 (1995)

STEVENS, J. . . . On April 27, 1988, Margaret McIntyre distributed leaflets to persons attending a public meeting at the Blendon Middle School in Westerville, Ohio. At this meeting, the superintendent of schools planned to discuss an imminent referendum on a proposed school tax levy. The leaflets expressed Mrs. McIntyre's opposition to the levy. There is no suggestion that the text of her message was false, misleading, or libelous. She had composed and printed it on her home computer and had paid a professional printer to make additional copies. Some of the handbills identified her as the author; others merely purported to express the views of "CONCERNED PARENTS AND TAX PAYERS." Except for the help provided by her son and a friend, who placed some of the leaflets on car windshields in the school parking lot, Mrs. McIntyre acted independently.

While Mrs. McIntyre distributed her handbills, an official of the school district, who supported the tax proposal, advised her that the unsigned leaflets did not conform to the Ohio election laws. Undeterred, Mrs. McIntyre appeared at another meeting on the next evening and handed out more of the handbills.

The proposed school levy was defeated at the next two elections, but it finally passed on its third try in November 1988. Five months later, the same school official filed a complaint with the Ohio Elections Commission charging that Mrs. McIntyre's distribution of unsigned leaflets violated § 3599.09(A) of the Ohio Code [which prohibited the distribution of political literature without the name and address of the person or organization responsible for the distribution]. The commission agreed and imposed a fine of $100. . . .

Mrs. McIntyre passed away during the pendency of this litigation. Even though the amount in controversy is only $100, petitioner, as the executor of her estate, has pursued her claim in this Court. Our grant of certiorari reflects our agreement with his appraisal of the importance of the question presented. . . .

Ohio maintains that the statute under review is a reasonable regulation of the electoral process. . . .

"Anonymous pamphlets, leaflets, brochures and even books have played an important role in the progress of mankind." *Talley v. California*. Great works of literature have frequently been produced by authors writing under assumed names.[100] Despite readers' curiosity and the public's interest in identifying the creator of a work of art, an author generally is free to decide whether or not to disclose his or her true identity. The decision in favor of anonymity may be motivated by fear of economic or official retaliation, by concern about social ostracism, or merely by a desire to preserve as much of one's privacy as possible. Whatever the motivation may be, at least in the field of literary endeavor, the interest in having anonymous works enter the marketplace of ideas unquestionably outweighs any public interest in requiring disclosure as a condition of entry. Accordingly, an author's decision to remain anonymous, like other decisions concerning omissions or additions to the content of a publication, is an aspect of the freedom of speech protected by the First Amendment.

. . . On occasion, quite apart from any threat of persecution, an advocate may believe her ideas will be more persuasive if her readers are unaware of her identity. Anonymity thereby provides a way for a writer who may be personally unpopular to ensure that readers will not prejudge her message simply because they do not like its proponent. Thus, even in the field of political rhetoric, where "the identity of the speaker is an important component of many attempts to persuade," the most effective advocates have sometimes opted for anonymity. The specific holding in *Talley* related to advocacy of an economic boycott, but the Court's reasoning embraced a respected tradition of anonymity in the advocacy of political causes.[101] This tradition is perhaps best exemplified by the secret ballot, the hard-won right to vote one's conscience without fear of retaliation. . . .

. . . [Section] 3599.09(A) of the Ohio Code does not control the mechanics of the electoral process. It is a regulation of pure speech. Moreover, even though this provision applies evenhandedly to advocates of differing viewpoints, it is a direct regulation of the content of speech. Every written document covered by the

---

[100] American names such as Mark Twain (Samuel Langhorne Clemens) and O. Henry (William Sydney Porter) come readily to mind. Benjamin Franklin employed numerous different pseudonyms. Distinguished French authors such as Voltaire (François Marie Arouet) and George Sand (Amandine Aurore Lucie Dupin), and British authors such as George Eliot (Mary Ann Evans), Charles Lamb (sometimes wrote as "Elia"), and Charles Dickens (sometimes wrote as "Boz"), also published under assumed names. . . .

[101] That tradition is most famously embodied in the Federalist Papers, authored by James Madison, Alexander Hamilton, and John Jay, but signed "Publius." Publius' opponents, the Anti-Federalists, also tended to publish under pseudonyms. . . .

statute must contain "the name and residence or business address of the chairman, treasurer, or secretary of the organization issuing the same, or the person who issues, makes, or is responsible therefor." Furthermore, the category of covered documents is defined by their content — only those publications containing speech designed to influence the voters in an election need bear the required markings. Consequently, we are not faced with an ordinary election restriction; this case "involves a limitation on political expression subject to exacting scrutiny." . . .

When a law burdens core political speech, we apply "exacting scrutiny," and we uphold the restriction only if it is narrowly tailored to serve an overriding state interest. . . .

Nevertheless, the State argues that, even under the strictest standard of review, the disclosure requirement in § 3599.09(A) is justified by two important and legitimate state interests. Ohio judges its interest in preventing fraudulent and libelous statements and its interest in providing the electorate with relevant information to be sufficiently compelling to justify the anonymous speech ban. These two interests necessarily overlap to some extent, but it is useful to discuss them separately.

Insofar as the interest in informing the electorate means nothing more than the provision of additional information that may either buttress or undermine the argument in a document, we think the identity of the speaker is no different from other components of the document's content that the author is free to include or exclude. . . . The simple interest in providing voters with additional relevant information does not justify a state requirement that a writer make statements or disclosures she would otherwise omit. Moreover, in the case of a handbill written by a private citizen who is not known to the recipient, the name and address of the author add little, if anything, to the reader's ability to evaluate the document's message. . . .

Under our Constitution, anonymous pamphleteering is not a pernicious, fraudulent practice, but an honorable tradition of advocacy and of dissent. Anonymity is a shield from the tyranny of the majority. It thus exemplifies the purpose behind the Bill of Rights, and of the First Amendment in particular: to protect unpopular individuals from retaliation — and their ideas from suppression — at the hand of an intolerant society. . . .

SCALIA, J. joined by REHNQUIST, C.J. dissenting. . . . The Court's unprecedented protection for anonymous speech does not even have the virtue of establishing a clear (albeit erroneous) rule of law. . . . It may take decades to work out the shape of this newly expanded right-to-speak-incognito, even in the elections field. And in other areas, of course, a whole new boutique of wonderful First Amendment litigation opens its doors. Must a parade permit, for example, be issued to a group that refuses to provide its identity, or that agrees to do so only under assurance that the identity will not be made public? Must a municipally owned theater that is leased for private productions book anonymously sponsored presentations? Must a government periodical that has a "letters to the editor" column disavow the policy that most newspapers have against the publication of anonymous letters? Must a public university that makes its facilities available for a speech by Louis Farrakhan or David Duke refuse to disclose the on-campus or off-campus group that has sponsored or paid for the speech? Must a municipal "public-access" cable channel permit anonymous (and masked) performers? The silliness that follows upon a generalized right to anonymous speech has no end. . . .

The Court says that the State has not explained "why it can more easily enforce the direct bans on disseminating false documents against anonymous authors and distributors than against wrongdoers who might use false names and addresses in an attempt to avoid detection." I am not sure what this complicated comparison means. I am sure, however, that (1) a person who is required to put his name to a document is much less likely to lie than one who can lie anonymously, and (2) the distributor of a leaflet which is unlawful because it is anonymous runs much more risk of immediate detection and punishment than the distributor of a leaflet which is unlawful because it is false. Thus, people will be more likely to observe a signing requirement than a naked "no falsity" requirement; and, having observed that requirement, will then be significantly less likely to lie in what they have signed. . . .

I do not know where the Court derives its perception that "anonymous pamphleteering is not a pernicious, fraudulent practice, but an honorable tradition of advocacy and of dissent." I can imagine no reason why an anonymous leaflet is any more honorable, as a general matter, than an anonymous phone call or an anonymous letter. It facilitates wrong by eliminating accountability, which is ordinarily the very purpose of the anonymity. . . .

NOTES & QUESTIONS

1. ***Why Is Anonymity in Speaking Protected by the First Amendment?*** *Talley* and *McIntyre* conclude that anonymous speech is protected under the First Amendment but do so based on different rationales. What are those rationales? Which rationale seems most persuasive to you?
2. ***Identification Requirements.*** In *Buckley v. ACLF*, 525 U.S. 182 (1999), the Court struck down part of a Colorado statute requiring individuals handing out petitions to wear name tags. The Court reasoned:

   > [T]he name badge requirement forces circulators to reveal their identities at the same time they deliver their political message, it operates when reaction to the circulator's message is immediate and may be the most intense, emotional, and unreasoned. . . . The injury to speech is heightened for the petition circulator because the badge requirement compels personal name identification at the precise moment when the circulator's interest in anonymity is the greatest.

   In *Watchtower Bible & Tract Society v. Village of Stratton,* 536 U.S. 150 (2002), a local ordinance required all solicitors of private residences to obtain a permit, which required that the individuals supply data about their cause as well as their name, home addresses, and employers or affiliated organizations. The Supreme Court held that the ordinance violated the First Amendment because there was insufficient evidence that door-to-door solicitation significantly increased fraud or crime.

3. ***Anonymity of Petitions.*** In *Doe v. Reed*, 130 S. Ct. 1886 (2010), the State of Washington passed a law that provided rights to same-sex domestic partners. A group of petitioners, called "Protect Marriage Washington," collected signatures to put a referendum on the ballot to nullify the law. The group collected more than 137,000 signatures, a sufficient amount to put the referendum (R-71) on the ballot. Several groups sought to obtain copies of the petition and the names and addresses of the people who signed it. The groups indicated they planned to post the names online. Protect Marriage Washington and several signers sought to enjoin the release of the petitions as a violation of the First Amendment. The Supreme Court held that because the plaintiffs sought to bar the state from making all referendum petitions available to the public, the plaintiffs were challenging the disclosure facially rather than as applied. The Court held that the plaintiffs' First Amendment interests were implicated but that their facial challenge to the disclosure was outweighed by the state's interest in "preserving the integrity of the electoral process." The state's interest encompassed fraud prevention and "promoting transparency and accountability in the electoral process."

   The Court left open whether the plaintiffs would prevail on a separate "as applied" challenge to the disclosure. The plaintiffs' facial challenge involved the disclosure requirement generally, without proof of specific harm to specific plaintiffs. In contrast, an "as applied" challenge would require specific plaintiffs to prove they were chilled in their speech.

4. ***Anonymity in Cyberspace and "John Doe" Lawsuits.*** E-mail and the Internet enable people to communicate anonymously with ease. People can send e-mail or post messages to electronic bulletin boards under pseudonyms. However, this anonymity is quite fragile, and in some cases illusory. Websites log the IP address of the computers of visitors of the site, and these IP addresses can be traced back to a person. An individual's Internet Service Provider (ISP) has information linking IP addresses to particular account holders. Under federal wiretap law, an ISP must disclose information identifying a particular user to the government pursuant to a subpoena. However, no subpoena is required for private parties. An ISP "may disclose a record or other information pertaining to a subscriber . . . to any person other than a governmental entity." 18 U.S.C. § 2703(c)(1)(A).

   In what is known as a "John Doe" lawsuit, plaintiffs can sue to find out the identity of an anonymous or pseudonymous speaker in order to pursue a defamation or privacy action. Plaintiffs bring a lawsuit against anonymous speakers (the John Does) and then seek civil subpoenas or court orders to compel ISPs to reveal the identities of these speakers. Courts must consider the First Amendment rights of the speakers when determining whether plaintiffs are entitled to discover the identities of speakers people allege have defamed them or invaded their privacy.[102] What standard should courts use to make this determination? The case below addresses this issue.

---

[102] Lyrissa Barnett Lidsky, *Silencing John Doe: Defamation and Discourse in Cyberspace*, 49 Duke L.J. 855 (2000).

DOE V. CAHILL

884 A.2d 451 (Del. 2005)

STEELE, C.J. . . . On November 2, 2004, the plaintiffs below, Patrick and Julia Cahill, both residents of Smyrna, Delaware, filed suit against four John Doe defendants asserting defamation and invasion of privacy claims. This appeal involves only one of the John Doe defendants, John Doe No. 1 below and "Doe" in this opinion. Using the alias "Proud Citizen," Doe posted two statements on an internet website sponsored by the Delaware State News called the "Smyrna/Clayton Issues Blog" concerning Cahill's performance as a City Councilman of Smyrna. The "Guidelines" at the top of the blog stated "[t]his is your hometown forum for opinions about public issues." The first of Doe's statements, posted on September 18, 2004, said:

> If only Councilman Cahill was able to display the same leadership skills, energy and enthusiasm toward the revitalization and growth of the fine town of Smyrna as Mayor Schaeffer has demonstrated! While Mayor Schaeffer has made great strides toward improving the livelihood of Smyrna's citizens, Cahill has devoted all of his energy to being a divisive impediment to any kind of cooperative movement. *Anyone who has spent any amount of time with Cahill would be keenly aware of such character flaws, not to mention an obvious mental deterioration.* Cahill is a prime example of failed leadership — his eventual ousting is exactly what Smyrna needs in order to move forward and establish a community that is able to thrive on its own economic stability and common pride in its town.

The next day, Doe posted another statement:

> *Gahill* [sic] *is as paranoid* as everyone in the town thinks he is. The mayor needs support from his citizens and protections from unfounded attacks. . . .

Pursuant to Superior Court Rule 30, the Cahills sought and obtained leave of the Superior Court to conduct a pre-service deposition of the owner of the internet blog, Independent Newspapers. After obtaining the IP addresses associated with the blog postings from the blog's owner, the Cahills learned that Comcast Corporation owned Doe's IP address. An IP address is an electronic number that specifically identifies a particular computer using the internet. IP addresses are often owned by internet service providers who then assign them to subscribers when they use the internet. These addresses are unique and assigned to only one ISP subscriber at a time. Thus, if the ISP knows the time and the date that postings were made from a specific IP address, it can determine the identity of its subscriber.

Armed with Doe's IP address, the Cahills obtained a court order requiring Comcast to disclose Doe's identity. As required by Federal Statute,[103] when Comcast received the discovery request, it notified Doe. On January 4, 2005, Doe filed an "Emergency Motion for a Protective Order" seeking to prevent the Cahills from obtaining his identity from Comcast. . . .

---

[103] 47 U.S.C. 551(c)(2) requires a court order to a cable ISP and notice to the ISP subscriber before an ISP can disclose the identity of its subscriber to a third party.

It is clear that speech over the internet is entitled to First Amendment protection. This protection extends to anonymous internet speech. Anonymous internet speech in blogs or chat rooms in some instances can become the modern equivalent of political pamphleteering. . . .

It also is clear that the First Amendment does not protect defamatory speech. . . . Certain classes of speech, including defamatory and libelous speech, are entitled to no Constitutional protection. . . . Accordingly, we must adopt a standard that appropriately balances one person's right to speak anonymously against another person's right to protect his reputation. . . .

In this case, this Court is called upon to adopt a standard for trial courts to apply when faced with a public figure plaintiff's discovery request that seeks to unmask the identity of an anonymous defendant who has posted allegedly defamatory material on the internet. Before this Court is an entire spectrum of "standards" that could be required, ranging (in ascending order) from a good faith basis to assert a claim, to pleading sufficient facts to survive a motion to dismiss, to a showing of *prima facie* evidence sufficient to withstand a motion for summary judgment, and beyond that, hurdles even more stringent. . . . [W]e hold that a defamation plaintiff must satisfy a "summary judgment" standard before obtaining the identity of an anonymous defendant.

We are concerned that setting the standard too low will chill potential posters from exercising their First Amendment right to speak anonymously. The possibility of losing anonymity in a future lawsuit could intimidate anonymous posters into self-censoring their comments or simply not commenting at all. A defamation plaintiff, particularly a public figure, obtains a very important form of relief by unmasking the identity of his anonymous critics. The revelation of identity of an anonymous speaker "may subject [that speaker] to ostracism for expressing unpopular ideas, invite retaliation from those who oppose her ideas or from those whom she criticizes, or simply give unwanted exposure to her mental processes." Plaintiffs can often initially plead sufficient facts to meet the good faith test applied by the Superior Court, even if the defamation claim is not very strong, or worse, if they do not intend to pursue the defamation action to a final decision. After obtaining the identity of an anonymous critic through the compulsory discovery process, a defamation plaintiff who either loses on the merits or fails to pursue a lawsuit is still free to engage in extra-judicial self-help remedies; more bluntly, the plaintiff can simply seek revenge or retribution.

Indeed, there is reason to believe that many defamation plaintiffs bring suit merely to unmask the identities of anonymous critics. As one commentator has noted, "[t]he sudden surge in John Doe suits stems from the fact that many defamation actions are not really about money." "The goals of this new breed of libel action are largely symbolic, the primary goal being to silence John Doe and others like him." This "sue first, ask questions later" approach, coupled with a standard only minimally protective of the anonymity of defendants, will discourage debate on important issues of public concern as more and more anonymous posters censor their online statements in response to the likelihood of being unmasked. . . .

Long-settled doctrine governs this Court's review of dismissals under Rule 12(b)(6). Under that doctrine, the threshold for the showing a plaintiff must make to survive a motion to dismiss is low. Delaware is a notice pleading jurisdiction.

Thus, for a complaint to survive a motion to dismiss, it need only give "general notice of the claim asserted." A court can dismiss for failure to state a claim on which relief can be granted only if "it appears with reasonable certainty that the plaintiff could not prove any set of facts that would entitle him to relief." On a motion to dismiss, a court's review is limited to the well-pleaded allegations in the complaint. An allegation, "though vague or lacking in detail" can still be well-pleaded so long as it puts the opposing party on notice of the claim brought against it. Finally, in ruling on a motion to dismiss under Rule 12(b)(6), a trial court must draw all reasonable factual inferences in favor of the party opposing the motion. . . .

We conclude that the summary judgment standard is the appropriate test by which to strike the balance between a defamation plaintiff's right to protect his reputation and a defendant's right to exercise free speech anonymously. We accordingly hold that before a defamation plaintiff can obtain the identity of an anonymous defendant through the compulsory discovery process he must support his defamation claim with facts sufficient to defeat a summary judgment motion.

. . . [T]o the extent reasonably practicable under the circumstances, the plaintiff must undertake efforts to notify the anonymous poster that he is the subject of a subpoena or application for order of disclosure. The plaintiff must also withhold action to afford the anonymous defendant a reasonable opportunity to file and serve opposition to the discovery request. Moreover, when a case arises in the internet context, the plaintiff must post a message notifying the anonymous defendant of the plaintiff's discovery request on the same message board where the allegedly defamatory statement was originally posted. . . .

[T]o obtain discovery of an anonymous defendant's identity under the summary judgment standard, a defamation plaintiff "must submit sufficient evidence to establish a *prima facie* case for each essential element of the claim in question." In other words, the defamation plaintiff, as the party bearing the burden of proof at trial, must introduce evidence creating a genuine issue of material fact for all elements of a defamation claim *within the plaintiff's control.*

Under Delaware law, a public figure defamation plaintiff in a libel case must plead and ultimately prove that: 1) the defendant made a defamatory statement; 2) concerning the plaintiff; 3) the statement was published; and 4) a third party would understand the character of the communication as defamatory. In addition, the public figure defamation plaintiff must plead and prove that 5) the statement is false and 6) that the defendant made the statement with actual malice. Finally, "[p]roof of damages proximately caused by a publication deemed libelous need not be shown in order for a defamed plaintiff to recover nominal or compensatory damages." . . .

[W]e are mindful that public figures in a defamation case must prove that the defendant made the statements with actual malice. Without discovery of the defendant's identity, satisfying this element may be difficult, if not impossible. Consequently, we do NOT hold that the public figure defamation plaintiff is required to produce evidence on this element of the claim. We hold only that a public figure plaintiff must plead the first five elements and offer *prima facie* proof on each of the five elements to create a genuine issue of material fact requiring trial. In other words, a public figure defamation plaintiff must only plead and prove facts with regard to elements of the claim that are within his control. . . .

Having adopted a summary judgment standard, we now apply it to the facts of this case. . . .

In deciding whether or not a statement is defamatory we determine, "*first,* whether alleged defamatory statements are expressions of fact or protected expressions of opinion; and [*second*], whether the challenged statements are capable of a defamatory meaning." . . .

Applying a good faith standard, the trial judge concluded, "it is enough to meet the 'good faith' standard that the Cahills articulate a legitimate basis for claiming defamation in the context of their particular circumstances." He continued "[g]iven that Mr. Cahill is a married man, [Doe's] statement referring to him as "Gahill" might reasonably be interpreted as indicating that Mr. Cahill has engaged in an extra-marital same-sex affair. Such a statement may form the basis of an actionable defamation claim." We disagree. Using a "G" instead of a "C" as the first letter of Cahill's name is just as likely to be a typographical error as an intended misguided insult. Under the summary judgment standard, no reasonable person would interpret this statement to indicate that Cahill had an extra-marital same-sex affair. With respect to Doe's other statements, the trial judge noted:

> Again, the context in which the statements were made is probative. [Doe's] statements might give the reader the impression that [Doe] has personal knowledge that Mr. Cahill's mental condition is deteriorating and that he is becoming "paranoid." Given that Mr. Cahill is a member of the Smyrna Town Council, an elected position of public trust, the impression that he is suffering from diminished mental capacity might be deemed capable of causing harm to his reputation, particularly when disseminated over the internet for all of his constituents to read.

We agree that the context in which the statements were made is probative, but reach the opposite conclusion. Given the context, no reasonable person could have interpreted these statements as being anything other than opinion. The guidelines at the top of the blog specifically state that the forum is dedicated to *opinions* about issues in Smyrna. . . .

Accordingly, we hold that as a matter of law a reasonable person would not interpret Doe's statements as stating facts about Cahill. The statements are, therefore, incapable of a defamatory meaning. Because Cahill has failed to plead an essential element of his claim, he *ipso facto* cannot produce *prima facie* proof of that first element of a libel claim, and thus, cannot satisfy the summary judgment standard we announce today. . . .

NOTES & QUESTIONS

1. ***Postscript.*** The anonymous speaker in *Doe v. Cahill* turned out to be Mayor Schaeffer's 25-year-old stepdaughter. Her identity was revealed inadvertently in discovery. The Schaeffers and Cahills were next-door neighbors, and they had feuded since 2003. Until the mayor's stepdaughter was unmasked, he had denied that anybody in his household made the statements against Cahill.

Subsequently, Cahill settled his defamation lawsuit against Schaeffer's stepdaughter.

After the Delaware Supreme Court decision was issued, Patrick and Julia Cahill were arrested following a shouting match with the Schaeffers. The Cahills were charged with terroristic threatening, harassment, and disorderly conduct. They were subsequently acquitted of these charges, but Patrick Cahill was convicted of violating a police order to avoid contacting the Schaeffers. He was fined $100 and sentenced to a year of probation.

2. ***The Standard for Unmasking an Anonymous Speaker.*** Courts have established different standards for a plaintiff to find out the identity of an anonymous speaker. The most common include:

   (a) *The Motion to Dismiss Standard.* The plaintiff must establish that the case would survive a motion to dismiss. *See Columbia Insurance Co. v. Seescandy.com*, 185 F.R.D. 573 (N.D. Cal. 1999).

   (b) *The Prima Facie Case Standard.* The plaintiff must produce evidence showing a prima facie case on all elements and must demonstrate that revealing the identity of the anonymous speaker will not severely harm the speaker's free speech or privacy rights and will be "necessary to enable plaintiff to protect against or remedy serious wrongs." *Highfields Capital Mgmt., LP v. Doe*, 385 F. Supp. 2d 969 (N.D. Cal. 2005); *Dendrite Int'l v. Doe No. 3*, 775 A.2d 756 (N.J. Super. App. Div. 2001).

   (c) *The Summary Judgment Standard.* The plaintiff must prove the case could survive a motion for summary judgment. *See Doe v. Cahill, supra.*

   (d) *The Variable Standard.* This standard varies depending upon the nature of the speech, with commercial speech being protected by a much lower standard than non-commercial speech. *See In re Anonymous Online Speakers*, 611 F.3d 653 (9th Cir. 2010) (known as the "*Quixtar*" case).

   What are the pros and cons of each approach?

3. ***The Identities of Third Parties to the Litigation.*** In *Doe v. 2TheMart.com, Inc.* 140 F. Supp. 2d 1088 (W.D. Wash. 2001), shareholders of 2TheMart.com, Inc. brought a derivative class action against the corporation. The company, in preparing its defense, subpoenaed the identity of 23 anonymous speakers who posted messages on an online message board. These postings were very critical of 2TheMart. One of the anonymous speakers challenged the subpoena. The court concluded:

   > The Court will consider four factors in determining whether the subpoena should issue. These are whether: (1) the subpoena seeking the information was issued in good faith and not for any improper purpose, (2) the information sought relates to a core claim or defense, (3) the identifying information is directly and materially relevant to that claim or defense, and (4) information sufficient to establish or to disprove that claim or defense is unavailable from any other source. . . .
   >
   > Only when the identifying information is needed to advance core claims or defenses can it be sufficiently material to compromise First Amendment

> rights. If the information relates only to a secondary claim or to one of numerous affirmative defenses, then the primary substance of the case can go forward without disturbing the First Amendment rights of the anonymous Internet users.
>
> The information sought by TMRT does not relate to a core defense. Here, the information relates to only one of twenty-seven affirmative defenses raised by the defendant, the defense that "no act or omission of any of the Defendants was the cause in fact or the proximate cause of any injury or damage to the plaintiffs." . . .
>
> [Moreover,] TMRT has failed to demonstrate that the identity of the Internet users is directly and materially relevant to a core defense. These Internet users are not parties to the case and have not been named as defendants as to any claim, cross-claim or third-party claim. . . .

Should the standard for unmasking non-parties to the litigation be stricter than that for parties to a case?

4. ***Can Being Anonymous Online Be Criminalized?*** In *ACLU v. Miller,* 977 F. Supp. 1228 (N.D. Ga. 1997), plaintiffs challenged a law that criminalized falsely identifying oneself in online communications. The court held that the law ran afoul of the First Amendment:

> Defendants allege that the statute's purpose is fraud prevention, which the Court agrees is a compelling state interest. However, the statute is not narrowly tailored to achieve that end and instead sweeps innocent, protected speech within its scope. Specifically, by its plain language the criminal prohibition applies regardless of whether a speaker has any intent to deceive or whether deception actually occurs. Therefore, it could apply to a wide range of transmissions which "falsely identify" the sender, but are not "fraudulent" within the specific meaning of the criminal code. . . .

5. ***The WHOIS Database.*** Currently, the Internet Corporation for Assigned Names and Numbers (ICANN) Registrar Accreditation Agreement (RAA) requires that the identity and addresses of domain name holders be publicly disclosed, as well as the identities, addresses, e-mail addresses, and telephone numbers for technical and administrative contacts. Domain names are the names assigned to particular websites (e.g., cnn.com). In other words, an individual who wants to create her own website must publicly disclose personal information and cannot remain anonymous. The registration scheme extends to anyone who owns a domain name, including commercial services and publishers of political newsletters.

Dawn Nunziato observes that the ICANN identification policy was enacted "[a]t the behest of interested intellectual property owners, who were concerned about their ability to police infringing content on the Internet." She argues:

> Because of the important role anonymous speech serves within expressive forums — which in turn are integral to democratic governments — ICANN should, in reevaluating its policies to accord meaningful protection for freedom of expression, revise its policy requiring domain name holders publicly to disclose their names and addresses. While protecting anonymous Internet speech is clearly an important component of free speech within the

> United States, it is even more important for ICANN to protect the identity of speakers from countries that are more inclined to retaliate against speakers based on the ideas they express.

Nunziato suggests that ICANN should still collect registrants' names and addresses, but only make public their e-mail addresses. Only upon a "heightened showing by a rights holder" should ICANN release a registrant's name and address.[104]

Should registrants of Internet domain names be able to obtain "proxy registrations" that hide their information from the general public? In February 2005, the National Telecommunication and Information Administration of the Department of Commerce decided that registrars, such as Go Daddy, could not offer proxy registrations for the U.S. domain. Does this decision implicate First Amendment interests?

6. ***Anonymity vs. Pseudonymity.*** Tal Zarsky argues that anonymity "come[s] at a high price to society" because "[i]n an anonymous society where locations, interactions, and transactions are hidden behind a veil of anonymity, the lack of accountability will spread to all areas of conduct, interfering with the formation of business and other relationships and allowing individuals to act without inhibitions." Zarsky contends that "traceable pseudonymity" is preferable because it "allows us to interact with consistent personalities" yet protects our "physical identity" and because it provides "accountability with partial anonymity."[105] What are the relative benefits and costs of traceable pseudonymity versus anonymity?

(b) Reporter's Privilege

Another instance where anonymity plays an important role in promoting First Amendment rights is anonymity of sources who share information with journalists. One of the most famous anonymous sources was Deep Throat, the source that revealed information about the Watergate burglary and cover-up by the Nixon Administration to Bob Woodward and Carl Bernstein, reporters at *The Washington Post.* Their reporting ultimately lead to President Nixon's resignation.

In criminal and civil cases, there are often demands on journalists to reveal the identity of an anonymous source. Journalists have sought protection from divulging the information in what is called "reporter's privilege," "journalist privilege," or "journalist-source privilege."

First Amendment and Federal Recognition of Reporter's Privilege. In *Branzburg v. Hayes*, 408 U.S. 665 (1972), the Supreme Court held that there is no First Amendment reporter's privilege against grand jury requests for evidence. However, at the conclusion of the opinion, the Court noted that:

---

[104] Dawn C. Nunziato, *Freedom of Expression, Democratic Norms, and Internet Governance*, 52 Emory L.J. 187, 202, 257, 259 (2003).

[105] Tal Z. Zarsky, *Thinking Outside the Box: Considering Transparency, Anonymity, and Pseudonymity as Overall Solutions to the Problems of Information Privacy in the Internet Society*, 58 U. Miami L. Rev. 991, 1028, 1032, 1044 (2004).

> [N]ews gathering is not without its First Amendment protections, and grand jury investigations if instituted or conducted other than in good faith, would pose wholly different issues for resolution under the First Amendment. . . . Grand juries are subject to judicial control and subpoenas to motions to quash. We do not expect courts will forget that grand juries must operate within the limits of the First Amendment as well as the Fifth.

Justice Powell, the swing vote in the 5-4 majority, wrote a concurrence to note that the "Court does not hold that newsmen, subpoenaed to testify before a grand jury, are without constitutional rights with respect to the gathering of news or in safeguarding their sources. . . . In short, the courts will be available to newsmen under circumstances where legitimate First Amendment interests require protection." Powell wrote that privilege claims should be assessed "by the striking of a proper balance between freedom of the press and the obligation of all citizens to give relevant testimony with respect to criminal conduct. The balance of these vital constitutional and societal interests on a case-by-case basis accords with the tried and traditional way of adjudicating such questions."

Following *Branzburg,* many federal circuit courts have recognized a qualified reporter's privilege. The reporter's privilege has fared much better in civil cases than in criminal ones.

State Recognition of Reporter's Privilege. In the states, the reporter's privilege has been recognized, with sources in state constitutions, state statutes, and common law. Forty-nine states and the District of Columbia have recognized it.[106] In most states, there is a qualified reporter's privilege, which can be overridden if the government establishes that it has no alternative way to obtain the information and that there is a compelling interest to do so. About 13 states have an absolute privilege, which cannot be overridden.

Currently, there is no reporter's privilege recognized under the Federal Rules of Evidence. In calling for such a privilege Geoffrey Stone argues that at "the hands of unrestrained federal prosecutors, journalists have taken a serious battering." He contends:

> A strong and effective journalist-source privilege is essential to a robust and independent press and to a well-functioning democratic society. It is in society's interest to encourage those who possess information of significant public value to convey it to the public, but without a journalist-source privilege, such communication will often be chilled because sources fear retribution, embarrassment or just plain getting "involved."[107]

Do you think that such a privilege should exist? Would sources with important information about companies come forward if they risked potential losing their jobs? Would sources come forward with information about the government if they risked criminal prosecution? On the other hand, if sources

---

[106] Geoffrey R. Stone, *We Need a Federal Journalist-Source Privilege NOW,* Huffington Post (Feb. 21, 2007), http://www.huffingtonpost.com/geoffrey-r-stone/we-need-a-federal-journal_b_41747.html.

[107] *Id.*

remain anonymous, would that allow them to divulge information and escape punishment?

The Valerie Plame Leak. In 2003, when former Ambassador Joseph Wilson disputed White House claims about weapons of mass destruction in Iraq. White House officials leaked to several reporters the fact that his wife, Valerie Plame, was a CIA agent, blowing her cover. Among the journalists receiving the information was the conservative pundit Robert Novak as well as *Time* magazine reporter Matthew Cooper and *New York Times* reporter Judith Miller.

Leaking the identity of a CIA agent is a crime, and a grand jury was convened to investigate. It subpoenaed from the reporters the identities of their sources. Cooper and Miller refused to comply with the subpoenas. District Court Judge Thomas Hogan ordered that the reporters comply or else face jail time for contempt. *Time* magazine announced that against the wishes of Cooper, it would turn over his notes. Should the journalists be required to hand over the notes?

The leak in this case was not by a source desiring to blow the whistle or reveal government corruption. Instead, the leak was done by government officials to retaliate against Wilson. Should leaks for purposes such as this one be denied the protection of reporter's privilege? If so, how would such an exception be defined?

Should the focus be on whether it is a crime to leak? In many instances, leaking is a crime, such as the Pentagon Papers leak as well as the leak by Edward Snowden. Should the focus be on whether the leak is in the public interest? How should the public interest be defined?

2. PRIVACY OF READING AND INTELLECTUAL EXPLORATION

Privacy is also central to the exploration of ideas. Neil Richards contends that the First Amendment protects what he calls "intellectual privacy." According to Richards:

> Intellectual privacy is the ability, whether protected by law or social circumstances, to develop ideas and beliefs away from the unwanted gaze or interference of others. Surveillance or interference can warp the integrity of our freedom of thought and can skew the way we think, with clear repercussions for the content of our subsequent speech or writing.[108]

To what extent does the First Amendment protect a person's right to privacy in reading, Web-surfing, and exploration of ideas?

STANLEY V. GEORGIA

394 U.S. 557 (1969)

MARSHALL, J. . . . An investigation of appellant's alleged bookmaking activities led to the issuance of a search warrant for appellant's home. Under authority of this warrant, federal and state agents secured entrance. They found very little

[108] Neil M. Richards, *Intellectual Privacy,* 87 Tex. L. Rev. 387, 389 (2008).

evidence of bookmaking activity, but while looking through a desk drawer in an upstairs bedroom, one of the federal agents, accompanied by a state officer, found three reels of eight-millimeter film. Using a projector and screen found in an upstairs living room, they viewed the films. The state officer concluded that they were obscene and seized them. Since a further examination of the bedroom indicated that appellant occupied it, he was charged with possession of obscene matter and placed under arrest. He was later indicted for "knowingly hav(ing) possession of . . . obscene matter" in violation of Georgia law. Appellant was tried before a jury and convicted. . . .

Appellant argues here . . . that the Georgia obscenity statute, insofar as it punishes mere private possession of obscene matter, violates the First Amendment. . . . [W]e agree that the mere private possession of obscene matter cannot constitutionally be made a crime. . . .

It is true that *Roth* does declare, seemingly without qualification, that obscenity is not protected by the First Amendment. That statement has been repeated in various forms in subsequent cases. However, neither *Roth* nor any subsequent decision of this Court dealt with the precise problem involved in the present case. Roth was convicted of mailing obscene circulars and advertising, and an obscene book, in violation of a federal obscenity statute. . . . None of the statements cited by the Court in *Roth* for the proposition that "this Court has always assumed that obscenity is not protected by the freedoms of speech and press" were made in the context of a statute punishing mere private possession of obscene material; the cases cited deal for the most part with use of the mails to distribute objectionable material or with some form of public distribution or dissemination. Moreover, none of this Court's decisions subsequent to *Roth* involved prosecution for private possession of obscene materials. Those cases dealt with the power of the State and Federal Governments to prohibit or regulate certain public actions taken or intended to be taken with respect to obscene matter. . . .

In this context, we do not believe that this case can be decided simply by citing *Roth*. . . .

It is now well established that the Constitution protects the right to receive information and ideas. "This freedom (of speech and press) . . . necessarily protects the right to receive. . . ." This right to receive information and ideas, regardless of their social worth, is fundamental to our free society. Moreover, in the context of this case — a prosecution for mere possession of printed or filmed matter in the privacy of a person's own home — that right takes on an added dimension. . . .

These are the rights that appellant is asserting in the case before us. He is asserting the right to read or observe what he pleases — the right to satisfy his intellectual and emotional needs in the privacy of his own home. He is asserting the right to be free from state inquiry into the contents of his library. Georgia contends that appellant does not have these rights, that there are certain types of materials that the individual may not read or even possess. Georgia justifies this assertion by arguing that the films in the present case are obscene. But we think that mere categorization of these films as "obscene" is insufficient justification for such a drastic invasion of personal liberties guaranteed by the First and Fourteenth Amendments. Whatever may be the justifications for other statutes regulating obscenity, we do not think they reach into the privacy of one's own home. If the First Amendment means anything, it means that a State has no business telling a man, sitting alone in his own house, what books he may read or what films he may watch. Our whole constitutional heritage rebels at the thought of giving government the power to control men's minds. . . .

We hold that the First and Fourteenth Amendments prohibit making mere private possession of obscene material a crime. *Roth* and the cases following that decision are not impaired by today's holding. As we have said, the States retain broad power to regulate obscenity; that power simply does not extend to mere possession by the individual in the privacy of his own home. Accordingly, the judgment of the court below is reversed and the case is remanded for proceedings not inconsistent with this opinion.

NOTES & QUESTIONS

1. ***Possession of Obscenity Outside the Home.*** Stanley possessed obscene material that Georgia could constitutionally outlaw because the First Amendment does not protect obscenity. According to the Court, states can ban obscene films outside the home. Thus, were Stanley to step outside the door with his films, a police officer could arrest him. Should Stanley's location inside his home make any difference? Suppose Stanley possessed and used illegal narcotics in his home. Does the state have any business telling a person, sitting alone in her home, what substances she may or may not ingest?
2. ***The Limits of* Stanley.** In *Osborne v. Ohio,* 495 U.S. 103 (1990), the Court held that the rule in *Stanley* does not apply to the possession of child pornography in the home:

   > In *Stanley,* Georgia primarily sought to proscribe the private possession of obscenity because it was concerned that obscenity would poison the minds of its viewers. We responded that "[w]hatever the power of the state to control public dissemination of ideas inimical to the public morality, it cannot constitutionally premise legislation on the desirability of controlling a person's private thoughts." The difference here is obvious: The State does not rely on a paternalistic interest in regulating Osborne's mind. Rather, Ohio has enacted § 2907.323(A)(3) in order to protect the victims of child pornography; it hopes to destroy a market for the exploitative use of children.

3. ***The First Amendment and Postal Mail.*** In *Lamont v. Postmaster General of the United States*, 381 U.S. 301 (1965), a 1962 federal statute required that all mail (except sealed letters) that originates or is prepared in a foreign country and is determined by the Secretary of the Treasury to be "communist political propaganda" be detained at the post office. The addressee would be notified of the matter, and the mail would be delivered to the addressee only upon her request. The Court struck down the statute on First Amendment grounds:

   > We rest on the narrow ground that the addressee in order to receive his mail must request in writing that it be delivered. This amounts in our judgment to an unconstitutional abridgment of the addressee's First Amendment rights. The addressee carries an affirmative obligation which we do not think the

> Government may impose on him. This requirement is almost certain to have a deterrent effect, especially as respects those who have sensitive positions. Their livelihood may be dependent on a security clearance. Public officials like schoolteachers who have no tenure, might think they would invite disaster if they read what the Federal Government says contains the seeds of treason. Apart from them, any addressee is likely to feel some inhibition in sending for literature which federal officials have condemned as "communist political propaganda." The regime of this Act is at war with the "uninhibited, robust, and wide-open debate and discussion" that are contemplated by the First Amendment.

4. *Anonymous Reading and Receiving of Ideas.* In *Tattered Cover, Inc. v. City of Thornton,* 44 P.3d 1044 (Colo. 2002), law enforcement officials (local City of Thornton police and a federal DEA agent) suspected that a methamphetamine lab was being operated out of a trailer home. On searching through some garbage from the trailer, an officer discovered evidence of drug operations and a mailing envelope from the Tattered Cover bookstore addressed to one of the suspects (Suspect A). There was an invoice and order number corresponding to the books shipped in the envelope, but no evidence about what those books were. Subsequently, a search warrant was obtained for the trailer home. In the bedroom, the police discovered a methamphetamine laboratory and drugs. Although there were a number of suspects, the police believed that Suspect A occupied the bedroom. Among the items seized from the bedroom were two books: *Advanced Techniques of Clandestine Psychedelic and Amphetamine Manufacture*, by Uncle Fester, and *The Construction and Operation of Clandestine Drug Laboratories*, by Jack B. Nimble.

The officers believed that these books were the ones mailed to Suspect A in the mailing envelope from the Tattered Cover found in the trash. The officers served The Tattered Cover with a DEA administrative subpoena, but Tattered Cover refused to comply, citing concern for its customers' privacy and First Amendment rights. The City then obtained a search warrant to search the bookstore's records. The Tattered Cover sued to enjoin the officers from executing the warrant.

The Colorado Supreme Court held that Colorado's First Amendment protects "the right to receive information and ideas." According to the court, "Everyone must be permitted to discover and consider the full range of expression and ideas available in our 'marketplace of ideas.' " The court further reasoned:

> Bookstores are places where a citizen can explore ideas, receive information, and discover myriad perspectives on every topic imaginable. When a person buys a book at a bookstore, he engages in activity protected by the First Amendment because he is exercising his right to read and receive ideas and information. Any governmental action that interferes with the willingness of customers to purchase books, or booksellers to sell books, thus implicates First Amendment concerns. . . .
>
> The need to protect anonymity in the context of the First Amendment has particular applicability to book-buying activity. . . . The right to engage in

> expressive activities anonymously, without government intrusion or observation, is critical to the protection of the First Amendment rights of book buyers and sellers, precisely because of the chilling effects of such disclosures. Search warrants directed to bookstores, demanding information about the reading history of customers, intrude upon the First Amendment rights of customers and bookstores because compelled disclosure of book-buying records threatens to destroy the anonymity upon which many customers depend. . . .

In contrast to the U.S. Supreme Court, which held in *Zurcher v. Stanford Daily*, 436 U.S. 547 (1978) that First Amendment concerns of government searches of expressive material can be satisfied by the government obtaining a search warrant, the Colorado Supreme Court concluded the state's First Amendment "requires a more substantial justification from the government," which must "demonstrate a sufficiently compelling need for the specific customer purchase record sought from the innocent, third-party bookstore."

In applying this standard to the facts of the case, the court noted that the government desired the evidence about the books to link Suspect A to the master bedroom where the lab was located along with the books. The court, however, concluded that physical evidence and witnesses could have been used to establish this fact.

The City also argued that proof that Suspect A purchased the books would link him to the crime. But the court rejected this argument:

> The dangers, both to Suspect A and to the book-buying public, of permitting the government to access the information it seeks, and to use this proof of purchase as evidence of Suspect A's guilt, are grave. Assuming that Suspect A purchased the books in question, he may have done so for any of a number of reasons, many of which are in no way linked to his commission of any crime. He might have bought them for a friend or roommate, unaware that they would subsequently be placed in the vicinity of an illegal drug lab. He might have been curious about the process of making drugs, without having any intention to act on what he read. It may be that none of these scenarios is as likely as that suggested by the City, that Suspect A bought the books intending to use them to help him make an illegal drug. Nonetheless, Colorado's long tradition of protecting expressive freedoms cautions against permitting the City to seize the Tattered Cover's book purchase record. . . .

Do you agree with the decision in *Tattered Cover* that, in addition to the right to speak anonymously, there is also a right to read anonymously? Does such a right follow logically from the Supreme Court's freedom of association and anonymity cases?

Consider the following argument by Julie Cohen:

> For the most part, First Amendment jurisprudence has defined readers' rights only incidentally. Historically, both courts and commentators have been more concerned with protecting speakers than with protecting readers. . . .
>
> When the two readers choose to express their own views, the First Amendment protects both speakers equally. Logically, that zone of protection should encompass the entire series of intellectual transactions through which they formed the opinions they ultimately chose to express. Any less protection would chill inquiry, and as a result, public discourse, concerning politically

> and socially controversial issues — precisely those areas where vigorous public debate is most needed, and most sacrosanct. . . .
>
> The freedom to read anonymously is just as much a part of our tradition, and the choice of reading materials just as expressive of identity, as the decision to use or withhold one's name.[109]

How far can the rationale of *Tattered Cover* be extended? Suppose the police obtained a search warrant for one's home and sought to seize a person's diary? Would such a seizure be subject to strict scrutiny? What about the search of one's computer, which can reveal anonymous speech as well as one's online reading activities? Isn't the government's questioning of various witnesses to whom a person spoke also likely to interfere with that person's expressive activities? Why are books different (or are they)?

---

[109] Julie E. Cohen, *A Right to Read Anonymously: A Closer Look at "Copyright Management" in Cyberspace*, 28 Conn. L. Rev. 981 (1996); *see also* Marc Jonathan Blitz, *Constitutional Safeguards For Silent Experiments in Living Libraries, the Right to Read, and a First Amendment Theory for an Unaccompanied Right to Receive Information*, 74 U. Mo. Kan. City L. Rev. 799, 881-82 (2006).

INDEX